Ways *of* Reading WORDS AND IMAGES

Ways *of* Reading
WORDS AND IMAGES

David Bartholomae
UNIVERSITY OF PITTSBURGH

Anthony Petrosky
UNIVERSITY OF PITTSBURGH

BEDFORD / ST. MARTIN'S
Boston ♦ New York

For Bedford / St. Martin's
Developmental Editor: John Sullivan
Production Editor: Lori Chong Roncka
Senior Production Supervisor: Dennis Conroy
Marketing Manager: Brian Wheel
Editorial Assistant: Christine Turnier-Vallecillo
Production Assistants: Kerri Cardone and Tina Lai
Copyeditor: Tara L. Masih
Text Design: Anna George
Cover Design: Mark McKie
Cover Art: Robert Rauschenberg, *Catch (Urban Bourbon)*, 1993. Acrylic on mirrored and enameled aluminum. Licensed by VAGA, New York, NY.
Composition: Pine Tree Composition, Inc.
Printing and Binding: R.R. Donnelley & Sons Company

President: Joan E. Feinberg
Editorial Director: Denise B. Wydra
Editor in Chief: Karen S. Henry
Director of Marketing: Karen Melton
Director of Editing, Design, and Production: Marcia Cohen
Managing Editor: Elizabeth M. Schaaf

Library of Congress Control Number: 2002112255

Manufactured in the United States of America.

7 6 5 4 3 2
f e d c b a

For information, write: Bedford / St. Martin's, 75 Arlington Street, Boston, MA 02116 (617-399-4000)

ISBN: 0-312-40381-X

ACKNOWLEDGMENTS

Preface

Ways of Reading Words and Images focuses on the interplay of text and image. We began to think about a separate, briefer version of *Ways of Reading* that examines this subject after noting the enthusiasm our students showed for the assignment sequence in *Ways of Reading* that was built around the work of Robert Coles and W. J. T. Mitchell. We found this not only in our own teaching, but also in that of our colleagues on campus and in the responses we received from teachers around the country. Students were interested in the intellectual project—in thinking about history and about documentary "truth" as represented in photographs. More than this, however, they showed great interest (and wit and skill) in preparing documentary essays, essays where they were responsible for combining words and images, including photographs of their own. We were impressed by the care and energy that went into this work; we were impressed by the quality of the writing and thinking; and, with digital technology, we were impressed by the final products, essays where the images had a quality of reproduction that made them important to the text. Words and images do, in fact, exist together inside computers, inside the now standard environment for the work of composition.

Once we decided to propose this new book, we let the selections from Coles and Mitchell (essays we had taught several times) suggest possible additional materials. We added extended selections from their key sources:

James Agee and Walker Evans, Roland Barthes, Dorothea Lange and Paul S. Taylor. Next, we pulled in some of the writers whose work we had taught in preparing for the sixth edition of *Ways of Reading:* Edward Said and Jean Mohr, John Berger, and Marianne Hirsch. We believe these selections can help prepare students to learn to read images, to write with them, to think with them, to make them a part of argument, inquiry, report, and story.

Ways of Reading Words and Images is designed for a course where students are given the opportunity to work on what they read, and to work on it by writing. When we began developing such courses, we realized the problems our students had when asked to write or talk about what they read were not "reading problems," at least not as these are strictly defined. Our students knew how to move from one page to the next. They could read sentences. They had, obviously, been able to carry out many of the versions of reading required for their education—skimming textbooks, cramming for tests, strip-mining books for term papers.

Our students, however, felt powerless in the face of serious writing, in the face of long and complicated texts—the kinds of texts we thought they should find interesting and challenging. We thought (as many teachers have thought) that if we just, finally, gave them something good to read—something rich and meaty—they would change forever their ways of thinking about English. It didn't work, of course. The issue is not only *what* students read, but what they can learn to *do* with what they read. We learned that the problems our students had lay not in the reading material (it was too hard) or in the students (they were poorly prepared) but in the classroom—in the ways we and they imagined what it meant to work on an essay.

There is no better place to work on reading than in a writing course, and this book is intended to provide occasions for readers to write. You will find a number of distinctive features in *Ways of Reading Words and Images.* For one thing, it contains selections you don't usually see in a college reader: long, powerful, mysterious pieces like John Berger's "Appearances" and the excerpt from Roland Barthes's *Camera Lucida.* These are the sorts of readings we talk about when we talk with our colleagues. We have learned that we can talk about them with our students as well.

When we chose the essays, we were looking for "readable" texts—that is, texts that leave some work for a reader to do. We wanted selections that invite students to be active, critical readers, that present powerful readings of common experience, that open up the familiar world and make it puzzling, rich, and problematic. We wanted to choose selections that invite students to be active readers and to take responsibility for their acts of interpretation. So we avoided the short set-pieces you find in so many anthologies. In a sense, those short selections misrepresent the act of reading. They can be read in a single sitting; they make arguments that can be easily paraphrased; they solve all the problems they raise; they wrap up Life and put it into a box; and so they turn reading into an act of appreciation, where the most that seems to be required is a nod of the head. And they suggest that a writer's job is to do just that, to write a piece that is similarly tight and neat and self-contained. We wanted to avoid pieces that were so plainly written or tightly bound that there was little for students to do but "get the point."

We learned that if our students had reading problems when faced with long and complex texts, the problems lay in the way they imagined a reader—the role a reader plays, what a reader does, why a reader reads (if not simply to satisfy the requirements of a course). When, for example, our students were puzzled by what they read, they took this as a sign of failure. ("It doesn't make any sense," they would say, as though the sense were supposed to be waiting on the page, ready for them the first time they read through.) And our students were haunted by the thought that they couldn't remember everything they had read (as though one could store all of a thirty-page chapter or essay in memory); or if they did remember bits and pieces, they felt that the fragmented text they possessed was evidence that they could not do what they were supposed to do. Our students were confronting the experience of reading, in other words, but they were taking the problems of reading—problems all readers face—and concluding that there was nothing for them to do but give up.

As expert readers, we have all learned what to do with a complex text. We know that we can go back to a text; we don't have to remember it—in fact, we've learned to mark up a text to ease that re-entry. We know that a reader is a person who puts together fragments. Those coherent readings we construct begin with confusion and puzzlement, and we construct those readings by writing and rewriting—by working on a text.

These are the lessons our students need to learn, and this is why a course in reading is also a course in writing. Our students need to learn that there is something they can do once they have first read through a complicated text; successful reading is not just a matter of "getting" an essay the first time. In a very real sense, you can't begin to feel the power a reader has until you realize the problems, until you realize that no one "gets" Mitchell or Barthes or Coles all at once. You work on what you read, and then what you have at the end is something that is yours, something you made. And this is what the teaching apparatus in *Ways of Reading Words and Images* is designed to do. In a sense, it says to students, "OK, let's get to work on these essays; let's see what you can make of them."

This, then, is the second distinctive feature you will find in *Ways of Reading Words and Images:* reading and writing assignments designed to give students access to the essays. After each selection, for example, you will find "Questions for a Second Reading." We wanted to acknowledge that rereading is a natural way of carrying out the work of a reader, just as rewriting is a natural way of completing the work of a writer. It is not something done out of despair or as a punishment for not getting things right the first time. The questions we have written highlight what we see as central textual or interpretive problems. Mitchell, for example, divides his essay into six sections. By going back through the essay with this in mind and by asking what he is doing in each case (what his method is and what it enables him to accomplish), a student is in a position to see the essay as the enactment of a method and not just as a long argument with its point hidden away at the end. These questions might serve as preparations for class discussion or ways of directing students' work in journals. Whatever the case, they both honor and direct the work of rereading.

Each selection is also followed by two sets of writing assignments, "Assignments for Writing" and "Making Connections." The first set directs students back into the work they have just read. While the assignments vary, there are some basic principles behind them. They ask students to work on the essay by focusing on difficult or problematic moments in the text; they ask students to work on the author's examples, extending and testing his or her methods of analysis; or they ask students to apply the method of the essay (its way of seeing and understanding the world) to settings or experiences of their own. Students are asked, for instance, to work in imitation of Agee and Evans, to take or select photographs like Walker Evans's and arrange them and write prose like Agee's to accompany them. In this project, they offer their work, as appropriate to their experience and place in time, as an engaged response to Agee and Evans's. The last assignments — "Making Connections" — invite students to read one essay in the context of another, to see, for example, if W. J. T. Mitchell's case studies of photographic essays can be used to frame a reading of larger sections of the works by James Agee and Walker Evans, Robert Coles, and Edward Said and Jean Mohr. In a sense, then, the essays are offered as models, but not as "prose models" in the strictest sense. What they model is a way of seeing or reading the world, of both imagining problems and imagining methods to make those problems available to a writer.

At the end of the book, we have included five assignment sequences. All the sequences include several of the essays in the anthology and require a series of separate drafts and revisions. In academic life, readers seldom read single essays in isolation, as though one were "finished" with a topic after a week or two. Rather, they read with a purpose—with a project in mind or a problem to solve. The assignment sequences are designed to give students a feel for the rhythm and texture of an extended academic project. They offer, that is, one more way of reading and writing. Because these sequences lead students through intellectual projects proceeding from one week to the next, they enable them to develop authority as specialists, to feel the difference between being an expert and being a "common" reader on a single subject. And, with the luxury of time available for self-reflection, students can look back on what they have done, not only to revise what they know, but also to take stock and comment on the value and direction of their work.

Because of their diversity, it is difficult to summarize the assignment sequences. Perhaps the best way to see what we have done is to turn to the back of the book and look at them. They are meant to frame a project for students but to leave open possibilities for new directions. You should feel free to add or drop readings, to mix sequences, and to revise the assignments to fit your course and your schedule.

You will also notice that there are no "glosses" appended to the essays. We have not added editors' notes to define difficult words or to identify names or allusions to other authors or artists. We've omitted them because their presence suggests something we feel is false about reading. They suggest that good readers know all the words or pick up all the allusions or recognize every name that is mentioned. This is not true. Good readers do what they can and try their best to fill in the blanks; they ignore seemingly unimportant references and look up the important ones. There is no reason for students to feel they lack the knowledge necessary to complete a reading of these texts. We have translated foreign phrases and glossed some technical terms, but we have kept the selections as clean and open as possible.

We have been asked on several occasions whether the readings aren't finally just too hard for students. The answer is no. Students will have to work on the selections, but that is the point of the course and the reason, as we said before, why a reading course is also a course in writing. College students want to believe that they can strike out on their own, make their mark, do something they have never done before. They want to *be* experts, not just hear from them. This is the great pleasure, as well as the great challenge, of undergraduate instruction. It is not hard to convince students they ought to be able to speak alongside of (or even speak back to) Robert Coles or Roland Barthes. And, if a teacher is patient and forgiving—willing, that is, to let a student work out a reading, willing to keep from saying, "No, that's not it," and filling the silence with the "right" reading—then students can, with care and assistance, learn to speak for themselves. It takes a certain kind of classroom, to be sure. A teacher who teaches this book will have to be comfortable turning the essays over to the students, even with the knowledge that they will not do immediately on their own what a professional could do—at least not completely, or with the same grace and authority.

In our own teaching, we have learned that we do not have to be experts on every figure or every area of inquiry represented in this book. And, frankly, that has come as a great relief. We can have intelligent, responsible conversations about essays or chapters on specialized topics without being experts. We read often in areas beyond our expertise; there has to be some way of reading an author for the first time. We can help our students by our willingness to admit where we are tentative and what we don't know. The most appropriate preparation for any of the essays in *Ways of Reading Words and Images* is to prepare to engage and direct students as readers and as writers. This is not the same thing as preparing a lecture. The classes we have been teaching, and they have been some of the most exciting we have ever taught, have been classes where the students—together and with their instructors—work on what these essays might mean.

So here we are, imagining students working shoulder to shoulder with Said and Mohr, Barthes, and Hirsch, even talking back to them as the occasion arises. There is a wonderful Emersonian bravado in all this. But such is the case with strong and active readers. If we allow students to work on powerful texts, they will want to share the power. This is the heady fun of academic life, the real pleasure of thinking, reading, and writing. There is no reason to keep it secret from our students.

Acknowledgments. We owe much to the friendship and wisdom of our colleagues at the University of Pittsburgh. There are old friends and colleagues with whom we have worked for a very long time: Ellen Bishop, Jean Ferguson Carr, Steve Carr, Nick Coles, Kathryn Flannery, Paul Kameen, Margaret Marshall, Mariolina Salvatori, and Jim Seitz. We also want to thank students and colleagues who gave particular help and attention to the work in preparation of the sixth edition of *Ways of Reading* and this book: Molly Brown, John Champagne, Malkiel Choseed, Ashley Currier, Jean Grace, David Griffith, Lorraine Higgins, Linda Huff, Aitor Ibarrola, Deane Kern, Geeta Khothari, Jennifer Lee, Dana Och, Juli Parrish, Richard Purcell, Tanya Reyes, Suzette Roth, Lauren Skrabala, Patricia Sullivan, Steve Sutherland, Jocelyn Trachtenberg, Jennifer Trainor, Henry Veggian, Ellen Wadey, Stacey Waite, Chris Warnick, Kathleen Welsch, Matt Willen, and Lois Williams. Deborah Galle helped significantly with the research for the headnotes.

And we owe much to colleagues at other schools who have followed our work with interest and offered their support and criticism. We are grateful for the notes, letters, and student papers.

We were fortunate to have outstanding reviewers on the project. We would like to thank Susan Glassow, Lane Community College; Stephanie Roach, University of Connecticut; Katherine Rogers-Carpenter, University of Kentucky; and Dawn Skorczewski, Emerson College.

Chuck Christensen of Bedford/St. Martin's is now in retirement. We wish him the very best in his new life. Joan Feinberg helped to shape this project from its very beginning. She is a fine and thoughtful friend as well as a fine and thoughtful editor. John Sullivan joined the group for the fifth edition. He had taught from an earlier edition of *Ways of Reading* and had, for us, a wonderful sense of the book's approach to reading, writing, and teaching. John is organized, resourceful, generous, quick to offer suggestions and to take on extra work. He soon became as much a collaborator as an editor. His care and dedication held everything together at times when we were falling apart. It was a real pleasure to work with him. Rose Corbett Gordon and Fred Courtright handled permissions. Caroline Thompson helped locate books, readings, and material for the headnotes. Coleen O'Hanley supervised the design and construction of the Web site; Christine Turnier-Vallecillo researched the links. Lori Chong Roncka expertly guided the manuscript through production. Tara L. Masih was an excellent copyeditor, sensitive to the quirks of our prose and attentive to detail.

And, finally, we are grateful to Joyce and Ellen, and to Jesse, Dan, Kate, Matthew, and Ben, for their love and support.

Contents

Ways *of* Reading

WORDS AND IMAGES

Introduction

Making a Mark

*R*EADING involves a fair measure of push and shove. You make your mark on a book and it makes its mark on you. Reading is not simply a matter of hanging back and waiting for a piece, or its author, to tell you what the writing has to say. In fact, one of the difficult things about reading is that the pages before you will begin to speak only when the authors are silent and you begin to speak in their place, sometimes for them—doing their work, continuing their projects—and sometimes for yourself, following your own agenda.

This is an unusual way to talk about reading, we know. We have not mentioned finding information or locating an author's purpose or identifying main ideas, useful though these skills are, because the purpose of our book is to offer you occasions to imagine other ways of reading. We think of reading as a social interaction—sometimes peaceful and polite, sometimes not so peaceful and polite.

We'd like you to imagine that when you read the selections we've collected here, somebody is saying something to you, and we'd like you to imagine that you are in a position to speak back, to say something of your own in turn. In other words, we are not presenting our book as a miniature library (a place to find information) and we do not think of you, the reader, as a term-paper writer (a person looking for information to write down on three-by-five cards).

When you read, you hear an author's voice as you move along; you believe a person with something to say is talking to you. You pay attention, even when you don't completely understand what is being said, trusting that it will all make sense in the end, relating what the author says to what you already know or expect to hear or learn. Even if you don't quite grasp everything you are reading at every moment (and you won't), and even if you don't remember everything you've read (no reader does—at least not in long, complex pieces), you begin to see the outlines of the author's project, the patterns and rhythms of that particular way of seeing and interpreting the world.

When you stop to talk or write about what you've read, the author is silent; you take over—it is your turn to write, to begin to respond to what the author said. At that point this author and his or her text become something you construct out of what you remember or what you notice as you go back through the text a second time, working from passages or examples but filtering them through your own predisposition to see or read in particular ways.

Reading, in other words, can be the occasion for you to put things together, to notice this idea or theme rather than that one, to follow a writer's announced or secret ends while simultaneously following your own. When this happens, when you forge a reading of a story or an essay, you make your mark on it, casting it in your terms. But the story makes its mark on you as well, teaching you not only about a subject but about a way of seeing and understanding a subject. The text provides the opportunity for you to see through someone else's powerful language, to imagine your own familiar settings through the images, metaphors, and ideas of others.

Readers learn to put things together by writing. It is not something you can do, at least not to any degree, while you are reading. It requires that you work on what you have read, and that work best takes shape when you sit down to write. We will have more to say about this kind of thinking in a later section of the introduction, but for now let us say that writing gives you a way of going to work on the text you have read. To write about a story or essay, you go back to what you have read to find phrases or passages that define what for you are the key moments, that help you interpret sections that seem difficult or troublesome or mysterious. If you are writing an essay of your own, the work that you are doing gives a purpose and a structure to that rereading.

Writing also, however, gives you a way of going back to work on the text of your own reading. It allows you to be self-critical. You can revise not just to make your essay neat or tight or tidy but to see what kind of reader you have been, to examine the pattern and consequences in the choices you have made. Revision, in other words, gives you the chance to work on your essay, but it also gives you an opportunity to work on your reading—to qualify or extend or question your interpretation of what you have read.

We can describe this process of "re-vision," or re-seeing, fairly simply. You should not expect to read the selections in this book once and completely understand them or know what you want to say. You will work out what you have to say while you write. And once you have constructed a reading—once you have completed a draft of your essay, in other words—you can step back, see what you have done, and go back to work on it. Through this activity—writing and rewriting—we have seen our students become strong, active, and critical readers.

Not everything a reader reads is worth that kind of effort. The readings we have chosen for this book all provide, we feel, powerful ways of seeing (or framing), or provide experiences, with texts and images. The selections cannot be quickly summarized. They are striking, surprising, sometimes troubling in how they challenge common ways of seeing. Some of them—such as James Agee and Walter Evans's *Let Us Now Praise Famous Men* and the selections "Old South" and "Plantation Under the Machine" from Dorothea Lange and Paul S. Taylor's *An American Exodus* have captured and altered the way our culture sees and understands its present and past. The essays have changed the way people think and write. In fact, every selection in the book is one that has given us, our students, and our colleagues that dramatic experience, almost like a discovery, when we suddenly saw things as we had never seen them before and, as a consequence, we had to work hard to understand what had happened and how our thinking had changed.

If we recall, for example, the first time we read Marianne Hirsch's essay, "Projected Memory: Holocaust Photographs in Personal and Public Fantasy" or Roland Barthes's *Camera Lucida,* we know that they have radically shaped our thinking. We carry these essays and their photographs with us in our minds, mulling over them, working through them, hearing Hirsch and Barthes in the sentences we write or sentences we read; we imagine their readings of the photographs in their essays as methods that we take into museums and other photographic essays; we are surprised, reading them for the third or fourth time, to find things we didn't see before. It's not that we failed to "get" these essays the first time around. In fact, we're not sure we have captured them yet, at least not in any final sense, and we disagree in basic ways about what Hirsch and Barthes are saying about photographs or about how these essays might best be used. Essays like these are not the sort that you can "get" like a loaf of bread at the store. We're each convinced that the essays are ours in that we know best what's going on in them, and yet we have also become theirs, creatures of these essays, because of the ways they have come to dominate our seeing, talking, reading, and writing. This captivity is something we welcome, yet it is also something we resist.

Our experience with these texts is a remarkable one and certainly hard to provide for others, but the challenges and surprises are reasons we read—we hope to be taken and changed in just these ways. Or, to be more accurate, it is why we read outside the daily requirements to keep up with the news or conduct our business. And it is why we bring reading into our writing courses.

Ways of Reading Words and Images

Before explaining how we organized this book, we would like to say more about the purpose and place of the kind of strong, aggressive, labor-intensive reading we've been referring to.

Readers face many kinds of experiences, and certain texts are written with specific situations in mind and invite specific ways of reading. Some texts, for instance, serve very practical purposes—they give directions or information. Others, like the short descriptive essays often used in English textbooks and anthologies, celebrate common ways of seeing and thinking and ask primarily to be admired. These texts seem self-contained; they announce their own meanings with little effort and ask little from the reader, making it clear how they want to be read and what they have to say. They ask only for a nod of the head or for the reader to take notes and give a sigh of admiration ("yes, that was very well said"). They are clear and direct. It is as though the authors could anticipate all the questions their own essays might raise and solve all the problems a reader might imagine. There is not much work for a reader to do, in other words, except, perhaps, to take notes and, in the case of textbooks, to work step-by-step, trying to remember as much as possible.

This is how assigned readings are often presented in university classrooms. Introductory textbooks (in biology or business, for instance) are good examples of books that ask little of readers outside of note-taking and memorization. In these texts the writers are experts and your job, as novice, is to digest what they have to say. And, appropriately, the task set before you is to summarize—so you can speak again what the author said, so you can better remember what you read. Essay tests are an example of the writing tasks that often follow this kind of reading. You might, for instance, study the human nervous system through textbook readings and lectures and then be asked to write a summary of what you know from both sources. Or a teacher might ask you during a class discussion to paraphrase a paragraph from a textbook describing chemical cell communication to see if you understand what you've read.

Another typical classroom form of reading is reading for main ideas. With this kind of reading you are expected to figure out what most people (or most people within a certain specialized group of readers) would take as the main idea of a selection. There are good reasons to read for main ideas. For one, it is a way to learn how to imagine and anticipate the values and habits of a particular group—test-makers or, if you're studying business, Keynesian economists, perhaps. If you are studying business, to continue this example, you must learn to notice what Keynesian economists notice—for instance, when they analyze the problems of growing government debt—to share key terms, to know the theoretical positions they take, and to adopt for yourself their common examples and interpretations, their jargon, and their established findings.

There is certainly nothing wrong with reading for information or reading to learn what experts have to say about their fields of inquiry. These are not, however, the only ways to read, although they are the ones most often taught. Perhaps because we think of ourselves as writing teachers, we are concerned with presenting other ways of reading in the college and university curriculum.

A danger arises in assuming that reading is only a search for information or main ideas. There are ways of thinking through problems and working with written texts which are essential to academic life, but which are not represented by summary and paraphrase or by note-taking and essay exams.

Student readers, for example, can take responsibility for determining the meaning of the text. They can work as though they were doing something other than finding ideas already there on the page, and they can be guided by their own impressions or questions as they read. We are not, now, talking about finding hidden meanings. If such things as hidden meanings can be said to exist, they are hidden by readers' habits and prejudices (by readers' assumptions that what they read should tell them what they already know), or by readers' timidity and passivity (by their unwillingness to take the responsibility to speak their minds and say what they notice).

Reading to locate meaning in the text places a premium on memory, yet a strong reader is not necessarily a person with a good memory. This point may seem minor, but we have seen too many students haunted because they could not retain a complete essay in their minds. A reader could set herself the task of remembering as much as she could from Roland Barthes's book *Camera Lucida,* but a reader could also do other things with that book; a reader might use the book to think about Barthes's approach to photographs as a lesson in how to make a personal, quirky way of reading photographs into interesting intellectual work. Students who read Barthes's prose as a memory test end up worrying about bits and pieces (bits and pieces they could go back and find if they had to) and turn their attention away from the more pressing problem of how to make sense of a difficult and often ambiguous essay.

A reader who needs to have access to something in a book can use simple memory aids. A reader can go back and scan, for one thing, to find passages or examples that might be worth reconsidering. Or a reader can construct a personal index, making marks in the margin or underlining passages that seem interesting or mysterious or difficult. A mark is a way of saying, "This is something I might want to work on later." If you mark the selections in this book as you read them, you will give yourself a working record of what, at the first moment of reading, you felt might be worth a second reading.

If Edward Said's essay (to change our example) presents problems for a reader, they are problems of a different order from summary and recall altogether. The essay is not the sort that tells you what it says. You would have difficulty finding one sentence that sums up or announces, in a loud and clear voice, what he is talking about. At the point you think Said is about to summarize, he turns to one more example, or he inserts a Jean Mohr photograph, that complicates what he's saying, as though what he is discussing defines his attempts to sum things up. If Said has a point to make, it cannot be stated in a sentence or two.

In fact, Said's essay is challenging reading in part because it does not have a single, easily identifiable main idea. A reader could infer that it has several points to make, none of which can be said easily and some of which, perhaps, are contradictory. To search for information, or to ignore the rough edges in search of a single, paraphrasable idea, is to divert attention from the task at hand, which is not to remember what Said says but to speak about the essay and what it means to you, the reader. In this sense, the Said essay is not the sum of its individual parts; it is, more accurately, what its readers make of it.

A reader could go to an expert on Palestine or on photographic essays to solve the problem of what to make of the essay—perhaps to a teacher, perhaps to a book in the library. And if the reader pays attention, he could remember what the expert said or he could put down notes on paper. But in doing either, the reader only rehearses what he has been told, abandoning the responsibility to make the essay meaningful. There are ways of reading, in other words, in which Said's essay "States," from *After the Last Sky,* is not what it means to the experts but what it means to you as a reader willing to take the chance to construct a reading that moves back and forth between Said's prose and the photographs in the text. You can be the authority on Said; you don't have to turn to others. The meaning of the essay, then, is something you develop as you go along, something for which you must take final responsibility. The meaning is forged from reading the essay, to be sure, but it is determined by what you do with the essay, by the connections you can make and your explanation of why those connections are important, and by your account of what Said might mean when he talks about "exile" and "dispossession," or "the striking thing about Palestinian prose and prose fiction is its formal instability (words and phrases Said uses as key terms in the essay). This version of Said's essay will finally be yours; it will not be exactly what Said said. (Only his words in the order he wrote them would say exactly what he said). You will choose the path to take through his essay and support it as you would with arguments, explanations, examples, and commentary.

If an essay or a story is not the sum of its parts but something you as a reader create by putting together those parts that seem to matter personally, then the way to begin, once you have read a selection in this collection, is by reviewing what you recall, by going back to those places that stick in your memory—or, perhaps, to those sections you marked with checks or notes in the margins. You begin by seeing what you can make of these memories and notes. You should realize that with essays as long and complex as those we've included in this book, you will never feel, after a single reading, as though you have command of everything you read. This is not a problem. After four or five readings (should you give any single essay that much attention), you may still feel that there are parts you missed or don't understand. This sense of incompleteness is part of the experience of reading, at least the experience of reading serious work. And it is part of the experience of a strong reader. No reader could retain one of these essays in her mind, no matter how proficient her memory or how experienced she might be. No reader, at least no reader we would trust, would admit that she understood everything Marianne Hirsch or W. J. T. Mitchell had to say, or that she knew exactly what to make of John Berger's claims that good photographs are long quotations from reality. What strong readers know is that they have to begin, and they have to begin regardless of their doubts or hesitations. What you have after your first reading of an essay is a starting place, and you begin with your marked passages or examples or notes, with questions to answer, or with problems to solve. Strong readings, in other words, put a premium on individual acts of attention and composition.

Strong Readers, Strong Texts

We chose texts for this book that invite strong readings. Our selections require more attention (or a different form of attention) than a written summary, a reduction to gist, or a recitation of main ideas. They are not "easy" reading. The challenges they present, however, do not make them inaccessible to college students. The essays are not specialized studies; they have interested, pleased, or piqued general and specialist audiences alike. To say that they are challenging is to say, then, that they leave some work for a reader to do. They are designed to teach a reader new ways to read (or to step outside habitual ways of reading), and they anticipate readers willing to take the time to learn. These readers need not be experts on the subject matter. Perhaps the most difficult problem for students is to believe that this is true.

You do not need experts to explain these texts, although you could probably go to the library and find an expert guide to most of the selections we've included. Let's take, for example, an argument made by Marianne Hirsch in her essay "Projected Memory: Holocaust Photographs in Personal and Public Fantasy." Hirsch studies images of children from the Holocaust and the ways in which certain of these have become "public images" that allow people to identify with and fantasize about them. She coins the term "postmemory" to stand for the way these images affect "the experiences of those who grow up dominated by narratives that preceded their birth, whose own belated stories are displaced by the stories of the previous generation, shaped by traumatic events that they can neither understand nor re-create." You could go to the library to find out how Hirsch is regarded by experts, literary critics, or Holocaust historians, for example; you could learn how her work fits into an established body of work on Holocaust writing and the influences of public photographs on people's fantasies. You could see what others have said about the writers and photographers she cites: Lorie Novak, Art Spiegelman, Marjorie Agosín, or Bruno Bettelheim. You could see how others have interpreted the photographs she includes as part of her argument. You could look for standard definitions of key terms like "postmemory" or "fantasy."

Though it is often important to seek out other texts and to know what other people are saying or have said, it is often necessary and even desirable to begin on your own. Hirsch can also be read outside any official system of interpretation. She is talking, after all, about our daily experience. And when she addresses the reader, she addresses a person—not a term-paper writer. When she writes, "As we look at the face of the child victim—Anne Frank, or the little boy from Warsaw—do we not also see there what the child saw?" she refers to us and what we know and how we know and see these images.

The question, then, is not what Hirch's words might mean to a literary critic, or generally to those who study images of the Holocaust. The question is what you, the reader, can make of those words and Hirsch's use of them in the essay, given your experience, your goals, and the work you do with what she has written. In this sense, "Projected Memory" is not what it means to others (those who have already decided what it means) but what it means to you, and this meaning is something you compose when you write about the essay; it is your account of what Hirsch says and how what she says might be said to make sense.

A teacher, poet, and critic we admire, I. A. Richards, once said, "Read as though it made sense and perhaps it will." To take command of complex material like the selections in this book, you need not subordinate yourself to experts; you can assume the authority to provide such a reading on your own. This means you must allow yourself a certain tentativeness and recognize your limits. You should not assume that it is your job to solve the problems between men and women. You can speak with authority while still acknowledging that complex issues *are* complex.

There is a paradox here. On the one hand, the essays are rich, magnificent, too big for anyone to completely grasp all at once, and before them, as before inspiring spectacles, it seems appropriate to stand humbly, admiringly. And yet, on the other hand, a reader must speak with authority.

In "The American Scholar," Ralph Waldo Emerson says, "Meek young men grow up in libraries, believing it their duty to accept the views which Cicero, which Locke, which Bacon, have given, forgetful that Cicero, Locke, and Bacon were only young men in libraries when they wrote these books." What Emerson offers here is not a fact but an attitude. There is creative reading, he says, as well as creative writing. It is up to you to treat authors as your equals, as people who will allow you to speak too. At the same time, you must respect the difficulty and complexity of their texts and of the issues and questions they examine. Little is to be gained, in other words, by turning one of the selections that follow into a message that would fit on a poster in a dorm room: "Live Your Own Life" or "Beware of Public Images."

Reading with and against the Grain

From this pushing and shoving with and against texts, we come then to a difficult mix of authority and humility. A reader takes charge of a text; a reader gives generous attention to someone else's (a writer's) key terms and methods, commits his time to her examples, tries to think in her language, imagines that this strange work is important, compelling, at least for the moment.

To read generously, to work inside someone else's system, to see your world in someone else's terms—we call this "reading with the grain." It is a way of working *with* a writer's ideas, in conjunction with someone else's text. As a way of reading, it can take different forms. In the reading and writing assignments that follow the selections in this book, you will sometimes be asked to summarize and paraphrase, to put others' ideas into your terms, to provide your account of what they are saying. This is a way of getting a tentative or provisional hold on a text, its examples and ideas; it allows you a place to begin to work. And sometimes you will be asked to extend a writer's project—to add your examples to someone else's argument, to read your experience through the frame of another's text, to try out the key terms and interpretive schemes in another writer's work.

We have also asked students to read against the grain, to read critically, to turn back, for example, *against* a writer's project, to ask questions they believe might come as a surprise, to look for the limits of the writer's vision, to provide alternate readings of his or her examples, to find examples that challenge the writer's argument, to engage the writer, in other words, in dialogue.

This, we've found, is the most difficult work for students to do, this work against the grain. For good reasons and bad, students typically define their skill by reproducing rather than questioning or revising the work of their teachers (or the work of those their teachers ask them to read). It is important to read generously and carefully and to learn to submit to projects that others have begun. But it is also important to know what you are doing—to understand where this work comes from, whose interests it serves, how and where it is kept together by will rather than desire, and what it might have to do with you. To fail to ask the fundamental questions—Where am I in this? how can I make my mark? whose interests are represented? what can I learn by reading with or against the grain?—to fail to ask these questions is to mistake skill for understanding, and it is to misunderstand the goals of a liberal education. All of the essays in this book, we would argue, ask to be read, not simply reproduced; they ask to be read and to be read with a difference. Our goal is to make that difference possible.

Reading and Writing: The Questions and Assignments

Strong readers, we've said, remake what they have read to serve their own ends, putting things together, figuring out how ideas and examples relate, explaining as best they can material that is difficult or problematic, translating phrases into their own terms. At these moments, it is hard to distinguish the act of reading from the act of writing. In fact, the connection between reading and writing can be seen as almost a literal one, since the best way you can show your reading of a rich and dense essay is by writing down your thoughts, placing one idea against another, commenting on what you've done, taking examples into account, looking back at where you began, perhaps changing your mind, and moving on.

Readers, however, seldom read a single essay in isolation, as though their only job were to arrive at some sense of what an essay has to say. Although we couldn't begin to provide examples of all the various uses of reading in academic life, it is often the case that readings provide information and direction for investigative projects, whether they are philosophical or scientific in nature. The reading and writing assignments that follow each selection in this book are designed to point you in certain directions, to give you ideas and projects to work with, and to challenge you to see one writer's ideas through another's.

Strong readers often read critically, weighing, for example, an author's claims and interpretations against evidence—evidence provided by the author in the text, evidence drawn from other sources, or the evidence that is assumed to be part of a reader's own knowledge and experience. Critical reading can produce results as far-reaching as a biochemist publicly challenging the findings and interpretations in an article on cancer research in the *New England Journal of Medicine* or as quiet as a student offering a personal interpretation of a story in class discussion.

You will find that the questions we have included in our reading and writing assignments often direct you to test what you think an author is saying by measuring it against your own experience. If the writers in this book are urging you to give strong readings of your common experience, you have access to what they say because they are talking not only to you but about you. You can try out their methods and their terms on examples of your own, continuing their arguments as though you were working with them on a common project. Or you can test their arguments as though you want to see not only where and how they will work but where and how they will not. You will also find questions that ask you to extend the argument of an essay by looking in detail at some of the essay's own examples.

Readers, as we have said, seldom read an essay in isolation, as though, having once worked out a reading of "Projected Memory" they could go on to something else, something unrelated. It is unusual for anyone, at least in an academic setting, to read in so random a fashion. Readers read most often because they have a project in hand—a question they are working on or a problem they are trying to solve.

In a sense, you do have the chance to become an expert reader, a reader with a project in hand, one who has already done some reading, who has watched others at work, and who has begun to develop a method of analysis and a set of key terms. You might read Roland Barthes's essay from *Camera Lucida,* for example, in the context of John Berger's "Appearances." Imagining yourself thinking about images and texts alongside some of the major figures in contemporary thought can be great fun and heady work—particularly when you have the occasion to speak back to those figures.

In every case, then, the material we provide to direct your work on the essay, or story will have you constructing a reading, but then doing something with what you have read—using the selection as a frame through which you can understand (through which you can "read") your own experience, the examples of others, or the ideas and methods of other writers.

You may find that you have to alter your sense of who a writer is and what a writer does as you work on your own writing. Writers are often told that they need to begin with a clear sense of what they want to do and what they want to say. The writing assignments we've written, we believe, give you a sense of what you want (or need) to do. We define a problem for you to work on, and the problem will frame the task for you. You will have to decide where you will go in the texts you have read to find materials to work with, the primary materials that will give you a place to begin as you work on your essay. It would be best, however, if you did not feel that you need to have a clear sense of what you want to say before you begin. You may begin to develop a sense of what you want to say while you are writing—as you begin, for example, to examine how and why Hirsch's prose could be said to be difficult to read, and what that difficulty might enable you to say about what Hirsch expects of a reader. It may also be the case, however, that the subjects you will be writing about are too big for you to assume that you need to have all the answers or that it is up to you to have the final word or to solve the problems once and for all. When you work on your essays, you should cast yourself in the role of one who is exploring a question, examining what might be said, and speculating on possible rather than certain conclusions. If you consider your responses to be provisional, examples of what might be said by a bright and serious student at this point in time, you will be in a position to learn more, as will those who read what you write. Think of yourself, then, as a writer intent on opening a subject up rather than closing one down.

Let us turn briefly now to the four categories of reading and writing assignments you will find in the book.

Questions for a Second Reading

Immediately following each selection are questions designed to guide your second reading. You may, as we've said, prefer to follow your own instincts as you search for the materials to build your understanding of the essay or story. These questions are meant to assist that process or develop those instincts. Most of the selections in this book are longer and more difficult than those you may be accustomed to reading. They are difficult enough that any reader would have to reread them and work to understand them; these questions are meant to suggest ways of beginning that work.

The second reading questions characteristically ask you to consider the relations between ideas and examples in what you have read or to test specific statements in the essays against your own experience (so that you can get a sense of the author's habit of mind, his or her way of thinking about subjects that are available to you, too). Some turn your attention to what we take to be key terms or concepts, asking you to define these terms by observing how the writer uses them throughout the essay.

These are the questions that seemed "natural" to us; they reflect our habitual way of reading and, we believe, the general habits of mind of the academic community. These questions have no simple answers; you will not find a correct answer hidden somewhere in the selection. In short, they are not the sorts of questions asked on SAT or ACT exams. They are real questions, questions that ask about the basic methods of an essay or about the issues the essay raises. They pose problems for interpretation or indicate sections where, to our minds, there is some interesting work for a reader to do. They are meant to reveal possible ways of reading the text, not to indicate that there is only one correct way, and that we have it.

You may find it useful to take notes as you read through each selection a second time, perhaps in a journal you can keep as a sourcebook for more formal written work.

Assignments for Writing

At the end of each selection, you will also find a set of writing assignments that ask you to write about a single selection. All of these assignments serve a dual purpose. Like the second reading questions, they suggest a way for you to reconsider what you have read; they give you access from a different perspective. The assignments also encourage you to be a strong reader and actively interpret what you have read. In one way or another, they all invite you to use a story or an essay as a way of framing experience, as a source of terms and methods to enable you to interpret something else—some other text, events and objects around you, or your own memories and experience.

When we talk with teachers and students using our books, we are often asked about the wording of these assignments. The assignments are long. The wording is often unusual, unexpected. The assignments contain many questions, not simply one. The directions seem indirect, confusing. "Why?" we're asked. "How should we work with these?" When we write assignments, our goal is to point students toward a project, to provide a frame for their reading, a motive for writing, a way of asking certain kinds of questions. In that sense, the assignments should not be read as a set of directions to be followed literally. In fact, they are written to resist that reading, to forestall a writer's desire to simplify, to be efficient, to settle for the first clear line toward the finish. We want to provide a context to suggest how readers and writers might take time, be thoughtful. And we want the projects students work on to become their own. We hope to provoke varied responses, to leave the final decisions to the students. So the assignments try to be open and suggestive rather than narrow and direct. We ask lots of questions, but students don't need to answer them all (or any of them) once they begin to write. Our questions are meant to suggest ways of questioning, starting points.

"What do you want?" Our own students ask this question. We want writers to make the most they can of what they read, including our questions and assignments.

Making Connections

The connections questions will have you work with two or more readings at a time. These are not so much questions that ask you to compare or contrast the essays as they are directions on how you might use one text as the context for interpreting another. W. J. T. Mitchell, for example, in "The Photographic Essay: Four Case Studies" examines *Let Us Now Praise Famous Men,* the photographic essay by James Agee and Walker Evans, as well as *Camera Lucida* by Roland Barthes and *After the Last Sky,* a photographic essay by Edward Said and Jean Mohr. Selections from these three photographic essays are also included in this book. So there is an assignment that asks you first to read the relationship of words and images in Roland Barthes's *Camera Lucida,* as your own project, and to reread, then, the relationship through Mitchell's essay, dealing in his ideas about "the dialectic of exchange and resistance" between words and images in photographic essays. You are invited to treat Mitchell's work as a source for your essay, a source that you might borrow from, comment on, or critique as a part of your writing about the relationship of words and images in *Camera Lucida.* There are assignments, then, such as this one, that ask you to extend and to test Mitchell's understanding of the relationship between words and images through your readings of other, "thicker" selections from each of three of the texts he uses for his case studies. In another assignment, you are asked to consider different ways of writing about the ways photographs create meaning by trying out, for example, the way Roland Barthes reads photographs so that you can test his claims against those made by John Berger, in his essay *Appearances,* after you try out Berger's way of reading photographs. You do this work so that you can imagine how Berger might comment on Barthes's understanding of the photographs he reads and how Barthes might comment on Berger's readings.

The purpose of all these assignments is to demonstrate how the work of one author can be used as a frame for reading and interpreting the work of another. This can be exciting work, and it demonstrates a basic principle of liberal arts education: students should be given the opportunity to adopt different points of view, including those of scholars and writers who have helped shape modern thought. These kinds of assignments give you the chance, even as a novice, to try your hand at the work of professionals.

The Assignment Sequences

The assignments in a sequence build on one another, each relying on the ones before, bringing the reading together in a scholarly project. The five sequences suggested at the end of this book, for example, bring together very different kinds of texts and authors: an essay on documentary work from an author who has devoted his life to such work (Coles); a section from two quite different book-length photographic essays on the American Depression by photographers and writers who caught the world's attention (Lange and Taylor; Agee and Evans); a photographic essay on the strange phenomenon of "postmemory" and the children of Holocaust survivors (Hirsch); two photographic essays by two leading intellectuals of our times who turn their attention to the ways we understand photographs (Berger and Barthes); a challenging analysis of the relationship of words and images that uses examples from other photographic essays in this book (Mitchell); and an essay on Palestine accompanied by photographs the author could not take himself (Said and Mohr). These are pieces that would not "normally" be read together. They are written for different audiences; they represent different genres, although they all deal in some way with the relationships of words and images, and they come from different times and places. Here, in this book, they are read as part of a number of projects looking at how writing and images coexist in essays, shaping each other, and the ways in which the authors of these essays imagine the purposes and uses of words and images together.

The questions we ask in the sequences of assignments, then, ask for something other than comparison and contrast. They direct your attention back to the texts you have read (so that you can understand them better or better understand how they do their work); they direct your attention from the book back out to your world, so that you can think about local texts, photographs, scenes, and figures through the terms and examples provided by your reading; and they ask you to read one selection in relation to another. John Berger, for example, writes around a set of photographs that seem to him to quote from appearances. He argues that the meaning of a significant photograph resides in the way it confirms individual subjectivity while, at the same time, it captures a "residue of continuous experience" that is more than any individual reader's response to it. Berger's reading of photographs and the terms he uses to describe the way he reads them provides a powerful context for a reader looking at essays and photographs by other authors, like Roland Barthes or Dorothea Lange and Paul Taylor. There are, then, assignments that ask you both to extend and to test Berger's reading through your reading of alternative photographs. In another assignment, you are asked to consider different ways of understanding photographs by looking at the work in two very different texts: James Agee and Walker Evans's *Let Us Now Praise Famous Men* and Roland Barthes's excerpt from *Camera Lucida.* The work of Agee and Evans "documenting" the Depression has an urgency and social agenda quite different from Roland Barthes's self-assigned project to come to some understanding of why he likes the photographs he likes.

The purpose of these assignments is to demonstrate how the work of one author can be used as a frame for reading and interpreting the work of another. This can be exciting work, and it demonstrates a basic principle of liberal arts education: students should be given the opportunity to adopt different points of view, including those of scholars and writers who have helped to shape modern thought.

Each assignment sequence links several reading and writing assignments and directs them toward a single goal. The assignments allow you to work on projects that require more time and incorporate more readings than would be possible in a single assignment. And they encourage you to develop your own point of view in concert with those of the professionals who wrote the selections you are reading.

The assignments allow you to participate in an extended academic project, one in which you take a position, revise it, look at a new example, hear what someone else has to say, revise it again, and see what conclusions you can draw about your subject. These projects always take time—they go through stages and revisions as a writer develops a command over his or her material, pushing against habitual ways of thinking, learning to examine an issue from different angles, rejecting quick conclusions, seeing the power of understanding that comes from repeated effort, and feeling the pleasure writers take when they find their own place in the context of others whose work they admire. This is the closest approximation we can give you of the rhythm and texture of academic life, and we offer our book as an introduction to its characteristic ways of reading, seeing, thinking, and writing.

The Readings

JAMES AGEE and WALKER EVANS

FRESH OUT OF HARVARD in 1932, James Agee (1909–1955) landed a job with Fortune *magazine, a publication dedicated to the service of wealth and power. The early thirties, however, was the time of the Great Depression. By 1932, approximately one out of every four Americans was unemployed. Agee, like many writers and intellectuals of his generation, struggled to come to terms with the gap between rich and poor, with what was happening in the country, and with a sense of his own powerlessness and complicity. In June 1936, he was given the assignment to travel to the Deep South with Walker Evans, the photographer, to do a story on "an average white family of tenant farmers." That evening, he wrote of his excitement to Father James Flyte, his former teacher and lifelong friend: "Best break I ever had on* Fortune. *Feel terrific personal responsibility toward story; considerable doubts of my ability to bring it off; considerable more of* Fortune's *ultimate willingness to use it as it seems (in theory) to me."*

With their assignment in hand, Agee and Evans headed out to meet the poor—not an easy task, particularly given Agee's concern to show proper respect for his subject and to produce work that was not simply exploiting their poverty for his and Evans's gain. Hence his feeling that they were "spies" in rural Alabama. With considerable awkwardness and a touch of good luck, Agee and Evans won the trust of three families and spent eight weeks taking notes and pictures.

The article they prepared was never published. Agee's editor rejected the draft he submitted and ordered a rewrite. Agee refused and proposed to take the project to a book publisher, but Fortune *owned the rights to the story and refused to release Agee from his contract. In 1937,* Fortune *relented; Agee began work again on the project, and in 1939 he and Evans submitted a book manuscript to the publisher under the title* Three Tenant Families. *Again the manuscript was rejected, largely as a result of the oddness of the writing and the demands it placed on its readers. It was also the case, however, that others—novelists (including John Steinbeck) and photographers (like Margaret Bourke-White)—had been publishing books on the plight of the rural poor. And, with the growing attention to events in Europe (Hitler had attacked Poland), the public's attention was drifting elsewhere. By 1941, Agee was writing for* Time *magazine. Through friends, Agee made contact with an editor for the Houghton Mifflin Company, who believed in the project, including the experiment in writing, and agreed to publish the manuscript with very few revisions.*

The book met with very limited success. The critics objected to the prose—"the choicest recent example of how to write self-inspired, self-conscious, and self-indulgent prose"—and the sales were poor. However, one influential critic, Lionel Trilling (then a professor of English at Columbia), wrote, "I feel sure that this is a great book."

> *Agee has a sensibility so precise, so unremitting, that it is sometimes appalling; and though nothing can be more tiresome than protracted sensibility, Agee's never wearies us: I think this is because it is brilliantly normal and because it is a moral rather than a physical sensibility. . . . The book is full of marvelous writing which gives a kind of hot pleasure that words can do so much.*

For Agee, the writing in Let Us Now Praise Famous Men *was an experiment, an attempt to represent real life and real people and to do so beyond the limits of traditional journalism. At an early stage in the project, he wrote that the text*

> *is to be as exhaustive a reproduction and analysis of personal experience, including the phases and problems of memory and recall and revisitation and the problems of writing and of communication, as I am capable of, with constant bearing on two points: to tell everything possible as accurately as possible: and to invent nothing. It involves therefore as total a suspicion of "creative" and "artistic" as of "reportorial" attitudes and methods, and it is likely therefore to involve the development of some more or less new forms of writing and of observation.*

It was not until the 1960s, when the book was reprinted, that Let Us Now Praise Famous Men *found its broad audience, initially made up of young Northern civil rights workers making a trip to the South, as Agee and Evans had done, with the hope of doing some good. And the prose became an early model for what we now think of as the "New Journalism" or "Creative Nonfiction." James Agee's books include the autobiographical novels* The Morning Watch *(1951) and* A Death in the Family *(1957) and a collection of film criticism,* Agee on Film *(1958–60); his work as a screenwriter includes* The African Queen *(1951) and* The Night of the Hunter *(1955).*

In 1935, Walker Evans (1903–1975) had been hired as a photographer by the Resettlement Administration (later known as the Farm Security Agency or FSA) to document the conditions faced by displaced farmers. These documentary projects, sponsored by the federal government as part of President Franklin D. Roosevelt's New Deal programs, were designed to bring the reality of rural poverty into the homes of urban Americans, with the goal of creating a national sense of crisis and providing visual evidence of the changes in rural life brought about by the Depression, the Dust Bowl, and farm mechanization. Roy Striker, the director of the photography unit, said, "We are going to have to turn to new devices, the movie and the still pictures and other things . . . to tell the rest of the world that there is a lower third [and] that they are human beings like the rest of us. . . ." The unflinching, heads-on, grim black-and-white style of photography that we associate with photographic "realism" is a product of the work of this era. From 1935 to 1937, Evans worked for the FSA's photographic survey of rural America and traveled throughout the South taking pictures.

In 1936, he took a leave of absence to work with James Agee on the project for Fortune *that later became* Let Us Now Praise Famous Men. *While Agee struggled with his end of the project, Evans worked fairly quickly. After the summer in the field, he returned to New York in the fall and printed and organized his shots, dividing the photographs selected for the volume into the four categories represented by the following sections, with particular attention to sequence. There was great care in the framing and printing of the images. It is important to consider also the care in their organization and presentation. Evans later said that his work in the 1930s was "neither journalistic [n]or political in technique and intention. It was reflective rather than tendentious and, in a certain way, disinterested."*

Evans worked for Time *magazine from 1943 to 1945 and then for* Fortune *from 1945 to 1965 as Special Photographic Editor, producing both portfolios and photographic essays. After his retirement from* Fortune, *Evans taught photography at Yale. Walker Evans published two books of photographs:* American Photographs *(1938) and* Many Are Called *(1966). His work has since been collected in a number of editions and was the subject of a recent show at the Metropolitan Museum of Art in New York City.*

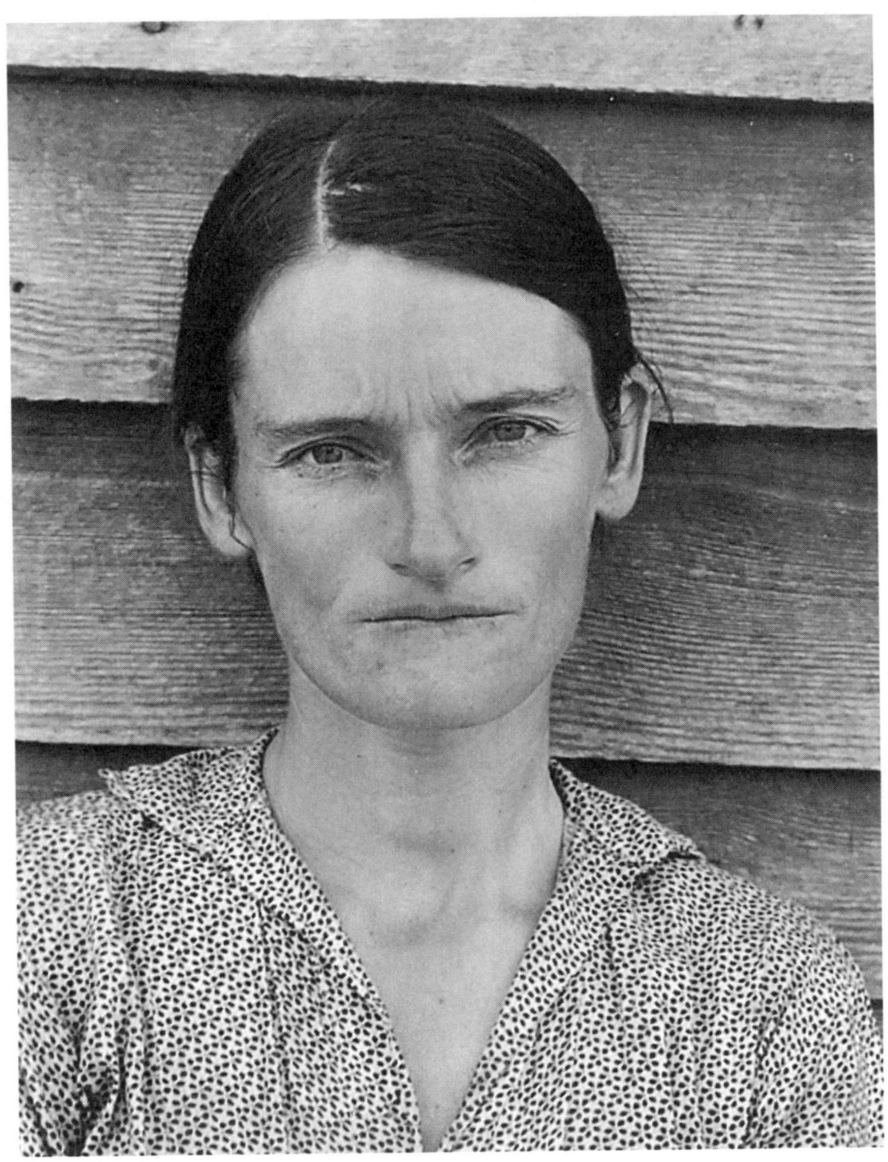

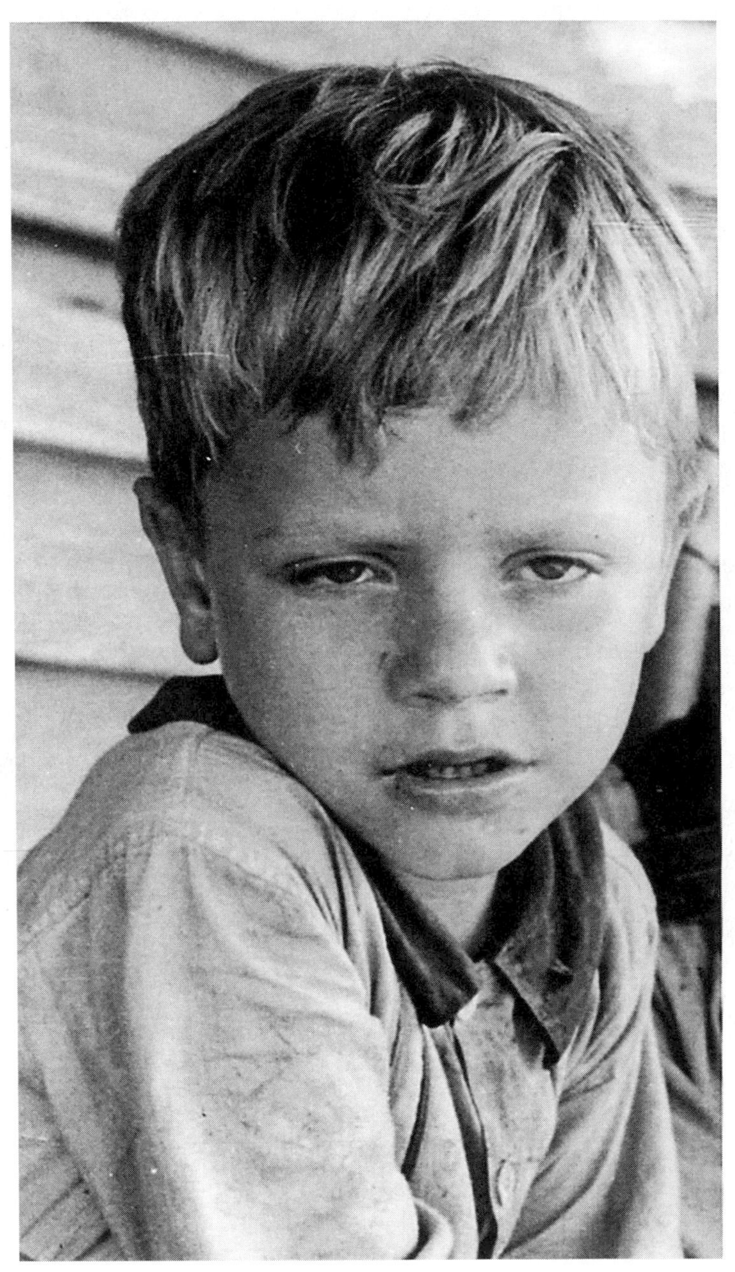

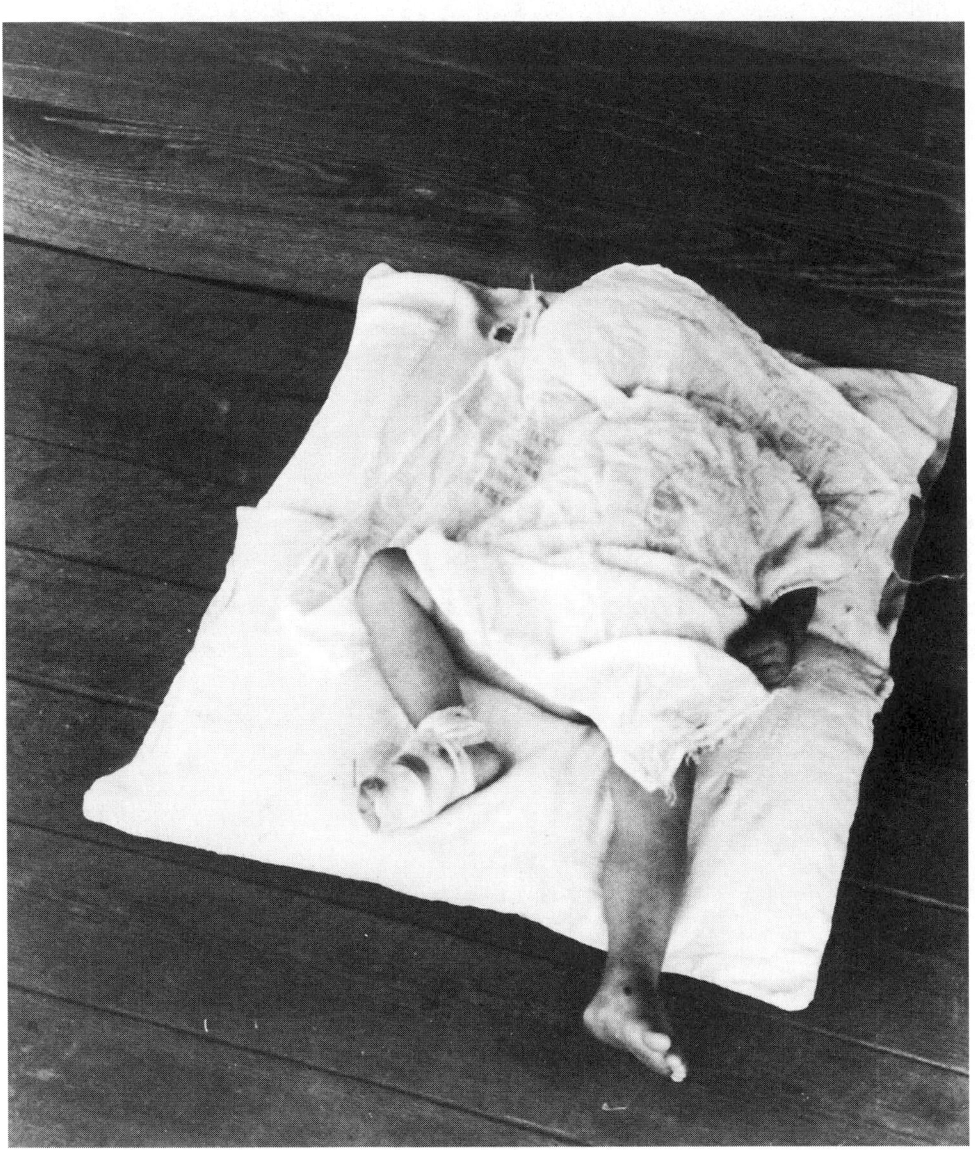

AVONDALE

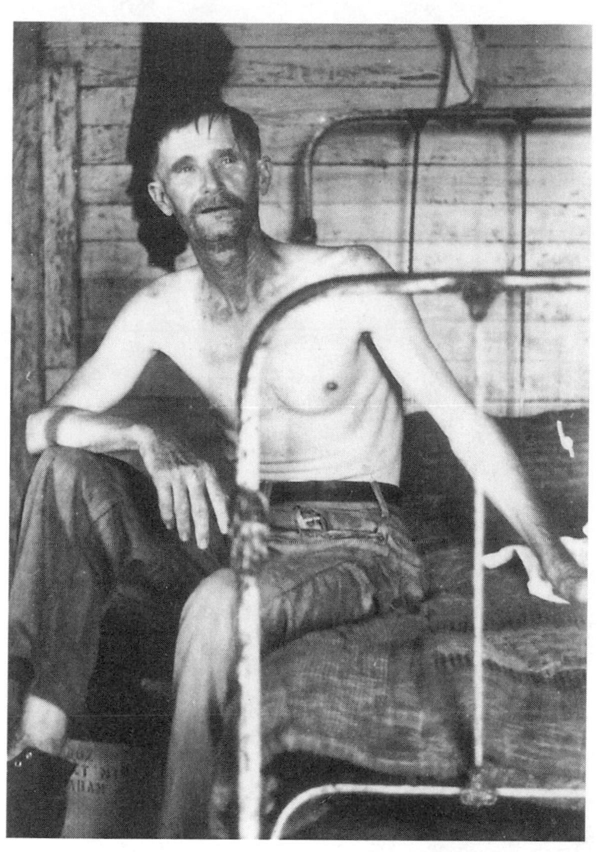

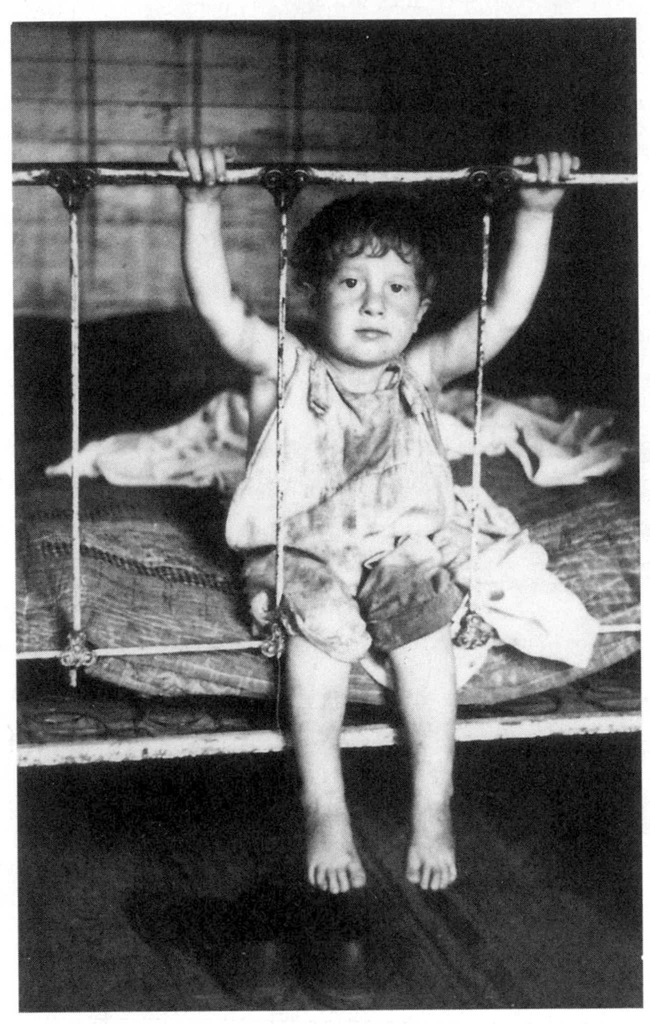

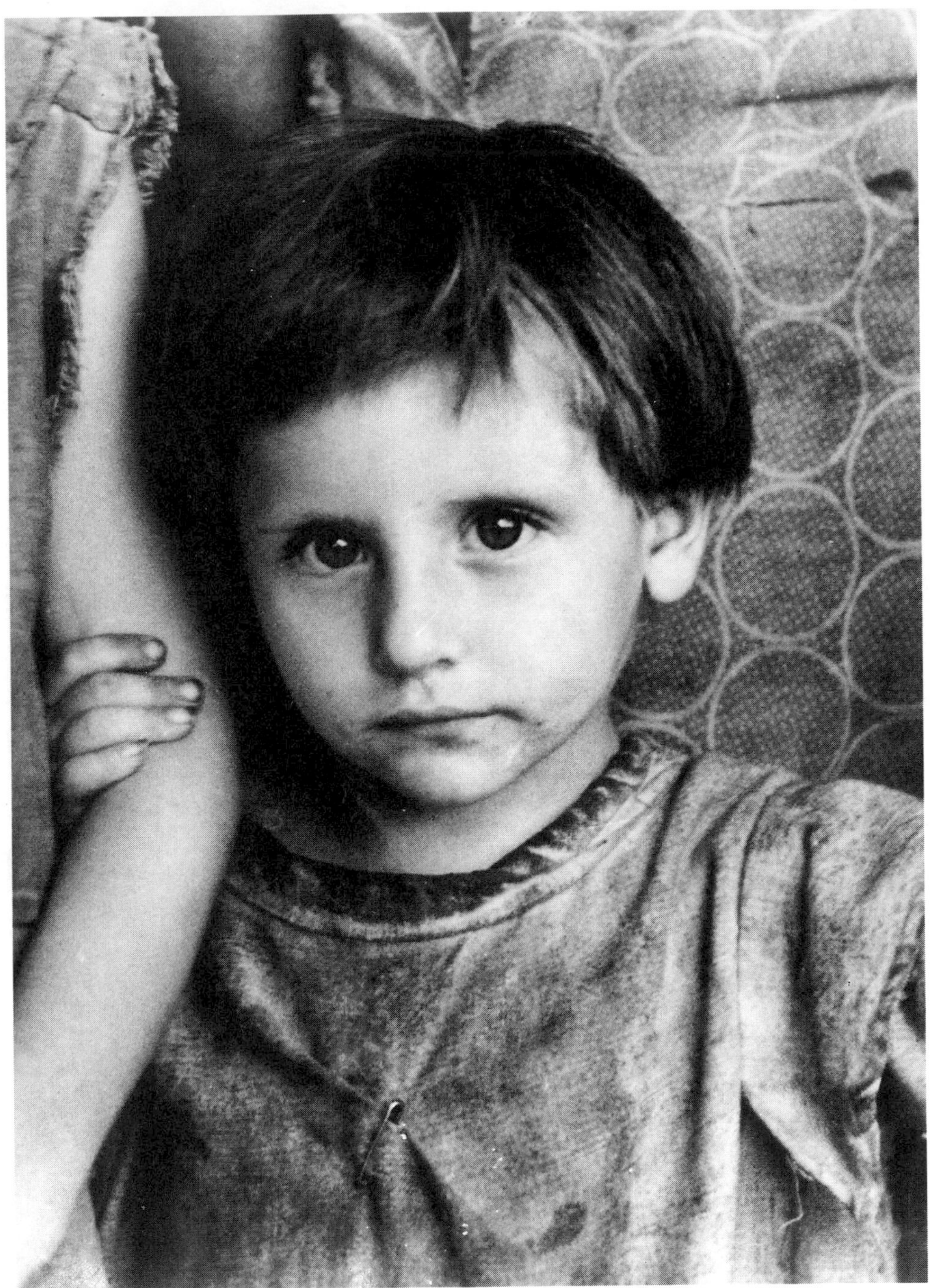

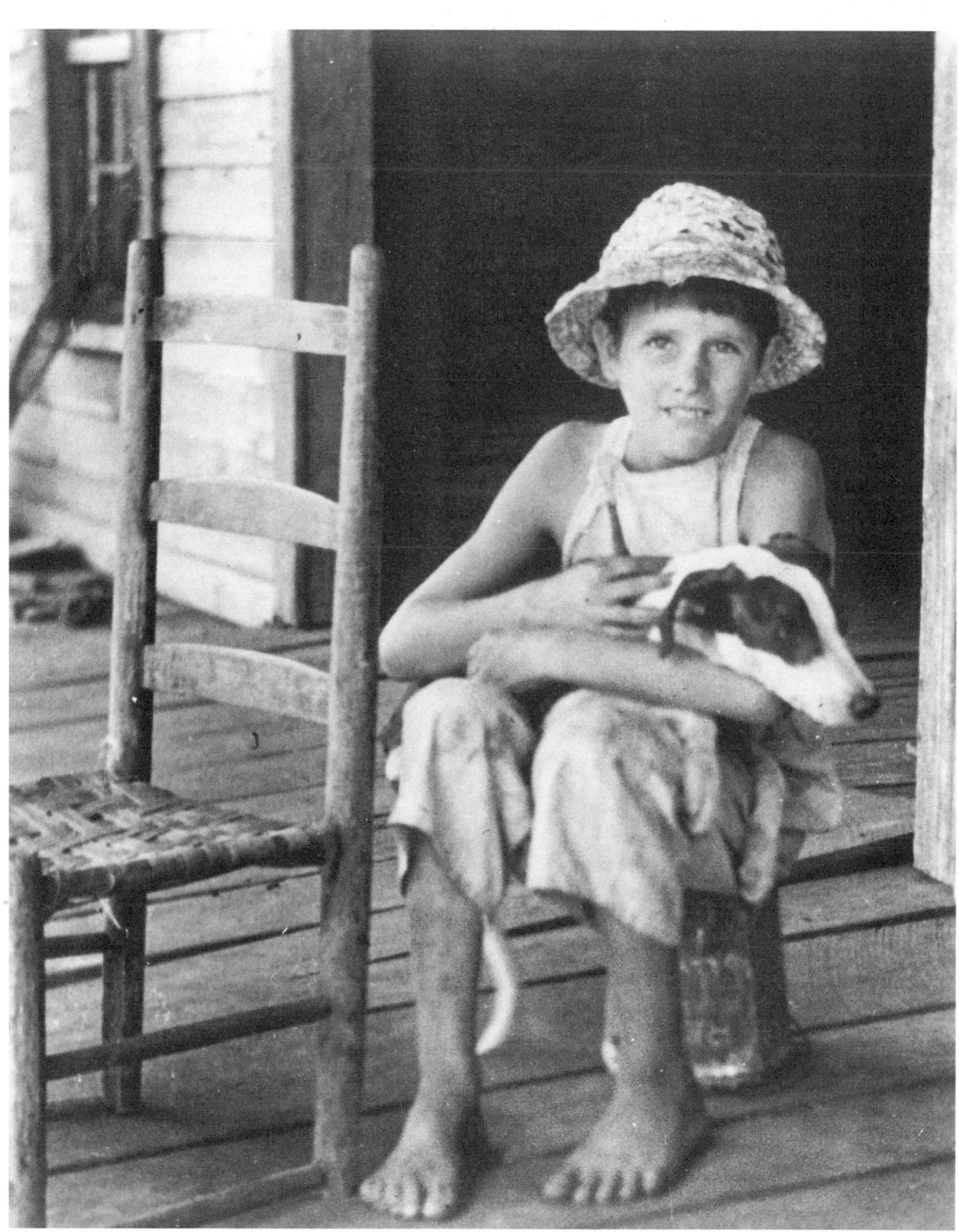

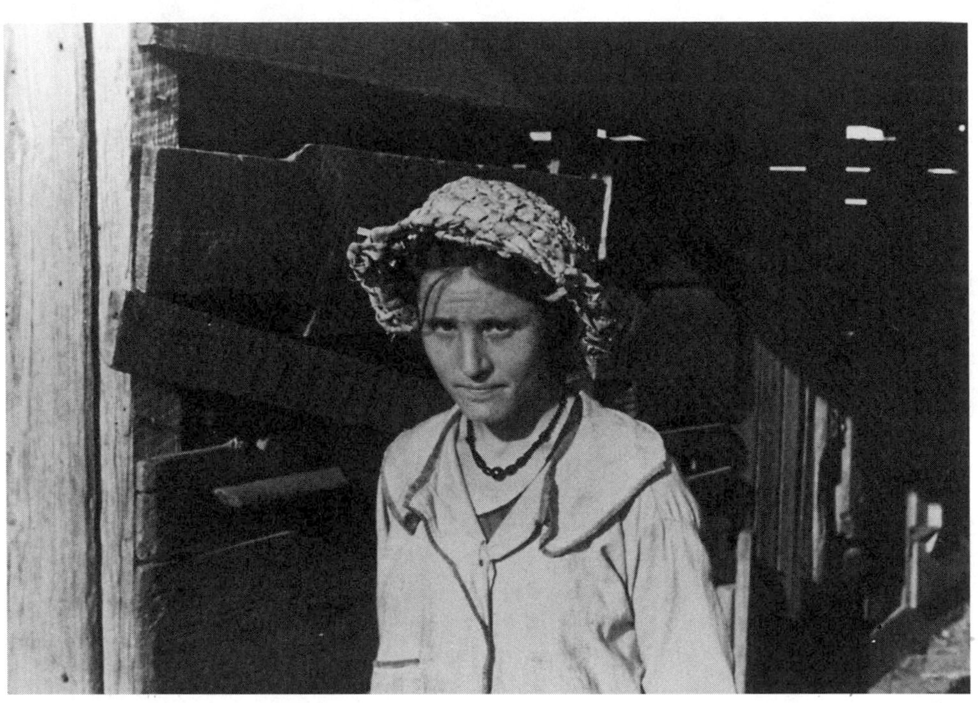

PLEASE BE
QUITE Every
body is Welcome

ogressive Farmer
RAUGHT
BILIOUSNESS
1935
AUGUST
Alka-Seltzer
Famous
Family Laxative
1936 JULY 1936
CARDUI
Owens & Owens
A Purely Vegetable Medicin
JUNE

C.A. JOHNSON & SON
McCOLLUM GROCERY CO.
Coca-Cola

Coca-Cola
NEHI

FREE
DANCE

MAYORS OFFICE

DRINK
Coca-Cola
DRINK
NEHI
GROVES
CHILL
TONIC
MONTGOMERY
RINGLING
BROS

666
COLDS
FEVER

ST. MATTHEW
SCHOOL.

BARBER
SHOP
SHOE SHINE

SILAS GREEN SHOW
ORLEANS

C.LEAN HILL
SCHOOL

U.S. POST OFFICE SPROTT ALA.
Coca-Cola
PAN-AM

Let Us Now Praise Famous Men

Preface

(Serious readers are advised to proceed to the book-proper after finishing the first section of the Preface. A later return will do no harm.)

During July and August 1936 Walker Evans and I were traveling in the middle south of this nation, and were engaged in what, even from the first, has seemed to me rather a curious piece of work. It was our business to prepare, for a New York magazine,[1] an article on cotton tenantry in the United States, in the form of a photographic and verbal record of the daily living and environment of an average white family of tenant farmers. We had first to find and to live with such a family; and that was the object of our traveling.

We found no one family through which the whole of tenantry in that country could be justly represented, but decided that through three we had come to know, our job might with qualified adequacy be done. With the most nearly representative of the three we lived a little less than four weeks, seeing them and the others intimately and constantly. At the end of August, long before we were willing to, we returned into the north and got our work ready.

For reasons which will not be a part of this volume the article was not published. At the end of the year it was, however, released to us; and in the spring of 1938 an agreement was reached with a New York publisher for an expansion of the same material in book form. At the end of another year and a half, for reasons which, again, will receive later attention, the completed manuscript was rejected, or withdrawn. In the spring of 1940 it was accepted by those who now publish it, on condition that certain words be deleted which are illegal in Massachusetts.

The authors found it possible to make this concession and, since it rather enhanced a deception, to permit prominence to the immediate, instead of the generic, title.

• • •

[1] Evans was on loan from the Federal Government. [All footnotes are from the original, unless otherwise noted.]

This volume is designed in two intentions: as the beginning of a larger piece of work; and to stand of itself, independent of any such further work as may be done.

The title of this volume is *Let Us Now Praise Famous Men.*

The title of the work as a whole, this volume included, is *Three Tenant Families.*

The nominal subject is North American cotton tenantry as examined in the daily living of three representative white tenant families.

Actually, the effort is to recognize the stature of a portion of unimagined existence, and to contrive techniques proper to its recording, communication, analysis, and defense. More essentially, this is an independent inquiry into certain normal predicaments of human divinity.

The immediate instruments are two: the motionless camera, and the printed word. The governing instrument—which is also one of the centers of the subject—is individual, anti-authoritative human consciousness.

Ultimately, it is intended that this record and analysis be exhaustive, with no detail, however trivial it may seem, left untouched, no relevancy avoided, which lies within the power of remembrance to maintain, of the intelligence to perceive, and of the spirit to persist in.

Of this ultimate intention the present volume is merely portent and fragment, experiment, dissonant prologue. Since it is intended, among other things, as a swindle, an insult, and a corrective, the reader will be wise to bear the nominal subject, and his expectation of its proper treatment, steadily in mind. For that is the subject with which the authors are dealing, throughout. If complications arise, that is because they are trying to deal with it not as journalists, sociologists, politicians, entertainers, humanitarians, priests, or artists, but seriously.

The photographs are not illustrative. They, and the text, are coequal, mutually independent, and fully collaborative. By their fewness, and by the impotence of the reader's eye, this will be misunderstood by most of that minority which does not wholly ignore it. In the interests, however, of the history and future of photography, that risk seems irrelevant, and this flat statement necessary.

The text was written with reading aloud in mind. That cannot be recommended; but it is suggested that the reader attend with his ear to what he takes off the page: for variations of tone, pace, shape, and dynamics are here particularly unavailable to the eye alone, and with their loss, a good deal of meaning escapes.

It was intended also that the text be read continuously, as music is listened to or a film watched, with brief pauses only where they are self-evident.

Of any attempt on the part of the publishers, or others, to disguise or in any other way to ingratiate this volume, the authors must express their regret, their intense disapproval, and, as observers awaiting new contributions to their subject, their complaisance.

This is a *book* only by necessity. More seriously, it is an effort in human actuality, in which the reader is no less centrally involved than the authors and those of whom they tell. Those who wish actively to participate in the subject, in whatever degree of understanding, friendship, or hostility, are invited to address the authors in care of the publishers. In material that is used, privately or publicly, names will be withheld on request.

Poor naked wretches, wheresoe'er you are,
That bide the pelting of this pitiless storm,
How shall your houseless heads and unfed sides,
Your loop'd and window'd raggedness, defend you
From seasons such as these? O! I have ta'en
Too little care of this! Take physick, pomp;
Expose thyself to feel what wretches feel,
That thou may'st shake the superflux to them,
And show the heavens more just.

Workers of the world, unite and fight. You have nothing to lose but your chains, and a world to win.[2]

[2]These words are quoted here to mislead those who will be misled by them. They mean, not what the reader may care to think they mean, but what they say. They are not dealt with directly in this volume; but it is essential that they be used here, for in the pattern of the work as a whole, they are, in the sonata form, the second theme; the poetry facing them is the first. In view of the average reader's tendency to label, and of topical dangers to which any man, whether honest, or intelligent, or subtle, is at present liable, it may be well to make the explicit statement that neither these words nor the authors are the property of any political party, faith, or faction.

1. The Great Ball on Which We Live

The world is our home. It is also the home of many, many other children, some of whom live in far-away lands. They are our world brothers and sisters. . . .

2. Food, Shelter, and Clothing

What must any part of the world have in order to be a good home for man? What does every person need in order to live in comfort? Let us imagine that we are far out in the fields. The air is bitter cold and the wind is blowing. Snow is falling, and by and by it will turn into sleet and rain. We are almost naked. We have had nothing to eat and are suffering from hunger as well as cold. Suddenly the Queen of the Fairies floats down and offers us three wishes.

What shall we choose?

"I shall wish for food, because I am hungry," says Peter.

"I shall choose clothes to keep out the cold," says John.

"And I shall ask for a house to shelter me from the wind, the snow, and the rain," says little Nell with a shiver.

Now everyone needs food, clothing, and shelter. The lives of most men on the earth are spent in getting these things. In our travels we shall wish to learn what our world brothers and sisters eat, and where their food comes from. We shall wish to see the houses they dwell in and how they are built. We shall wish also to know what clothing they use to protect themselves from the heat and the cold.[3]

---

[3]These are the opening sentences of *Around the World With the Children*, by F. B. Carpenter (published by The American Book Company), a third-grade geography textbook belonging to Louise Gudger, aged ten, daughter of a cotton tenant.

Persons and Places

FRED GARVRIN RICKETTS: a two-mule tenant farmer, aged fifty-four.
SADIE (WOODS) RICKETTS: his wife, aged forty-nine.
MARGARET: aged twenty.
PARALEE: aged nineteen.
JOHN GARVRIN: aged twelve.
RICHARD: aged eleven.
FLORA MERRY LEE: aged ten.
KATY: aged nine.
CLAIR BELL: aged four.
THOMAS GALLATIN WOODS (BUD): a one-mule tenant farmer, aged fifty-nine.
IVY WOODS: his second wife; middle twenties.
MISS-MOLLY: her mother; early fifties.
GALLATIN: Woods' son by first marriage; a half-cropper; middle thirties.
EMMA: a daughter of the first marriage; aged eighteen; married.
PEARL: Ivy's daughter by common-law marriage to a man prior to Woods; aged eight.
THOMAS: son of Woods and second wife; aged three.
ELLEN: child of second marriage; aged twenty months.
GEORGE GUDGER: a one-mule half-cropper; aged thirty-one.
ANNIE MAE (WOODS) GUDGER: his wife, aged twenty-seven.
MAGGIE LOUISE: aged ten.
GEORGE JUNIOR: aged eight.
BURT WESTLY: aged four.
VALLEY FEW (SQUINCHY): aged twenty months.
CHESTER BOLES: Gudger's landlord.
T. HUDSON MARGRAVES: ⎤
MICHAEL MARGRAVES: ⎦— landlords to Woods and Ricketts.
HARMON: a landowner and New Deal executive.
ESTELLE: a middle-class young woman.
JAMES AGEE: a spy, traveling as a journalist.

WALKER EVANS: a counter-spy, traveling as a photographer.

WILLIAM BLAKE
LOUIS-FERDINAND CÉLINE
RING LARDNER
JESUS CHRIST
SIGMUND FREUD
LONNIE JOHNSON
IRVINE UPHAM
OTHERS

— unpaid agitators.

BIRMINGHAM: a large Southern industrial city.
CHEROKEE CITY: a county seat; population *c.* 7000.
CENTERBORO: county seat for these tenants; *c.* 1500.
COOKSTOWN: their landlords' town, and theirs; *c.* 300.
MADRID: a crossroads; two stores, four houses.
HOBE'S HILL: a low plateau of clay, where the tenants live.

It is two miles to the highway; three to Madrid; seven to Cookstown; seventeen to Centerboro; twenty-seven to Cherokee City; eighty to Birmingham. Transportation, for these families, is by mule or by mule wagon or on foot. This is not far from the geographic center of the North American Cotton Belt.

Sadie Ricketts is a half-sister of Woods; Annie Mae Gudger is his daughter.

Since none of the characters or incidents of this volume are fictitious, the names of most persons, and nearly all names of places, are altered.

The ages given, and tenses throughout, save where it is otherwise obvious or deliberately ambiguous, are as of the summer of 1936.

Design of the Book[4]

VERSES

PREAMBLE

ALL OVER ALABAMA

(On the Porch: 1

July 1936

LATE SUNDAY MORNING

AT THE FORKS

NEAR A CHURCH

PART ONE: *A Country Letter*

COLON

PART TWO: *Some Findings and Comments*

MONEY

SHELTER

[4]The excerpts that follow the "Preamble" are drawn from Part One: *A Country Letter* and Part Two: *Some Findings and Comments,* "Shelter." [Editors' note]

(On the Porch: 2

CLOTHING

EDUCATION

WORK

INTERMISSION: *Conversation in the Lobby*

PART THREE: *Inductions*

SHADY GROVE ALABAMA

TWO IMAGES

TITLE STATEMENT

NOTES AND APPENDICES

(On the Porch: 3

Preamble[5]

"I spoke of this piece of work we were doing as 'curious.' I had better amplify this.

It seems to me curious, not to say obscene and thoroughly terrifying, that it could occur to an association of human beings drawn together through need and chance and for profit into a company, an organ of journalism, to pry intimately into the lives of an undefended and appallingly damaged group of human beings, an ignorant and helpless rural family, for the purpose of parading the nakedness, disadvantage and humiliation of these lives before another group of human beings, in the name of science, of 'honest journalism' (whatever that paradox may mean), of humanity, of social fearlessness, for money, and for a reputation for crusading and for unbias which, when skillfully enough qualified, is exchangeable at any bank for money (and in politics, for votes, job patronage, abelincolnism, etc.;[6] and that these people could be capable of meditating this prospect without the slightest doubt of their qualification to do an 'honest' piece of work, and with a conscience better than clear, and in the virtual certitude of almost unanimous public approval. It seems curious, further, that the assignment of this work should have fallen to persons having so extremely different a form of respect for the subject, and responsibility toward it, that from the first and inevitably they counted their employers, and that Government likewise to which one of them was bonded, among their most dangerous enemies, acted as spies, guardians, and cheats,[7] and trusted no judgment, however authoritative it claimed to be, save their own: which in many aspects of the task before them was untrained and uninformed. It seems further curious that realizing the extreme corruptness and difficulty of the circumstances, and the unlikelihood of achieving in any untainted form what they wished to achieve, they ac-

---

[5] The title, "Preamble," was indicated in the "Design of the Book" but was not included in the original. We've added a title here for ease of reference. [Editors' note]

[6] Money.

[7] Une chose permise ne peut pas être pure.
L'illégal me va.
– *Essai de Critique Indirecte*

cepted the work in the first place. And it seems curious still further that, with all their suspicion of and contempt for every person and thing to do with the situation, save only for the tenants and for themselves, and their own intentions, and with all their realization of the seriousness and mystery of the subject, and of the human responsibility they undertook, they so little questioned or doubted their own qualifications for this work.

All of this, I repeat, seems to me curious, obscene, terrifying, and unfathomably mysterious.

So does the whole course, in all its detail, of the effort of these persons to find, and to defend, what they sought: and the nature of their relationship with those with whom during the searching stages they came into contact; and the subtlety, importance, and almost intangibility of the insights or revelations or oblique suggestions which under different circumstances could never have materialized; so does the method of research which was partly evolved by them, partly forced upon them; so does the strange quality of their relationship with those whose lives they so tenderly and sternly respected, and so rashly undertook to investigate and to record.

So does the whole subsequent course and fate of the work: the causes for its non-publication, the details of its later acceptance elsewhere, and of its design; the problems which confronted the maker of the photographs; and those which confront me as I try to write of it: the question, Who are you who will read these words and study these photographs, and through what cause, by what chance, and for what purpose, and by what right do you qualify to, and what will you do about it; and the question, Why we make this book, and set it at large, and by what right, and for what purpose, and to what good end, or none: the whole memory of the South in its six-thousand-mile parade and flowering outlay of the façades of cities, and of the eyes in the streets of towns, and of hotels, and of the trembling heat, and of the wide wild opening of the tragic land, wearing the trapped frail flowers of its garden of faces; the fleet flush and flower and fainting of the human crop it raises; the virulent, insolent, deceitful, pitying, infinitesimal and frenzied running and searching, on this colossal peasant map, of two angry, futile and bottomless, botched and overcomplicated youthful intelligences in the service of an anger and of a love and of an undiscernible truth, and in the frightening vanity of their would-be purity; the sustaining, even now, and forward moving, lifted on the lifting of this day as ships on a wave, above whom, in a few hours, night once more will stand up in his stars, and they decline through lamplight and be dreaming statues, of those, each, whose lives we knew and whom we love and intend well toward, and of whose living we know little in some while now, save that quite steadily, in not much possible change for better or much worse, mute, innocent, helpless and incorporate among that small-moted and inestimable swarm and pollen stream and fleet of single, irreparable, unrepeatable existences, they are led, gently, quite steadily, quite without mercy, each a littler farther toward the washing and the wailing, the sunday suit and the prettiest dress, the pine box, and the closed clay room whose frailly decorated roof, until rain has taken it flat into oblivion, wears the shape of a ritual scar and of an inverted boat: curious, obscene, terrifying, beyond all search of dream unanswerable, those problems which stand thickly forth like light from all matter, triviality, chance, intention, and record in the body, of being, of truth, of conscience, of hope, of hatred, of beauty, of indignation, of guilt, of betrayal, of innocence, of forgiveness, of vengeance, of guardianship, of an indenominable fate, predicament, destination, and God.

Therefore it is in some fear that I approach those matters at all, and in much confusion. And if there are questions in my mind how to undertake this communication, and there are many, I must let the least of them be, whether I am boring you, or whether I am taking too long getting started, and too clumsily. If I bore you, that is that. If I am clumsy, that may indicate partly the difficulty of my subject, and the seriousness with which I am trying to take what hold I can of it; more certainly, it will indicate my youth, my lack of mastery of my so-called art or craft, my lack perhaps of talent. Those matters, too, must reveal themselves as they may. However they turn out, they cannot be otherwise than true to their conditions, and I would not wish to conceal these conditions even if I could, for I am interested to speak as carefully and as near truly as I am able. No doubt I shall worry myself that I am taking too long getting started, and shall seriously distress myself over my inability to create an organic, mutually sustaining and dependent, and as it were musical, form: but I must remind myself that I started with the first word I wrote, and that the centers of my subject are shifty; and, again, that I am no better an "artist" than I am capable of being, under these circumstances, perhaps under any other; and that this again will find its measurement in the facts as they are, and will contribute its own measure, whatever it may be, to the pattern of the effort and truth as a whole.

I might say, in short, but emphatically not in self-excuse, of which I wish entirely to disarm and disencumber myself, but for the sake of clear definition, and indication of limits, that I am only human. Those works which I most deeply respect have about them a firm quality of the superhuman, in part because they refuse to define and limit and crutch, or admit themselves as human. But to a person of my uncertainty, undertaking a task of this sort, that plane and manner are not within reach, and could only falsify what by this manner of effort may at least less hopelessly approach clarity, and truth."

"For in the immediate world, everything is to be discerned, for him who can discern it, and centrally and simply, without either dissection into science, or digestion into art, but with the whole of consciousness, seeking to perceive it as it stands: so that the aspect of a street in sunlight can roar in the heart of itself as a symphony, perhaps as no symphony can: and all of consciousness is shifted from the imagined, the revisive, to the effort to perceive simply the cruel radiance of what is.

This is why the camera seems to me, next to unassisted and weaponless consciousness, the central instrument of our time; and is why in turn I feel such rage at its misuse: which has spread so nearly universal a corruption of sight that I know of less than a dozen alive whose eyes I can trust even so much as my own."

"If I had explained myself clearly you would realize by now that through this non-'artistic' view, this effort to suspend or destroy imagination, there opens before consciousness, and within it, a universe luminous, spacious, incalculably rich and wonderful in each detail, as relaxed and natural to the human swimmer, and as full of glory, as his breathing: and that it is possible to capture and communicate this universe not so well by any means of art as through such open terms as I am trying it under.

In a novel, a house or person has his meaning, his existence, entirely through the writer. Here, a house or a person has only the most limited of his meaning through me: his true meaning is much huger. It is that he *exists,* in actual being, as you do and as I do, and as no character of the imagination can possibly exist. His great weight, mystery, and dignity are in this fact. As for me, I can tell you of him only what I saw, only so accurately as in my terms I know how: and this in turn has its chief stature not in any ability of mine but in the fact that I too exist, not as a work of fiction, but as a human being. Because of his immeasurable weight in actual existence, and because of mine, every word I tell of him has inevitably a kind of immediacy, a kind of meaning, not at all necessarily 'superior' to that of imagination, but of a kind so different that a work of the imagination (however intensely it may draw on 'life') can at best only faintly imitate the least of it."

"The communication is not by any means so simple. It seems to me now that to contrive techniques appropriate to it in the first place, and capable of planting it cleanly in others, in the second, would be a matter of years, and I shall probably try none of it or little, and that very tortured and diluted, at present. I realize that, with even so much involvement in explanations as this, I am liable seriously, and perhaps irretrievably, to obscure what would at best be hard enough to give its appropriate clarity and intensity; and what seems to me most important of all: namely, that these I will write of are human beings, living in this world, innocent of such twistings as these which are taking place over their heads; and that they were dwelt among, investigated, spied on, revered, and loved, by other quite monstrously alien human beings, in the employment of still others still more alien; and that they are now being looked into by still others, who have picked up their living as casually as if it were a book, and who were actuated toward this reading by various possible reflexes of sympathy, curiosity, idleness, et cetera, and almost certainly in a lack of consciousness, and conscience, remotely appropriate to the enormity of what they are doing.

If I could do it, I'd do no writing at all here. It would be photographs; the rest would be fragments of cloth, bits of cotton, lumps of earth, records of speech, pieces of wood and iron, phials of odors, plates of food and of excrement. Booksellers would consider it quite a novelty; critics would murmur, yes, but is it art; and I could trust a majority of you to use it as you would a parlor game.

A piece of the body torn out by the roots might be more to the point.

As it is, though, I'll do what little I can in writing. Only it will be very little. I'm not capable of it; and if I were, you would not go near it at all. For if you did, you would hardly bear to live.

As a matter of fact, nothing I might write could make any difference whatever. It would only be a 'book' at the best. If it were a safely dangerous one it would be 'scientific' or 'political' or 'revolutionary.' If it were really dangerous it would be 'literature' or 'religion' or 'mysticism' or 'art,' and under one such name or another might in time achieve the emasculation of acceptance. If it were dangerous enough to be of any remote use to the human race it would be merely 'frivolous' or 'pathological,' and that would be the end of that. Wiser and more capable men than I shall ever be have put their findings before you, findings so rich and so full of anger, serenity, murder, healing, truth, and love that it seems incredible the world were not destroyed and fulfilled in the instant, but you are too much for them: the weak in courage are strong in cunning; and one by one, you have absorbed and have captured and dishonored, and have distilled of your deliverers the most ruinous of all your poisons; people hear Beethoven in concert halls, or over a bridge game, or to relax; Cézannes are hung on walls, reproduced, in natural wood frames; van Gogh is the man who cut off his ear and whose yellows became recently popular in window decoration; Swift loved individuals but hated the human race; Kafka is a fad; Blake is in the Modern Library; Freud is a Modern Library Giant; Dovschenko's *Frontier* is disliked by those who demand that it fit the Eisenstein esthetic; *nobody* reads Joyce any more; Céline is a madman who has incurred the hearty dislike of Alfred Kazin, reviewer for the *New York Herald Tribune* book section, and is, moreover, a fascist; I hope I need not mention Jesus Christ, of whom you have managed to make a dirty gentile.

However that may be, this is a book about 'sharecroppers,' and is written for all those who have a soft place in their hearts for the laughter and tears inherent in poverty viewed at a distance, and especially for those who can afford the retail price; in the hope that the reader will be edified, and may feel kindly disposed toward any well-thought-out liberal efforts to rectify the unpleasant situation down South, and will somewhat better and more guiltily appreciate the next good meal he eats; and in the hope, too, that he will recommend this little book to really sympathetic friends, in order that our publishers may at least cover their investment and that (just the merest perhaps) some kindly thought may be turned our way, and a little of your money fall to poor little us."

"Above all else: in God's name don't think of it as Art.

Every fury on earth has been absorbed in time, as art, or as religion, or as authority in one form or another. The deadliest blow the enemy of the human soul can strike is to do fury honor. Swift, Blake, Beethoven, Christ, Joyce, Kafka, name me a one who has not been thus castrated. Official acceptance is the one unmistakable symptom that salvation is beaten again, and is the one surest sign of fatal misunderstanding, and is the kiss of Judas.

Really it should be possible to hope that this be recognized as so, and as a mortal and inevitably recurrent danger. It is scientific fact. It is disease. It is avoidable. Let a start be made. And then exercise your perception of it on work that has more to tell you than mine has. See how respectable Beethoven is; and by what right any wall in museum, gallery, or home presumes to wear a Cézanne; and by what idiocy Blake or work even of such intention as mine is ever published and sold. I will tell you a test. It is unfair. It is untrue. It stacks all the cards. It is out of line with what the composer intended. All so much the better.

Get a radio or a phonograph capable of the most extreme loudness possible, and sit down to listen to a performance of Beethoven's Seventh Symphony or of Schubert's C-Major Symphony. But I don't mean just sit down and listen. I mean this: Turn it on as loud as you can get it. Then get down on the floor and jam your ear as close into the loudspeaker as you can get it and stay there, breathing as lightly as possible, and not moving, and neither eating nor smoking nor drinking. Concentrate everything you can into your hearing and into your body. You won't hear it nicely. If it hurts you, be glad of it. As near as you will ever get, you are inside the music; not only inside it, you are it; your body is no longer your shape and substance, it is the shape and substance of the music.

Is what you hear pretty? or beautiful? or legal? or acceptable in polite or any other society? It is beyond any calculation savage and dangerous and murderous to all equilibrium in human life as human life is; and nothing can equal the rape it does on all that death; nothing except anything, anything in existence or dream, perceived anywhere remotely toward its true dimension."

"Beethoven said a thing as rash and noble as the best of his work. By my memory, he said: 'He who understands my music can never know unhappiness again.' I believe it. And I would be a liar and a coward and one of your safe world if I should fear to say the same words of my best perception, and of my best intention.

Performance, in which the whole fate and terror rests, is another matter."

A Country Letter

It is late in a summer night, in a room of a house set deep and solitary in the country; all in this house save myself are sleeping; I sit at a table, facing a partition wall; and I am looking at a lighted coal-oil lamp which stands on a table close to the wall, and just beyond the sleeping of my relaxed left hand; with my right hand I am from time to time writing, with a soft pencil, into a school-child's composition book; but just now, I am entirely focused on the lamp, and light.

It is of glass, light metal colored gold, and cloth of heavy thread.

The glass was poured into a mold, I guess, that made the base and bowl, which are in one piece; the glass is thick and clean, with icy lights in it. The base is a simply fluted, hollow skirt; stands on the table; is solidified in a narrowing, a round inch of pure thick glass, then hollows again, a globe about half flattened, the globe-glass thick, too; and this holds oil, whose silver line I see, a little less than half down the globe, its level a very little—for the base is not quite true—tilted against the axis of the base.

This "oil" is not at all oleaginous, but thin, brittle, rusty feeling, and sharp; taken and rubbed between forefinger and thumb, it so cleanses their grain that it sharpens their mutual touch to a new coin edge, or the russet nipple of a breast erected in cold; and the odor is clean, cheerful and humble, less alive by far than that of gasoline, even a shade watery: and a subtle sweating of this oil is on the upward surface of the globe, as if it stood through the glass, and as if the glass were a pitcher of cool water in a hot room. I do not understand nor try to deduce this, but I like it; I run my thumb upon it and smell of my thumb, and smooth away its streaked print on the glass; and I wipe my thumb and forefinger dry against my pants, and keep on looking.

In this globe, and in this oil that is clear and light as water, and reminding me of creatures and things once alive which I have seen suspended in jars in a frightening smell of alcohol—serpents, tapeworms, toads, embryons, all drained one tan pallor of absolute death; and also of the serene, scarved flowers in untroubled wombs (and pale-tanned too, flaccid, and in the stench of exhibited death, those children of fury, patience and love which stand in the dishonors of accepted fame, and of the murdering of museum staring); in this globe like a thought, a dream, the future, slumbers the stout-weft strap of wick, and up this wick is drawn the oil, toward heat; through a tight, flat tube of tin, and through a little slotted smile of golden tin, and there ends fledged with flame, in the flue; the flame, a clean, fanged fan:

I:

The light in this room is of a lamp. Its flame in the glass is of the dry, silent, and famished delicateness of the latest lateness of the night, and of such ultimate, such holiness of silence and peace that all on earth and within extremest remembrance seems suspended upon it in perfection as upon reflective water: and I feel that if I can by utter quietness succeed in not disturbing this silence, in not so much as touching this plain of water, I can tell you anything within realm of God, whatsoever it may be, that I wish to tell you, and that what so ever it may be, you will not be able to help but understand it.

It is the middle and pure height and whole of summer and a summer night, the held breath, of a planet's year; high shored sleeps the crested tide: what day of the month I do not know, which day of the week I am not sure, far less what hour of the night. The dollar watch I bought a few days ago, as also from time to time I buy a ten cent automatic pencil, and use it little before I lose all track of it, ran out at seventeen minutes past ten the day before yesterday morning, and time by machine measure was over for me at that hour, and is a monument. I know of the lateness and full height by the quietly starved brightness of my senses, which some while ago made the transition past any need for sleep without taking much notice of it, as, in the late darkness, the long accustomed liner loses the last black headland, and quietly commends her forehead upon the long open home of the sea: and by a quality in the night itself not truly apparent to any one of the senses, yet, by some indirection, to every sense in one, of a most complete and universally shared withdrawal to source, like that brief paralysis which enchants a city while wreaths are laid to a cenotaph, and, muted, a bugle's inscription shines, in the tightening just before the relaxation of this swarmed, still, silence, till, hats-on, gears grow and smooth, the lifted foot arrested in the stop-shot completes its step, once more the white mane of the drayhorse flurrs in the sunny air: now vibrates all that vast stone hive: into resumption, reassumption, of casual living.

And it is in these terms I would tell you, at all leisure, and in all detail, whatever there is to tell: of where I am; of what I perceive.

Lamplight here, and lone, late: the odor is of pine that has stood shut on itself through the heat of a hot day: the odor of an attic at white noon: and all of the walls save that surface within immediate touch of the lamp, where like water slept in lantern light the grain is so sharply discerned in its retirement beyond the sleep of the standing shape of pines, and the pastings and pinnings of sad ornaments, are a most dim scarce-color of grayed silver breathed in yellow red which is the hue and haze in the room; and above me, black; where, beyond bones of rafters underlighted, a stomach sucked against the spine in fear, the roof draws up its peak: and this is a frightening dark, which has again to do with an attic: for it is the darkness that stands just up the stairs, sucking itself out of sight of the light, from an attic door left ajar, noticed on your way to bed, and remembered after you are there: so that I muse what not quite creatures and what not quite forms are suspended like bats above and behind my bent head; and how far down in their clustered weight they are stealing while my eyes are on this writing; and how skillfully swiftly they suck themselves back upward into the dark when I turn my head: and above all, why they should be so coy, who, with one slather of cold membranes drooping, could slap out light and have me: and who own me since all time's beginning. Yet this mere fact of thinking holds them at distance, as crucifixes demons, so lightly and well that I am almost persuaded of being merely fanciful; in which exercise I would be theirs most profoundly beyond rescue, not knowing, and not fearing, I am theirs.

Above that shell and carapace, more frail against heaven than fragilest membrane of glass, nothing, straight to the terrific stars: whereof all heaven is chalky; and of whom the nearest is so wild a reach my substance wilts to think on: and we, this Arctic flower snow-rooted, last matchflame guarded on a windy plain, are seated among these stars alone: none to turn to, none to make us known; a little country settlement so deep, so lost in shelve and shade of dew, no one so much as laughs at us. Small wonder how pitiably we love our home, cling in her skirts at night, rejoice in her wide star-seducing smile, when every star strikes us sick with the fright: do we really exist at all?

> This world is not my home, I'm, only passing through,
> My treasures and my hopes, are, all, beyond the sky,
> I've many, friends, and kindreds, that's gone, along before,
> And I can't, feel, at home, in this world, any, more.

And thus, too, these families, not otherwise than with every family in the earth, how each, apart, how inconceivably lonely, sorrowful, and remote! Not one other on earth, nor in any dream, that can care so much what comes to them, so that even as they sit at the lamp and eat their supper, the joke they are laughing at could not be so funny to anyone else; and the littlest child who stands on the bench solemnly, with food glittering all over his cheeks in the lamplight, this littlest child I speak of is not there, he is of another family, and it is a different woman who wipes the food from his cheeks and takes his weight upon her thighs and against her body and who feeds him, and lets his weight slacken against her in his heavying sleep; and the man who puts another soaked cloth to the skin cancer on his shoulder; it is his wife who is looking on, and his child who lies sunken along the floor with his soft mouth broad open and his nakedness up like a rolling dog, asleep: and the people next up the road cannot care in the same way, not for any of it: for they are absorbed upon themselves: and the negroes down beyond the spring have drawn their shutters tight, the lamplight pulses like wounded honey through the seams into the soft night, and there is laughter: but nobody else cares. All over the whole round earth and in the settlements, the towns, and the great iron stones of cities, people are drawn inward within their little shells of rooms, and are to be seen in their wondrous and pitiful actions through the surfaces of their lighted windows by thousands, by millions, little golden aquariums, in chairs, reading, setting tables, sewing, playing cards, not talking, talking, laughing inaudibly, mixing drinks, at radio dials, eating, in shirt-sleeves, carefully dressed, courting, teasing, loving, seducing, undressing, leaving the room empty in its empty light, alone and writing a letter urgently, in couples married, in separate chairs, in family parties, in gay parties, preparing for bed, preparing for sleep: and none can care, beyond that room; and none can be cared for, by any beyond that room: and it is small wonder they are drawn together so cowardly close, and small wonder in what dry agony of despair a mother may fasten her talons and her vampire mouth upon the soul of her struggling son and drain him empty, light as a locust shell: and wonder only that an age that has borne its children and must lose and has lost them, and lost life, can bear further living; but so it is:

A man and a woman are drawn together upon a bed and there is a child and there are children:

First they are mouths, then they become auxiliary instruments of labor: later they are drawn away, and become the fathers and mothers of children, who shall become the fathers and mothers of children:

Their father and their mother before them were, in their time, the children each of different parents, who in their time were each children of parents:

This has been happening for a long while: its beginning was before stars:

It will continue for a long while: no one knows where it will end:

While they are still drawn together within one shelter around the center of their parents, these children and their parents together compose a family:

This family must take care of itself; it has no mother or father: there is no other shelter, nor resource, nor any love, interest, sustaining strength or comfort, so near, nor can anything happy or sorrowful that comes to anyone in this family possibly mean to those outside it what it means to those within it: but it is, as I have told, inconceivably lonely, drawn upon itself as tramps are drawn round a fire in the cruelest weather; and thus and in such loneliness it exists among other families, each of which is no less lonely, nor any less without help or comfort, and is likewise drawn in upon itself:

Such a family lasts, for a while: the children are held to a magnetic center:

Then in time the magnetism weakens, both of itself in its tiredness of aging and sorrow, and against the strength of the growth of each child, and against the strength of pulls from outside, and one by one the children are drawn away:

Of those that are drawn away, each is drawn elsewhere toward another: once more a man and a woman, in a loneliness they are not liable at that time to notice, are tightened together upon a bed: and another family has begun:

Moreover, these flexions are taking place every where, like a simultaneous motion of all the waves of the water of the world: and these are the classic patterns, and this is the weaving, of human living: of whose fabric each individual is a part: and of all parts of this fabric let this be borne in mind:

Each is intimately connected with the bottom and the extremest reach of time:

Each is composed of substances identical with the substance of all that surrounds him, both the common objects of his disregard, and the hot centers of stars:

All that each person is, and experiences, and shall never experience, in body and in mind, all these things are differing expressions of himself and of one root, and are identical: and not one of these things nor one of these persons is ever quite to be duplicated, nor replaced, nor has it ever quite had precedent: but each is a new and incommunicably tender life, wounded in every breath, and almost as hardly killed as easily wounded: sustaining, for a while, without defense, the enormous assaults of the universe:

So that how it can be that a stone, a plant, a star, can take on the burden of being; and how it is that a child can take on the burden of breathing; and how through so long a continuation and cumulation of the burden of each moment one on another, does any creature bear to exist, and not break utterly to fragments of nothing: these are matters too dreadful and fortitudes too gigantic to meditate long and not forever to worship:

Just a half-inch beyond the surface of this wall I face is another surface, one of the four walls which square and collaborate against the air another room, and there lie sleeping, on two iron beds and on pallets on the floor, a man and his wife and her sister, and four children, a girl, and three harmed boys. Their lamp is out, their light is done this long while, and not in a long while has any one of them made a sound. Not even straining, can I hear their breathing: rather, I have a not quite sensuous knowledge of a sort of suspiration, less breathing than that indiscernible drawing-in of heaven by which plants live, and thus I know they rest and the profundity of their tiredness, as if I were in each one of these seven bodies whose sleeping I can almost touch through their wall, and which in the darkness I so clearly see, with the whole touch and weight of my body: George's red body, already a little squat with the burden of thirty years, knotted like oakwood, in its clean white cotton summer union suit that it sleeps in; and his wife's beside him, Annie Mae's, slender, and sharpened through with bone, that ten years past must have had such beauty, and now is veined at the breast, and the skin of the breast translucent, delicately shriveled, and blue, and she and her sister Emma are in plain cotton shifts; and the body of Emma, her sister, strong, thick and wide, tall, the breasts set wide and high, shallow and round, not yet those of a full woman, the legs long, thick and strong; and Louise's green lovely body, the dim breasts faintly blown between wide shoulders, the thighs long, clean and light in their line from hip to knee, the head back steep and silent to the floor, the chin highest, and the white shift up to her divided thighs; and the tough little body of Junior, hardskinned and gritty, the feet crusted with sores; and the milky and strengthless littler body of Burt whose veins are so bright in his temples; and the shriveled and hopeless, most pitiful body of Squinchy, which will not grow:

But it is not only their bodies but their postures that I know, and their weight on the bed or on the floor, so that I lie down inside each one as if exhausted in a bed, and I become not my own shape and weight and self, but that of each of them, the whole of it, sunken in sleep like stones; so that I know almost the dreams they will not remember, and the soul and body of each of these seven, and of all of them together in this room in sleep, as if they were music I were hearing, each voice in relation to all the others, and all audible, singly, and as one organism, and a music that cannot be communicated: and thus they lie in this silence, and rest.

Burt half-woke, whimpering before he was awake, an inarticulated soprano speaking through not quite weeping in complaint to his mother as before a sure jury of some fright of dream: the bed creaked and I heard her bare feet slow, the shuffling soles, and her voice, not whispering but stifled and gentle, Go to sleep now, git awn back to sleep, they aint nothing agoin to pester ye, git awn back to sleep, in that cadence of strength and sheltering comfort which anneals all fence of language and surpasses music; and George's grouched, sleepy voice, and hers to him, no words audible; and the shuffling; and a twisting in beds, and grumbling of weak springs; and the whimpering sinking, and expired; and the sound of breathing, strong, not sleeping, now, slowed, shifted across into sleep, now, steadier; and now, long, long, drawn off as lightest lithest edge of bow, thinner, thinner, a thread, a filament; nothing: and once more that silence wherein more deep than starlight this home is foundered.

I am fond of Emma, and very sorry for her, and I shall probably never see her again after a few hours from now. I want to tell you what I can about her.

She is a big girl, almost as big as her sister is wiry, though she is not at all fat: her build is rather that of a young queen of a child's magic story who throughout has been coarsened by peasant and earth living and work, and that of her eyes and her demeanor, too, kind, not fully formed, resolute, bewildered, and sad. Her soft abundant slightly curling brown hair is cut in a square bob which on her large fine head is particularly childish, and indeed Emma is rather a big child, sexual beyond propriety to its years, than a young woman; and this can be seen in a kind of dimness of definition in her features, her skin, and the shape of her body, which will be lost in a few more years. She wears a ten cent store necklace and a sunday cotton print dress because she is visiting, and is from town, but she took off her slippers as soon as she came, and worked with Annie Mae. According to her father she is the spitn image of her mother when her mother was young; Annie Mae favors her father and his people, who were all small and lightly built.

Emma is very fond of her father and very sorry for him, as her sister is, and neither of them can stand his second wife. I have an idea that his marrying her had a lot to do with Emma's own marriage, which her father so strongly advised her against. He married the second time when Emma was thirteen, and for a long while they lived almost insanely, as I will tell you of later, far back in a swamp: and when Emma was sixteen she married a man her father's age, a carpenter in Cherokee City. She has been married to him two years; they have no children. Emma loves good times, and towns, and people her own age, and he is jealous and mean to her and suspicious of her. He has given her no pretty dresses nor the money to buy cloth to make them. Every minute he is in the house he keeps his eye right on her as if she was up to something, and when he goes out, which is as seldom as he can, he locks her in: so that twice already she has left him and come home to stay, and then after a while he has come down begging, and crying, and swearing he'll treat her good, and give her anything she asks for, and that he'll take to drink or kill himself if she leaves him, and she has gone back: for it isn't any fun at home, hating that woman the way she does, and she can't have fun with anyone else because she is married and nobody will have fun with her that way: and now (and I think it may be not only through the depression but through staying in the house because of jealousy and through fear of living in a town with her, and so near a home she can return to), her husband can no longer get a living in Cherokee City; he has heard of a farm on a plantation over in the red hills in Mississippi and has already gone, and taken it, and he has sent word to Emma that she is to come in a truck in which a man he knows, who has business to drive out that way, is moving their furniture; and this truck is leaving tomorrow. She doesn't want to go at all, and during the past two days she has been withdrawing into rooms with her sister and crying a good deal, almost tearlessly and almost without voice, as if she knew no more how to cry than how to take care for her life; and Annie Mae is strong against her going, all that distance, to a man who leaves her behind and then just sends for her, saying, Come on along, now; and George too is as committal over it as he feels will appear any right or business of his to be, he a man, and married, to the wife of another man, who is no kin to him, but only the sister of his wife, and to whom he is himself unconcealably attracted: but she is going all the same, without at all understanding why. Annie Mae is sure she won't stay out there long, not all alone in the country away from her kinfolks with that man; that is what she keeps saying, to Emma, and to George, and even to me; but actually she is surer than not that she may never see her young sister again, and she grieves for her, and for the loss of her to her own loneliness, for she loves her, both for herself and her dependence and for that softness of youth which already is drawn so deep into the trap, and in which Annie Mae can perceive herself as she was ten years past; and she gives no appearance of noticing the clumsy and shamefaced would-be-subtle demeanors of flirtation which George is stupid enough to believe she does not understand for what they are: for George would only be shocked should she give him open permission, and Emma could not be too well trusted either. So this sad comedy has been going on without comment from anyone, which will come to nothing: and another sort has been going on with us, of a kind fully as helpless. Each of us is attractive to Emma, both in sexual immediacy and as symbols or embodiments of a life she wants and knows she will never have; and each of us is fond of her, and attracted toward her. We are not only strangers to her, but we are strange, unexplainable, beyond what I can begin yet fully to realize. We have acted toward her with the greatest possible care and shyness and quiet, yet we have been open or "clear" as well, so that she knows we understand her and like her and care for her almost intimately. She is puzzled by this and yet not at all troubled, but excited; but there is nothing to do about it on either side. There is tenderness and sweetness and mutual pleasure in such a "flirtation" which one would not for the world restrain or cancel, yet there is also an essential cruelty, about which nothing can be done, and strong possibility of cruelty through misunderstanding, and inhibition, and impossibility, which can be restrained, and which one would rather die than cause any of: but it is a cruel and ridiculous and restricted situation, and everyone to some extent realizes it. Everyone realizes it, I think, to such a degree even as this: supposing even that nothing can be helped about the marriage, supposing she is going away and on with it, which she shouldn't, then if only Emma could spend her last few days alive having a gigantic good time in bed, with George, a kind of man she is best used to, and with Walker and with me, whom she is curious about and attracted to, and who are at the same moment tangible and friendly and not at all to be feared, and on the other hand have for her the mystery or glamour almost of mythological creatures. This has a good many times in the past couple ot days come very clearly through between all of us except the children, and without fear, in sudden and subtle but unmistakable expressions of the eyes, or ways of smiling: yet not one of us would be capable of trusting ourselves to it unless beyond any doubt each knew all the others to be thus capable: and even then how crazily the conditioned and inferior parts of each of our beings would rush in, and take revenge. But this is just a minute specialization of a general brutal pity: almost any person, no matter how damaged and poisoned and blinded, is infinitely more capable of intelligence and of joy than he can let himself be or than he usually knows; and even if he had no reason to fear his own poisons, he has those that are in others to fear, to assume and take care for, if he would not hurt both himself and that other person and the pure act itself beyond cure.

But here I am going to shift ahead of where I am writing, to a thing which is to happen, or which happened, the next morning (you mustn't be puzzled by this, I'm writing in a continuum), and say what came of it.

The next morning was full of the disorganized, half listless, yet very busy motions of ordinary life broken by an event: Emma's going away. I was going to take her and Annie Mae to her brother Gallatin's house near Cookstown, where she was to meet the man with his truck, and I was waiting around on the front porch in the cool-hot increasing morning sunlight, working out my notes, while the morning housework was done up in special speed. (George was gone an hour or more ago, immediately after the breakfast they had all sat through, not talking much. There had been a sort of lingering in eating and in silences, and a little when the food was done, broken by talk to keep the silences from becoming too frightening; I had let the breakfast start late by telling him I would take him in the car; then abruptly he got up saying, "Well, Jimmy, if you—" Whether he would kiss Emma good-bye, as a sort of relative, was on everybody's mind. He came clumsily near it: she half got from her chair, and their bodies were suddenly and sharply drawn toward each other a few inches: but he was much too shy, and did not even touch her with the hand he reached out to shake hers. Annie Mae drawled, smiling, What's wrong with ye George; she ain't agoin' to bite ye; and everyone laughed, and Emma stood up and they embraced, laughing, and he kissed her on her suddenly turned cheek, a little the way a father and an adolescent son kiss, and told her good-bye and wished her good luck, and I took him to work in the car, and came back. And now here I was, as I have said, on the porch.) Here I was on the porch, diddling around in a notebook and hearing the sounds of work and the changing patterns of voices inside, and the unaccustomed noise of shoeleather on the floor, because someone was dressed up for travel; and a hen thudded among dried watermelon seeds on the oak floor, looking, as they usually do, like a nearsighted professor; and down hill beyond the open field a little wind laid itself in a wall against the glistening leaves of the high forest and lay through with a long sweet granular noise of rustling water; and the hen dropped from the ledge of the porch to the turded dirt with a sodden bounce, and an involuntary cluck as her heaviness hit the ground on her sprung legs; and the long lithe little wind released the trees and was gone on, wandering the fringed earth in its affairs like a saturday schoolchild in the sun, and the leaves hung troubling in the aftermath; and I heard footsteps in the hall and Emma appeared, all dressed to go, looking somehow as if she had come to report a decision that had been made in a conference, for which I, without knowing it, seemed to have been waiting. She spoke in that same way, too, not wasting any roundabout time or waiting for an appropriate rhythm, yet not in haste, looking me steadily and sweetly in the eyes, and said, I want you and Mr. Walker to know how much we all like you, because you make us feel easy with you; we don't have to act any different from what it comes natural to act, and we don't have to worry what you're thinking about us, it's just like you was our own people and had always lived here with us, you all are so kind, and nice, and quiet, and easygoing, and we wisht you wasn't never going to go away but stay on here with us, and I just want to tell you how much we all keer about you; Annie Mae says that same, and you please tell Mr. Walker, too, if I don't see him afore I go. (I knew she could never say it over again, and I swore I certainly would tell him.)

What's the use trying to say what I felt. It took her a long time to say what she wanted so much to say, and it was hard for her, but there she stood looking straight into my eyes, and I straight into hers, longer than you'd think it would be possible to stand it. I would have done anything in the world for her (that is always characteristic, I guess, of the seizure of the strongest love you can feel: pity, and the wish to die for a person, because there isn't anything you can do for them that is at all measurable to your love), and all I could do, the very most, for this girl who was so soon going on out of my existence into so hopeless a one of hers, the very most I could do was not to show all I cared for her and for what she was saying, and not to even try to do, or to indicate the good I wished I might do her and was so utterly helpless to do. I had such tenderness and such gratitude toward her that while she spoke I very strongly, as something steadier than an "impulse," wanted in answer to take her large body in my arms and smooth the damp hair back from her forehead and to kiss and comfort and shelter her like a child, and I can swear that I now as then almost believe that in that moment she would have so well understood this, and so purely and quietly met it, that now as then I only wish to God I had done it; but instead the most I did was to stand facing her, and to keep looking into her eyes (doing her the honor at least of knowing that she did not want relief from this), and, managing to keep the tears from running down my face, to smile to her and say that there was nothing in my whole life that I had cared so much to be told, and had been so grateful for (and I believe this is so); and that I wanted her to know how much I liked them, too, and her herself, and that I certainly felt that they were my own people, and wanted them to be, more than any other kind of people in the world, and that if they felt that of me, and that I belonged with them, and we all felt right and easy with each other and fond of each other, then there wasn't anything in the world I could be happier over, or be more glad to know (and this is so, too); and that I knew I could say all of the same of Walker (and this, too, I know I was true in saying). I had stood up, almost without realizing I was doing it, the moment she appeared and began to speak, as though facing some formal, or royal, or ritual action, and we stayed thus standing, not leaning against or touching anything, about three feet apart, facing each other. I went on to say that whatever might happen to her or that she might do in all her life I wished her the best luck anyone could think of, and not ever to forget it, that nobody has a right to be unhappy, or to live in a way that makes them unhappy, for the sake of being afraid, or what people will think of them, or for the sake of anyone else, if there is any way they can possibly do better, that won't hurt other people too much. She slowly and lightly blushed while I spoke and her eyes became damp and bright, and said that she sure did wish me the same. Then we had nothing to say, unless we should invent something, and nothing to do, and quite suddenly and at the same instant we smiled, and she said well, she reckoned she'd better git on in and help Annie Mae, and I nodded, and she went, and a half-hour later I was driving her, and Annie Mae, and her father, and Louise, and Junior, and Burt, and the baby, to her brother's house near Cookstown. The children were silent and intent with the excitement of riding in the car, stacked on top of each other around their mother on the back seat and looking out of the windows like dogs, except Louise, whose terrible gray eyes met mine whenever I glanced for them in the car mirror. Emma rode between me and her father, her round sleeveless arms cramped a little in front of her. My own sleeves were rolled high, so that in the crowding our flesh touched. Each of us at the first few of these contacts drew quietly away, then later she relaxed her arms, and her body and thighs as well, and so did I, and for perhaps fifteen minutes we lay quietly and closely side to side, and intimately communicated also in our thoughts. Our bodies were very hot, and the car was packed with hot and sweating bodies, and with a fine salt and rank odor like that of crushed grass: and thus in a short while, though I knew speed was not in the mood of anyone and was going as slowly as I felt I could with propriety, we covered the short seven mileage of clay, then slag, to Cookstown, and slowed through the town (eyes, eyes on us, of men, from beneath hatbrims), and down the meandering now sandy road to where her brother lived. I had seen him once before, a man in his thirties with a bitter, intelligent, skull-formed face; and his sour wife, and their gold skinned children: and now here also was another man, forty or so, leathery-strong, black-shaven, black-hatted, booted, his thin mouth tightened round a stalk of grass showing gold stained teeth, his cold, mean eyes a nearly white blue; and he was sardonically waiting, and his truck, loaded with chairs and bed-iron, stood in the sun where the treeshade had slid beyond it. He was studying Emma coldly and almost without furtiveness, and she was avoiding his eyes. It was impossible to go quite immediately. We all sat around a short while and had lemonade from a pressed-glass pitcher, from which he had already taken at least two propitiatory glasses. It has been made in some hope of helping the leavetaking pass off as a sort of party, from two lemons and spring water, without ice, and it was tepid, heavily sweetened (as if to compensate the lack of lemons), and scarcely tart; there was half a glass for each of us, out of five tumblers, and we all gave most of it to the children. The children of the two families stayed very quiet, shy of each other; the others, save the black-hatted man, tried to talk, without managing much; they tried especially hard when Emma got up, as suddenly as if she had to vomit, and went into the next room and shut the door, and Annie Mae followed her. Gallatin said it was mighty hard on a girl so young as that leaving her kinfolks so far behind. The man in the hat twisted his mouth on the grass and, without opening his teeth, said Yeah-ah, as if he had his own opinions about that. We were trying not to try to hear the voices in the next room, and that same helpless, frozen, creaky weeping I had heard before; and after a little it quieted; and after a little more they came out, Emma flourily powdered straight to the eyes, and the eyes as if she had cried sand instead of tears; and the man said—it was the first kind gesture I had seen in him and one of the few I suspect in his life, and I am sure it was kind by no intention of his: "Well, we can't hang around here all day. Reckon you'd better come on along, if you're coming."

With that, Emma and her father kiss, shyly and awkwardly, children doing it before parents; so do she and her brother; she and Annie Mae embrace; she and I shake hands and say good-bye: all this in the sort of broken speed in which a family takes leave beside the black wall of a steaming train when the last crates have been loaded and it seems certain that at any instant the windows, and the leaned unpitying faces, will begin to slide past on iron. Emma's paper suitcase is lifted into the truck beside the bedsprings which will sustain the years on years of her cold, hopeless nights; she is helped in upon the hard seat beside the driver above the hot and floorless engine, her slippered feet propped askew at the ledges of that pit into the road; the engine snaps and coughs and catches and levels on a hot white moistureless and thin metal roar, and with a dreadful rending noise that brings up the mild heads of cattle a quarter of a mile away the truck rips itself loose from the flesh of the planed dirt of the yard and wrings into the road and chucks ahead, we waving, she waving, the black hat straight ahead, she turned away, not bearing it, our hands drooped, and we stand disconsolate and emptied in the sun; and all through these coming many hours while we slow move within the anchored rondures of our living, the hot, screaming, rattling twenty-mile-an-hour traveling elongates steadily crawling, a lost, earnest, and frowning ant, westward on red roads and on white in the febrile sun above no support, suspended, sustained from falling by force alone of its outward growth, like that long and lithe incongruous slender runner a vine spends swiftly out on the vast blank wall of the earth, like snake's head and slim stream feeling its way, to fix, and anchor, so far, so wide of the strong and stationed stalk: and that is Emma.

But as yet this has not happened, and now she sleeps, here in this next room, among six others dear in their lives to me, and if I were but to section and lift away a part of this so thin shell and protection of wall, there they would be as in a surgery, or a medical drawing, the brain beneath the lifted, so light helmet of the skull, the deep-chambered, powerful and so vulnerable, so delicately ruined, emboweled, most vital organs, behind the placid lovedelighting skin; and a few hours past, they were going to bed, and not long before, they were eating supper, and because of their sadness, and because of the excitement of her being here, supper had in its speaking and its whole manner a tone out of the ordinary, a quality of an occasion, almost of a party, almost of gaiety, with a pale chocolate pudding, made out of cocoa and starch, for dessert, and a sort of made-conversation and joking half forced by fear of sadness, and half genuinely stimulated by her presence and by a shyness and liking for us: and in the middle of the table stood the flower of the lighted lamp, more kind, more friendly in the still not departed withering daylight and more lovely, than may be set in words beneath its fact: and when the supper was finished, it disintegrated without suture or transition into work, sleep, rest: Annie Mae, Emma, Louise, the three women, rising to the work they had scarcely ceased during the meal (for they had served us, eating betweentimes), clearing, scraping, crumbing the damp oilcloth with damp cloth in the light, dishwashing, meanwhile talking (Louise not talking, listening to them, the older women, absorbing, absorbing deeply, grain by grain, ton by ton, that which she shall not escape): the women lifting themselves from their chairs into this work; the children meanwhile sinking and laid out five fathom five mile deep along the exhausted floor: and we, following manners, transferred with George, a few feet beyond the kitchen door, in the open porch hall, leaned back in chairs against the wall, or leaned between our knees and our planted feet, he, with his work shoes off, his feet taking, thirstily drinking like the sunken heads of horses at the trough, the cool and beauty quiet of the grained and gritted boards of the floor; and he talking a little, but too tired for talk, and rolling a damp cigarette and smoking its short sweetness through to the scorching of the stony thumb, with a child's body lifted sleeping between his knees:

and when the women are through, they may or may not come out too, with their dresses wet in front with the dishwashing and their hard hands softened and seamed as if withered with water, and sit a little while with the man or the men: and if they do, it is not for long, for everyone is much too tired, and has been awake and at work since daylight whitened a little behind the trees on the hill, and it is now very close to dark, with daylight scarcely more than a sort of tincture on the air, and this diminishing, and the loudening frogs, and the locusts, the crickets, and the birds of night, tentative, tuning, in that great realm of hazy and drowned dew, who shall so royally embroider the giant night's fragrant cloud of earthshade: and so, too, the talking is sporadic, and sinks into long unembarrassed silences; the sentences, the comments, the monosyllables, drawn up from deepest within them without thought and with faint creaking of weight as if they were wells, and spilled out in a cool flat drawl, and quietly answered; and a silence; and again, some words: and it is not really talking, or meaning, but another and profounder kind of communication, a rhythm to be completed by answer and made whole by silence, a lyric song, as horses who nudge one another in pasture, or like drowsy birds who are heavying a dark branch with their tiredness before sleep: and it is their leisure after work; but it does not last; and in fifteen minutes, or a half-hour at most, it is done, and they draw themselves into motion for bed:

one by one, in a granite-enameled, still new basin which is for that single purpose, they wash their feet in cold water—for this is a very cleanly and decent family—and begin to move into the bedroom: first the children, then the women, last George: the pallets are laid; the lamp is in the bedroom; George sits in the porch dark, smoking another cigarette. Junior, morose and whimpering and half blind with sleep, undresses himself, sliding the straps from his shoulders and the overalls from his nakedness and sinking in his shirt asleep already, along the thin cotton pallet. Burt scarcely half awakens as his sister strips him, a child of dough, and is laid like a corpse beside his cruel brother. Squinchy is drugged beyond doomcrack: his heavy tow head falls back across her bent arm loose as that of a dead bird, the mouth wide open, the eyelids oily gleaming, as his mother slips from his dwarf body the hip length, one-button dress; and the women, their plain shifts lifted from the closet nails, undress themselves, turned part away from each other, and careful not to look: the mother, whose body already at twenty-seven is so wrung and drained and old, a scrawny, infinitely tired, delicate animal, the poor emblems of delight no longer practicable to any but most weary and grunting use: her big young sister, childless still, and dim, soft as a bloomed moon, and still in health, who emanates some disordering or witless violation: and the still inviolate, lyric body of a child, very much of the earth, yet drawn into that short and seraphic phase of what seems unearthliness which it will so soon lose: each aware of herself and of the others, and each hiding what shames or grieves her: and the two elder talking (and the child, the photographic plate, receiving: These are women, I am a woman, I am not a child any more, I am undressing with women, and this is how women are, and how they talk), talking ahead, the two women, in flat, secure, drawled, reedy voices, neither shy nor deliberately communicative, but utterly communicative, the talk loosening out of them serenely and quietly steady and in no restraint of uncertainty of one another like the alternate and plaited music of two slow-dribbling taps; and they are in bed and George throws his cigarette, hurtling its spark into the night yard, and comes in, and they turn their faces away while he undresses; and he takes the clean thin union suit from its nail by the scrolled iron head of the bed; and he slides between the coarse sheets and lets down his weight; and for a little while more, because they are stimulated, they keep talking, while the children sleep, and while Louise lies looking and listening, with the light still on, and there is almost volubility in the talk, and almost gaiety again, and inaudible joking, and little runs of laughter like startled sparrows; and gradually this becomes more quiet, and there is a silence full of muted thought; and George, says; Well; and fluffs out the lamp, and its light from the cracks in my wall, and there is silence; and George speaks, low, and is answered by both women; and a silence; and Emma murmurs something; and after a few seconds Annie Mae murmurs a reply; and there is a silence, and a slow and constrained twisting on springs and extension of a body, and silence; and a long silence in the darkness of the peopled room that is chambered in the darkness of the continent before the unwatching stars; and Louise says, Good night Immer, and Emma says, Good night Louise; and Louise says, Good night mamma; and Annie Mae says, Good night Louise; and Louise says, Good night daddy; and George says, Good night Louise; good night George; night, Immer; night, Annie Mae; night, George; night, Immer; night, Annie Mae; night, Louise; night; good night, good night:

The Gudger House

The house is left alone

Slowly they diminished along the hill path, she, and her daughter, and her three sons, in leisured enfilade beneath the light. The mother first, her daughter next behind, her eldest son, her straggler, whimpering; their bare feet pressed out of the hot earth gentle explosions of gold. She carried her youngest child, his knees locked simian across her, his light hands at her neck, and his erected head, hooded with night, next hers, swiveled mildly upon the world's globe, a periscope. The dog, a convoy, plaited his wanderings round them through the briars. She wore the flowerlike beauty of the sunbonnet in which she is ashamed to appear before us. At length, well up the hill, their talking shrank and became inaudible, and at that point will give safe warning on the hill of their return. Their slanted bodies slowly straightened, one by one, along the brim, and turned into the east, a slow frieze, and sank beneath the brim in order of their height, masts foundered in a horizon; the dog, each of the walking children, at length; at last, the guileless cobra gloatings of the baby, the mother's tall, flared head.

They are gone.

No one is at home, in all this house, in all this land. It is a long while before their return. I shall move as they would trust me not to, and as I could not, were they here. I shall touch nothing but as I would touch the most delicate wounds, the most dedicated objects.

The silence of the brightness of this middle morning is increased upon me moment by moment and upon this house, and upon this house the whole of heaven is drawn into one lens; and this house itself, in each of its objects, it, too, is one lens.

I am being made witness to matters no human being may see.

There is a cold beating at my solar plexus. I move in exceeding slowness and silence that I shall not dishonor nor awaken this house: and in every instant of silence, it becomes more entirely perfected upon itself under the sun. I take warmed water from the bucket, without sound, and it brings the sweat out sharply and I wipe it away, remembering in shame his labor, George, at this instant, hard, in the strenuous heat, and upon the tanned surface of this continent, this awful field where cotton is made, infinitesimal, the antlike glistening of the sweated labors of nine million. I remember how in hot early puberty, realizing myself left alone the whole of a cavernous and gloomed afternoon in my grandfather's large unsentineled home, I would be taken at the pit of the stomach with a most bitter, criminal gliding and cold serpent restiveness, and would wander from vacant room to vacant room examining into every secrecy from fungoid underearth to rarehot roof and from the roof would gaze in anguish and contempt upon the fronded suffocations of the midsummer city; trying to read; trying to play the piano; ravening upon volumes of soft-painted nudes; staring hungrily and hatefully into mirrors; rifling drawers, closets, boxes, for the mere touch at the lips and odor of fabrics, pelts, jewels, switches of hair; smoking cigars, sucking at hidden liquors; reading the piteous enthusiasms of ribboned letters stored in attic trunks: at length I took off all my clothes, lay along the cold counterpanes of every bed, planted my obscenities in the cold hearts of every mirror in foreknowledge, what unseen words and acts lurked ambushed in those deep white seas before the innocent fixtures of a lady's hair: I permitted nothing to escape the fingering of my senses nor the insulting of the cold reptilian fury of the terror of lone desire which was upon me:

It is not entirely otherwise now, in this inhuman solitude, the nakedness of this body which sleeps here before me, this tabernacle upon whose desecration I so reverentially proceed: yet it differs somewhat: for there is here no open sexual desire, no restiveness, nor despair: but the quietly triumphant vigilance of the extended senses before an intricate task of surgery, a deep stealthfulness, not for shame of the people, but in fear and in honor of the house itself, a knowledge of being at work. And by this same knowledge, along with the coldness, the adoration, the pity, the keen guilt at the heart, complete casualness. I am merely myself, a certain young man, standing in my sweated clothes in the rear of a dividing porch of a certain house, foundered as stone in sea in deepest Alabamian rurality, beneath the white scorch of a calm white morning; the leaves, sluicing most gently in their millions what open breadth of earth I see, beneath upward coilings of transparent air, and here, their home; and they have gone; and it is now my chance to perceive this, their home, as it is, in whose hollow heart resounds the loud zinc flickering heartbeat of the cheap alarm two hours advanced upon false time; a human shelter, a strangely lined nest, a creature of killed pine, stitched together with nails into about as rude a garment against the hostilities of heaven as a human family may wear.

We stand first facing it, squarely in front of it, in the huge and peaceful light of this August morning:

And it stands before us, facing us, squarely in front of us, silent and undefended in the sun.

In front of the house: Its general structure

Two blocks, of two rooms each, one room behind another. Between these blocks a hallway, floored and roofed, wide open both at front and rear: so that these blocks are two rectangular yoked boats, or floated tanks, or coffins, each, by an inner wall, divided into two squared chambers. The roof, pitched rather steeply from front and rear, its cards met and nailed at a sharp angle. The floor faces the earth closely. On the left of the hall, two rooms, each an exact square. On the right a square front room and, built later, behind it, using the outward weatherboards for its own front wall, a leanto kitchen half that size.

At the exact center of each of the outward walls of each room, a window. Those of the kitchen are small, taller than wide, and are glassed. Those of the other rooms are exactly square and are stopped with wooden shutters.

From each room a door gives on the hallway. The doors of the two front rooms are exactly opposite: the doors of the rear rooms are exactly opposite. The two rooms on either side of the hallway are also connected inwardly by doors through their partition walls.

Out at the left of the house, starting from just above the side window of the front room, a little roof is reached out and rested on thin poles above bare ground: shelter for wagon or for car.

At the right of the house, just beneath the side window of the front room, a commodious toolbox, built against the wall. It is nailed shut.

The hallway yields onto a front porch about five feet long by ten wide, reaching just a little short of the windows at either side, set at dead center of the front of the house. A little tongue of shingles, the same size, is stuck out slightly slanted above it, and is sustained on four slender posts from which most of the bark has been stripped.

Three steps lead down at center; they are of oak: the bottom one is cracked and weak, for all its thickness. Stones have been stacked beneath it, but they have slid awry, and it goes to the ground sharply underfoot. Just below and beyond it is a wide flat piece of shale the color of a bruise. It is broken several ways across and is sunken into the dirt.

The forty-foot square of land in front of the house, the "front yard," is bare of any trees or bushes; there is nothing at all near the house of its own height, or bestowing of any shade. This piece of land is hunched a little on itself in a rondure. Through the dry haze of weeds and flowering fennels its dead red yellowness glows quietly, a look of fire in sunlight, and it is visible how intricately it is trenched and seamed with sleavings of rain; as if, the skull lifted off, the brain were exposed, of some aged not intellectual being who had lived a long time patiently and with difficulty.

Where we stand, square toward the front, the house is almost perfectly symmetrical. Its two front walls, square, balanced, each of a size, cloven by hallway; the lifted roof; at center of each wall, a square window, the shutters closed; the porch and its roof and the four little posts like candles:

Each window is framed round with a square of boards.

Ten or twelve feet out in this yard, and precisely in line with these front windows, as if they were projections of them, and of about the same size, two hollow squares of wood are laid upon the earth and are sunk level with it:

and these are in fact two projections and are related with these windows, and indeed are windows, of a sort: for they are intended to let through their frames from the blank wall and darkness of the earth a particular and gracious, pleasing light; they are flower-beds. The one at the left is sprung through with the same indiscriminate fennels of the yard; the one on the right, the same. But here among this rambling of bastardy stands up, on its weak stem, one fainting pale magenta petunia, which stares at its tired foot; and this in the acreage of these three farms is the one domestic flower.

Now raising the eyes, slowly in face of this strength of sun, to look the house in its blind face:

In front of the house: The façade

The porch: stands in its short square shade:

The hall: it is in shadow also, save where one wall, fifteen feet back, is slantingly slashed with light:

At the far end of this well of hall, the open earth, lifted a little, bald hard dirt; the faced frontages of the smokehouse and the henhouse, and a segment of the barn: and all of this framed image a little unnaturally brilliant and vital, as all strongly lighted things appear through corridors of darkness:

And this hall between, as the open valve of a sea creature, steadfastly flushing the free width of ocean through its infinitesimal existence: and on its either side, the square boxes, the square front walls, raised vertical to the earth, and facing us as two squared prows of barge or wooden wings, shadow beneath their lower edge and at their eaves; and the roof:

And these walls:

Nailed together of boards on beams, the boards facing the weather, into broad cards of wood inlet with windows stopped with shutters: walls, horizontals, of somewhat narrow weatherboarding; the windows bounded by boards of that same width in a square: the shutters, of wide vertical boards laid edge to edge, not overlapped: each of these boards was once of the living flesh of a pine tree; it was cut next the earth, and was taken between the shrieking of saws into strict ribbons; and now, which was vertical, is horizontal to the earth, and another is clamped against the length of its outward edge and its downward clamps another, and these boards, nailed tightly together upon pine beams, make of their horizontalities a wall: and the sun makes close horizontal parallels along the edges of these weatherboards, of sharp light and shade, the parallels strengthened here in slight straight-line lapse from level, in the subtle knife-edged curve of warping loose in another place: another irregular "pattern" is made in the endings and piecings-out of boards:

And the roof:

It is of short hand-hewn boards so thick and broad, they are shingles only of a most antique sort: crosswise upon rigid beams, laths have been nailed, not far apart, and upon these laths, in successive rows of dozens and of hundreds, and here again, though regularly, with a certain shuffling of erratism pure symmetry, these broad thick shingles are laid down overlapping from the peak to the overhung edge like the plumage of a bird who must meet weather: and not unlike some square and formalized plumage, as of a holy effigy, they seem, and made in profligate plates of a valuable metal; for they have never been stained, nor otherwise touched or colored save only by all habits of the sky: nor has any other wood of this house been otherwise ever touched: so that, wherever the weathers of the year have handled it, the wood of the whole of this house shines with the noble gentleness of cherished silver, much as where (yet differently), along the floors, in the pathings of the millions of soft wavelike movements of naked feet, it can be still more melodiously charmed upon its knots, and is as wood long fondled in a tender sea:

Upon these structures, light:

It stands just sufficiently short of vertical that every leaf of shingle, at its edges, and every edge of horizontal plank (blocked, at each center, with squared verticals) is a most black and cutting ink: and every surface struck by light is thus: such an intensity and splendor of silver in the silver light, it seems to burn, and burns and blinds into the eyes almost as snow; yet in none of that burnishment or blazing whereby detail is lost: each texture in the wood, like those of bone, is distinct in the eye as a razor: each nail-head is distinct: each seam and split; and each slight warping; each random knot and knothole: and in each board, as lovely a music as a contour map and unique as a thumbprint, its grain, which was its living strength, and these wild creeks cut stiff across by saws; and moving nearer, the close-laid arcs and shadows even of those tearing wheels: and this, more poor and plain than bone, more naked and noble than sternest Doric, more rich and more variant than watered silk, is the fabric and the stature of a house.

It is put together out of the cheapest available pine lumber, and the least of this is used which shall stretch a skin of one thickness alone against the earth and air; and this is all done according to one of the three or four simplest, stingiest, and thus most classical plans contrivable, which are all traditional to that country: and the work is done by half-skilled, half-paid men under no need to do well, who therefore take such vengeance on the world as they may in a cynical and part willful apathy; and this is what comes of it: Most naïve, most massive symmetry and simpleness. Enough lines, enough off-true, that this symmetry is strongly yet most subtly sprained against its centers, into something more powerful than either full symmetry or deliberate breaking and balancing of "monotonies" can hope to be. A look of being most earnestly hand-made, as a child's drawing, a thing created out of need, love, patience, and strained skill in the innocence of a race. Nowhere one ounce or inch spent with ornament, not one trace of relief or of disguise: a matchless monotony, and in it a matchless variety, and this again throughout restrained, held rigid: and of all this, nothing which is not intrinsic between the materials of structure, the earth, and the open heaven. The major lines of structure, each horizontal of each board, and edge of shingle, the strictness yet subtle dishevelment of the shingles, the nail-heads, which are driven according to geometric need, yet are not in perfect order, the grain, differing in each foot of each board and in each board from any other, the many knots in this cheap lumber: all these fluencies and irregularities, all these shadows of pattern upon each piece of wood, all these in rectilinear ribbons caught into one squared, angled, and curled music, compounding a chord of four chambers upon a soul and center of clean air: and upon all these masses and edges and chances and flowerings of grain, the changes of colorings of all weathers, and the slow complexions and marchings of pure light.

Or by another saying:

"In all this house:

"In all of this house not any one inch of lumber being wasted on embellishment, or on trim, or on any form of relief, or even on any doubling of walls: it is, rather, as if a hard thin hide of wood has been stretched to its utmost to cover exactly once, or a little less than once, in all six planes the skeletal beams which, with the inside surface of the weatherboarding, are the inside walls; and no touch, as I have said, of any wash or paint, nor, on the floors, any kind of covering, nor, to three of the rooms, any kind of ceiling, but in all places left bare the plain essences of structure; in result all these almost perfect symmetries have their full strength, and every inch of the structure, and every aspect and placement of the building materials, comes inevitably and purely through into full esthetic existence, the one further conditioner, and discriminator between the functions and proprieties of indoors and out, being the lights and operations of the sky."

Or by a few further notes:

"On symmetry: the house is rudimentary as a child's drawing, and of a bareness, cleanness, and sobriety which only Doric architecture, so far as I know, can hope to approach: this exact symmetry is sprung slightly and subtly, here and there, one corner of the house a little off vertical, a course of weatherboarding failing the horizontal between parallels, a window frame not quite square, by lack of skill and by weight and weakness of timber and time; and these slight failures, their tensions sprung against centers and opposals of such rigid and earnest exactitude, set up intensities of relationship far more powerful than full symmetry, or studied dissymmetry, or use of relief or ornament, can ever be: indeed, the power is of another world and order than theirs, and there is, as I mentioned, a particular quality of a thing hand-made, which by comparison I can best suggest thus: by the grandeur that comes of the effort of one man to hold together upon one instrument, as if he were breaking a wild monster to bridle and riding, one of the larger fugues of Bach, on an organ, as against the slick collaborations and effortless climaxes of the same piece in the manipulations of an orchestra."

Or again by materials: and by surfaces and substances: the build and shape of walls, roof, window frames, verticals of shutters, opposals and cleavings of mass as I have said, and the surfaces and substances: "The front porch of oak two-by-twelves so hard they still carry a strong piercing fell of splinters; the four supporting posts which have the delicate bias and fluences of young trees and whose surface is close to that of rubbed ivory; in the musculatures of their stripped knots they have the flayed and expert strength of anatomical studies: and the rest of the house entirely of pine, the cheapest of local building material and of this material one of the cheapest grades: in the surfaces of these boards are three qualities of beauty and they are simultaneous, mutually transparent: one is the streaming killed strength of the grain, infinite, talented, and unrepeatable from inch to inch, the florid genius of nature which is incapable of error: one is the close-set transverse arcs, dozens to the foot, which are the shadows of the savage breathings and eatings of the circular saws; little of this lumber has been planed: one is the tone and quality the weather has given it, which is related one way to bone, another to satin, another to unpolished but smooth silver: all these are visible at once, though one or another may be strongly enhanced by degree and direction of light and by degree of humidity: moreover, since the lumber is so cheap, knots are frequent, and here and there among the knots the iron-hard bitter red center is lost, and there is, instead, a knothole; the grain near these knots goes into convulsions or ecstasies such as Beethoven's deafness compelled; and with these knots the planes of the house are badged at random, and again moreover, these wild fugues and floods of grain, which are of the free perfect innocence of nature, are sawn and stripped across into rigid ribbons and by rigid lines and boundaries, in the captive perfect innocence of science, so that these are closely collaborated and interinvolved in every surface: and at points strategic to structure: and regimented by need, and attempting their own symmetries, yet not in perfect line (such is the tortured yet again perfect innocence of men, caught between the pulls of nature and science), the patternings and constellations of the heads of the driven nails: and all these things, set in the twisted and cradling planet, take the benefit of every light and weather which the sky in their part of the world can bestow, this within its terms being subtly unrepeatable and probably infinite, and are qualified as few different structures can be, to make full use of these gifts. By most brief suggestion: in full symmetry of the sun, the surfaces are dazzling silver, the shadows strong as knives and India ink, yet the grain and all detail clear: in slanted light, all slantings and sharpenings of shadow: in smothered light, the aspect of bone, a relic: at night, the balanced masses, patient in the base world: from rain, out of these hues of argent bone the colors of agate, the whole wall, one fabric and mad zebra of quartered minerals and watered silks: and in the sheltered yet open hallway, a granite gray and seeming of nearly granitic hardness, the grain dim, the sawmarks very strong; in the strength of these marks and peculiar sobriety of the color, a look as if there has been a slow and exact substitution of calcium throughout all the substance: within the rooms, the wood holds much nearer its original colors of yellows, reds, and peasant golds drawn deep toward gray, yet glowing quietly through it as the clay world glows through summer."

But enough.

The room beneath the house

The rear edges of the house rest in part on stacked stones, in part on the dirt; in part they overhang this dirt a little. Beneath the house this dirt sinks gently, so that the flanks and forward edges are lifted to level in part on taller stacks of stone, in part on thick rounded sections of logs. The porch floor, and the forward parts of the house, are about two and a half feet off the ground.

This cold plaque of earth beneath, which wears the shape of the house and is made different from other earth, as that part of a wall against which a picture has been hung for years: which might have been field, pasture, forest, mere indiscriminate land: by chance:

At a bright time in sun, and in a suddenness alien to those rhythms the land had known these hundred millions of years, lumber of other land was brought rattling in yellow wagonloads and caught up between hammers upon air before unregarding heaven a hollow altar, temple, or poor shrine, a human shelter, which for the space of a number of seasons shall hold this shape of earth denatured: yet in whose history this house shall have passed soft and casually as a snowflake fallen on black spring ground, which thaws in touching.

There in the chilly and small dust which is beneath porches, the subtle funnels of doodlebugs whose teasing, of a broomstraw, is one of the patient absorptions of kneeling childhood, and there, in that dust and the damper dust and the dirt, dead twigs of living, swept from the urgent tree, signs, and relics: bent nails, withered and knobbed with rust; a bone button, its two eyes torn to one; the pierced back of an alarm clock, greasy to the touch; a torn fragment of pictured print; an emptied and flattened twenty-gauge shotgun shell, its metal green, lettering still visible; the white tin eyelet of a summer shoe; and thinly scattered, the desiccated and the still soft excrement of hens, who stroll and dab and stand, shimmying, stabbing at their lice, and stroll out again into the sun as vacantly as they departed it. And other things as well: a long and slender infinitesimally rustling creek and system of ants in their traffic: the underside of the house, so sparsely lifted even at the front, and meeting the quietly swollen earth so close there is scarcely light at all at the rear: and here the earth is cold, continually damp, and in the odors of mold and of a well, and there are cold insects, sutured and plated, rapid on many feet that run in a rill and nimbus along their narrow bodies; and strong spiders here, and dead ones, pale as mushrooms, suspended in the ruins of their lives, or strong, avid, distinct among their clean constructions, still, slowly palpitant in their thick bodies, watching you with a poison sharpness of eye you cannot be sure you see, sudden to movement and swift, and some who jump: and the clean pine underside of the house, blond like the floor of a turtle, that sun has never and weather has scarcely touched, so that it looks still new, as if as yet it had sustained no sorrow above, but only a hope that was still in process of approach, as once this whole house was, all fresh and bridal, four hollowed rooms brimmed with a light of honey:

(O therefore in the cleanly quiet, calm hope, sweet odor, awaiting, of each new dwelling squared by men on air, be sorrowful, as of the sprung trap, the slim wrist gnawn, the little disastrous fox:

It stands up in the sun and the bride smiles: quite soon the shelves are papered; the new forks taste in the food:

Ruin, ruin is in our hopes: nor hope, help, any healing:)

it is hung and strung with their frail structures, and closes with the cool damp dirt in almost darkness: and is of this noiseless and variegated underworld the flat scarce-lifted stone, the roof and firmament: and above:

This underside, and firmament, and shelter and graveyard of sharp alien and short lives, and drifting lot of orts of usage, and retirement of hens, and relief of dogs, and meditation space of children, and gradation of constant shade, and yielder upward of harsh winter damp, slid through likewise from time to time with snakes, and sterilizer of earth which contiguous, just beyond its region of rule, sick as it is, streams and inaudibly shrieks with green violence: this likewise on its upward surface is the floor and basis of still other living, a wide inch-thick plat of wood, swept with straws and not seldom scrubbed, soaped and spreaded with warmth of water, that drains in its seams, and kneeling, hard breathing, with hard straws scoured and pure: the walls stand up from its edges and face one another; and its surface sustains the distributed points and weights of the furnishings of living, and the motions and directions of desire, need, work, and listlessness: a floor, a sustainer of human living; whereto children and dogs droop in their tiredness and rest, and sleep, and on a pallet a baby lies, spread over with a floursack against infringement of flies, and sleeps, and here a moving camera might know, on its bareness, the standing of the four iron feet of a bed, the wood of a chair, the scrolled treadle of a sewing machine, the standing up at right angles of plain wood out of plain wood, the great and handsome grains and scars of this vertical and prostrate wood, the huge and noble motions of brooms and of knees and of feet, and how with clay, and animals, and the leaning face of a woman, these are among the earliest and profoundest absorptions of a very young child.

The hallway

Structure of four rooms

The hallway is long courses of weatherboard facing one another in walls six feet apart, featureless excepting two pair of opposite doors, not ceiled, but beneath the empty and high angling of the roof: perhaps because of the blankness of these walls, and their facing closeness relative to their parallel length, there is here an extremely strong sense of the nakedness and narrowness of their presence, and of the broad openness, exposing the free land, at either end. The floor is laid along beams rather wide apart. In all the rear end it yields to the ground under much weight: the last few feet lie solid to the ground, and this is a strong muck in wet weather.

The one static fixture in the hallway is at the rear, just beyond the kitchen door. It is a wooden shelf, waist-high, and on this shelf, a bucket, a dipper, a basin, and usually a bar of soap, and hanging from a nail just above, a towel. The basin is granite-ware, small for a man's hands, with rustmarks in the bottom. The bucket is a regular galvanized two-gallon bucket, a little dented, and smelling and touching a little of a fishy-metallic kind of shine and grease beyond any power of cleaning. It is half full of slowly heating water which was not very cold to begin with: much lower than this, the water tastes a little ticklish and nasty for drinking, though it is still all right for washing. The soap is sometimes strong tan "kitchen" soap, sometimes a cheap white gelatinous lavender face soap. It stands on the shelf in a china saucer. The dipper again is granite-ware, and again blistered with rust at the bottom. Sometimes it bobs in the bucket; sometimes it lies next the bucket on the shelf. The towel is half a floursack, with the blue and red and black printing still faint on it. Taken clean and dry, it is the pleasantest cloth I know for a towel. Beyond that, it is particularly clammy, clinging, and dirty-feeling.

A few notes of discrimination may be helpful:

The towels in such a farmhouse are always floursacks. "Kitchen" towels are of another world and class of farmer, and "face" and "turkish" towels of still another.

By no means all poor farmers use any sort of "toilet" soap. Some seldom use soap at all. When they use other than kitchen soap, it is of one of about three kinds, all of them of the sort available in five-and-tens and small-town general stores. One is "lava" or "oatmeal" soap, whose rough texture is pleasing and convincing of cleanliness to a person who works with his hands. The white soaps smell sharply of lye: again, the odor is cleansing. Or if the soap is more fancy, it is a pink or lemon or purple color, strongly and cheaply scented and giving a big lather. No cheap yet somewhat pleasantly scented soap such as lux is used.

Rather more often than not, the basin and the dipper are plain unenameled tin. I expect, but am not sure, that this is a few cents cheaper. In any case the odor, taste, and shiny, greasy texture soon become strong. The use of enamel ware is a small yet sharp distinction and symptom in "good taste," and in "class," and in a sort of semi-esthetic awareness, choice and will. The use of gray as against white is still another discriminative. That they bought small sizes, which are a very few cents cheaper, speaks for itself. So does the fact that they have afforded still another basin, not quite big enough for its use, to wash their feet in.

At times, there is also a mirror here, and a comb; but more often these are on the bedroom mantel.

The hall and front porch are a kind of room, and are a good deal used. Mrs. Gudger and her children sit in the porch in empty times of the morning and afternoon: back in the rear of the hall is the evening place to sit, before supper or for a little while just after it. There are few enough chairs that they have to be moved around the house to where they are needed, but ordinarily there is a rockingchair on the porch and a straight chair in the rear of the hall next the bedroom door. This rockingchair is of an inexpensive "rustic" make: sections of hickory sapling with the bark still on. On the hard and not quite even porch floor the rocking is stony and cobbled, with a little of the sound of an auto crossing a loose wooden bridge. Three of the straight chairs are strong, plain, not yet decrepit hickory-bottoms, which cost a dollar and a half new; there is also a kitchen-type chair with a pierced design in the dark scalloped wood at the head, and the bottom broken through.

When we first knew the Gudgers they had their eating-table in the middle of the hall, for only in the hall is there likely to be any sort of breeze, and the kitchen, where nearly all farm families eat, was so hot that they could at times hardly stand to eat in it. This was only an experiment though, and it was not successful. The hall is too narrow for any comfort in it for a whole family clenched round a table. If it were even two feet wider, it would be much more use to them, but this would not have occurred to those who built it, nor, if it had, would anything have been done about it.

Four rooms make a larger tenant house than is ordinary: many are three; many are two; more are one than four: and three of these rooms are quite spacious, twelve feet square. For various reasons, though, all of which could easily enough have been avoided in the building of the house, only two of these rooms, the kitchen and the rear bedroom, are really habitable. There is no ceiling to either of the front rooms, and the shingles were laid so unskillfully, and are now so multitudinously leaky, that it would be a matter not of repairing but of complete relaying to make a solid roof. Between the beams at the eaves, along the whole front of the house, and the top of the wall on which the beams rest, there are open gaps. In the front room on the right, several courses of weatherboarding have been omitted between the level of the eaves and the peak of the roof: a hole big enough for a cow to get through. The walls, and shutters, and floors, are not by any means solid: indeed, and beyond and aside from any amount of laborious calking, they let in light in many dozens of places. There are screens for no windows but one, in the rear bedroom. Because in half the year the fever mosquitoes are thick and there are strong rainstorms, and in the other half it is cold and wet for weeks on end with violent slanted winds and sometimes snow, the right front room is not used to live in at all and the left front room is used only dubiously and irregularly, though the sewing machine is there and it is fully furnished both as a bedroom and as a parlor. The children use it sometimes, and it is given to guests (as it was to us), but storm, mosquitoes, and habit force them back into the other room where the whole family sleeps together.

But now I want to take these four rooms one by one, and give at least a certain rough idea of what is in each of them and of what each is "like," though I think I should begin this with a few more general remarks.

Odors

Bareness and space

The Gudgers' house, being young, only eight years old, smells a little dryer and cleaner, and more distinctly of its wood, than an average white tenant house, and it has also a certain odor I have never found in other such houses: aside from these sharp yet slight subtleties, it has the odor or odors which are classical in every thoroughly poor white southern country house, and by which such a house could be identified blindfold in any part of the world, among no matter what other odors. It is compacted of many odors and made into one, which is very thin and light on the air, and more subtle than it can seem in analysis, yet very sharply and constantly noticeable. These are its ingredients. The odor of pine lumber, wide thin cards of it, heated in the sun, in no way doubled or insulated, in closed and darkened air. The odor of woodsmoke, the fuel being again mainly pine, but in part also, hickory, oak, and cedar. The odors of cooking. Among these, most strongly, the odors of fried salt pork and of fried and boiled pork lard, and second, the odor of cooked corn. The odors of sweat in many stages of age and freshness, this sweat being a distillation of pork, lard, corn, woodsmoke, pine, and ammonia. The odors of sleep, of bedding and of breathing, for the ventilation is poor. The odors of all the dirt that in the course of time can accumulate in a quilt and mattress. Odors of staleness from clothes hung or stored away, not washed. I should further describe the odor of corn: in sweat, or on the teeth, and breath, when it is eaten as much as they eat it, it is of a particular sweet stuffy fetor, to which the nearest parallel is the odor of the yellow excrement of a baby. All these odors as I have said are so combined into one that they are all and always present in balance, not at all heavy, yet so searching that all fabrics of bedding and clothes are saturated with them, and so clinging that they stand softly out of the fibers of newly laundered clothes. Some of their components are extremely "pleasant," some are "unpleasant"; their sum total has great nostalgic power. When they are in an old house, darkened, and moist, and sucked into all the wood, and stacked down on top of years of a moldering and old basis of themselves, as at the Ricketts,' they are hard to get used to or even hard to bear. At the Woods,' they are blowsy and somewhat moist and dirty. At the Gudgers,' as I have mentioned, they are younger, lighter, and cleaner-smelling. There too, there is another and special odor, very dry and edged: it is somewhere between the odor of very old newsprint and of a victorian bedroom in which, after long illness, and many medicines, someone has died and the room has been fumigated, yet the odor of dark brown medicines, dry-bodied sickness, and staring death, still is strong in the stained wallpaper and in the mattress.

Bareness and space (and spacing) are so difficult and seem to me of such greatness that I shall not even try to write seriously or fully of them. But a little, applying mainly to the two bedrooms.

The floors are made of wide planks, between some of which the daylighted earth is visible, and are naked of any kind of paint or cloth or linoleum covering whatever, and paths have been smoothed on them by bare feet, in a subtly uneven surface on which the polished knots are particularly beautiful. A perfectly bare floor of broad boards makes a room seem larger than it can if the floor is covered, and the furniture too, stands on it in a different and much cleaner sort of relationship. The walls as I have said are skeleton; so is the ceiling in one of these rooms; the rooms are twelve feet square and are meagerly furnished, and they are so great and final a whole of bareness and complete simplicity that even the objects on a crowded shelf seem set far apart from each other, and each to have a particularly sharp entity of its own. Moreover, all really simple and naïve people[8] incline strongly toward exact symmetries, and have some sort of instinctive dislike that any one thing shall touch any other save what it rests on, so that chairs, beds, bureaus, trunks, vases, trinkets, general odds and ends, are set very plainly and squarely discrete from one another and from walls, at exact centers or as near them as possible, and this kind of spacing gives each object a full strength it would not otherwise have, and gives their several relationships, as they stand on shelves or facing, in a room, the purest power such a relationship can have. This is still more sharply true with such people as the Gudgers, who still have a little yet earnest wish that everything shall be as pleasant and proper to live with as possible, than with others such as the Woods and Ricketts, who are disheveled and wearied out of any such hope or care.

• • • • • • • • • • • •

QUESTIONS FOR A SECOND READING

1. Walker Evans's photographs stand at the head of the book *Let Us Now Praise Famous Men,* before the title page. We have reproduced this format. The photographs, then, have no introduction; there are no captions; there is nothing to verbally prepare a reader or to establish a tie to the book that follows. They are just there, as though they could or should or must speak for themselves. (And James Agee's written text does not refer directly to the photographs. It doesn't gloss them or explain them or even describe them.)

[8] And many of the most complex, and not many between.

Look back carefully through the photographs. Think of yourself as a reader reading the images, their presentation, and their arrangement. What do they say? How are you expected to read them? or prepared to read them?

Here are some questions you might ask. The blank pages divide the photographs into four clusters: How are the individual clusters different and how are they the same? Is there an order within each cluster? Do the clusters have a similar order? Is there an argument or narrative that develops as you turn the pages? Are you given a key or a theme or a topic that can organize your understanding of the photographs?

2. We have provided most of the frontmatter of the book. This is the written text that follows the photographs and precedes the first chapter. The frontmatter is made up of the "Preface," several verses and quotations, a list of persons and places, the odd table of contents called "Design of the Book," and the "Preamble." This is where Agee prepares a reader for the book to follow; it is where he describes the problems the book presented for the writers and the problems the book will, he feels, present to the reader. The work, he says, near the start of the "Preamble," is "curious, obscene, terrifying, and unfathomably mysterious." The writing is "clumsy." The camera has "spread so nearly universal a corruption of sight that I know of less than a dozen alive whose eyes I can trust even so much as my own."

   Reread this section in order to paraphrase and summarize Agee's sense of how, where, and why the book presents problems for the writer and for a reader. And then, as you reread the excerpts that follow, put him to the test. What are the difficulties (or pleasures) you experience as a reader? Are they anticipated in the "Preface" and "Preamble"? What does it take to learn to be a reader of this book? Has Agee helped to prepare you? What are the distinctive features of his writing? How would you explain them as part of his project or necessary to his project or the result of his project? Are his terms helpful in such an explanation?

3. We gave you two excerpts from the main body of the work: one from "A Country Letter" and one from "Shelter" on "The Gudger House." In the "Preface," Agee writes, "The photographs are not illustrative. They, and the text, are co-equal, mutually independent, and fully collaborative." (p. 87).

   How do you understand the relation the text provides (or invites) between words and images? As you reread the text, turn back to the photographs. In what ways might they be said to be "co-equal," "mutually independent," and/or "fully collaborative." Do you have other ways of describing the connections?

4. In the "Preface," Agee says of the book, "The nominal subject is North American cotton tenantry as examined in the daily living of three representative white tenant families." As you reread, think about how the book defines its subject. Agee refers to the "nominal" subject. What distinction is he making? and why? If the nominal subject is North American cotton tenantry, what might the real subject be? How would you know?

5. Agee's prose style is odd and distinctive. (By some standards, it is not standard English.) Here is a representative passage:

   > Burt half-woke, whimpering before he was awake, an inarticulated soprano speaking through not quite weeping in complaint to his mother as

> before a sure jury of some fright of dream: the bed creaked and I heard her bare feet slow, the shuffling soles, and her voice, not whispering but stifled and gentle, Go to sleep now, git awn back to sleep, they aint nothin agoin to pester ye, git awn back to sleep, in that cadence of strength and sheltering comfort which anneals all fence of language and surpasses music; and George's grouched, sleepy voice, and hers to him, no words audible; and the shuffling; and a twisting in beds, and grumbling of weak springs; and the whimpering sinking, and expired; and the sound of breathing, strong, not sleeping, now, slowed, shifted across into sleep, now, steadier; and now, long, long, drawn off as lightest lithest edge of bow, thinner, thinner, a thread, a filament; nothing: and once more that silence wherein more deep than starlight this home is foundered. (p. 108)

You can work with this passage or choose one of your own—one that interests you and that you feel is representative of Agee's prose style. There are two parts to this exercise:

a. Be prepared to read your passage aloud and to discuss what the language does—not what it *says*, but what it *does* as an act of attention or as a way of recording experience or as a way of organizing a reader's time and understanding. (Agee says in the "Preface," "The text was written with reading aloud in mind. . . . it is suggested that the reader attend with his ear to what he takes off the page: for variations of tone, pace, shape, and dynamics are here particularly unavailable to the eye alone, and with their loss, a good deal of meaning escapes" [p. 87].)

b. Write a similar passage, one that describes a moment you observe or recall. And what now, now that you have done this work from the inside, would you say that this way of writing allows a writer to *do*?

WRITING ASSIGNMENTS

1. Walker Evans's photographs stand at the head of the book *Let Us Now Praise Famous Men*, before the title page. There is no introduction; there are no captions; there is nothing to verbally prepare a reader or to establish a tie to the book that follows. They are just there, as though they could or should or must speak for themselves. (And James Agee's written text does not refer directly to the photographs. It doesn't gloss them or explain them or even describe them.)

   Write an essay about the photographs, about how you understand them (and the project they represent), and about their placement in the book. The questions we asked earlier (in the "Questions for a Second Reading") can serve here. Look back carefully through the photographs. Think of yourself as a reader reading the images, their presentation, and their arrangement. What do they say? How are you expected to read them? or prepared to read them?

   If it was appropriate to turn this assignment into a larger research project, you might also look to see what Walker Evans has said about those photographs and, in general, about his work as a photographer.

   Note: This assignment puts particular pressure on the first-person perspective of the essayist—you. You will need to write from your sense of the photographs and what might be said about them. It has been useful to our students to call attention to this from the very beginning. You might think of the "I" in your essay as a character, someone with a history, interests, a point of view, a style, someone of a particular age with a particular background in relation to photography, photographs, and Evans's subjects. And you might want to distinguish among your responses and others that you can imagine. It might become appropriate to acknowledge, in other words, that not everyone can, will, or should see these photographs the way you do.

2. The "Preface" ends with the following invitation:

> This is a *book* only by necessity. More seriously, it is an effort in human actuality, in which the reader is not less centrally involved than the authors and those of whom they tell. Those who wish actively to participate in the subject, in whatever degree of understanding, friendship, or hostility, are invited to address the authors in care of the publishers. In material that is used, privately or publicly, names will be withheld on request. (p. 87)

   Neither Agee nor Evans is around to receive a response. Still, you might prepare one for them, a letter or a proposal or a miniproject that speaks to your involvement with their work and proposes (and perhaps enacts or represents) a way of participating.

3. In the "Preface," Agee refers to *Let Us Now Praise Famous Men* as a "curious piece of work." To prepare for this assignment, you will need to have a close and precise sense of just what that work is. The preceding "Questions for a Second Reading" are designed to assist you in developing that sense.

   With that as preparation, prepare a similar project, a miniversion of the work of Agee and Evans. You will need a set of photographs. They could be yours or ones you gather from other sources (including the sources in this textbook). To be most in line with Agee and Evans, the photographs should be of a place, a people, a way of life and/or work that you urgently feel the need to make present to others. You will need to gather photographs and you will need to prepare a written text.

   You could think of this as a strict imitation, where you are arranging and selecting (perhaps taking) photographs in the manner of Walker Evans, and where you are writing prose in the style of Agee. Or you could think of this as an homage, or a response, or an argument, or a way of entering the conversation. You are offering your work, as appropriate to your experience and place in time, as an engaged response to theirs.

   It would be useful to prepare a brief preface to your project.

4. Walker Evans's photographs stand at the head of the book *Let Us Now Praise Famous Men*, before the title page. There is no introduction; there are no captions; there is nothing to verbally prepare a reader or to establish a tie to the book that follows. They are just there, as though they could or should or must speak for themselves.

   James Agee's written text does not refer directly to the photographs. It doesn't gloss them or explain them or even describe them. He does, however, refer to Evans, to photographs, and to photography in the "Preface" and the "Preamble."

   Write an essay in which you explain your understanding of the relationship between the photographs and the text. In doing so, you are providing a lesson to others in how one might best read this book (or the excerpts in *Ways of Reading Words and Images*). You should certainly consider what Agee says in the frontmatter. You should not be limited by or tied to his account, however.

Note: For this assignment, it might be best to assume that your reader is not yet familiar with Agee and Evans and *Let Us Now Praise Famous Men*. You will need to provide some introduction and context. For the written text, you will need to provide summary, paraphrase, and quotation. You should certainly feel free to reproduce images in the body of your essay.

5. Agee's prose style is odd and distinctive. The fifth "Question for a Second Reading" provides a distinctive passage and suggests that you prepare a reading and an imitation, all designed to give you access to thinking about what this prose *does* (as opposed to what it *says*). This exercise would be useful preparation for an essay on Agee's style. Your imitation, in fact, could be written into that essay as a case in point.

   Write an essay in which you present and discuss Agee's project as a writer in the excerpts we've provided from *Let Us Now Praise Famous Men*. You can turn to what he says about the project in the "Preface" and "Preamble," but you should certainly also turn to the example of the prose that follows. What is he doing at the level of the sentence? What is he doing beyond the sentence? How does this prose serve his "nominal" subject? How does it define or represent a "real" subject?

MAKING CONNECTIONS

1. In his chapter, "The Tradition: Fact and Fiction" (p. 212), Robert Coles gives a detailed account of the photographs in *Let Us Now Praise Famous Men*. For this assignment, we'd like you to write an essay in response to Coles. Perhaps the best way to do this is to write, first, about the photographs from your own perspective. The "Questions for a Second Reading" and the first "Writing Assignment" provide a context and some help toward such an essay. For the sake of convenience, we'll reproduce the writing assignment here:

   > Walker Evans's photographs stand at the head of the book *Let Us Now Praise Famous Men*, before the title page. There is no introduction; there are no captions; there is nothing to verbally prepare a reader or to establish a tie to the book that follows. They are just there, as though they could or should or must speak for themselves. (And James Agee's written text does not refer directly to the photographs. It doesn't gloss them or explain them or even describe them.)
   >
   > Write an essay about the photographs, about how you understand them (and the project they represent), and about their placement in the book. The questions we asked earlier . . . can serve here. Look back carefully through the photographs. Think of yourself as a reader reading the images, their presentation, and their arrangement. What do they say? How are you expected to read them? or prepared to read them?

Once you have written out, in draft, your understanding of the photographs, read Coles's account. Then write an essay in which you bring Coles's argument to bear on the work you have done with the photographs. What does he say? What does he say that you find useful? Where and how do you differ in approach or in conclusion? What might you make of these differences? (Or how, in your essay, might you define a relationship with an established scholar?)

In your essay, you should make it clear that Coles is serving *your* project. Your work is at the center. He is someone you are turning to after having developed (or in order to continue to develop) a position of your own. You need to be present in your essay as a scholar, in other words. Coles should not render you silent or make you disappear.

You should assume that your readers do not know (or remember) Coles's account of the photographs. You will need to present his case. Your reader may know something about *Let Us Now Praise Famous Men*, but they don't have a copy handy. It would be useful, therefore, to work some of the images into the body of your essay.

Note: This assignment puts particular pressure on the first-person perspective of the essayist—you. You will need to write from your sense of the photographs and what might be said about them. It has been useful to our students to call attention to this from the very beginning. You might think of the "I" in your essay as a character, someone with a history, interests, a point of view, a style, someone of a particular age with a particular background in relation to photography, photographs, and Evans's subjects.

2. *Let Us Now Praise Famous Men* is one of the "case studies" in W. J. T. Mitchell's "The Photographic Essay: Four Case Studies" (p. 332). He develops a theory about the relationship of photograph to text in Agee and Evans's book. For this assignment, we'd like you to write an essay in response to Mitchell. Perhaps the best way to do this is to first establish a position of your own. The "Questions for a Second Reading" and the fourth "Writing Assignment" provide a context and some help toward such an essay. For the sake of convenience, we'll reproduce the writing assignment here:

> Walker Evans's photographs stand at the head of the book *Let Us Now Praise Famous Men*, before the title page. There is no introduction; there are no captions; there is nothing to verbally prepare a reader or to establish a tie to the book that follows. They are just there, as though they could or should or must speak for themselves.
>
> James Agee's written text does not refer directly to the photographs. It doesn't gloss them or explain them or even describe them. He does, however, refer to Evans, to photographs, and to photography in the preface and the preamble.
>
> Write an essay in which you explain your understanding of the relationship between the photographs and the text. In doing so, you are providing a lesson to others in how one might best read this book (or the excerpts in *Ways of Reading Words and Images*). You should certainly consider what Agee says in the frontmatter. You should not be limited by or tied to his account, however.

Once you have written out, in draft, your understanding of the photographs, read Mitchell's account. And write an essay in which you bring Mitchell's argument to bear on the work you have done. What does he say? What does he say that you find useful? Where and how do you differ in approach or in conclusion? (Or how, in your essay, might you define a relationship with an established scholar?)

In your essay, you should make it clear that Mitchell is serving *your* project. Your work is at the center. He is someone you are turning to after having developed (or in order to continue to develop) a position of your own. You need to be present in your essay as a scholar, in other words. Mitchell should not render you silent or make you disappear.

Note: This assignment puts particular pressure on the first-person perspective of the essayist—you. It has been useful to our students to call attention to this from the very beginning. You might think of the "I" in your essay as a character, someone with a history, interests, a point of view, a style, someone of a particular age with a particular background in relation to photography, photographs, and Evans and Agee's subjects.

3. In "Projected Memory: Holocaust Photographs in Personal and Public Fantasy" (p. 261), Marianne Hirsch writes about the past as it is defined by (created by) photographs and our use of them. It is a cautionary essay; it is about the proper uses of the past, about how to understand the power and presence of photographs. Agee writes about photographs and the present. It, too, is full of cautions. Here, from the "Preamble," is a statement of particular urgency:

> "For in the immediate world, everything is to be discerned, for him who can discern it, and centrally and simply, without either dissection into science, or digestion into art, but with the whole of consciousness, seeking to perceive it as it stands: so that the aspect of a street in sunlight can roar in the heart of itself as a symphony, perhaps as no symphony can: and all of consciousness is shifted from the imagined, the revisive, to the effort to perceive simply the cruel radiance of what is.
>
> This is why the camera seems to me, next to unassisted and weaponless consciousness, the central instrument of our time; and is why in turn I feel such rage at its misuse: which has spread so nearly universal a corruption of sight that I know of less than a dozen alive whose eyes I can trust even so much as my own." (p. 98)

Write an essay that works with these two selections and their possible uses for you (and people like you) at this point in time, a time filled with photographic images. What do the writers say about photography? What do they say about the dangers and powers in photographic images and our uses of them? What do they show or enact in their writing about these images? And where are you with these lessons? What makes sense to you?

Note: You should write for readers who have read neither Hirsch's nor Agee and Evans's work. You will need to provide context, paraphrase, quotation, image, and example.

4. In both *Let Us Now Praise Famous Men* (Agee and Evans) and "States" (Edward Said and Jean Mohr, " p. 378), the photographs prompt many pages of writing—and the writing is not simply caption or introduction or even commentary. The writing has its own force and agenda. Reread both "States" and

Let Us Now Praise Famous Men, looking for interesting and representative passages that can be placed next to the photographs and used to talk about the achieved relation between words and images.

With these examples as your primary material, write an essay that examines the different ways Agee and Said understand their projects, their relationship to the images, to their subject, to their audience, and to history—to the broad set of political concerns that are served by each project. You should assume that your readers have some familiarity with Agee and Said as figures but that they don't have the writers' books with them and can't be expected to remember all that they say (or show). You will need to present your examples, in other words, as you use them as the objects of discussion.

ROLAND BARTHES

ROLAND BARTHES (1915–1980) was born in Cherbourg, France, and studied French literature and classics at the University of Paris. He taught French in Romania and Egypt before joining the Centre National de la Recherche Scientifique to work in sociology and linguistics. After the success of his early work in the 1960s, Barthes taught at the Sorbonne, the University of Paris, the Collège de France, and Johns Hopkins University in Baltimore.

Barthes was a distinguished scholar ("the founder of French and modern semiotics"), but he was also a public figure, a brilliant, extravagant, and popular essayist whose work was read widely outside the academy. There was plenty to read. In his lifetime he published over 150 articles and seventeen books, including Writing Degree Zero, Elements of Semiology, The Pleasure of the Text, The Fashion System, Image-Music-Text, Mythologies, *and* Camera Lucida, *from which the following excerpts were taken. He was also a contributor to* Tel Quel, *the influential French journal.*

Barthes wrote about language, linguistics, and literature, about music, film, and painting, but he was also instrumental in extending the study of culture to the everyday, particularly in Mythologies, *where he demonstrated possibilities for reading the common material of culture: the Eiffel Tower, the face of Greta Garbo, an advertisement for margarine. In the introduction to* Mythologies, *Barthes says, "The starting point of these reflections was usually a feeling of impatience at the sight of the 'naturalness' with which newspapers, art and common sense constantly dress up a reality which, even though it is the one we live in, is undoubtedly determined by history. . . . I resented seeing Nature and History confused at every turn, and I wanted to track down, in the decorative display of* what-goes-without-saying, *the ideological abuse, which, in my view, is hidden there."*

Barthes's work asks us to think of predictable, routine, organized events like the taking of photographs (or the viewing of photographs) as though they were texts, texts created not by a single author but by some other, larger agency (called "history" in the passage just quoted). These "texts" reproduce a tradition, assume an audience, and must be read, Barthes argues. He asks us to "read" a photograph, for example, in the same way we'd read a literary text. When we fail to "read" these nonlinguistic texts, we mistake "History" for "Nature." We forget that nonlinguistic texts are written—even if we cannot find their author, they embody design and intention; they are constructed to create effects, to produce certain ends, shaping both what and how we think.

Camera Lucida (La Chambre Claire) *was Barthes's last book. It was written soon after the death of his mother, an event he refers to in the text: "Now, one November evening shortly after my mother's death, I was going through some photographs. I had no hope of 'finding' her. . . . I had acknowledged that fatality, one of the most agonizing features of mourning, which decreed that however often I might consult such images, I could never recall her features (summon them up as a totality)." Of these photographs, he says, "I could not even say that I loved them: I was not sitting down to contemplate them, I was not engulfing myself in them. I was sorting them, but none seemed to me really 'right': neither as a photographic performance nor as a living resurrection of the beloved face. If I were ever to show them to friends I could doubt that these photographs would* speak." Camera Lucida *was completed after his mother's death and shortly before his own, from an accident, in March 1980.*

The book is written in two parts. The first part announces the project: "I wanted to learn at all costs what Photography was 'in itself,' by what essential feature it was to be distinguished from the community of images" (including painting and cinema). And he decides to begin the study by examining his own experience and practice in 'looking' at photographic images. The following selection basically begins at that point: "I see photographs everywhere, like everyone else, nowadays; they come from the world to me, without my asking. . . ." As you'll see, he initially organizes the project by thinking about what he likes and what he doesn't like in photographs, and from that outlines a method, a way of paying attention (or promoting interest) that is centered in the person, in you, in the person looking.

Camera Lucida

6

I see photographs everywhere, like everyone else, nowadays; they come from the world to me, without my asking; they are only "images," their mode of appearance is heterogeneous. Yet, among those which had been selected, evaluated, approved, collected in albums or magazines and which had thereby passed through the filter of culture, I realized that some provoked tiny jubilations, as if they referred to a stilled center, an erotic or lacerating value buried in myself (however harmless the subject may have appeared); and that others, on the contrary, were so indifferent to me that by dint of seeing them multiply, like some weed, I felt a kind of aversion toward them, even of irritation: there are moments when I detest Photographs: what have I to do with Atget's old tree trunks, with Pierre Boucher's nudes, with Germaine Krull's double exposures (to cite only the old names)? Further: I realized that I have never liked *all* the pictures by any one photographer: the only thing by Stieglitz that delights me (but to ecstasy) is his most famous image ("The Horse-Car Terminal," New York, 1893); a certain picture by Mapplethorpe led me to think I had found "my" photographer; but I hadn't—I don't like all of Mapplethorpe. Hence I could not accede to that notion which is so convenient when we want to talk history, culture, aesthetics—that notion known as an artist's style. I felt, by the strength of my "investments," their disorder, their caprice, their enigma, that Photography is an *uncertain* art, as would be (were one to attempt to establish such a thing) a science of desirable or detestable bodies.

I saw clearly that I was concerned here with the impulses of an overready subjectivity, inadequate as soon as articulated: *I like/I don't like:* we all have our secret chart of tastes, distastes, indifferences, don't we? But just so: I have always wanted to remonstrate with my moods; not to justify them; still less to fill the scene of the text with my individuality; but on the contrary, to offer, to extend this individuality to a science of the subject, a science whose name is of little importance to me, provided it attains (as has not yet occurred) to a generality which neither reduces nor crushes me. Hence it was necessary to take a look for myself.

"Only Stieglitz's most famous photograph delights me . . ."

A. Stieglitz: The Horse-Car Terminal. New York, 1893

7

I decided then to take as a guide for my new analysis the attraction I felt for certain photographs. For of this attraction, at least, I was certain. What to call it? Fascination? No, this photograph which I pick out and which I love has nothing in common with the shiny point which sways before your eyes and makes your head swim; what it produces in me is the very opposite of hebetude; something more like an internal agitation, an excitement, a certain labor too, the pressure of the unspeakable which wants to be spoken. Well, then? Interest? Of brief duration; I have no need to question my feelings in order to list the various reasons to be interested in a photograph; one can either desire the object, the landscape, the body it represents; or love or have loved the being it permits us to recognize; or be astonished by what one sees; or else admire or dispute the photographer's performance, etc.; but these interests are slight, heterogeneous; a certain photograph can satisfy one of them and interest me slightly; and if another photograph interests me powerfully, I should like to know what there is in it that sets me off. So it seemed that the best word to designate (temporarily) the attraction certain photographs exerted upon me was *advenience* or even *adventure*. This picture *advenes,* that one doesn't.

The principle of adventure allows me to make Photography exist. Conversely, without adventure, no photograph. I quote Sartre: "Newspaper photographs can very well 'say nothing to me.' In other words, I look at them without assuming a posture of existence. Though the persons whose photograph I see are certainly present in the photograph, they are so without existential posture, like the Knight and Death present in Dürer's engraving, but without my positing them. Moreover, cases occur where the photograph leaves me so indifferent that I do not even bother to see it 'as an image.' The photograph is vaguely constituted as an object, and the persons who figure there are certainly constituted as persons, but only because of their resemblance to human beings, without any special intentionality. They drift between the shores of perception, between sign and image, without ever approaching either."

In this glum desert, suddenly a specific photograph reaches me; it animates me, and I animate it. So that is how I must name the attraction which makes it exist: an *animation*. The photograph itself is in no way animated (I do not believe in "lifelike" photographs), but it animates me: this is what creates every adventure.

8

In this investigation of Photography, I borrowed something from phenomenology's project and something from its language. But it was a vague, casual, even cynical phenomenology, so readily did it agree to distort or to evade its principles according to the whim of my analysis. First of all, I did

"I understood at once
that this photograph's 'adventure'
derived from the co-presence of two elements . . ."

Koen Wessing: Nicaragua. 1979

not escape, or try to escape, from a paradox: on the one hand the desire to give a name to Photography's essence and then to sketch an eidetic science of the Photograph; and on the other the intractable feeling that Photography is essentially (a contradiction in terms) only contingency, singularity, risk: my photographs would always participate, as Lyotard says, in "something or other": is it not the very weakness of Photography, this difficulty in existing which we call banality? Next, my phenomenology agreed to compromise with a power, *affect;* affect was what I didn't want to reduce; being irreducible, it was thereby what I wanted, what I ought to reduce the Photograph *to;* but could I retain an affective intentionality, a view of the object which was immediately steeped in desire, repulsion, nostalgia, euphoria? Classical phenomenology, the kind I had known in my adolescence (and there has not been any other since), had never, so far as I could remember, spoken of desire or of mourning. Of course I could make out in Photography, in a very orthodox manner, a whole network of essences: material essences (necessitating the physical, chemical, optical study of the Photography), and regional essences (deriving, for instance, from aesthetics, from History, from sociology); but at the moment of reaching the essence of Photography in general, I branched off; instead of following the path of a formal ontology (of a Logic), I stopped, keeping with me, like a treasure, my desire or my grief; the anticipated essence of the Photograph could not, in my mind, be separated from the "pathos" of which, from the first glance, it consists. I was like that friend who had turned to Photography only because it allowed him to photograph his son. As *Spectator* I was interested in Photography only for "sentimental" reasons; I wanted to explore it not as a question (a theme) but as a wound: I see, I feel, hence I notice, I observe, and I think.

9

I was glancing through an illustrated magazine. A photograph made me pause. Nothing very extraordinary: the (photographic) banality of a rebellion in Nicaragua: a ruined street, two helmeted soldiers on patrol; behind them, two nuns. Did this photograph please me? Interest me? Intrigue me? Not even. Simply, it existed (for me). I understood at once that its existence (its "adventure") derived from the co-presence of two discontinuous elements, heterogeneous in that they did not belong to the same world (no need to proceed to the point of contrast): the soldiers and the nuns. I foresaw a structural rule (conforming to my own observation), and I immediately tried to verify it by inspecting other photographs by the same reporter (the Dutchman Koen Wessing): many of them attracted me because they included this kind of duality which I had just become aware of. Here a mother and daughter sob over the father's arrest (Baudelaire: "the emphatic truth of gesture in the great circumstances of life"), and this happens *out in the countryside* (where could they have learned the news? for whom are these gestures?). Here, on a torn-up pavement, a child's corpse under a white sheet;

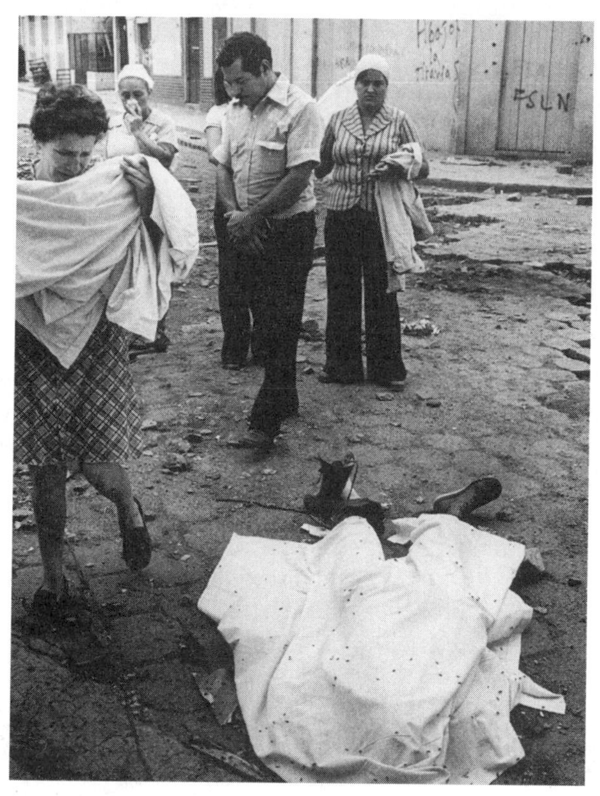

". . . the sheet carried by the weeping mother (why this sheet?) . . ."

Koen Wessing: Nicaragua. 1979

parents and friends stand around it, desolate: a banal enough scene, unfortunately, but I noted certain interferences: the corpse's one bare foot, the sheet carried by the weeping mother (why this sheet?), a woman in the background, probably a friend, holding a handkerchief to her nose. Here again, in a bombed-out apartment, the huge eyes of two little boys, one's shirt raised over his little belly (the excess of those eyes disturb the scene). And here, finally, leaning against the wall of a house, three Sandinists, the lower part of their faces covered by a rag (stench? secrecy? I have no idea, knowing nothing of the realities of guerrilla warfare); one of them holds a gun that rests on his thigh (I can see his nails); but his other hand is stretched out, open, as if he were explaining and demonstrating something. My rule applied all the more closely in that other pictures from the same reportage were less interesting to me; they were fine shots, they expressed the dignity and horror of rebellion, but in my eyes they bore no mark or sign: their homogeneity remained cultural: they were "scenes," rather *à la* Greuze, had it not been for the harshness of the subject.

10

My rule was plausible enough for me to try to name (as I would need to do) these two elements whose co-presence established, it seemed, the particular interest I took in these photographs.

The first, obviously, is an extent, it has the extension of a field, which I perceive quite familiarly as a consequence of my knowledge, my culture; this field can be more or less stylized, more or less successful, depending on the photographer's skill or luck, but it always refers to a classical body of information: rebellion, Nicaragua, and all the signs of both: wretched ununiformed soldiers, ruined streets, corpses, grief, the sun, and the heavy-lidded Indian eyes. Thousands of photographs consist of this field, and in these photographs I can, of course, take a kind of general interest, one that is even stirred sometimes, but in regard to them my emotion requires the rational intermediary of an ethical and political culture. What I feel about these photographs derives from an *average* affect, almost from a certain training. I did not know a French word which might account for this kind of human interest, but I believe this word exists in Latin: it is *studium,* which doesn't mean, at least not immediately, "study," but application to a thing, taste for someone, a kind of general, enthusiastic commitment, of course, but without special acuity. It is by *studium* that I am interested in so many photographs, whether I receive them as political testimony or enjoy them as good historical scenes: for it is culturally (this connotation is present in *studium*) that I participate in the figures, the faces, the gestures, the settings, the actions.

The second element will break (or punctuate) the *studium.* This time it is not I who seek it out (as I invest the field of the *studium* with my sovereign consciousness), it is this element which rises from the scene, shoots out of it like an arrow, and pierces me. A Latin word exists to designate this wound, this prick, this mark made by a pointed instrument: the word suits me all the better in that is also refers to the notion of punctuation, and because the photographs I am speaking of are in effect punctuated, sometimes even speckled with these sensitive points; precisely, these marks, these wounds are so many *points.* This second element which will disturb the *studium* I shall therefore call *punctum;* for *punctum* is also: sting, speck, cut, little hole—and also a cast of the dice. A photograph's *punctum* is that accident which pricks me (but also bruises me, is poignant to me).

Having thus distinguished two themes in Photography (for in general the photographs I liked were constructed in the manner of a classical sonata), I could occupy myself with one after the other.

11

Many photographs are, alas, inert under my gaze. But even among those which have some existence in my eyes, most provoke only a general and, so to speak, *polite* interest: they have no *punctum* in them: they please or displease me without pricking me: they are invested with no more than *studium.* The *studium* is that very wide field of unconcerned desire, of various interest, of inconsequential taste: *I like/I don't like.* The *studium* is of the order of *liking,* not of *loving;* it mobilizes a half desire, a demi-volition; it is the same sort of vague, slippery, irresponsible interest one takes in the people, the entertainments, the books, the clothes one finds "all right."

To recognize the *studium* is inevitably to encounter the photographer's intentions, to enter into harmony with them, to approve or disapprove of them, but always to understand them, to argue them within myself, for culture (from which the *studium* derives) is a contract arrived at between creators and consumers. The *studium* is a kind of education (knowledge and civility, "politeness") which allows me to discover the *Operator,* to experience the intentions which establish and animate his practices, but to experience them "in reverse," according to my will as a *Spectator.* It is rather as if I had to read the Photographer's myths in the Photograph, fraternizing with them but not quite believing in them. These myths obviously aim (this is what myth is for) at reconciling the Photograph with society (is this necessary?—Yes, indeed: the Photograph is *dangerous*) by endowing it with *functions,* which are, for the Photographer, so many alibis. These functions are: to inform, to represent, to surprise, to cause to signify, to provoke desire. And I, the *Spectator,* I recognize them with more or less pleasure: I invest them with my *studium* (which is never my delight or my pain).

12

Since the Photograph is pure contingency and can be nothing else (it is always *something* that is represented)—contrary to the text which, by the sudden action of a single word, can shift a sentence from description to reflection—it immediately yields up those "details" which constitute the very raw material of ethnological knowledge. When William Klein photographs "Mayday, 1959" in Moscow, he teaches me how Russians dress (which after all I don't know): I *note* a boy's big cloth cap, another's necktie, an old woman's scarf around her head, a youth's haircut, etc. I can enter still further into such details, observing that many of the men photographed by Nadar have long fingernails: an ethnographical question: how long were nails worn in a certain period? Photography can tell me this much better than painted portraits. It allows me to accede to an infra-knowledge; it supplies me with a collection of partial objects and can flatter a certain fetishism of mine: for this "me" which likes knowledge, which nourishes a kind of amorous preference for it. In the same way, I like certain biographical features which, in a writer's life, delight me as much as certain photographs; I have called these features "biographemes"; Photography has the same relation to History that the biographeme has to biography.

13

The first man who saw the first photograph (if we except Niepce, who made it) must have thought it was a painting: same framing, same perspective. Photography has been, and is still, tormented by the ghost of Painting (Mapplethorpe represents an iris stalk the way an Oriental painter might have done it); it has made Painting, through its copies and contestations, into the absolute, paternal Reference, as if it were born from the Canvas (this is true, technically, but only in part; for the painters' *camera obscura* is only one of the causes of Photography; the essential one, perhaps, was the chemical discovery). At this point in my investigation, nothing eidetically distinguishes a photograph, however realistic, from a painting. "Pictorialism" is only an exaggeration of what the Photograph thinks of itself.

Yet is it not (it seems to me) by Painting that Photography touches art, but by Theater. Niepce and Daguerre are always put at the origin of Photography (even if the latter has somewhat usurped the former's place); now Daguerre, when he took over Niepce's invention, was running a panorama theater animated by light shows and movements in the Place du Château. The *camera obscura,* in short, has generated at one and the same time perspective painting, photography, and the diorama, which are all three arts of the stage; but if Photography seems to me closer to the Theater, it is by way of a singular intermediary (and perhaps I am the only one who sees it): by way of Death. We know the original relation of the theater and the cult of the Dead: the first actors separated themselves from the community by playing the role of the Dead: to make oneself up was to designate oneself as a body simultaneously living and dead: the whitened bust of the totemic theater, the man with the painted face in the Chinese theater, the rice-paste makeup of the Indian Katha-Kali, the Japanese No mask . . . Now it is this same relation which I find in the Photograph; however "lifelike" we strive to make it (and this frenzy to be lifelike can only be our mythic denial of an

© WILLIAM KLEIN, COURTESY HOWARD GREENBERG GALLERY, NYC

"The photographer teaches me
how the Russians dress:
I note a boy's big cloth cap,
another's necktie,
an old woman's scarf around her head,
a youth's haircut . . ."

William Klein: Mayday, Moscow. 1959

apprehension of death), Photography is a kind of primitive theater, a kind of *Tableau Vivant,* a figuration of the motionless and made-up face beneath which we see the dead.

14

I imagine (this is all I can do, since I am not a photographer) that the essential gesture of the *Operator* is to surprise something or someone (through the little hole of the camera), and that this gesture is therefore perfect when it is performed unbeknownst to the subject being photographed. From this gesture derive all photographs whose principle (or better, whose alibi) is "shock"; for the photographic "shock" (quite different from the *punctum*) consists less in traumatizing than in revealing what was so well hidden that the actor himself was unaware or unconscious of it. Hence a whole gamut of "surprises" (as they are for me, the *Spectator;* but for the Photographer, these are so many "performances").

The first surprise is that of the "rare" (rarity of the referent, of course); a photographer, we are told admiringly, has spent four years composing a photographic anthology of monsters (man with two heads, woman with three breasts, child with a tail, etc.: all smiling). The second surprise is one habitual to Painting, which has frequently reproduced a gesture apprehended at the point in its course where the normal eye cannot arrest it (I have elsewhere called this gesture the *numen* of historical painting): Bonaparte has just touched the plague victims of Jaffa; his hand withdraws; in the same way, taking advantage of its instantaneous action, the Photograph immobilizes a rapid scene in its decisive instant: Apestéguy, during the Publicis fire, photographs a woman jumping out of a window. The third surprise is that of prowess: "For fifty years, Harold D. Edgerton has photographed the explosion of a drop of milk, to the millionth of a second (little need to admit that this kind of photography neither touches nor even interests me: I am too much of a phenomenologist to like anything but appearances to my own measure). A fourth surprise is the one which the photographer looks for from the contortions of technique: superimpressions, anamorphoses, deliberate exploitation of certain defects (blurring, deceptive perspectives, trick framing); great photographers (Germaine Krull, Kertész, William Klein) have played on these surprises, without convincing me, even if I understand their subversive bearing. Fifth type of surprise: the *trouvaille* or lucky find; Kertész photographs the window of a mansard roof; behind the pane, two classical busts look out into the street (I like Kertész, but I don't like whimsy, neither in music nor in photography); the scene can be arranged by the photographer, but in the world of illustrated media, it is a "natural" scene which the good reporter has had the genius, *i.e.,* the luck, to catch: an emir in native costume on skis.

All these surprises obey a principle of defiance (which is why they are alien to me): the photographer, like an acrobat, must defy the laws of probability or even of possibility; at the limit, he must defy those of the interesting: the photograph becomes "surprising" when we do not know why it has been taken; what motive and what interest is there in photographing a backlighted nude in a doorway, the front of an old car in the grass, a freighter at the dock, two benches in a field, a woman's buttocks at a farmhouse window, an egg on a naked belly (photographs awarded prizes at a contest for amateurs)? In an initial period, Photography, in order to surprise, photographs the notable; but soon, by a familiar reversal, it decrees notable whatever it photographs. The "anything whatever" then becomes the sophisticated acme of value.

15

Since every photograph is contingent (and thereby outside of meaning), Photography cannot signify (aim at a generality) except by assuming a mask. It is this word which Calvino correctly uses to designate what makes a face into the product of a society and of its history. As in the portrait of William Casby, photographed by Avedon: the essence of slavery is here laid bare: the mask is the meaning, insofar as it is absolutely pure (as it was in the ancient theater). This is why the great portrait photographers are great mythologists: Nadar (the French bourgeoisie), Sander (the Germans of pre-Nazi Germany), Avedon (New York's "upper crust").

Yet the mask is the difficult region of Photography. Society, it seems, mistrusts pure meaning: It wants meaning, but at the same time it wants this meaning to be surrounded by a noise (as is said in cybernetics) which will make it less acute. Hence the photograph whose meaning (I am not saying its effect, but its meaning) is too impressive is quickly deflected; we consume it aesthetically, not politically. The Photograph of the Mask is in fact critical enough to disturb (in 1934, the Nazis censored Sander because his "faces of the period" did not correspond to the Nazi archetype of the race), but it is also too discrete (or too "distinguished") to constitute an authentic and effective social critique, at least according to the exigencies of militantism: what committed science would acknowledge the interest of Physiognomy? Is not the very capacity to perceive the political or moral meaning of a face a class deviation? And even this is too much to say: Sander's Notary is suffused with self-importance and stiffness, his Usher with assertiveness and brutality; but no notary, no usher could ever have read such signs. As distance, social observation here assumes the necessary intermediary role in a delicate aesthetic, which renders it futile: no critique except among those who are already capable of criticism. This impasse is something like Brecht's: he was hostile to Photography because (he said) of the weakness of its critical power; but his own theater has never been able to be politically effective on account of its subtlety and its aesthetic quality.

If we except the realm of Advertising, where the meaning must be clear and distinct only by reason of its mercantile nature, the semiology of Photog-

"The mask is meaning,
insofar as it is absolutely pure . . ."
Richard Avedon: William Casby, Born a Slave. 1963

"The Nazis censored Sander because his 'faces of the period' did not correspond to the aesthetic of the Nazi race."

Sander: Notary

raphy is therefore limited to the admirable performances of several portraitists. For the rest, with regard to the heterogeneity of "good" photographs, all we can say is that the *object speaks,* it induces us, vaguely, to think. And further: even this risks being perceived as dangerous. At the limit, *no meaning at all* is safer: the editors of *Life* rejected Kertész's photographs when he arrived in the United States in 1937 because, they said, his images "spoke too much"; they made us reflect, suggested a meaning—a different meaning from the literal one. Ultimately, Photography is subversive not when it frightens, repels, or even stigmatizes, but when it is *pensive,* when it thinks.

16

An old house, a shadowy porch, tiles, a crumbling Arab decoration, a man sitting against the wall, a deserted street, a Mediterranean tree (Charles Clifford's "Alhambra"): this old photograph (1854) touches me: it is quite simply *there* that I should like to live. This desire affects me at a depth and according to roots which I do not know: Warmth of the climate? Mediterranean myth? Apollinism? Defection? Withdrawal? Anonymity? Nobility? Whatever the case (with regard to myself, my motives, my fantasy), I want to live there, *en finesse*—and the tourist photograph never satisfies that *esprit de finesse.* For me, photographs of landscape (urban or country) must be *habitable,* not visitable. This longing to inhabit, if I observe it clearly in myself, is neither oneiric (I do not dream of some extravagant site) nor empirical (I do not intend to buy a house according to the views of a real-estate agency); it is fantasmatic, deriving from a kind of second sight which seems to bear me forward to a utopian time, or to carry me back to somewhere in myself: a double movement which Baudelaire celebrated in *Invitation au voyage* and *La Vie antérieure.* Looking at these landscapes of predilection, it is as if *I were certain* of having been there or of going there. Now Freud says of the maternal body that "there is no other place of which one can say with so much certainty that one has already been there." Such then would be the essence of the landscape (chosen by desire): *heimlich,* awakening in me the Mother (and never the disturbing Mother).

17

Having thus reviewed the *docile interests* which certain photographs awaken in me, I deduced that the *studium,* insofar as it is not traversed, lashed, striped by a detail (*punctum*) which attracts or distresses me, engenders a very widespread type of photograph (the most widespread in the world), which we might call the *unary photograph.* In generative grammar, a transformation is unary if, through it, a single series is generated by the base: such as the passive, negative, interrogative, and emphatic transformations. The Photograph is unary when it emphatically transforms "reality" without doubling it, without making it vacillate (emphasis is a power of cohesion): no

"I want to live there . . . "

Charles Clifford: The Alhambra (Grenada). 1854–1856

duality, no indirection, no disturbance. The unary Photograph has every reason to be banal, "unity" of composition being the first rule of vulgar (and notably, of academic) rhetoric: "The subject," says one handbook for amateur photographers, "must be simple, free of useless accessories; this is called the Search for Unity."

News photographs are very often unary (the unary photograph is not necessarily tranquil). In these images, no *punctum:* a certain shock—the literal can traumatize—but no disturbance; the photograph can "shout," not wound. These journalistic photographs are received (all at once), perceived. I glance through them, I don't recall them; no detail (in some corner) ever interrupts my reading: I am interested in them (as I am interested in the world), I do not love them.

Another unary photograph is the pornographic photograph (I am not saying the erotic photograph: the erotic is a pornographic that has been disturbed, fissured). Nothing more homogeneous than a pornographic photograph. It is always a naïve photograph, without intention and without calculation. Like a shop window which shows only one illuminated piece of jewelry, it is completely constituted by the presentation of only one thing: sex: no secondary, untimely object ever manages to half conceal, delay, or distract . . . A proof *a contrario:* Mapplethorpe shifts his close-ups of genitalia from the pornographic to the erotic by photographing the fabric of underwear at very close range: the photograph is no longer unary, since I am interested in the texture of the material.

18

In this habitually unary space, occasionally (but alas all too rarely) a "detail" attracts me. I feel that its mere presence changes my reading, that I am looking at a new photograph, marked in my eyes with a higher value. This "detail" is the *punctum.*

It is not possible to posit a rule of connection between the *studium* and the *punctum* (when it happens to be there). It is a matter of a co-presence, that is all one can say: the nuns "happened to be there," passing in the background, when Wessing photographed the Nicaraguan soldiers; from the viewpoint of reality (which is perhaps that of the *Operator*), a whole causality explains the presence of the "detail": the Church implanted in these Latin-American countries, the nuns allowed to circulate as nurses, etc.; but from my *Spectator's* viewpoint, the detail is offered by chance and for nothing; the scene is in no way "composed" according to a creative logic; the photograph is doubtless dual, but this duality is the motor of no "development," as happens in classical discourse. In order to perceive the *punctum,* no analysis would be of any use to me (but perhaps memory sometimes would, as we shall see): it suffices that the image be large enough, that I do not have to study it (this would be of no help at all), that, given right there on the page, I should receive it right here in my eyes.

19

Very often the *punctum* is a "detail," *i.e.,* a partial object. Hence, to give examples of *punctum* is, in a certain fashion, to *give myself up.*

Here is a family of American blacks, photographed in 1926 by James Van der Zee. The *studium* is clear: I am sympathetically interested, as a docile cultural subject, in what the photograph has to say, for it *speaks* (it is a "good" photograph): it utters respectability, family life, conformism, Sunday best, an effort of social advancement in order to assume the White Man's attributes (an effort touching by reason of its naïveté). The spectacle interests me but does not prick me. What does, strange to say, is the belt worn low by the sister (or daughter)—the "solacing Mammy"—whose arms are crossed behind her back like a schoolgirl, and above all her *strapped pumps* (Mary Janes—why does this dated fashion touch me? I mean: to what date does it refer me?). This particular *punctum* arouses great sympathy in me, almost a kind of tenderness. Yet the *punctum* shows no preference for morality or good taste: the *punctum* can be ill-bred. William Klein has photographed children of Little Italy in New York (1954); all very touching, amusing, but what I stubbornly see are one child's bad teeth. Kertész, in 1926, took young Tzara's portrait (with a monocle); but what I notice, by that additional vision which is in a sense the gift, the grace of the *punctum,* is Tzara's hand resting on the door frame: a large hand whose nails are anything but clean.

However lightning-like it may be, the *punctum* has, more or less potentially, a power of expansion. This power is often metonymic. There is a photograph by Kertész (1921) which shows a blind gypsy violinist being led by a boy; now what I see, by means of this "thinking eye" which makes me add something to the photograph, is the dirt road; its texture gives me the certainty of being in Central Europe; I perceive the referent (here, the photograph really transcends itself: Is this not the sole proof of its art? To annihilate itself as *medium,* to be no longer a sign but the thing itself?), I recognize, with my whole body, the straggling villages I passed through on my long-ago travels in Hungary and Rumania.

There is another (less Proustian) expansion of the *punctum:* when, paradoxically, while remaining a "detail," it fills the whole picture. Duane Michals has photographed Andy Warhol: a provocative portrait, since Warhol hides his face behind both hands. I have no desire to comment intellectually on this game of hide-and-seek (which belongs to the *studium*); since for me, Warhol hides nothing; he offers his hands to read, quite openly; and the *punctum* is not the gesture but the slightly repellent substance of those spatulate nails, at once soft and hard-edged.

20

Certain details may "prick" me. If they do not, it is doubtless because the photographer has put them there intentionally. In William Klein's "Shinohiera, Fighter Painter" (1961), the character's monstrous head has nothing to

The strapped pumps

James Van der Zee. Family Portrait. 1926

"What I stubbornly see
are one boy's
bad teeth . . . "

William Klein: Little Italy, New York, 1954

say to me because I can see so clearly that it is an artifice of the camera angle. Some soldiers with nuns behind them served as an example to explain what the *punctum* was for me (here, quite elementary); but when Bruce Gilden photographs a nun and some drag queens together (New Orleans, 1973), the deliberate (not to say, rhetorical) contrast produces no effect on me, except perhaps one of irritation. Hence the detail which interests me is not, or at least not strictly, intentional, and probably must not be so; it occurs in the field of the photographed thing like a supplement that is at once inevitable and delightful; it does not necessarily attest to the photographer's art; it says only that the photographer was there, or else, still more simply, that he could not *not* photograph the partial subject at the same time as the total object (how could Kertész have "separated" the dirt road from the violinist walking on it?). The Photographer's "second sight" does not consist in "seeing" but in being there. And above all, imitating Orpheus, he must not turn back to look at what he is leading—what he is giving to me!

21

A detail overwhelms the entirety of my reading; it is an intense mutation of my interest, a fulguration. By the mark of *something,* the photograph is no longer "anything whatever." This *something* has triggered me, has provoked a tiny shock, a *satori,* the passage of a void (it is of no importance that its referent is insignificant). A strange thing: the virtuous gesture which seizes upon "docile" photographs (those invested by a simple *studium*) is an idle gesture (to leaf through, to glance quickly and desultorily, to linger, then to hurry on); on the contrary, the reading of the *punctum* (of the pricked photograph, so to speak) is at once brief and active. A trick of vocabulary: we say "to develop a photograph"; but what the chemical action develops is undevelopable, an essence (of a wound), what cannot be transformed but only repeated under the instances of insistence (of the insistent gaze). This brings the Photograph (certain photographs) close to the Haiku. For the notation of a haiku, too, is undevelopable: everything is given, without provoking the desire for or even the possibility of a rhetorical expansion. In both cases we might (we must) speak of an *intense immobility:* linked to a detail (to a detonator), an explosion makes a little star on the pane of the text or of the photograph: neither the Haiku nor the Photograph makes us "dream."

In Ombredane's experiment, the blacks see on his screen only the chicken crossing one corner of the village square. I too, in the photograph of two retarded children at an institution in New Jersey (taken in 1924 by Lewis H. Hine), hardly see the monstrous heads and pathetic profiles (which belong to the *studium*); what I see, like Ombredane's blacks, is the off-center detail, the little boy's huge Danton collar, the girl's finger bandage; I am a primitive, a child—or a maniac; I dismiss all knowledge, all culture, I refuse to inherit anything from another eye than my own.

"I recognize, with my whole body,
the straggling villages I passed through
on my long-ago travels
in Hungary and Rumania . . . "

A. Kertész: The Violinist's Tune. Abony, Hungary, 1921

© COURTESY GEORGE EASTMAN HOUSE

"I dismiss all knowledge
all culture . . . I see only
the boy's huge Danton collar,
the girl's finger bandage . . ."

Lewis H. Hine: Idiot Children in an Institution. New Jersey, 1924

22

The *studium* is ultimately always coded, the *punctum* is not (I trust I am not using these words abusively). Nadar, in his time (1882), photographed Savorgnan de Brazza between two young blacks dressed as French sailors; one of the two boys, oddly, has rested his hand on Brazza's thigh; this incongruous gesture is bound to arrest my gaze, to constitute a *punctum*. And yet it is not one, for I immediately code the posture, whether I want to or not, as "aberrant" (for me, the *punctum* is the other boy's crossed arms). What I can name cannot really prick me. The incapacity to name is a good symptom of disturbance. Mapplethorpe has photographed Robert Wilson and Philip Glass. Wilson *holds* me, though I cannot say why, *i.e.*, say *where:* is it the eyes, the skin, the position of the hands, the track shoes? The effect is certain but unlocatable, it does not find its sign, its name; it is sharp and yet lands in a vague zone of myself; it is acute yet muffled, it cries out in silence. Odd contradiction: a floating flash.

Nothing surprising, then, if sometimes, despite its clarity, the *punctum* should be revealed only after the fact, when the photograph is no longer in front of me and I think back on it. I may know better a photograph I remember than a photograph I am looking at, as if direct vision oriented its language wrongly, engaging it in an effort of description which will always miss its point of effect, the *punctum*. Reading Van der Zee's photograph, I thought I had discerned what moved me: the strapped pumps of the black woman in her Sunday best; but this photograph has *worked* within me, and later on I realized that the real *punctum* was the necklace she was wearing; for (no doubt) it was this same necklace (a slender ribbon of braided gold) which I had seen worn by someone in my own family, and which, once she died, remained shut up in a family box of old jewelry (this sister of my father never married, lived with her mother as an old maid, and I had always been saddened whenever I thought of her dreary life). I had just realized that however immediate and incisive it was, the *punctum* could accommodate a certain latency (but never any scrutiny).

Ultimately—or at the limit—in order to see a photograph well, it is best to look away or close your eyes. "The necessary condition for an image is sight," Janouch told Kafka; and Kafka smiled and replied: "We photograph things in order to drive them out of our minds. My stories are a way of shutting my eyes." The photograph must be silent (there are blustering photographs, and I don't like them): this is not a question of discretion, but of music. Absolute subjectivity is achieved only in a state, an effort, of silence (shutting your eyes is to make the image speak in silence). The photograph touches me if I withdraw it from its usual blah-blah: "Technique," "Reality," "Reportage," "Art," etc.: to say nothing, to shut my eyes, to allow the detail to rise of its own accord into affective consciousness.

"The punctum, *for me,*
is the second boy's
crossed arms . . ."

Nadar: Savorgnan de Brazza. 1882.

"Bob Wilson holds *me,*
but I cannot say why . . ."
R. Mapplethorpe: Phil Glass and Bob Wilson

23

Last thing about the *punctum:* whether or not it is triggered, it is an addition: it is what I add to the photograph and *what is nonetheless already there.* To Lewis Hine's retarded children, I add nothing with regard to the degenerescence of the profile: the code expresses this before I do, takes my place, does not allow me to speak; what I add—and what, of course, is already in the image—is the collar, the bandage. Do I add to the images in movies? I don't think so; I don't have time: in front of the screen, I am not free to shut my eyes; otherwise, opening them again, I would not discover the same image; I am constrained to a continuous voracity; a host of other qualities, but not *pensiveness;* whence the interest, for me, of the photogram.

Yet the cinema has a power which at first glance the Photograph does not have: the screen (as Bazin has remarked) is not a frame but a hideout; the man or woman who emerges from it continues living: a "blind field" constantly doubles our partial vision. Now, confronting millions of photographs, including those which have a good *studium,* I sense no blind field: everything which happens within the frame dies absolutely once this frame is passed beyond. When we define the Photograph as a motionless image, this does not mean only that the figures it represents do not move; it means that they do not *emerge,* do not *leave:* they are anesthetized and fastened down, like butterflies. Yet once there is a *punctum,* a blind field is created (is divined): on account of her necklace, the black woman in her Sunday best has had, for me, a whole life external to her portrait; Robert Wilson, endowed with an unlocatable *punctum,* is someone I want to meet. Here is Queen Victoria photographed in 1863 by George W. Wilson; she is on horseback, her skirt suitably draping the entire animal (this is the historical interest, the *studium*); but beside her, attracting my eyes, a kilted groom holds the horse's bridle: this is the *punctum;* for even if I do not know just what the social status of this Scotsman may be (servant? equerry?), I can see his function clearly: to supervise the horse's behavior: what if the horse suddenly began to rear? What would happen to the queen's skirt, *i.e.,* to *her majesty?* The *punctum* fantastically "brings out" the Victorian nature (what else can one call it?) of the photograph, it endows this photograph with a blind field.

The presence (the dynamics) of this blind field is, I believe, what distinguishes the erotic photograph from the pornographic photograph. Pornography ordinarily represents the sexual organs, making them into a motionless object (a fetish), flattered like an idol that does not leave its niche; for me, there is no *punctum* in the pornographic image; at most it amuses me (and even then, boredom follows quickly). The erotic photograph, on the contrary (and this is its very condition), does not make the sexual organs into a central object; it may very well not show them at all; it takes the spectator outside its frame, and it is there that I animate this photograph and that it animates me. The *punctum,* then, is a kind of subtle *beyond*—as if the image launched desire beyond what it permits us to see: not only toward "the rest" of the naked-

"Queen Victoria, entirely unesthetic . . ."
–*Virginia Woolf*

G. W. Wilson: Queen Victoria. 1863

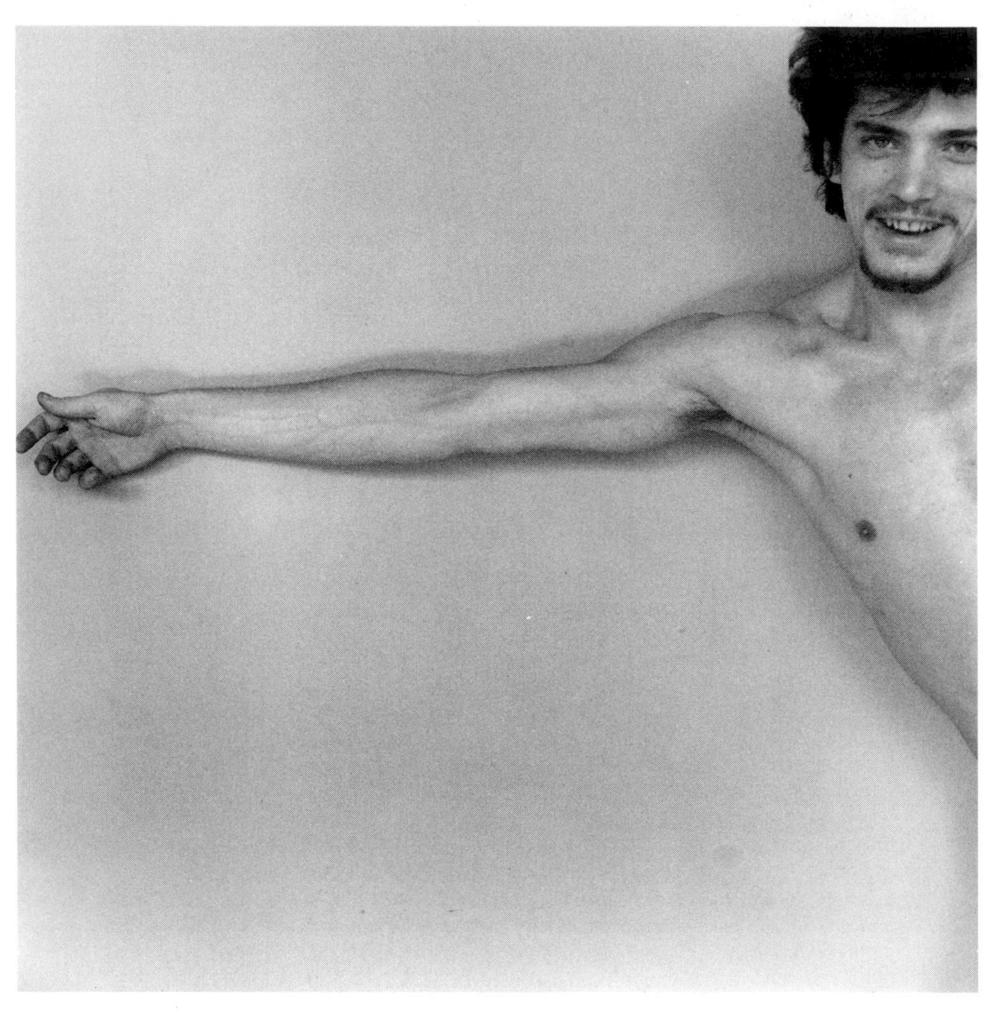

". . . the hand at
the right degree of openness,
the right density of abandonment . . ."

R. Mapplethorpe: Young Man with Arm Extended

ness, not only toward the fantasy of a *praxis*, but toward the absolute excellence of a being, body and soul together. This boy with his arm outstretched, his radiant smile, though his beauty is in no way classical or academic, and though he is half out of the photograph, shifted to the extreme left of the frame, incarnates a kind of blissful eroticism; the photograph leads me to distinguish the "heavy" desire of pornography from the "light" (good) desire of eroticism; after all, perhaps this is a question of "luck": the photographer has caught the boy's hand (the boy is Mapplethorpe himself, I believe) at just the right degree of openness, the right density of abandonment: a few millimeters more or less and the divined body would no longer have been offered with benevolence (the pornographic body shows itself, it does not give itself, there is no generosity in it): the photographer has found the *right moment*, the *kairos* of desire.

• • • • • • • • • • • •

QUESTIONS FOR A SECOND READING

1. It is interesting to follow Barthes as he sorts out distinctions between the photographs he admires and those that don't do a thing for him. His prose is a prose that presents the "I" as a key figure. This is the "I" of "I feel" or "I like/I don't like"; it is not simply the "I" of "I think." Here is a representative passage:

    > I see photographs everywhere, like everyone else, nowadays; they come from the world to me, without my asking; they are only "images," their mode of appearance is heterogeneous. Yet, among those which had been selected, evaluated, approved, collected in albums or magazines and which had thereby passed through the filter of culture, I realized that some provoked tiny jubilations, as if they referred to a stilled center, an erotic or lacerating value buried in myself (however harmless the subject may have appeared); and that others, on the contrary, were so indifferent to me that by dint of seeing them multiply, like some weed, I felt a kind of aversion toward them, even of irritation: there are moments when I detest Photographs: what have I to do with Atget's old tree trunks, with Pierre Boucher's nudes, with Germaine Krull's double exposures (to cite only the old names)? (p. 140)

    The writing here runs counter to the usual classroom accounts of writing, or "academic" writing—that a writer can't use the first person, that a writer's instincts or feelings are irrelevant, that a writer's thoughts are not easily welcomed in his or her prose.

    As you reread, pay close attention to how Barthes does his work—how he stages this performance of the "I" thinking. Could you do this? How would your writing change if you were to follow this pattern?

2. Barthes relies, often, on a specialized vocabulary. (The unusual, difficult, or Latin terms are in the original; the difficulty is not simply a product of bad translation.) As you reread, identify that set of unusual terms and phrases

you think are crucial to understanding Barthes's thoughts on photography. How does he use the terms? Can you work out definitions in context? What do the dictionaries say? And why do you think these terms are important? What do they allow him to do that "ordinary" terms would not? In a group, you might divide up these terms and prepare a glossary for others to use.

3. While *Camera Lucida* is not particularly long or dense, it is complex and its complexity resides, in part, in the way Barthes develops his argument. As you reread, trace out (perhaps in outline form) the twists and turns, the stages of his argument. Where does he begin? What is the next key point? and the next? and so on. What role do the photographs play?

4. *Studium* and *punctum* are key terms Barthes uses to refer to his varied responses to photographs. The definitions develop in range and depth as the essay proceeds. Or, to put it another way, Barthes defines them differently at various stages in the essay. As you reread, chart out the stages of definition. This will give you a sense of the range they cover; it will also provide a demonstration of how a writer works on, worries about, qualifies, and extends his terms.

5. The essay draws on the work of a wide range of photographers, from Stieglitz to Mapplethorpe. You could divide these up among a group in order to do some research and report back on these photographers, their work, and the sorts of things that have been said about their photographs (ideally the same photographs Barthes includes in his essay). What is there that is peculiar, distinctive, or unconventional in Barthes's writings on photography?

ASSIGNMENTS FOR WRITING

1. The selection we've provided from *Camera Lucida* is made up of numbered sections. These define a unit of writing that is larger than the paragraph and smaller than the essay. (What name might you give to this unit?) Choose one of these sections that seems characteristic and fun and write one of your own in imitation. Try to capture its form, method, structure of thought, energy, style. You can provide your own photographs or you can work with his. When you are done, take time to think about what this form of writing allows you to do. If possible, take time to share these thoughts with others in your class.

   With this as preparation, prepare a Barthes-like essay that is made up of three or four of these numbered sections.

2. Write an essay in which you present Barthes's argument to someone who has not read the text. This is a complicated task, since the argument has shifts and turns. You will need to give a sense of the progress of his essay, where he begins and ends, and a sense of his examples and of what he does with them.

   We would invite you to think of this summary as strategic. You are trying to get down on paper what Barthes is saying because you want to respond to it. (How to respond? You can imagine yourself in conversation with Barthes. You can respond as a reader, describing the experience of working with the text. You can extend his argument, or challenge it. You can turn from his concerns to yours—you, too, see photographs everywhere.) Just as Barthes is present in his essay, you should be present in yours. And give yourself plenty of time and space, certainly more than a single paragraph.

3. Working with "public photographs" (not family photos, in other words), present them through your deployment of Barthes's terms, *studium* and *punctum.* You may choose photographs from a book or a collection; you may work with photographs in this textbook (and you may draw some, but not all, from Barthes's essay).

   Write an essay in which you discuss these photographs in order to think about (and to think with) Barthes's example in *Camera Lucida.* In your essay you will need to set this up as a project. Where do these terms come from—*studium* and *punctum?* What interests you in trying them out? You should take plenty of time to work through your discussions of the photographs. And, in the end, you should talk about the exercise and what you can conclude from it. For example, as you move from Barthes's world to your own, how useful is this distinction (*studium* and *punctum*)? As you look at a newspaper or a magazine or still images on a television or a computer screen, or at "art" photographs in a book or a museum, how useful is the argument? As you think about new technologies (digital cameras, computer editing), does the argument need to be revised?

4. Choose one of the photographs in the selection from *Camera Lucida.* Write an essay in which you present, first, Barthes's discussion of it (with your introduction and commentary). Provide your own discussion, one that best represents your experience of and/or commitment to the photograph. Your discussion should be at least as long as his. Then, when you are done, write about the differences. You are different people, to be sure, but think about the differences as representative. You represent a particular generation, a particular set of interests, a particular set of experiences with photographs, a particular stage in a career, and Barthes represents something quite different.

MAKING CONNECTIONS

1. *Camera Lucida* is one of the "case studies" in W. J. T. Mitchell's "The Photographic Essay: Four Case Studies" (p. 332). For this assignment, we'd like you to write an essay on Barthes that represents your response to Mitchell.

   Perhaps the best way to do this is, first, to establish a position of your own. Take time to reread *Camera Lucida* to think about the staging, the placement, and the use of photographs. Choose examples you can use to think about the various relationships of image to word and word to image, and begin to explore, in draft form, your thoughts.

   Once you have written out, in draft, your understanding of the relationship of the photographs to text, read Mitchell's account. Then write an essay in which you bring Mitchell's argument to bear on the work you have done. What does Mitchell say? What does he say that you find useful? Where and how do you differ in approach or in conclusion? (Or how, in your essay, might you define a relationship with an established scholar?)

   In your essay, you should make it clear that Mitchell is serving *your* project. Your work is at the center. He is someone you are turning to after having developed (or in order to continue to develop) a position of your own. Mitchell should not render you silent or make you disappear.

Note: This assignment puts particular pressure on the first-person perspective of the essayist—you. It has been useful to our students to call attention to this from the very beginning. You might think of the "I" in your essay as a character, someone with a history, interests, a point of view, a style, someone of a particular age with a particular background in relation to photography and photographs.

2. Barthes begins with the questions, "What do I like? / What don't I like?" Dorothea Lange and Paul S. Taylor, in "Old South" and "Plantation Under the Machine," began their project with extensive fieldwork in the American South. Choose three of the photographs from either "Old South" (p. 291) and "Plantation Under the Machine" (p. 301) and write about them in the style and manner of Barthes, putting into play his terms *studium* and *punctum.*

   Lange and Taylor struggle to keep the "personal" out of their work, and they seem to be particularly suspicious of language—at least a language that is allowed to run free. They would never, for example, speak for the "unspoken thoughts" of their subjects. Barthes struggles to assert his desires against what he is supposed to think and feel. He is quick to want to turn the photographs to his own interests and his own ends.

   Write an essay in which you present the two approaches of Lange and Taylor and Roland Barthes. Use your exercises as central exhibits in your essay. How do Lange and Taylor and Barthes define one's responsibility to photographs? How do they imagine the proper use of photographs in service of politics, society, the general good? Would you say that Barthes' project serves or violates the work of Lange and Taylor?

3. John Berger, in his essay "Appearances" (p. 175), and Roland Barthes, in *Camera Lucida,* offer extended lessons in how to see, read, and understand photographic images. Write an essay that both presents these lessons and takes a position on their value or usefulness. You should be sure to offer at least one extended example from each essay (with the appropriate photograph). And it would be interesting to take a third photograph (of your choosing) and to provide a Berger-like and then a Barthes-like reading of it. In your conclusion, you might think about the value and usefulness of these lessons to those of your time and generation.

JOHN BERGER

JOHN BERGER (b. 1926), like few other art critics, elicits strong and contradictory reactions to his writing. He has been called (sometimes in the same review) "preposterous" as well as "stimulating," "pompous" yet "exciting." He has been accused of falling prey to "ideological excesses" and of being a victim of his own "lack of objectivity," but he has been praised for his "scrupulous" and "cogent" observations on art and culture. He is one of Europe's most influential Marxist critics, yet his work has been heralded and damned by leftists and conservatives alike. Although Berger's work speaks powerfully, its tone is quiet, thoughtful, measured. According to the poet and critic Peter Schjeldahl, "The most mysterious element in Mr. Berger's criticism has always been the personality of the critic himself, a man of strenuous conviction so loath to bully that even his most provocative arguments sit feather-light on the mind."

In 1972, Berger published his most widely read work, Ways of Seeing, *a book which began as a series on BBC television. In fact, the show was a forerunner of those encyclopedic television series later popular on public television stations in the United States:* Civilization, The Ascent of Man, Cosmos, The Civil War. *Berger's show was less glittery and ambitious, but in its way it was more serious in its claims to be educational. As you watched the screen, you saw a series of images (photographs and paintings). These were sometimes presented with commentary, but sometimes in silence, so that you constantly saw one image in the context of another—for example, classic presentations of women in oil paintings interspersed with images of women from contemporary art, advertising, movies, and "men's magazines." The goal of the exercise, according to Berger, was to "start a process of questioning," to focus his viewer's attention not on a single painting in isolation but on "ways of seeing" in general, on the ways we have learned to look at and understand the images that surround us, and on the culture that teaches us to see things as we do.*

Ways of Seeing *used images alone to establish a narrative or an argument, and it mixed words and images in such a way that they were interdependent. The book was a major contribution to the development of the photographic essay. These methods were used again by Berger and by his collaborator, the Swiss photographer Jean Mohr, in three other books:* A Fortunate Man *(1967), the story of an English country doctor;* A Seventh Man *(1975), an account of the migrant worker in Europe; and* Another Way of Telling *(1982), the book from which the following selection is drawn.*

Another Way of Telling *is the most fully articulated account of the collaboration between Mohr and Berger. The book has a subject, "the lives of mountain peasants," but it also contains essays by Mohr and Berger on photographs, photography, and the uses of the photographic image. The book is divided into five sections. Each relies on photographs, some include written text. The first, "Beyond My Camera," is by Jean Mohr and considers the relationships among the photographer, his subjects, and those who view and use his work. The second, "Appearances," by John Berger, is included here. The third part, "If each time. . . ," with photographs by Mohr and narrated by Mohr and Berger, consists of a sequence of a hundred and fifty photographs without words or captions. It is offered as a "reflection" on a peasant woman's life. It is not, they say, documentary or reportage. The fourth section, "Stories," by Berger, returns to the theoretical implications of the storytelling in "If each time. . . ." And the fifth, a poem and a photograph, is intended as a "reminder of the reality from which [they] began: the life work of peasants."*

Berger has written poems, novels, essays, and film scripts, including The Success and Failure of Picasso *(1965),* G. *(1971), and* About Looking *(1980). He lived and worked in England for years, but he currently lives in Quincy, a small peasant village in Haute-Savoie, France, where he wrote, over the course of several years, a trilogy of books on peasant life, titled* Into Their Labours. *The first book in the series,* Pig Earth *(1979), is a collection of essays, poems, and stories set in Haute-Savoie. The second,* Once in Europa *(1987), consists of five peasant tales that take love as their subject. The third and final book in the trilogy,* Lilac and Flag: An Old Wives' Tale of the City, *published in 1990, is a novel about the migration of peasants to the city. His most recent books are* About Looking *(1992);* Photocopies *(1996), a collection of short stories;* King: A Street Story *(1999), a novel;* I Send You This Cadmium Red: A Correspondence between John Berger and John Christie *(2000); and two collections of essays,* Selected Essays *(2000) and* The Shape of a Pocket *(2001).*

Appearances

This essay, although it appears under my name and is the culmination of many years' thinking about photography, nevertheless owes a great deal to the criticisms and encouragement of Gilles Aillaud, Anthony Barnett, Nella Bielski, Peter Fuller, Gérard Mordillat, Nicolas Philibert, Lloyd Spencer.

• • •

> Reason respects the differences and imagination the similitude of things.
>
> –SHELLEY

Nearly twenty years ago I had the project of taking a series of photographs which would accompany, and be interchangeable with, a sequence of love poems. Just as it was not clear whether the poems spoke with the voice of a woman or a man, so it should remain uncertain whether the image inspired the text or vice versa. My first interest in photography was passionate.

To learn how to use a camera, in order to be able to take these photographs, I went to see Jean Mohr. Alain Tanner gave me his address. Jean instructed me with great patience. And for two years I took hundreds of photographs in the hope of telling my love.

This is how my close interest in photography began. And I recall it now because, however theoretical and distanced some of my later remarks may appear to be, photography is still, first and foremost, for me a means of expression. The all-important question is: What kind of means?

Jean Mohr and I became friends and then collaborators. This is the fourth book we have made together. During this collaboration we have continually tried to examine its nature. How should a photographer and writer collaborate? What are the possible relations between images and text? How can we approach the reader together? These questions did not arise abstractly, they imposed themselves whilst we were working on books which we believed to be urgent. The implications of a certain relationship between doctor and patient, between cure and suffering. The state of the visual arts in the Soviet Union. The experience of migrant workers. And now, in this book, the way peasants look at themselves.

Faced with the problem of communicating experience, through a constant process of trial and error, we found ourselves having to doubt or reject many of the assumptions usually made about photography. We discovered that photographs did not work as we had been taught.

The Ambiguity of the Photograph

What makes photography a strange invention—with unforeseeable consequences—is that its primary raw materials are light and time.

Yet let us begin with something more tangible. A few days ago a friend of mine found this photograph and showed it to me.

I know nothing about it. The best way of dating it is probably by its photographic technique. Between 1900 and 1920? I do not know whether it was taken in Canada, the Alps, South Africa. All one can see is that it shows a smiling middle-aged man with his horse. Why was it taken? What meaning did it have for the photographer? Would it have had the same meaning for the man with the horse?

One can play a game of inventing meanings. The Last Mountie. (His smile becomes nostalgic). The Man Who Set Fire to Farms. (His smile becomes sinister.) Before the Trek of Two Thousand Miles. (His smile becomes a little apprehensive.) After the Trek of Two Thousand Miles. (His smile becomes modest.) . . .

The most definite information this photograph gives is about the type of bridle the horse is wearing, and this is certainly not the reason why it was taken. Looking at the photograph alone it is even hard to know to what use category it belonged. Was it a family-album picture, a newspaper picture, a traveller's snap?

Could it have been taken, not for the sake of the man, but of the horse? Was the man acting as a groom, just holding the horse? Was he a horse-dealer? Or was it a still photograph taken during the filming of one of the early Westerns?

The photograph offers irrefutable evidence that this man, this horse and this bridle existed. Yet it tells us nothing of the significance of their existence.

A photograph arrests the flow of time in which the event photographed once existed. All photographs are of the past, yet in them an instant of the past is arrested so that, unlike a lived past, it can never lead to the present. Every photograph presents us with two messages: a message concerning the event photographed and another concerning a shock of discontinuity.

Between the moment recorded and the present moment of looking at the photograph, there is an abyss. We are so used to photography that we no longer consciously register the second of these twin messages—except in special circumstances: when for example, the person photographed was familiar to us and is now far away or dead. In such circumstances the photograph is more traumatic than most memories or mementos because it seems to confirm, prophetically, the later discontinuity created by the absence or death. Imagine for a moment that you were once in love with the man with the horse and that he has now disappeared.

If, however, he is a total stranger, one thinks only of the first message, which here is so ambiguous that the event escapes one. What the photograph shows goes with any story one chooses to invent.

Nevertheless the mystery of this photograph does not quite end there. No invented story, no explanation offered will be quite as *present* as the banal appearances preserved in this photograph. These appearances may tell us very little, but they are unquestionable.

The first photographs were thought of as marvels because, far more directly than any other form of visual image, they presented the appearance of what was absent. They preserved the look of things and they allowed the look of things to be carried away. The marvel in this was not only technical.

Our response to appearances is a very deep one, and it includes elements which are instinctive and atavistic. For example, appearances alone—regardless of all conscious considerations—can sexually arouse. For example, the stimulus to action—however tentative it remains—can be provoked by the colour red. More widely, the look of the world is the widest possible confirmation of the *thereness* of the world, and thus the look of the world continually proposes and confirms our relation to that thereness, which nourishes our sense of Being.

Before you tried to read the photograph of the man with the horse, before you placed it or named it, the simple act of looking at it confirmed, however briefly, your sense of being in the world, with its men, hats, horses, bridles . . .

• • •

The ambiguity of a photograph does not reside within the instant of the event photographed: there the photographic evidence is less ambiguous than any eye-witness account. The photo-finish of a race is rightly decided by

what the camera has recorded. The ambiguity arises out of that discontinuity which gives rise to the second of the photograph's twin messages. (The abyss between the moment recorded and the moment of looking.)

A photograph preserves a moment of time and prevents it being effaced by the supersession of further moments. In this respect photographs might be compared to images stored in the memory. Yet there is a fundamental difference: whereas remembered images are the *residue* of continuous experience, a photograph isolates the appearances of a disconnected instant.

And in life, meaning is not instantaneous. Meaning is discovered in what connects, and cannot exist without development. Without a story, without an unfolding, there is no meaning. Facts, information, do not in themselves constitute meaning. Facts can be fed into a computer and become factors in a calculation. No meaning, however, comes out of computers, for when we give meaning to an event, that meaning is a response, not only to the known, but also to the unknown: meaning and mystery are inseparable, and neither can exist without the passing of time. Certainty may be instantaneous; doubt requires duration; meaning is born of the two. An instant photographed can

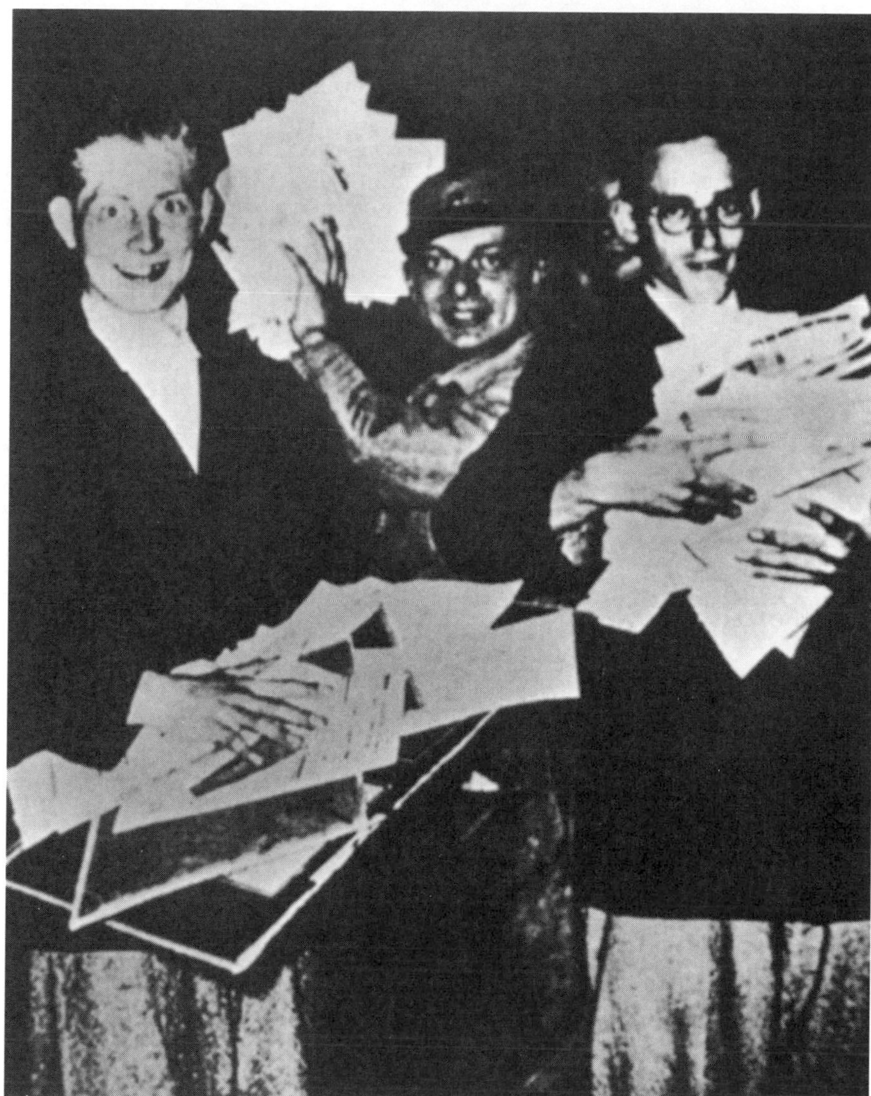

IMPERIAL WAR MUSEUM, NYP 68567

only acquire meaning insofar as the viewer can read into it a duration extending beyond itself. When we find a photograph meaningful, we are lending it a past and a future.

The professional photographer tries, when taking a photograph, to choose an instant which will persuade the public viewer to lend it an *appropriate* past and future. The photographer's intelligence or his empathy with the subject defines for him what is appropriate. Yet unlike the story-teller or painter or actor, the photographer only makes, in any one photograph, *a single constitutive choice:* the choice of the instant to be photographed. The photograph, compared with other means of communication, is therefore weak in intentionality.

A dramatic photograph may be as ambiguous as an undramatic one.

What is happening? It requires a caption for us to understand the significance of the event. "Nazis Burning Books." And the significance of the caption again depends upon a sense of history that we cannot necessarily take for granted.

All photographs are ambiguous. All photographs have been taken out of a continuity. If the event is a public event, this continuity is history; if it is personal, the continuity, which has been broken, is a life story. Even a pure landscape breaks a continuity: that of the light and the weather. Discontinuity always produces ambiguity. Yet often this ambiguity is not obvious, for as soon as photographs are used with words, they produce together an effect of certainty, even of dogmatic assertion.

In the relation between a photograph and words, the photograph begs for an interpretation, and the words usually supply it. The photograph, irrefutable as evidence but weak in meaning, is given a meaning by the words. And the words, which by themselves remain at the level of generalisation, are given specific authenticity by the irrefutability of the photograph. To-

gether the two then become very powerful; an open question appears to have been fully answered.

Yet it might be that the photographic ambiguity, if recognised and accepted as such, could offer to photography a unique means of expression. Could this ambiguity suggest another way of telling? This is a question I want to raise now and return to later.

• • •

Cameras are boxes for transporting appearances. The principle by which cameras work has not changed since their invention. Light, from the object photographed, passes through a hole and falls on to a photographic plate or film. The latter, because of its chemical preparation, preserves these traces of light. From these traces, through other slightly more complicated chemical processes, prints are made. Technically, by the standards of our century, it is a simple process. Just as the historically comparable invention of the printing press was, in its time, simple. What is still not so simple is to grasp the nature of the appearances which the camera transports.

Are the appearances which a camera transports a construction, a man-made cultural artifact, or are they, like a footprint in the sand, a trace *naturally* left by something that has passed? The answer is, both.

The photographer chooses the event he photographs. This choice can be thought of as a cultural construction. The space for this construction is, as it were, cleared by his rejection of what he did not chose to photograph. The construction is his reading of the event which is in front of his eyes. It is this reading, often intuitive and very fast, which decides his choice of the instant to be photographed.

Likewise, the photographed image of the event, when shown as a photograph, is also part of a cultural construction. It belongs to a specific social situation, the life of the photographer, an argument, an experiment, a way of explaining the world, a book, a newspaper, an exhibition.

Yet at the same time, the material relation between the image and what it represents (between the marks on the printing paper and the tree these marks represent) is an immediate and unconstructed one. And is indeed like a *trace.*

The photographer chooses the tree, the view of it he wants, the kind of film, the focus, the filter, the time-exposure, the strength of the developing solution, the sort of paper to print on, the darkness or lightness of the print, the framing of the print—all this and more. But where he does not intervene—and cannot intervene without changing the fundamental character of photography—is between the light, emanating from that tree as it passes through the lens, and the imprint it makes on the film.

It may clarify what we mean by a *trace* if we ask how a drawing differs from a photograph. A drawing is a translation. That is to say each mark on the paper is consciously related, not only to the real or imagined "model," but also to every mark and space already set out on the paper. Thus a drawn

or painted image is woven together by the energy (or the lassitude, when the drawing is weak) of countless judgements. Every time a figuration is evoked in a drawing, everything about it has been mediated by consciousness, either intuitively or systematically. In a drawing an apple is *made* round and spherical; in a photograph, the roundness and the light and shade of the apple are received as a given.

This difference between making and receiving also implies a very different relation to time. A drawing contains the time of its own making, and this means that it possesses its own time, independent of the living time of what it portrays. The photograph, by contrast, receives almost instantaneously—usually today at a speed which cannot be perceived by the human eye. The only time contained in a photograph is the isolated instant of what it shows.

There is another important difference within the times contained by the two kinds of images. The time which exists within a drawing is not uniform. The artist gives more time to what she or he considers important. A face is likely to contain more time than the sky above it. Time in a drawing accrues according to human value. In a photograph time is uniform: every part of the image has been subjected to a chemical process of uniform duration. In the process of revelation all parts were equal.

These differences between a drawing and a photograph relating to time lead us to the most fundamental distinction between the two means of communication. The countless judgements and decisions which constitute a drawing are systematic. That is to say that they are grounded in an existent language. The teaching of this language and its specific usages at any given time are historically variable. A master-painter's apprentice during the Renaissance learnt a different practice and grammar of drawing from a Chinese apprentice during the Sung period. But every drawing, in order to re-create appearances, has recourse to a language.

Photography, unlike drawing, does not possess a language. The photographic image is produced instantaneously by the reflection of light; its figuration is *not* impregnated by experience or consciousness.

Barthes, writing about photography, talked of "humanity encountering for the first time in its history *messages without a code.* Hence the photograph is not the last (improved) term of the great family of images; it corresponds to a decisive mutation of informational economics."[1] The mutation being that photographs supply information without having a language of their own.

Photographs do not translate from appearances. They quote from them.

• • •

It is because photography has no language of its own, because it quotes rather than translates, that it is said that the camera cannot lie. It cannot lie because it prints directly.

(The fact that there were and are faked photographs is, paradoxically, a proof of this. You can only make a photograph tell an explicit lie by elaborate tampering, collage, and re-photographing. You have in fact ceased to practise photography. Photography in itself has no language which can be *turned.*) And yet photographs can be, and are, massively used to deceive and misinform.

We are surrounded by photographic images which constitute a global system of misinformation: the system known as publicity, proliferating consumerist lies. The role of photography in this system is revealing. The lie is constructed before the camera. A "tableau" of objects and figures is assembled. This "tableau" uses a language of symbols (often inherited, as I have pointed out elsewhere,[2] from the iconography of oil painting), an implied narrative and, frequently, some kind of performance by models with a sexual content. This "tableau" is then photographed. It is photographed precisely because the camera can bestow authenticity upon any set of appearances, however false. The camera does not lie even when it is used to quote a lie. And so, this makes the lie *appear* more truthful.

The photographic quotation is, within its limits, incontrovertible. Yet the quotation, placed like a fact in an explicit or implicit argument, can misinform. Sometimes the misinforming is deliberate, as in the case of publicity; often it is the result of an unquestioned ideological assumption.

For example, all over the world during the nineteenth century, European travellers, soldiers, colonial administrators, adventurers, took photographs of "the natives," their customs, their architecture, their richness, their poverty, their women's breasts, their headdresses; and these images, besides provoking amazement, were presented and read as proof of the justice of the imperial division of the world. The division between those who organised and rationalised and surveyed, and those who *were* surveyed.

In itself the photograph cannot lie, but, by the same token, it cannot tell the truth; or rather, the truth it does tell, the truth it can by itself defend, is a limited one.

The idealistic early press photographers—in the twenties and thirties of this century—believed that their mission was to bring home the truth to the world.

> Sometimes I come away from what I am photographing sick at heart, with the faces of people in pain etched as sharply in my mind as on my negatives. But I go back because I feel it is my place to make such pictures. Utter truth is essential, and that is what stirs me when I look through the camera.
>
> –MARGARET BOURKE-WHITE

I admire the work of Margaret Bourke-White. And photographers, under certain political circumstances, have indeed helped to alert public opinion to the truth of what was happening elsewhere. For example: the degree of rural poverty in the United States in the 1930s; the treatment of Jews in the streets of Nazi Germany; the effects of U.S. napalm bombing in Vietnam. Yet to believe that what one sees, as one looks through a camera on to the experience of others, is the "utter truth" risks confusing very different levels of the truth. And this confusion is endemic to the present public use of photographs.

Photographs are used for scientific investigation: in medicine, physics, meteorology, astronomy, biology. Photographic information is also fed into systems of social and political control—dossiers, passports, military intelligence. Other photographs are used in the media as a means of public communication. The three contexts are different, and yet it has been generally assumed that the truthfulness of the photograph—or the way that this truth functions—is the same in all three.

In fact, when a photograph is used scientifically, its unquestionable evidence is an aid in coming to a conclusion: it supplies information *within the conceptual framework* of an investigation. It supplies a missing detail. When photographs are used in a control system, their evidence is more or less limited to establishing identity and presence. But as soon as a photograph is used as a means of communication, the nature of lived experience is involved, and then the truth becomes more complex.

An X-ray photograph of a wounded leg can tell the "utter truth" about whether the bones are fractured or not. But how does a photograph tell the "utter truth" about a man's experience of hunger or, for that matter, his experience of a feast?

At one level there are no photographs which can be denied. All photographs have the status of fact. What has to be examined is in what way photography can and cannot give meaning to facts.

• • •

Let us recall how and when photography was born, how, as it were, it was christened, and how it grew up.

The camera was invented in 1839. Auguste Comte was just finishing his *Cours de Philosophie Positive*. Positivism and the camera and sociology grew up together. What sustained them all as practices was the belief that observable quantifiable facts, recorded by scientists and experts, would one day offer man such a total knowledge about nature and society that he would be able to order them both. Precision would replace metaphysics, planning would resolve social conflicts, truth would replace subjectivity, and all that was dark and hidden in the soul would be illuminated by empirical knowledge. Comte wrote that theoretically nothing need remain unknown to man except, perhaps, the origin of the stars! Since then cameras have photographed even the formation of stars! And photographers now supply us with more facts every month than the eighteenth-century Encyclopaedists dreamt of in their whole project.

Yet the positivist utopia was not achieved. And the world today is less controllable by experts, who have mastered what they believe to be its mechanisms, than it was in the nineteenth century.

What *was* achieved was unprecedented scientific and technical progress and, eventually, the subordination of all other values to those of a world market which treats everything, including people and their labour and their lives and their deaths, as a commodity. The unachieved positivist utopia became, instead, the global system of late capitalism wherein all that exists becomes quantifiable—not simply because it *can be* reduced to a statistical fact, but also because it *has been* reduced to a commodity.

In such a system there is no space for experience. Each person's experience remains an individual problem. Personal psychology replaces philosophy as an explanation of the world.

Nor is there space for the social function of subjectivity. All subjectivity is treated as private, and the only (false) form of it which is socially allowed is that of the individual consumer's dream.

From this primary suppression of the social function of subjectivity, other suppressions follow: of meaningful democracy (replaced by opinion polls and market-research techniques), of social conscience (replaced by self-interest), of history (replaced by racist and other myths), of hope—the most subjective and social of all energies (replaced by the sacralisation of Progress as Comfort).

The way photography is used today both derives from and confirms the suppression of the social function of subjectivity. Photographs, it is said, tell the truth. From this simplification, which reduces the truth to the instantaneous, it follows that what a photograph tells about a door or a volcano belongs to the same order of truth as what it tells about a man weeping or a woman's body.

If no theoretical distinction has been made between the photograph as scientific evidence and the photograph as a means of communication, *this has been not so much an oversight as a proposal.*

The proposal was (and is) that when something is visible, it is a fact, and that facts contain the only truth.

Public photography has remained the child of the hopes of positivism. Orphaned—because these hopes are now dead—it has been adopted by the opportunism of corporate capitalism. It seems likely that the denial of the innate ambiguity of the photograph is closely connected with the denial of the social function of subjectivity.

A Popular Use of Photography

> "In our age there is no work of art that is looked at so closely as a photograph of oneself, one's closest relatives and friends, one's sweetheart," wrote Lichtwark back in 1907, thereby moving the inquiry out of the realm of aesthetic distinctions into that of social functions. Only now this vantage point can be carried further.
>
> –WALTER BENJAMIN,
> *A Small History of Photography* (1931)

A mother with her child is staring intently at a soldier. Perhaps they are speaking. We cannot hear their words. Perhaps they are saying nothing and

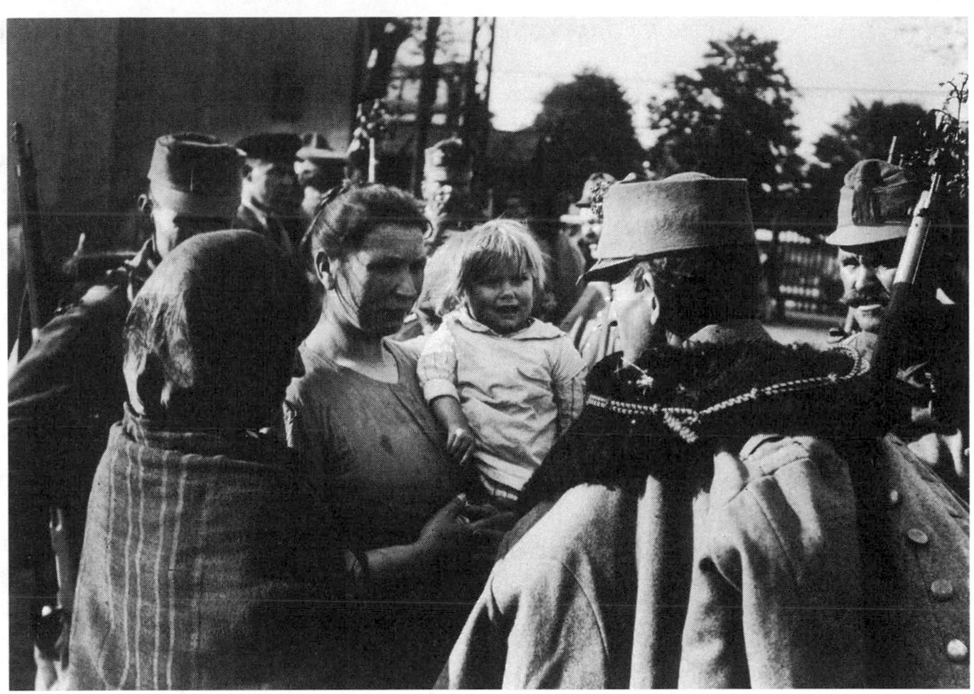

everything is being said by the way they are looking at each other. Certainly a drama is being enacted between them.

The caption reads: "A Red Hussar Leaving, June 1919, Budapest." The photograph is by André Kertész.

So, the woman has just walked out of their home and will shortly go back alone with the child. The drama of the moment is expressed in the difference between the clothes they are wearing. His for travelling, for sleeping out, for fighting; hers for staying at home.

The caption can also entail other thoughts. The Hapsburg monarchy had fallen the previous autumn. The winter had been one of the extreme shortages (especially of fuel in Budapest) and economic disintegration. Two months before, in March, the socialist Republic of Councils had been declared. The Western allies in Paris, fearful lest the Russian and now the Hungarian example of revolution should spread throughout Eastern Europe and the Balkans, were planning to dismantle the new republic. A blockade was already imposed. General Foch himself was planning the military invasion being carried out by Rumanian and Czech troops. On June 8th Clemenceau telegraphed an ultimatum to Béla Kun demanding a Hungarian military withdrawal which would have left the Rumanians occupying the eastern third of their country. For another six weeks the Hungarian Red Army fought on, but it was finally overwhelmed. By August, Budapest was occupied and very soon after, the first European fascist regime under Horthy was established.

If we are looking at an image from the past and we want to relate it to ourselves, we need to know something of the history of that past. And so the foregoing paragraph—and much more than that might be said—is relevant to the reading of Kertész's photograph. Which is presumably why he gave it the caption he did and not just the title "Parting." Yet the photograph—or rather, the way this photograph demands to be read—cannot be limited to the historical.

Everything in it is historical: the uniforms, the rifles, the corner by the Budapest railway station, the identity and biographies of all the people who are (or were) recognisable—even the size of the trees on the other side of the fence. And yet it also concerns a resistance to history: an opposition.

This opposition is not the consequence of the photographer having said Stop! It is not that the resultant static image is like a fixed post in a flowing river. We know that in a moment the soldier will turn his back and leave; we presume that he is the father of the child in the woman's arms. The significance of the instant photographed is already claiming minutes, weeks, years.

The opposition exists in the parting look between the man and the woman. This look is not directed towards the viewer. We witness it as the older soldier with the moustache and the woman with the shawl (perhaps a sister) do. The exclusivity of this look is further emphasised by the boy in the mother's arms; he is watching his father, and yet he is excluded from their look.

This look, which crosses before our eyes, is holding in place what *is,* not specifically what is there around them outside the station, but what *is* their life, what *are* their lives. The woman and the soldier are looking at each other so that the image of what *is* now shall remain for them. In this look their being *is* opposed to their history, even if we assume that this history is one they accept or have chosen.

• • •

How can one be opposed to history? Conservatives may oppose with force changes in history. But there is another kind of opposition. Who can read Marx and not feel his hatred towards the historical processes he discovered and his impatience for the end of history when, he believed, the realm of necessity would be transformed into the realm of freedom?

An opposition to history may be partly an opposition to what happens in it. But not only that. Every revolutionary protest is also a project against people being the objects of history. And as soon as people feel, as the result of their desperate protest, that they are no longer such objects, *history ceases to have the monopoly of time.*

> Imagine the blade of a giant guillotine as long as the diameter of the city. Imagine the blade descending and cutting a section through everything that is there—walls, railway lines, wagons, workshops, churches, crates of fruit, trees, sky, cobblestones. Such

> a blade has fallen a few yards in front of the face of everyone who is determined to fight. Each finds himself a few yards from the precipitous edge of an infinitely deep fissure which only he can see. The fissure, like a deep cut into the flesh, is unmistakably itself; there can be no doubting what has happened. But there is no pain at first.
>
> The pain is the thought of one's own death probably being very near. It occurs to the men and women building the barricades that what they are handling, and what they are thinking, are probably being handled and thought by them for the last time. As they build the defences, the pain increases.
>
> . . . At the barricades the pain is over. The transformation is complete. It is completed by a shout from the rooftops that the soldiers are advancing. Suddenly there is nothing to regret. The barricades are between their defenders and the violence done to them throughout their lives. There is nothing to regret because it is the quintessence of their past which is now advancing against them. On their side of the barricades it is already the future.[3]

Revolutionary actions are rare. Feelings of opposition to history, however, are constant, even if unarticulated. They often find their expression in what is called private life. A home has become not only a physical shelter but also a teleological shelter, however frail, against the remorselessness of history; a remorselessness which should be distinguished from the brutality, injustice, and misery the same history often contains.

People's opposition to history is a reaction (even a protest, but a protest so intimate that it has no direct social expression and the indirect ones are often mystified and dangerous: both fascism and racism feed upon such protests) against a violence done to them. The violence consists in conflating time and history so that the two become indivisible, so that people can no longer read their experience of either of them separately.

This conflation began in Europe in the nineteenth century, and has become more complete and more extensive as the rate of historical change has increased and become global. All popular religious movements—such as the present mounting Islamic one against the materialism of the West—are a form of resistance to the violence of this conflation.

What does this violence consist in? The human imagination which grasps and unifies time (before imagination existed, each time scale—cosmic, geological, biological—was disparate) has always had the capacity of undoing time. This capacity is closely connected with the faculty of memory. Yet time is undone not only by being remembered but also by the living of certain moments which defy the passing of time, not so much by becoming unforgettable but because, within the experience of such moments there is an imperviousness to time. They are experiences which provoke the words *for ever, toujours, siempre, immer.* Moments of achievement, trance, dream, passion, crucial ethical decision, prowess, near-death, sacrifice, mourning, music, the visitation of *duende.* To name some of them.

Such moments have continually occurred in human experience. Although not frequently in any one lifetime, they are common. They are the material of *all* lyrical expression (from pop music to Heine and Sappho). Nobody has lived without experiencing such moments. Where people differ is in the confidence with which they credit importance to them. I say confidence since I believe that intimately, if not publicly, no one fails to allow them some importance. They are summit moments and they are intrinsic to the relation imagination/time.

Before time and history were conflated, the rate of historical change was slow enough for an individual's awareness of time passing to remain quite distinct from her or his awareness of historical change. The sequences of an individual life were surrounded by the relatively changeless, and the relatively changeless (history) was in its turn surrounded by the timeless.

History used to pay its respects to mortality: the enduring honoured the value of what was brief. Graves were a mark of such respect. Moments which defied time in the individual life were like glimpses through a window; these windows, let into the life, looked *across* history, which changed slowly, towards the timeless which would never change.

When in the eighteenth century the rate of historical change began to accelerate, causing the principle of historical progress to be born, the timeless or unchanging was claimed by and gradually incorporated into historical time. Astronomy arranged the stars historically. Renan historicised Christianity. Darwin made every origin historical. Meanwhile, actively, through imperialism and proletarianisation, other cultures and ways of life and work, which embodied different traditions concerning time, were being destroyed. The factory which works all night is a sign of the victory of a ceaseless, uniform, and remorseless time. The factory continues even during the time of dreams.

The principle of historical progress insisted that the elimination of all other views of history save its own was part of that progress. Superstition, embedded conservatism, so-called eternal laws, fatalism, social passivity, the fear of eternity so skillfully used by churches to intimidate, repetition and ignorance: all these had to be swept away and replaced by the proposal that man could make his own history. And indeed this did—and does—represent progress, in that social justice cannot be fully achieved without such an awareness of the historical possibility, and this awareness depends upon historical explanations being given.

Nevertheless a deep violence was done to subjective experience. And to argue that this is unimportant in comparison with the objective historical possibilities created is to miss the point because, precisely, the modern anguished form of the distinction subjective/objective begins and develops with this violence.

Today what surrounds the individual life can change more quickly than the brief sequences of that life itself. The timeless has been abolished, and history itself has become ephemerality. History no longer pays its respects to the dead: the dead are simply what it has passed through. (A study of the comparative number of public monuments erected during the last hundred years in the West would show a startling decline during the last twenty-five.) There is no longer any generally acknowledged value longer than that of a life, and most are shorter. The worldwide phenomenon of inflation is symptomatic in this respect: an unprecedented modern form of economic transience.

Consequently the common experience of those moments which defy time is now denied by everything which surrounds them. Such moments have ceased to be like windows looking across history towards the timeless. Experiences which prompt the term *for ever* have now to be assumed alone and privately. Their role has been changed: instead of transcending, they isolate. The period in which photography has developed corresponds to the period in which this uniquely modern anguish has become commonplace.

Yet fortunately people are never only the passive objects of history. And apart from popular heroism, there is also popular ingenuity. In this case such ingenuity uses whatever little there is at hand, to preserve experience, to recreate an area of "timelessness," to insist upon the permanent. And so, hundreds of millions of photographs, fragile images, often carried next to the heart or placed by the side of the bed, are used to refer to that which historical time has no right to destroy.

The private photograph is treated and valued today as if it were the materialisation of that glimpse through the window which looked across history towards that which was outside time.

• • •

The photograph of the woman and the red hussar represents an idea. The idea was not Kertész's. It was being lived in front of his eyes and he was receptive to it.

What did he see?

Summer sunlight.

The contrast between her dress and the heavy greatcoats of the soldiers who will have to sleep out.

The men waiting with a certain heaviness.

Her concentration—she looks at him as if already into the distance which will claim him.

Her scowl, which will not give way to weeping.

His modesty—one reads it by his ear and the way he holds his head—because at this moment she is stronger than he.

Her acceptance, in the stance of her body.

The boy, surprised by the father's uniform, aware of the unusual occasion.

Her hair arranged before coming out, her worn dress.

The limits of their wardrobe.

It is only possible to itemise the things seen, for if they touch the heart, they do so essentially through the eye. For example, the appearance of the woman's hands clasped over her stomach tells how she might peel potatoes, how one of her hands might lie when asleep, how she would put up her hair.

PÊCHES SUR UNE ASSIETTE, CÉZANNE

The woman and the soldier are recognising one another. How close a parting is to a meeting! And through that act of recognition, such as perhaps they have never experienced before, each hopes to take away an image of the other which will withstand anything that may happen. An image that nothing can efface. This is the idea being lived before Kertész's camera. And this is what makes this photograph paradigmatic. It shows a moment which is explicitly about what is implicit in all photographs that are not simply enjoyed but loved.

All photographs are possible contributions to history, and any photograph, under certain circumstances, can be used in order to break the monopoly which history today has over time.

The Enigma of Appearances

To read what has never been written.
–HOFMANNSTHAL

We have looked at two different uses of photography. An ideological use, which treats the positivist evidence of a photograph as if it represented the ultimate and only truth. And in contrast, a popular but private use which cherishes a photograph to substantiate a subjective feeling.

I have not considered photography as an art. Paul Strand, who was a great photographer, thought of himself as an artist. In recent years art museums have begun to collect and show photographs. Man Ray said: "I photograph what I do not wish to paint, and I paint what I cannot photograph." Other equally serious photographers, like Bruce Davidson, claim it as a virtue that their pictures do not "pose as art."

The arguments, put forward from the nineteenth century onwards, about photography sometimes being an art have confused rather than clarified the issue because they have always led to some kind of comparison with the art of painting. And an art of translation cannot usefully be compared to an art of quotation. Their resemblances, their influence one upon the other, are purely formal; functionally they have nothing in common.

Yet however true this may be, a crucial question remains: why can photographs of unknown subjects move us? If photographs do not function like paintings, how do they function? I have argued that photographs quote from appearances. This may suggest that appearances themselves constitute a language.

What sense does it make to say this?

Let me first try to avoid a possible misunderstanding. In his last book Barthes wrote: "Each time when having gone a little way with a language, I have felt that its system consists in, and in that way is slipping towards, a kind of reductionism and disapproval, I have quietly left and looked elsewhere."[4]

Unlike their late master, some of Barthes' structuralist followers love closed systems. They would maintain that in my reading of Kertész's photograph, I relied upon a number of semiological systems, each one being a social/cultural construct: the sign-language of clothes, of facial expressions, of bodily gestures, of social manners, of photographic framing, etc. Such semiological systems do indeed exist and are continually being used in the making and reading of images. Nevertheless the sum total of these systems cannot exhaust, does not begin to cover, all that can be read in appearances. Barthes himself was of this opinion. The problem of appearances constituting something like a language cannot be resolved simply by reference to these semiological systems.

So we are left with the question: what sense does it make to say that appearances may constitute a language?

Appearances cohere. At the first degree they cohere because of common laws of structure and growth which establish visual affinities. A chip of rock can resemble a mountain; grass grows like hair; waves have the form of valleys; snow is crystalline; the growth of walnuts is constrained in their shells somewhat like the growth of brains in their skulls; all supporting legs and feet, whether static or mobile, visually refer to one another; etc., etc.

At the second degree, appearances cohere because as soon as a fairly

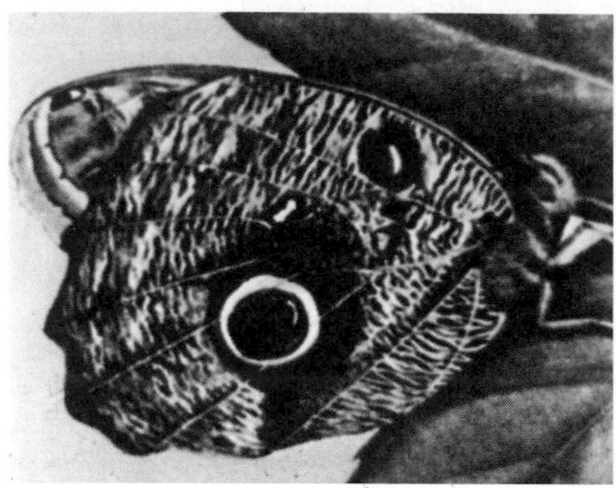

developed eye exists, visual imitation begins. All natural camouflage, much natural colouring, and a wide range of animal behaviour derive from the principle of appearances fusing or being suggestive of other appearances. On the underside of the wings of the Brassolinae, there are markings which imitate, with great accuracy, the eyes of an owl or another large bird. When attacked, these butterflies flick their wings and their attackers are intimidated by the flashing eyes.

Appearances both distinguish *and* join events.

During the second half of the nineteenth century, when the coherence of appearances had been largely forgotten, one man understood and insisted upon the significance of such a coherence. "Objects interpenetrate each other. They never cease to live. Imperceptibly they spread intimate reflections around them." Cézanne.

Appearances also cohere within the mind as perceptions. The sight of any single thing or event entrains the sight of other things and events. To recognise an appearance requires the memory of other appearances. And these memories, often projected as expectations, continue to qualify the seen long

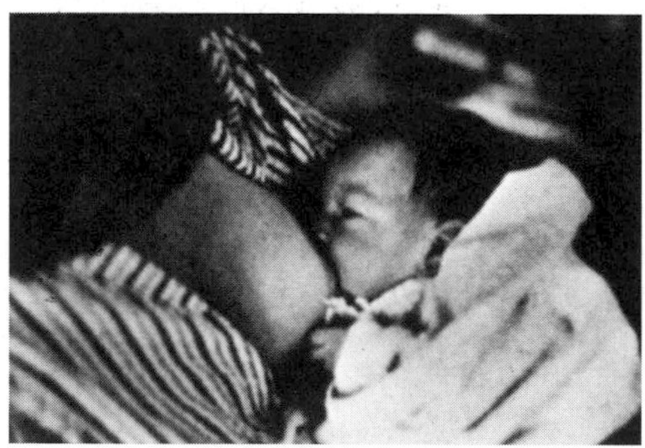

after the stage of primary recognition. Here for example, we recognise a baby at the breast, but neither our visual memory nor our visual expectations stop there. One image interpenetrates another.

As soon as we say that appearances *cohere* this *coherence* proposes a unity not unlike that of a language.

• • •

Seeing and organic life are both dependent upon light, and appearances are the face of this mutuality. And so appearances can be said to be doubly systematic. They belong to a natural affinitive system which exists as such because of certain universal structural and dynamic laws. This is why, as already noted, all legs resemble one another. Secondly, they belong to a perceptive system which organises the mind's experience of the visible.

The primary energy of the first system is natural reproduction, always thrusting towards the future; the primary energy of the second system is memory, continually retaining the past. In all perceived appearances there is the double traffic of both systems.

We now know that it is the right hemisphere of the human brain which "reads" and stores our visual experience. This is significant because the areas and centres where this takes place are structurally identical with those in the left hemisphere which process our experience of words. The apparatus with which we deal with appearances is identical with that with which we deal with verbal language. Furthermore, appearances in their unmediated state—that is to say, before they have been interpreted or perceived—lend themselves to reference systems (so that they may be stored at a certain level in the memory) which are comparable to those used for words. And this again prompts one to conclude that appearances possess some of the qualities of a code.

All cultures previous to our own treated appearances as signs addressed to the living. All was *legend:* all was there to be *read* by the eye. Appearances revealed resemblances, analogies, sympathies, antipathies, and each of these conveyed a message. The sum total of these messages explained the universe.

The Cartesian revolution overthrew the basis for any such explanation. It was no longer the relation between the look of things which mattered. What mattered was measurement and difference, rather than visual correspondences. The purely physical could no longer in itself reveal meaning, it could do so only if investigated by reason, which was the probe of the spiritual. Appearances ceased to be double-faced like the words of a dialogue. They became dense and opaque, requiring dissection.

Modern science became possible. The visible, however, deprived of any ontological function, was philosophically reduced to the area of aesthetics. Aesthetics was the study of sensuous perceptions as they affected an individual's feelings. Thus, the reading of appearances became fragmented; they were no longer treated as a signifying whole. Appearances were reduced to contingency, whose meaning was purely personal.

The development may help to explain the fitfulness and erratic history of nineteenth-century and twentieth-century visual art. For the first time ever, visual art was severed from the belief that it was in the very nature of appearances to be meaningful.

If, however, I persist in maintaining that appearances resemble a language, considerable difficulties arise. Where, for example, are its *universals?* A language of appearance implies an encoder; if appearances are there to be read, who wrote them?

It was a rationalist illusion to believe that in dispensing with religion, mysteries would be reduced. What has happened, on the contrary, is that mysteries multiply. Merleau-Ponty wrote:

> We must take literally what vision teaches us, namely that through it we come in contact with the sun and the stars, that we are everywhere all at once, and that even our power to imagine ourselves elsewhere . . . borrows from vision and employs means we owe to it. Vision alone makes us learn that beings that are different, "exterior," foreign to one another, are yet absolutely *together,* are "simultaneity"; this is a mystery psychologists handle the way a child handles explosives.[5]

There is no need to disinter ancient religious and magical beliefs which held that the visible is *nothing except a coded message.* These beliefs, being ahistorical, ignored the coincidence of the historical development of eye *and* brain. They also ignored the coincidence that both seeing and organic life are dependent upon light. Yet the enigma of appearances remains, whatever our historical explanations. Philosophically, we can evade the enigma. But we cannot *look* away from it.

• • •

One looks at one's surroundings (and one is always surrounded by the visible, even in dreams) and one reads what is there, according to circumstances, in different ways. Driving a car draws out one kind of reading; cutting down a tree another; waiting for a friend another. Each activity motivates its own reading.

At other times the reading, or the choices which make a reading, instead of being directed towards a goal, are the consequence of an event that has already occurred. Emotion or mood motivates the reading, and the appearances, thus read, become *expressive.* Such moments have often been described in literature, but they do not belong to literature, they belong to the visible.

Ghassan Kanafani, the Palestinian writer, describes a moment when everything he was looking at became expressive of the same pain and determination:

> Never shall I forget Nadia's leg, amputated from the top of the thigh. No! Nor shall I forget the grief which had moulded her face and merged into its traits for ever. I went out of the hospital in Gaza that day, my hand clutched in silent derision on the two

> pounds I had brought with me to give Nadia. The blazing sun filled the streets with the colour of blood. And Gaza was brand new, Mustafa! You and I never saw it like this. The stones piled up at the beginning of the Shajiya quarter where we lived had a meaning, and they seemed to have been put there for no other reason but to explain it. This Gaza in which we had lived and with whose good people we had spent seven years of defeat was something new. It seemed to me just a beginning. I don't know why I thought it was just a beginning. I imagined that the main street that I walked along on the way back home was only the beginning of a long, long road leading to Safad. Everything in this Gaza throbbed with sadness which was not confined to weeping. It was a challenge; more than that, it was something like reclamation of the amputated leg.[6]

In every act of looking there is an expectation of meaning. This expectation should be distinguished from a desire for an explanation. The one who looks may explain *afterwards;* but, prior to any explanation, there is the expectation of what appearances themselves may be about to reveal.

Revelations do not usually come easily. Appearances are so complex that only the search which is inherent in the act of looking can draw a reading out of their underlying coherence. If, for the sake of a temporary clarification, one artificially separates appearances from vision (and we have seen that in fact this is impossible), one might say that in appearances everything that can be read is already there, but undifferentiated. It is the search, with its choices, which differentiates. And *the seen,* the revealed, is the child of both appearances and the search.

Another way of making this relation clearer would be to say that appearances in themselves are oracular. Like oracles they go beyond, they insinuate further than the discrete phenomena they present, and yet their insinuations are rarely sufficient to make any more comprehensive reading indisputable. The precise meaning of an oracular statement depends upon the quest or need of the one who listens to it. Everyone listens to an oracle alone, even when in company.

The one who looks is essential to the meaning found, *and yet can be surpassed by it.* And this surpassing is what is hoped for. Revelation was a visual category before it was a religious one. The hope of revelation—and this is particularly obvious in every childhood—is the stimulus to the *will* to all looking which does not have a precise functional aim.

Revelation, when what we see does surpass us, is perhaps less rare than is generally assumed. By its nature, revelation does not easily lend itself to verbalisation. The words used remain aesthetic exclamations! Yet whatever its frequency, our expectation of revelation is, I would suggest, a human constant. The form of this expectation may historically change, but in itself, it is a constituent of *the relation between the human capacity to perceive and the coherence of appearances.*

The totality of this relationship is perhaps best indicated by saying that appearances constitute a half-language. Such a formulation, suggesting both a resemblance to and a difference from a full language, is both clumsy and imprecise, but at least it opens up a space for a number of ideas.

• • •

The positivist view of photography has remained dominant, despite its inadequacies, because no other view is possible unless one comes to terms with the revelational nature of appearances. All the best photographers worked by intuition. In terms of their work, this lack of theory did not matter much. What did matter is that the photographic possibility remained theoretically hidden.

What is this possibility?

The single constitutive choice of a photographer differs from the continuous and more random choices of someone who is looking. Every photographer knows that a photograph simplifies. The simplifications concern focus, tonality, depth, framing, supersession (what is photographed does not change), texture, colour, scale, the other senses (their influence on sight is excluded), the play of light. A photograph quotes from appearances but, in quoting, simplifies them. This simplification can increase their legibility. Everything depends upon the quality of the quotation chosen.

The photograph of the man with the horse quotes very briefly. Kertész's photograph outside Budapest railway station quotes at length.

The "length" of the quotation has nothing to do with exposure time. It is not a temporal length. Earlier we saw that a photographer, through the choice of the instant photographed, may try to persuade the viewer to lend that instant a past and a future. Looking at the man with the horse, we have no clear idea of what has just happened or what is about to happen. Looking at the Kertész, we can trace a story backwards for years and forwards for at least a few hours. This difference in the narrative range of the two images is important, yet although it may be closely associated with the "length" of the quotation, it does not in itself represent that length. It is necessary to repeat that the length of the quotation is in no sense a temporal length. It is not time that is prolonged but meaning.

The photograph cuts across time and discloses a cross-section of the event or events which were developing at that instant. We have seen that the instantaneous tends to make meaning ambiguous. But the cross-section, if it is wide enough, and can be studied at leisure, allows us to see the interconnectedness and related coexistence of events. Correspondences, which ultimately derive from the unity of appearances, then compensate for the lack of sequence.

This may become clearer if I express it in a diagrammatic, but necessarily highly schematic, way.

In life it is an event's development in time, its duration, which allows its meaning to be perceived and felt. If one states this actively, one can say that the event moves towards or through meaning. This movement can be represented by an arrow.

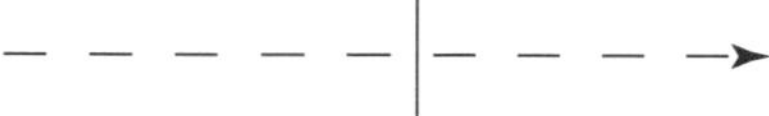

Normally a photograph arrests this movement and cuts across the appearances of the event photographed. Its meaning becomes ambiguous.

Only by the spectator's lending the frozen appearances a supposed past and future can the arrow's movement be hypothesised.

Above I represented the photographic cut by a vertical line. If, however, one thinks of this cut as a cross-section of the event, one can represent it frontally, as it were, instead of from the side, as a circle. One then has a diagram like this.

The diameter of the circle depends upon the amount of information to be found in the event's instantaneous appearances. The diameter (the amount of information received) may vary according to the spectator's personal relation to the photographed event. When the man with the horse is a stranger, the diameter remains small, the circle a very reduced one. When the same man is your son, the amount of information gleaned, and the diameter of the circle, increase dramatically.

The exceptional photograph which quotes at length increases the diameter of the circle even when the subject is totally unknown to the spectator.

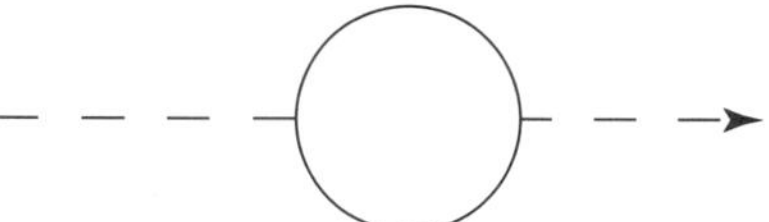

This increase is achieved by the coherence of the appearances—as photographed at that precise conjuncture—extending the event beyond itself. The appearances of the event photographed implicate other events. It is the energy of these simultaneous connections and cross-references which enlarge the circle beyond the dimension of instantaneous information.

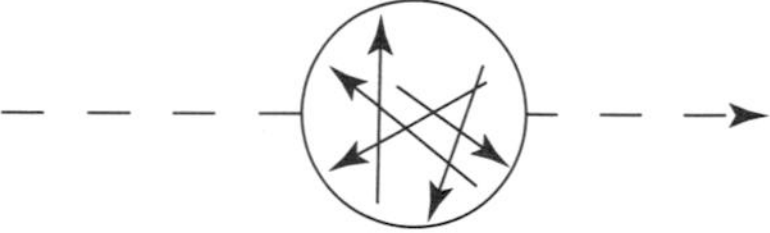

Thus, the discontinuity which is the result of the photographic cut is no longer destructive, for in the photograph of the long quotation another kind of meaning has become possible. The particular event photographed implicates other events by way of an idea born of the appearances of the first event. This idea cannot be merely tautologous. (An image of a person weeping and the idea of suffering would be tautologous.) The idea, confronting the event, extends and joins it to other events, thus widening the diameter.

How is it possible for appearances to "give birth" to ideas? Through their specific coherence at a given instant, they articulate a set of *correspondences* which provoke in the viewer a recognition of some past experience. This recognition may remain at the level of a tacit agreement with memory, or it may become conscious. When this happens, it is formulated as an idea.

A photograph which achieves expressiveness thus works dialectically: it preserves the particularity of the event recorded, and it chooses an instant when the correspondences of those particular appearances articulate a general idea.

In his *Philosophy of Right*,[7] Hegel defines individuality as follows:

> Every self-consciousness knows itself (1) as universal, as the potentiality of abstracting from everything determinate, and (2) as particular, with a determinate object, content and aim. Still, both these moments are only abstractions; what is concrete and true (and everything true is concrete) is the universality which has the particular as its opposite, but the particular which by its reflection into itself has been equalised with the universal. This unity is individuality.

In every expressive photograph, in every photograph which quotes at length, the particular, by way of a general idea, has been *equalised with the universal.*

• • •

A young man is asleep at the table in a public place, perhaps a café. The expression on his face, his character, the way the light and shade dissolve him and his clothes, his open shirt and the newspaper on the table, his health and his fatigue, the time of night: all these are visually present in this event and are particular.

Emanating from the event and confronting it is the general idea. In this photograph the idea concerns legibility. Or, more precisely, the distinction, the stroke, between legibility/illegibility.

Remove the newspapers on the table and on the wall behind the sleeping figure, and the photograph will no longer be expressive—until or unless what replaces them instigates another idea.

The event instigates the idea. And the idea, confronting the event, urges it to go beyond itself and to represent the generalisation (what Hegel calls the abstraction) carried within the idea. We see a particular young man asleep. And seeing him, we ponder on sleep in general. Yet this pondering does not take us away from the particular; on the contrary, it has been instigated by it and everything we continue to read is in the interest of the particular. We think or feel or remember *through the appearances* recorded in the photograph, and *with* the idea of legibility/illegibility which was instigated by them.

The print of the newspaper the young man was reading before he fell asleep, the print of the newspapers hanging on the wall, which we can almost read even from this distance—all written news, all written regulations and time-tables—have for him become temporarily unreadable. And at the

Boy Sleeping, May 25, 1912, Budapest (André Kertész)

same time, what is going on in his sleeping mind, the way he is recovering from his fatigue, are unreadable for us, or for anybody else who was waiting in the waiting-room. Two legibilities. Two illegibilities. The idea of the photograph oscillates (like his breathing) between the two poles.

None of this was constructed or planned by Kertész. His task was to be to that degree receptive to the coherence of appearances at that instant from that position in that place. The correspondences, which emerge from this coherence, are too extensive and too interwoven to enumerate very satisfactorily in words. (One cannot take photographs with a dictionary.) Paper corresponds with cloth, with folds, with facial features, with print, with darkness, with sleep, with light, with legibility. In the quality of Kertész's *receptivity* here, one sees how a photograph's lack of intentionality becomes its strength, its lucidity.

A young boy in 1917 playing in a field with a lamb. He is clearly aware of being photographed. He is both exuberant and innocent.

What makes this photograph memorable? Why does it provoke memories in us? We, who are not Hungarian shepherd boys born before the First World War. It is not memorable, as most picture-editors might assume, because the boy's expression and gestures are happy and charming. When isolated, photographed gestures and expressions become either mute or caricatural. Here, however, they are not isolated. They contain and are confronted by an idea.

FRIENDS, SEPTEMBER 3, 1917, ESZTERGAN (ANDRÉ KERTÉSZ)

What we see of the lamb—what makes the animal instantly recognisable as a lamb—is the texture of its fleece: that very texture which the boy's hand is stroking and which has attracted him to play with the animal in the way he is. Simultaneously with the texture of the fleece, we notice—or the photograph insists that we notice—the texture of the stubble on which the boy is rolling and which he must feel through his shirt.

The idea within the event, the idea to which Kertész was here receptive, concerns the sense of touch. And how in childhood, everywhere, this sense of touch is especially acute. The photograph is lucid because it speaks, through an idea, to our fingertips, or to our memory of what our fingertips felt.

Event and idea are naturally, actively connected. The photograph frames them, excluding everything else. A particular is being equalised with the universal.

In "A Red Hussar Leaving" the idea concerns stillness. Everything is read as movement: the trees against the sky, the folds of their clothes, the scene of departure, the breeze that ruffles the baby's hair, the shadow of the trees, the woman's hair on her cheek, the angle at which the rifles are being carried. And within this flux, the idea of stillness is instigated by the look passing between the woman and the man. And the lucidity of this idea makes us ponder on the stillness which is born in every departure.

A pair of lovers are embracing on a park bench (or in a garden?). They are an urban middle-class couple. They are probably unaware of being photographed. Or if they are aware, they have now almost forgotten the camera. They are discreet—as the conventions of their class would demand on any public occasion, with or without cameras—and yet, at the same time, desire (or the longing for desire) is making them (might make them) abandoned. Such is the not uncommon event. What makes it an uncommon photograph is that the special coherence of everything we see in it—the concealing screen of the hedge behind them, her gloves, the cuffs of their jackets with the same buttons on them, the movements of their hands, the touching of their noses, the darkness which marries their tailored clothes and the shade of the hedge, the light which illuminates leaves and skin—this coherence instigates the idea of the stroke dividing decorum/desire, clothed/unclothed, occasion/privacy. And such a division is a universal adult experience.

Kertész himself said: "The camera is my tool. Through it I give reason to everything around me." It may be possible to construct a theory upon the specific photographic process of "giving a reason."

Let us summarise. Photographs quote from appearances. The taking-out of the quotation produces a discontinuity, which is reflected in the ambiguity of a photograph's meaning. All photographed events are ambiguous, except to those whose personal relation to the event is such that their own lives supply the missing continuity. Usually, in public the ambiguity of photographs is hidden by the use of words which explain, less or more truthfully, the pictured events.

LOVERS, MAY 15, 1915, BUDAPEST (ANDRÉ KERTÉSZ)

The expressive photograph—whose expressiveness can contain its ambiguity of meaning and "give reason" to it—is a long quotation from appearances: the length here to be measured not by time but by a greater extension of meaning. Such an extension is achieved by turning the photograph's discontinuity to advantage. The narration is broken. (We do not know why the young man asleep is waiting for a train, supposing that that is what he is doing.) Yet the very same discontinuity, by preserving an instantaneous set of appearances, allows us to read across them and to find a synchronic coherence. A coherence which, instead of narrating, instigates ideas. Appearances have this coherent capacity because they constitute something approaching a language. I have referred to this as a half-language.

The half-language of appearances continually arouses an expectation of further meaning. We seek revelation with our eyes. In life this expectation is only rarely met. Photography confirms this expectation and confirms it in a way which can be shared (as we shared the reading of these photographs by Kertész). In the expressive photograph, appearances cease to be oracular and become elucidatory. It is this confirmation which moves us.

Apart from the event photographed, apart from the lucidity of the idea, we are moved by the photograph's fulfilment of an expectation which is intrinsic to the will to look. The camera completes the half-language of appearances and articulates an unmistakable meaning. When this happens we suddenly find ourselves at home amongst appearances, as we are at home in our mother tongue.

NOTES

[1] Roland Barthes, *Image-Music-Text* (London: Fontana, 1977), p. 45.

[2] John Berger, *Ways of Seeing* (London: British Broadcasting Corporation and Penguin Books Ltd, 1972), pp. 134, 141.

[3] John Berger, *G.* (London: Weidenfeld & Nicolson, 1972), pp. 71–72.

[4] Roland Barthes, *Reflections on Photography* (New York: Farrar, Strauss & Giroux, 1981).

[5] Maurice Merleau-Ponty, *The Primacy of Perception* (Evanston, Ill.: Northwestern University Press, 1964), p. 187.

[6] G. Kanafani, *Men in the Sun* (London: Heinemann Educational Books, 1978), p. 79.

[7] Georg W. F. Hegel, *Philosophy of Right* (London: Oxford University Press, 1975), p. 7.

• • • • • • • • • • • •

QUESTIONS FOR A SECOND READING

1. Early in his essay, as he comments on his collaborative work with the photographer Jean Mohr, Berger says they had to "doubt or reject many of the assumptions usually made about photography." He states, "We discovered that photographs did not work as we had been taught" (p. 175). As you reread this essay, mark those moments where Berger identifies assumptions about photographs that his project in "Appearances" leads him to doubt or reject. What are the assumptions? Why does he question them? What does he learn about photography by asking those questions?

2. Rereading "Appearances" brings us into close contact with our own assumptions about photography, its use and value. Before you read the essay, make a list of the assumptions that you hold about photography. Then, as you reread, use the writing to prompt your thinking. Are your assumptions the same as Berger's? Do his examples or arguments give you grounds for changing your own? Do you differ? For those of your time and generation, in what ways might Berger's essay be said to be convincing or compelling?

3. As Berger writes about photography, he introduces a special terminology: "residue of continuous experience," "expectations of meaning," "language," "half-language," "quotation," "semiotics," "positivism." As you reread, identify the set of unusual terms and phrases that you think are crucial to understanding Berger's thinking. How does he use them? Can you work out definitions in context? What do the dictionaries say? Why do you think these terms are important? What do they allow him to do that "ordinary" terms would not? In a group, you might divide up these terms and prepare a glossary for others to use.

4. While "Appearances" is not particularly long or dense, it is complex and its complexity resides, in part, in the way Berger develops his argument. There is a summary of his argument at the very end; you might start there. And then, as you reread, trace out (perhaps in outline form) the twists and turns, the stages of his argument. Where does he begin? What is the next key point? and the next? and so on? What role do the photographs play?
5. At one point, Berger says, "One can play the game of invented meanings." Choose an image from "Appearances" (or any other image in this textbook) and be prepared to play this game. And beyond the "game," there are the readings Berger presents with care and detail: "A mother with her child is staring intently at a soldier. Perhaps they are speaking" (p. 186); or, "A young man is asleep at the table in a public place, perhaps a café. The expression on his face, his character, the way the light and shade dissolve him and his clothes, his open shirt and the newspaper on the table, his health and his fatigue, the time of night: all these are visibly present in this event and are particular" (p. 200). Taking one of these quotes in full, and working with an image of your own choosing (perhaps one from this textbook), be prepared to provide a full Berger-like reading of a photograph.

ASSIGNMENTS FOR WRITING

1. Berger uses metaphors of reading and writing to explain how photographs express (or can be made to express) meaning. He writes that "photographs quote from appearances" (p. 193). He says that the longer the quotation, the greater the possibilities for the extension of meaning. Photographs that constitute a shorter quotation, then, don't offer as much for viewers to "read" or "give reason to." Photographs are treated as texts. The photograph of the long quotation, he says, makes ideas possible, ideas that are discontinuous with the content of the photograph. "A photograph which achieves expressiveness thus works dialectically: it preserves the particularity of the event recorded, and it chooses an instant when the correspondences of the particular appearances articulate a general idea" (p. 200).

   This is a difficult argument. His demonstration of the expressiveness of certain photographs is achieved in his own writing. As you prepare to summarize Barthes's argument, you might look at his written account of "Boy Sleeping" (p. 200), "Friends" (p. 202), "Lovers" (p. 203), or, with a significant difference, "A Red Hussar Leaving, June 1919, Budapest" (p. 186).

   For this assignment, choose two public photographs, photographs for which you do not have any personal connections. Choose one that Berger might call a short quotation and choose another that might be called a long quotation. Use these to test his claims and to try out his style. Write about each, using his writing as a model. And from these exercises, write an essay in which you present, test, and extend Berger's argument. How might Berger account for their "length," for the "extension" of meaning they allow? How would he value this? And what about you? How would you explain what you have done? How might you explain its value to you and to people like you, people of your generation?

2. Berger makes the development of photography (and the uses of photographs) part of a larger history, one that involves "positivism," "corporate capitalism," and the "social function of subjectivity." In the end, he offers a use of photographic images that at least appears to be positive, even redemptive:

   > Apart from the event photographed, apart from the lucidity of the idea, we are moved by the photograph's fulfilment of an expectation which is intrinsic to the will to look. The camera completes the half-language of appearances and articulates an unmistakable meaning. When this happens we suddenly find ourselves at home amongst appearances, as we are at home in our mother tongue. (p. 205)

   Reread with a particular concern to understand and to be able to speak for this history. (The fourth "Question for a Second Reading" might help prepare you for this.) You should locate key passages and work with the difficult terms and concepts. Write an essay in which you discuss this history Berger describes. How does it engage and involve photography? What are the consequences, dangers, and the possibilities, according to Berger, of the use of photographic images? Why are photographs important, and not just decorations or ways of passing time?

   And, finally, where are you with this? Does his account make sense to you? illuminate your own experience? Is there an argument here that you would want to make in response to his work, one addressed to other students and on behalf of your generation?

3. Crucial to Berger's argument are the existence of "expressive photographs," photographs that quote the particular at length and whose particular appearances articulate a "general idea." His demonstration of the expressiveness of these photographs is achieved in his own writing. You might look at his written account of "Boy Sleeping" (p. 200), "Friends" (p. 202), "Lovers" (p. 203), or, with a significant difference, "A Red Hussar Leaving, June 1919, Budapest" (p. 186). The written accounts have a particular pattern to them: "A mother with her child is staring intently at a soldier. Perhaps they are speaking" (p. 186); or, "A young man is asleep at the table in a public place, perhaps a café. The expression on his face, his character, the way the light and shade dissolve him and his clothes, his open shirt and the newspaper on the table, his health and his fatigue, the time of night: all these are visibly present in this event and are particular" (p. 200).

   For this assignment, write an essay that considers three photographs:

   a. Take time to find and consider a photograph you believe to be "expressive," in Berger's terms. This should not be something, or so Berger would argue, from your family album. Write about this photograph with Berger as your model.

   b. Choose an advertising photograph, a photograph of "dogmatic assertion," like the champagne ad on page 180. Write about it following Berger's line of argument.

   c. Choose, then, a photograph that is (or could be) from your family album—a photograph of particular and immediate meaning to you. (Why doesn't Berger do this, do you suppose?) And write about that photograph. You don't have to use Berger as your model, but you should be working toward an idea, a sense of how such a photograph might be read and how it might be valued.

With these three photographs (and your written accounts) as your primary sources, prepare an essay on the "cultural work" of photographs, the ways they function and serve contemporary culture. This is your essay. You are the primary spokesperson. Berger is a source, someone you've read, who has influenced (even inspired) your work. Be sure you don't let him have all the good lines.

4. Early in his essay, as he comments on his collaborative work with the photographer Jean Mohr, Berger says they had to "doubt or reject many of the assumptions usually made about photography." He states, "We discovered that photographs did not work as we had been taught" (p. 175). To prepare for this assignment, think about the assumptions you (and people like you) have about photography. Talk to your friends, to the people in your class; make a list. And, as you reread Berger's essay, mark those moments where he identifies assumptions about photographs that his project in "Appearances" leads him to doubt or reject. Think also about the particular uses of photography, including digital photography, in your world—a world Berger couldn't have known when he was writing.

   Write an essay in which you use Berger's work to test your (and your generation's) assumptions about photography. You should assume that you are writing for readers who have not yet read Berger's essay. You'll need to provide some background, introduction, summary, and paraphrase. You should provide a sense of what the issues are for him and a sense of what he sees and does with the photographs that matter to him. Why, in other words, should he be read at this point in time? What does he have to say to you and to students of our generation? What do you need to say in return?

MAKING CONNECTIONS

1. There are photographs in "Appearances" that are directly acknowledged in the text. Not all the photographs get equal time, however. And there are photographs without direct acknowledgment. We should assume they were carefully chosen and carefully arranged, that this essay is, in fact, an example of a "photographic essay." Take time to reread "Appearances" and think about the staging, the placement, and the use of the photographs. Choose examples you can use to think about the various relationships of image to word and word to image.

   When you are done, reread W. J. T. Mitchell's "The Photographic Essay: Four Case Studies" (p. 332), and read it with the thought that "Appearances" might serve as a fifth case study. You should assume that you are writing for an audience familiar with neither text. You will, then, need to take care to present each, its key terms, examples, and arguments. And you should use Mitchell to think about Berger and his project. How might Mitchell classify "Appearances" in his account of the "dialectic of exchange and resistance between photography and language"? Where might he place "Appearances" in relation to the other four case studies? Both Barthes and Mitchell express an urgency in their discussion of how we use and understand images. Are there connections? Is this urgency something you might share?

2. In John Berger's "Appearances" and in Roland Barthes's *Camera Lucida* (p. 140), the authors give an extended demonstration of how they look at ("read") and value photographs. There is a personal urgency in each. Each author, that is, is working out something important; each provides an example of research driven by interest and desire. And both authors, it seems safe to say, are offering lessons. They are urging action. They are not just filing a report. Both "Appearances" and *Camera Lucida* are available to teach others how to read and value photographs; both offer methods, justification, motive, examples.

   Write an essay in which you present the work of Barthes and Berger to students of your generation. You should assume that your readers have not read these works, but that they share an interest in photographic images and their use. You'll need to guide them through each author, choosing representative examples. You might provide a Barthes-like and a Berger-like reading of a set of common examples, either their photographs or ones you provide or a mixture of both. You'll need to urge your readers to see what you see in these examples, perhaps to take the sides that you take, or to hold similar reservations, or to share a particular passion or concern.

3. Both John Berger, in "Appearances," and Edward Said, in "States" (p. 378), are concerned with how photographs might be used to yield ideas, to produce understanding. Write an essay in which you work closely with an example from each writer, one where he is providing a written account of a photograph. In what context are they providing this "reading" of a photograph? How, that is, do they understand goal and the importance of their work? And what is represented in the act, in the writing? How might the writing be seen to work between image and idea in the service of understanding?

   It would probably be best to assume that your readers are not familiar with the work of either Berger or Said. You will need to provide an introduction; you will need to take care to introduce their projects and your interest in them.

ROBERT COLES

*EARLY IN HIS CAREER as a psychologist, Robert Coles spent seven years following migrant workers north from Florida to gather material for the second volume—*Migrants, Sharecroppers, Mountaineers*—of his remarkable, Pulitzer Prize–winning series of books,* Children of Crisis. *He learned about the workers' lives, he said, by visiting "certain homes week after week until it [had] come to pass that I [had] known certain families for many years." The sacrifice, patience, compassion, and discipline required for his massive documentary projects—the eight volumes of the* Children of Crisis *series and, later,* The Inner Lives of Children*—transform the usual business of research into something magnificent.*

Coles's project began when he was stationed at Keesler Air Force Base in Biloxi, Mississippi. He was, he says, a "rather smug and all too self-satisfied child psychiatrist, just out of medical training." He was in the South at the beginning of the civil rights movement, and the scenes he witnessed, the experience, for example, of black children taunted and threatened as they walked into newly desegregated schools, led him to abandon his plans to return to New England and to remain instead in the South to find out how children responded to crisis. He began with standard psychiatric questions, such as "How did these children respond to stress?" but soon realized, he said, "that I was meeting families whose assumptions, hopes, fears, and expectations were quite definitely strange to me. I realized, too, how arbitrarily I was fitting the lives of various individuals into my psychiatric categories—a useful prac-

tice under certain circumstances, but now, for me, a distinct hindrance. I was unwittingly setting severe, maybe crippling, limits on what I would allow myself to see, try to comprehend." He learned, through the children, to abandon his carefully rehearsed questions and to talk and listen. The stories he learned to tell are remarkable and moving and have an authority few writers achieve.

Born in 1929, Coles graduated from Harvard University in 1950, earned an M.D. degree from Columbia University in 1954, and began his career as a child psychiatrist. He is currently the James Agee Professor of Social Ethics at Harvard University and a founding member of the Center of Documentary Studies at Duke University. An essayist, poet, and scholar, Coles has published over fifty books, including Women of Crisis (1978), coauthored with his wife, Jane Hallowell Coles, The Call of Stories: Teaching and the Moral Imagination *(1989),* Harvard Diary *(1990),* The Call of Service: A Witness to Idealism *(1994),* School *(1998), and* The Children of Crisis Reader *(2001). Coles is also the editor of the documentary magazine* DoubleTake.

The essay that follows is a chapter from Coles's book Doing Documentary Work *(1997). Coles first presented it in 1996 in a series of lectures given at the New York Public Library. The chapter draws on the last twenty years of his teaching, including courses in the "literary-documentary tradition" at Harvard and at the Center for Documentary Studies at Duke. When Coles refers to "documentary work" he is referring to any attempt to engage, represent, and understand the lives of others. His reference, then, extends to journalists, poets, novelists, and filmmakers; to sociologists, anthropologists, and historians; to physicians, psychologists, and social workers; to anyone who is charged to know deeply and to speak and act for others. There is an urgency in Coles's work, a sense of mission and service, that is rare in academia and in contemporary intellectual life. You can feel this urgency in his conclusion to "The Tradition: Fact and Fiction":*

> *And so it goes, then—doing documentary work is a journey, and is a little more, too, a passage across boundaries (disciplines, occupational constraints, definitions, conventions all too influentially closed for traffic), a passage that can become a quest, even a pilgrimage, a movement toward the sacred truth enshrined not only on tablets of stone, but in the living hearts of those others whom we can hear, see, and get to understand. Thereby, we hope to be confirmed in our own humanity—the creature on this earth whose very nature it is to make just that kind of connection with others during the brief stay we are permitted here.*

The Tradition: Fact and Fiction

The heart of the matter for someone doing documentary work is the pursuit of what James Agee called "human actuality"—rendering and representing for others what has been witnessed, heard, overheard, or sensed. Fact is "the quality of being actual," hence Agee's concern with actuality. All documentation, however, is put together by a particular mind whose capacities, interests, values, conjectures, suppositions and presuppositions, whose memories, and, not least, whose talents will come to bear directly or indirectly on what is, finally presented to the world in the form of words, pictures, or even music or artifacts of one kind or another. In shaping an article or a book, the writer can add factors and variables in two directions: social and cultural and historical on the one hand, individual or idiosyncratic on the other. As Agee reminds us in his long "country letter," his aria: "All that each person is, and experiences, and shall ever experience, in body and in mind, all these things are differing expressions of himself and of one root, and are identical: and not one of these things nor one of these persons is ever quite to be duplicated, nor replaced, nor has it ever quite had precedent: but each is a new and incommunicably tender life, wounded in every breath, and almost as hardly killed as easily wounded: sustaining, for a while, without defense, the enormous assaults of the universe."

Such an emphasis on human particularity would include the ups and downs of a life, even events (both internal and external) in that life that would seem to have nothing to do with the objectivity of, say, the world of central Alabama, but everything to do with the world of the writer or the photographer who will notice, ignore, take seriously, or find irrelevant Alabama's various moments, happenings, acts and deeds and comments, scenes. Events are filtered through a person's awareness, itself not uninfluenced by a history of private experience, by all sorts of aspirations, frustrations, and yearnings, by those elusive, significant "moods" as they can affect and even sway what we deem of interest or importance, not to mention how we assemble what we have learned into something to present to others—to editors, museum curators first of all, whose personal attitudes, not to mention the nature of their jobs or the values and desires of *their* bosses, all help shape their editorial or curatorial judgment. The web of one kind of human complexity (that of life in Hale County, Alabama) connects with, is influenced by, the web of another kind of human complexity (Agee and Evans and all that informs not only their lives but those of their magazine and book editors).

So often in our discussion of documentary work my students echo Agee, emphasize the "actuality" of the work—its responsibility to fact. They commonly pose for themselves the familiar alternative of fiction, as though we were dealing in clear-cut opposites: if not the true as against the false, at least the real as against the imaginary. But such opposites or alternatives don't quite do justice either conceptually or pragmatically to the aspect of "human actuality" that has to do with the vocational life of writers, photographers, folklorists, musicologists, and filmmakers, those who are trying to engage with people's words, their music, gestures, movements, and overall appearance and then let others know what they have learned. No one going anywhere, on a journalistic trip, on a documentary assignment, for social-science research, or to soak up the atmosphere of a place to aid in the writing of a story or a novel, will claim to be able to see and hear everything, or even claim to be able to notice all that truly matters. Who we are, to some variable extent, determines what we notice and, at another level of intellectual activity, what we regard as worthy of notice, what we find significant. Nor will technology help us all that decisively. I can arrive in America's Alabama or England's Yorkshire, I can find my way to a South Seas island or to central Africa, I can go visit a nearby suburban mall with the best tape recorder in the world, with cameras that take superb pictures, and even with a clear idea of what I am to do, and still I face the matter of looking *and* overlooking, paying instant heed *and* letting something slip by; and I face the matter of sorting out what I *have* noticed, of arranging it for emphasis—the matter, really, of *composition,* be it verbal or visual, the matter of re-presenting; and here that all-important word *narrative* enters. Stories heard or seen now have to turn into stories put together with some guiding intelligence and discrimination: I must select *what* ought to be present; decide on the *tone* of that presentation, its *atmosphere* or *mood.* These words can be as elusive as they are compelling to an essay, an exhibition of pictures, or a film.

Even if the strict limits of oral history are never suspended (*only* the taped interviews with informants are used in a given article or book, or any comments from the practitioner of oral history are confined to an introduction or to explanatory footnotes) there still remains that challenge of selection, with its implications for the narrative: which portions of which tapes are to be used, and with what assertive or clarifying or instructional agenda in mind (in the hope, for instance, of what popular or academic nod of comprehension or applause). How does one organize one's "material," with what topics in mind, what broader themes? How does one deal with the mix of factuality and emotionality that any taped interview presents, never mind a stock of them, and how does one arrange and unfold the events, the incidents: a story's pace, its plot, its coherence, its character development and portrayal, its suggestiveness, its degree of inwardness, its degree of connection to external action, and, all in all, its dramatic power, not to mention its moral authority?

The above words and phrases are summoned all the time by writers and teachers of fiction. Fictional devices, that is, inform the construction of nonfiction, and of course, fiction, conversely, draws upon the actual, the "real-life." A novelist uses his or her lived experience and the observations he or she has made and is making in the course of living a life as elements of a writing life. I remember William Carlos Williams pausing, after a home visit, to write down not only medical notes but a writer's notes: words heard; a revealing moment remembered; the appearance of a room on a particular day, or of a face brimming with surprise or happiness, a head lowered in dismay, a look of anticipation or alarm or dread, fear on a child's face, those details of life, of language, of appearance, of occurrence for which novelists are known, but which the rest of us also crave or require, as readers, of course, but also in our working lives: we all survive and prevail through a mastery of certain details, or fail by letting them slip through our fingers.

A novelist has to have those details at constant hand. He or she has had occasion in so-called real life to become aware of them but now has to fit this personal learning into a story, a narrative that requires both imagination and an idea of what will reach and touch readers persuasively. Nonfiction involves the same process, though we have to be careful of how we use words such as *experience, observation,* and, certainly, *imagination* when discussing nonfiction. A documentarian's report will be strengthened by what has been witnessed, but will be fueled, surely, by what those observations come to mean in his or her head: we absorb sights and sounds, and they become *our* experience, unique to us, in that we, their recipients, are unique. What we offer others in the way of our documentary reports, then, is *our* mix of what we have observed and experienced, as we have assembled it, that assembly having to do, again, with our imaginative capability, our gifts as writers, as editors, as storytellers, as artists. Oscar Lewis and Studs Terkel, working with taped interviews, pages and pages of transcripts, put all of that together in such a way that makes us readers marvel, not only at what we're told but at how it gets told—and, before that, at how it was elicited from the various individuals these two met and from anyone who worked with them (Lewis trained a team of colleagues to help him out). Others of us might have met the same people but obtained from them different stories, maybe fewer in number or less interesting, less revealing.

I remember well what one of my psychoanalytic supervisors, Elizabeth Zetzel, who was a rather solidly conventional physician with a mind George Eliot would have called "theoretic," told me as she contemplated my protocols (my daily notes of what I had heard from a particular patient). Psychoanalysis, she said, is not only the uncovering of psychological material; it is two people doing so. Therefore, anyone's analysis, undertaken with a particular analyst, is only one of a possible series of hypothetical analyses, depending on who *else* might be the analyst, and what might be looked at and concluded on the basis of that other person's presence as the analyst, rather than the one now being consulted. I had been zealously on the prowl for certain memories that would, frankly, confirm my clinical notion of what had happened earlier in a certain patient's life, and to what effect. Dr. Zetzel had realized (I would later realize) that this was not only *an* inquiry, or the "correct" inquiry, but *my* inquiry—that someone else might have had other clinical interests, other kinds of memories to pursue, other clinical destinations in mind and, very important, would no doubt have engaged with this patient in a different way. (Nietzsche's aphorism holds here: "It takes two to make a truth.")

Moreover, what I make of what I hear from any patient has to do with what I've learned, and with what I have brought from my life to what has been taught me. Psychoanalysis, then, is a person's continuing narrative, however "meandering" rather than formally structured, as it is prompted by and shaped by his or her life, of course, but also as it responds to a particular listener or observer who has his or her own narrative interests and capacities and intentions (his or her observations, experiences, and, as with artists, talent and imagination—ways of sensing and of phrasing what is sensed, skill at putting him- or herself in another's shoes). A profession also has its narrative as well as its intellectual and emotional demands, and it, too, affects a particular practitioner, here a psychoanalyst, in influential ways: an agreed-upon language; an agreed-upon story called a diagnosis or a clinical interpretation or summary, namely, how we (are trained to) tell ourselves what we're hearing before we get around to letting our patients know what we think. Put differently, we develop, as psychiatric or psychoanalytic listeners, a professional narrative, which is offered in response to the narratives we hear in that unusual room where matters of utter intimacy and privacy become a shared documentary experience limited to two people. Others may be brought into the "act," however, since patients talk to people they know, and so do we, in our professional lives (at meetings) and in our writing lives: we share case histories with our colleagues and stories with readers, and surely we tailor our stories to elicit readers' interest—a tradition that goes back to Freud's first books and accounts for those of the many who have followed throughout this profession's now hundred-year history.

All of the above is as intricate and knotty, but also as evident and ordinary, as what happens every day when any two people talk to each other. The words and the pictorial sense vary on both sides, depending upon who the people are; and if one or both of the two talks to a third or a fourth person, that "report" will also vary depending on the person then doing the listening. We have words for the gross distortions of this process: rumor, gossip. We are less likely to account for the almost infinite possible variations on an encounter that constitute a human exchange, or a human response to the nonhuman world of the landscape or the multihuman world of a social scene. Naturally, a novelist does go one significant step further—reserves the right to use his or her imagination more freely than a documentarian, and to call upon the imaginary as a matter of course: personal fantasies, made-up voices given to made-up characters with made-up names, and scenes described out of the mind's visual reveries, even as its verbal ones supply words. All of the above has to be done with judgment as well as provocative ingenuity and boldness. The imaginary life, like the real one, requires a teller's thoughtfulness, canniness, sensitivity, and talent for dealing with language, or with the visual. What emerges, if it is done successfully, is a kind of truth, sometimes (as in Tolstoy, George Eliot, Dickens; we each make our choices from among these storytellers) an enveloping and unforgettable wisdom that strikes the reader as realer than real, a truth that penetrates deep within one, that leaps beyond verisimilitude or incisive portrayal, appealing and recognizable characterization, and lands on a terrain where the cognitive, the emotional, the reflective, and the moral live side-by-side. "I make up stories all day," I hear a wonderfully able novelist say at a seminar on "documentary studies." "Some people would say I tell lies—my 'business' is to write them down and sell them, with the help of a publisher." We all demur, but he rejects what he hears as an evasive politeness on our part. "All right," he provokes us further, "I do a good job, so I get published, and you like what you read. But there are talented storytellers out there, let's call them that, who spend their lives telling stories, persuading people to get wrapped up in them, just like they talk of getting wrapped up in a good novel . . . and they are telling what you and I would call lies, a string of them, or falsehoods, or *un*truths. Some of them do enough of it that they become known chiefly, essentially, for what they tell *as*—they are 'con artists.' Am I a version of such a person, a successful, socially sanctioned, 'sublimated' version? Is that a useful way of thinking about stories and novels—cleverly or entertainingly put together lies?"

This writer, this novelist who was also a teacher and an effective conversationalist, was forcefully putting a big subject before us. He had, after a fashion, constructed a small story about the matter of storytelling in which he highlighted the matter of fiction as something made up—though often quite full of facts, observations, accurately recalled happenings, and also made up, potentially, of truth, even the highest kind of truth, as many of us would insist. Others in the seminar, of course, spoke of journalism and social science, their claims to another kind of truth, one that pertains to an observed world unconnected to an imagined one; though, again, the journalist's, the photographer's, the social scientist's imagination can all the time influence how a news story or a research project is done, what is obtained in the way of information, remarks, photographs, and how all of that is relayed to others.

I tried, in that seminar, to make sense of my own work, to figure out its nature, and so did we all: this was the purpose of the seminar. During the early 1960s, as I mentioned earlier, I was trying hard to learn how Southern schoolchildren, both black and white, were managing under the stresses of court-ordered desegregation in the South, and how civil rights activists were dealing with their special, often dangerous, even fatally dangerous lives of constant protest. I was doing psychiatric research and beginning to write up my findings for presentation to professional audiences and journals. By then, I'd also been interviewed by newspaper reporters, because I was immersed in a serious educational, social, and racial crisis. I was privileged (I only gradually realized) to be watching a moment of history. Soon I was not only taking what I heard from children, teachers, parents, and young activists and fitting it all into a language, a way of thinking, a theoretical or conceptual apparatus of sorts (lists of defense mechanisms, signs of various symptoms, evidence of successful adaptation); I was developing a general thesis on what makes for collapse in children under duress and what makes for "resiliency." I had developed a list of "variables," aspects of a life that tended to make a child worthy of being described as such by me: a resilient child. Eventually, with enough knowledge of enough children, I had in mind a broader claim, a more ambitious one, a statement on "*the* resilient child."

I was also seeing, in some newspapers, quotations correctly attributed to me that weren't always my words, and that seemed a bit foreign to me because they had been hurriedly scribbled as I talked. Even my exactly transcribed words, *taped* words, sometimes seemed strange to me, because they appeared out of context; they were deprived of the explanatory remarks, the narrative sequence, that had preceded and followed them. My wife would say, "You said *that?*" I would say yes, and then the refrain: "but the reporter used what I said for his purposes"—and I wasn't necessarily being critical. I had tried to explain something, had tried to speak with some qualifications or even with skepticism, second thoughts, or outright misgivings about my own thoughts, themselves being constantly modified by interviews, by conversations with colleagues, by *consideration* of this or that matter, the reflective aspect of what gets called experience.

The reporters, needless to say, had their own purposes to consider, their own experiences; they had gradually accumulated manners of hearing and remembering, of listening to tapes, based on notions of what they were meant to do professionally. I was meant to move from hearing children talk about what was on their minds to thinking about the *projections* these children summoned, the *denials* or *reaction-formations* to which they resorted; a journalist is used to hearing me, and soon enough, asking me pointed questions that aim for an opinion, an explanation, stated as plainly and unequivocally as possible. *Why* is this child doing so well, given the pressures she has to endure? Why is *that* child not doing so well? What is your explanation for the difference? If my explanation was too long-winded, evasive, abstract, or, finally, unconvincing, the reporter pressed, rephrased, got me to reconsider, to say things differently—until what I said helped him or her understand the subject at hand (and would presumably help his or her editor and readers, who inhabit his or her mind, understand). Sometimes I was not only surprised by the printed result, as my wife was, but grateful. Those reporters pushed me to think (and to put things) in ways not familiar to me, and when I remembered what I said, seeing it presented in the context of a story, a part of the reporter's own take on the subject, I found myself learning something, regarding matters with a different emphasis or point of view, responding, it can be said, to the "truth" of that particular interview. All interviews, one hopes, become jointly conducted!

The harder I struggled to make sense of my work, never mind make sense of what others might make of it, the more confused I became: what was I doing, what was I learning, what was I trying to say? I was a child psychiatrist and was learning to be a psychoanalyst, but I wasn't working with patients in an office or a clinic; I was visiting children and their parents in their homes, talking with teachers in schools, and, through SNCC [Student Nonviolent Coordinating Committee], doing things regarded by cities and states of the South as illegal, a challenge both to laws and to long-standing customs. On the one hand, I had to answer to a certain kind of psychiatric voice in me: why *are* you doing all this? On the other hand, I had to answer to the collective voices of civil rights workers: why are you concentrating your energies on *us*, when there's a "sick" society out there; for example, look at your own profession, the utterly segregated universities, medical schools, residency training programs, psychoanalytic institutes—why don't you study all that! Then, I had to contend with my great teacher Dr. W. C. Williams, to whom (1961, 1962) I'd sent some drafts of my psychiatric reports. "For God's sake," he told me once, "try to find a cure for that passive voice you use, for the third person, for all that technical language—it's a syndrome!" My apologies and chagrin and self-pity only elicited this: "Take your readers in hand, take them where you've been, tell them what you've seen, give them some stories you've heard. Most of all, write for *them*, the ordinary folks out there, not for yourself and your buddies in the profession of psychiatry." I can still recall my sense of futility and inadequacy as I thought about those admonishing remarks. I had always known that Dr. Williams could be irritable with people he knew and wanted to help (I'd seen him be so with patients), but now I felt critically judged, and unable to do anything in keeping with the advice given me—lest I lose my last link with my medical and psychiatric and psychoanalytic life: my capacity to write articles that would earn me (not to mention the work I was doing) a hearing, some acceptance.

What Dr. Williams urged, my wife, a high-school teacher of English and history, also urged. She began listening to the tapes we'd collected (she and I worked together, full-time, until our sons were born in 1964, 1966, and 1970). She marked up certain moments in the transcripts which she found interesting, pulled them together, and wrote from memory some descriptions of the scenes in which those comments were made: times, places, details such as the weather, the casual talk exchanged, the food so generously served us, the neighborhood excursions we took—to churches, to markets, a world explored with the help of embattled people who knew that if we were really to understand them, we had to go beyond those clinical questions that I wanted so much to ask them. In time Jane had assembled "moments," she called them, for me to read: a mix of descriptive writing and edited versions of interviews, with suggestions for what she called "personal reflection" on my part. "You'll have some old-fashioned essays," she wrote. "Nothing to be afraid of!"

Plenty to be afraid of, I thought. It took me a couple of years to overcome that apprehension and worry. I was taught and rallied and reassured by Jane, badgered by Dr. Williams, until he died (March 4, 1963), challenged by some of the friends I'd made in SNCC, who kept telling me I should "tell their stories," not try to "shrink" them, and encouraged by Margaret Long, a novelist who worked for the Southern Regional Council, an interracial group long devoted to standing up in many ways to segregation. In 1963 the Council published my first nonprofessional piece (as I thought of it back then) on the work I was doing: "Separate But Equal Lives." The very title signified a break for me, a departure from the heavyweight jargon I'd learned to use as an expression of professional arrival. With this new kind of writing, I began to think differently about the very nature of the work I was doing. The point now was not only to analyze what children said, or the drawings they made, but to learn about their *lives,* in the hope of being able to describe them as knowingly and clearly as possible to anyone who cares to read of them rather than to my colleagues in child psychiatry.

In 1970, well along in such writing, I heard this from one of my old supervisors at the Children's Hospital in Boston, George Gardner: "You're doing documentary work, documentary child psychiatry, I suppose you could call it." I was pleased, though also worried—haunted by the judgmental self, its appearance often a measure of careerist anxiety. When I told my wife what Dr. Gardner had said, she laughed and said, "When Dr. Gardner settles for 'documentary work' alone, you'll be there!" But where is her "there"? We never discussed that question at the time. I was almost afraid to think about what she had in mind, even as I know in retrospect what she was suggesting—that I try to respond more broadly (less clinically) to these children, give them their due as individuals, as human beings, rather than patients. After all, they weren't "sick," or coming to me in a hospital or a clinical setting for "help"; they were "out there," living their lives, and I had come to them in an effort to learn how they "got along." Those two words increasingly became my methodological description of intent, my rationale of sorts: to try to ascertain as best I could the character of particular lives, the way they are lived, the assumptions held, the hopes embraced, the fears and worries borne—in Flannery O'Connor's felicitous phrase, the particular "habit of being" that informs *this* person's existence, *that* one's. To render such lives requires that one take a stand with respect to them—that of the observer, first and foremost, so that they can be apprehended, but that of the *distanced* observer, the editor, the critic (not of them, but of them as the subject of a story). What of their lives to offer others, and in what manner of delivery? As I asked that question I could hear one of Dr. Williams's refrains: "the language, the language!" Williams was forever trying to do justice both to what he heard from others, and to what he heard in his own head: the narrative side of documentary work, the exposition of a particular effort at exploration.

Documentary work, then, ultimately becomes, for most of us, documentary writing, documentary photographs, a film, a taped series of folk songs, a collection of children's drawings and paintings: reports of what was encountered for the ears and eyes of others. Here we weed and choose from so very much accumulated. Here we connect ourselves critically with those we have come to know—we arrange and direct their debut on the stage, and we encourage and discourage by selecting some segments and eliminating others. Moreover, to repeat, some of us add our own two cents (or more); we work what others have become to *us* into *our* narrative—the titles we give to photographs, the introductions we write for exhibitions, the statements we make with films. Even if our work is presented as only about *them,* we have been at work for weeks, for months, discarding and thereby concentrating what we retain: its significance mightily enhanced because so much else has been taken away.

It is not unfair, therefore, for an Oscar Lewis or a Studs Terkel or a Fred Wiseman to be known as the one who is "responsible" for what are supposedly documentary reports about all those others who were interviewed or filmed. Those others, in a certain way, have become "creations" of Lewis, Terkel, Wiseman—even if we have no explanatory comments from any of them about what they have done, and how, and with what purpose in mind. The stories such documentarians tell us are, in a way, the surviving remnants of so very much that has been left aside. We who cut, weave, edit, splice, crop, sequence, interpolate, interject, connect, pan, come up with our captions and comments, have our say (whenever and wherever and however) have thereby linked our lives to those we have attempted to document, creating a joint presentation for an audience that may or may not have been asked to consider all that has gone into what they are reading, hearing, or viewing.

I remember, a wonderfully enlightening afternoon spent with labor economist Paul Taylor in 1972, while I was working on a biographical study of Dorothea Lange. Jane and I sat in Taylor's spacious, comfortable Berkeley home, the one he and Dorothea Lange occupied together until her death of cancer in 1965. He took me, step by step, through their work together, the work that culminated in *American Exodus* (1939). We examined many of Lange's photographs, some of them prints that were never published or shown. We were looking at an artist's sensibility, as it informed the selections she had made—which picture really worked, really got across what the photographer intended for us to contemplate.

I studied her iconic "migrant mother," a picture known throughout the world, a visual rallying ground of sorts for those who want to be reminded and remind others of jeopardy's pensive life [Fig. 1, p. 221]. There she sits, her right hand touching her lower right cheek, the lady of Nipoma, caught gazing, in March of 1936, one of her children to her left, one to her right, head turned away from us, disinclined to look at the camera and, through it, the legions of viewers with whom it connects. The three figures seem so close, so "tight," it would be said in the South, yet each seems lost to the others: the children lost in the private world they secure by hiding their eyes, the mother lost in a look that is seemingly directed at no one and everyone, a look that is inward and yet that engages with us who look at her, and maybe with her, or through her, at the kind of life she has been living. But only minutes before Lange took that famous picture, she had taken others. At furthest remove [Fig. 2, p. 222] we are shown the same mother and her children in the makeshift tent that is their home; two others, a bit closer, show her with another child who has just been suckling at her breast and now has settled into

FIGURE [1]

a sleep. In one picture [Fig. 3, p. 223] the mother is alone with that child; in the next, [Fig. 4, p. 224] another of her children has come to her side, its face on her left shoulder. I return to the picture Lange has selected: now the older children are alongside their mother, but her appearance commands our attention—her hair lightly combed, her strong nose and broad forehead and wide mouth giving her face authority, her informally layered plainclothes, her

FIGURE [2]

worker's arms and fingers telling us that this is someone who every day has to take life on with no conviction of success around any corner.

Dorothea Lange has, in a sense, removed that woman from the very world she is meant, as a Farm Security Administration (FSA) photographer, to document. The tent is gone, and the land on which it is pitched, and the utensils. The children, in a way, are gone, their backs turned to us, their backs a sort of screen upon which we may project our sense of what is happening to them, what they feel. But one child's head is slightly lowered, and the other has covered her face with her right arm—and so a feeling of their sadness, become the viewer's sadness, has surely seized so many of us who have stared and stared at that woman, who is herself staring, and maybe, as in a Rodin sculpture, doing some serious thinking: struggling for a vision, dealing with an apprehension, experiencing a premonition or a nightmarish moment of foreboding. We are told by Lange that she is a "migrant mother," because otherwise she could be quite another kind of working (or nonworking) mother, yet she has been at least somewhat separated from sociological clues, and so she becomes psychologically more available to us, kin to us. A photographer has edited and cropped her work in order to make it more accessible to her anticipated view-

FIGURE [3]

ers. As a documentarian, Lange snapped away with her camera, came back with a series of pictures that narrate a kind of white migrant life in the mid-1930s—and then, looking for one picture that would make the particular universal, that would bring us within a person's world rather than keep us out (as pitying onlookers), she decided upon a photograph that allows us to move from well-meant compassion to a sense of respect, even awe: we see a stoic dignity, a thoughtfulness whose compelling survival under such circumstances is itself something to ponder, something to find arresting, even miraculous.

Another well-known Lange picture that Paul Taylor and I studied was "Ditched, Stalled, and Stranded," taken in California's San Joaquin Valley in 1935. Taylor first showed me the uncropped version of that picture [Fig. 5, p. 225], with a man seated at the steering wheel of a car, his wife beside him. He has a wool cap on, of a kind today more commonly worn in Europe than here. He has a long face with a sturdy nose, and with wide eyes he stares past his wife (the right car door open) toward the viewer. The woman's right hand is in the pocket of her coat, which has a fur collar, and she is looking at an angle to the viewer. She has a round face, and seems to be of ample size. A bit of her dress and her right leg appear beyond the bottom limit of the coat. My dad, politically conservative, had seen that version of the picture years ago, and had pointed out to me that he was not impressed by Lange's title:

FIGURE [4]

here, after all, in the middle of the 1930s, at the height of the Great Depression, a worldwide phenomenon, were a couple who seemed well-clothed, well-fed—and who had a car. Did I realize, he wondered, how few people in the entire world, even in America, could be so described at that time? An automobile and a fur-collared coat to him meant something other than being "ditched, stalled, and stranded."

FIGURE [5]

Lange chose to crop that photograph for presentation in various exhibitions and books [Fig. 6, p. 226]. She removed the woman, save a touch of her coat (the cloth part), so the driver looks directly at us. Like the migrant mother, his gaze connects with our gaze, and we wonder who this man is, and where he wants to go, or is headed, and why he is described by the photographer as so thoroughly at an impasse. The photographer, in turn, tries to provide an answer. The man's left hand holds lightly onto the steering mechanism just below the wheel, and he seems almost an extension of that wheel, the two of them, along with the title given them, a metaphor for a troubled nation gone badly awry: whither his direction, and will he even be able to get going again, to arrive where he would like to be? Once more, Lange turns a photograph into a melancholy statement that embraces more than the population of a California agricultural region. She does so by cropping (editing)

FIGURE [6]

her work, by denying us the possibility of a married couple in which one spouse seems reasonably contented, by reducing a scene to a driver who is readily seen as forlorn, and also as deeply introspective, eager for us, his fellow citizens, to return the intensity of his (moral) introspection.

I remember Paul Taylor gazing intently at the migrant mother and the man who was "ditched, stalled, and stranded"—a return on his part to a 1930s world, but also a moment's opportunity to reflect upon an entire documentary tradition, in which *American Exodus* figures importantly. No question, Paul and Jane reminded me, social observers and journalists have been journeying into poor neighborhoods, rural and urban, for generations, and in so doing have connected their written reports to a visual effort of one kind or another. Henry Mayhew's sensitively rendered *London Labour and the London Poor,* which describes nineteenth-century London, was accompanied by the drawings of Cruikshank, the well-known English illustrator—an inquiry that included a pictorial response. When George Orwell's *The Road to Wigan Pier* was first published in 1937, its text was supplemented by photographs, poorly reproduced, their maker unacknowledged—yet surely some who read Orwell's provocative and suggestive text were grateful for a glimpse of the world this great essayist had visited.

By the 1930s, under the auspices of the Farm Security Administration, and especially Roy Stryker, who had a keen sense of the relationship between politics and public awareness, a number of photographers were roaming the American land eager to catch sight of, and then, through their cameras, catch hold of a country struggling mightily with the consequences of the Great Depression—in the words of President Franklin Delano Roosevelt (1937) "one-third of a nation ill-housed, ill-clad, ill-nourished." So it is that Russell Lee and Ben Shahn and Arthur Rothstein and Walker Evans and Marion Post Wolcott, and, not least, Dorothea Lange became part of a significant photographic and cultural moment—the camera as an instrument of social awareness, of political ferment.

Though some photographers place great store by the titles they attach to their pictures, or write comments that help locate the viewer, help give him or her a sense of where the scene is or even provide a bit of context (how the person taking the picture happened to be at a particular place at a particular time), most photographers are content to let their work stand on its own, a silent confrontation of us all-too-wordy folk, for whom language (in the form of abstractions and recitations) can sometimes become an obstacle rather than a pathway to the lived truth of various lives. But Dorothea Lange's work in the 1930s, quite able, of course, to stand on its own, became part of something quite unique and important; and that connection (her photographs and the statements of some of the men and women whose pictures she took, joined to text written by Paul Taylor) would become a major achievement in the annals of fieldwork, of social-science research, of public information as rendered by a photographer and an academic (who in this case happened to be husband and wife).

It is possible to take much for granted as one goes through the pages of the 1939 edition of *American Exodus* (it was re-issued in 1969 with a foreword by Paul Taylor). The pictures are still powerful, even haunting, and some of them have become absorbed in an American iconography of sorts—the one titled "U.S. 54 in Southern New Mexico" [Fig. 7, p. 228], for instance, or the one taken in the Texas Panhandle in 1938 that shows a woman in profile, her right hand raised to her brow, her left to her neck: a portrait of perplexity, if not desperation [Fig. 8, p. 229]. That woman is quoted as saying "If you die, you're

FIGURE [7]

dead—that's all," and we, over half a century later, are apt to forget that in the 1930s there was no solid tradition of interviewing the subjects of a photographic study, linking what someone has to say to her or his evident circumstances as rendered by the camera. Again and again Dorothea Lange asked questions, wrote down what she heard (or overheard). Her sharp ears were a match for her shrewd and attentive eyes, and she knew to let both those aspects of her humanity connect with the people she had tried to understand.

Meanwhile, her husband was daring to do an original kind of explorative social science. As he accompanied her, he learned about the individuals, the locales she was photographing: how much workers got paid for picking crops, how much they paid for living in a migratory labor camp, and, more broadly, what had happened in the history of American agriculture from the earliest years of this century to the late 1930s. This was a study, after all, of a nation's fast-changing relationship to its land, of a major shift both in land usage and population: from the old South and the Plains states to California and Arizona, and from small farms or relatively genteel plantations to so-called factory-farms that now utterly dominate our grain and food (and animal) production. A combination of the economic collapse of the 1930s and the disastrous drought of that same time dislodged hundreds of thousands of Americans, some of whom sought jobs in cities, but many of whom embarked on the great trek westward, the last of the major migrations in that direction. For Paul Taylor, such an economic disaster was also a human one,

FIGURE [8]

and he knew how to do justice to both aspects of what was truly a crisis for humble small-farm owners or sharecroppers or tenant farmers or field hands. Taylor wanted to let his fellow citizens know the broader social and economic and historical facts and trends that had culminated in the 1930s "exodus"; Lange wanted us to see both the world being left and the world being sought, and to attend the words of the participants in a tragedy (for some) and an opportunity (for others).

Although these two observers and researchers concentrated on the largely white families that departed the plains because a once enormously fertile expanse had become scorched earth, we are also asked to remember the Delta of the South, parts of Mississippi and Louisiana and Arkansas, and, by implication, the especially burdensome life of blacks, whose situation in the 1930s, even for progressives, was of far less concern than it would become a generation later, in the 1960s. The New Deal, it must be remembered, was very much sustained, politically, by the (white) powers-that-be of the South, and black folk, then, as now, on the very bottom of the ladder, were not even voters. Nevertheless, Lange and Taylor paid them heed, and did so prophetically—took us with them to the cities, to Memphis, to show us another exodus, that of millions of such people from the old rural South to its urban centers, or, more commonly, to those up North.

Also prophetically, these two original-minded social surveyors were at pains to attend what we today call the environment—what happens to the land, the water, that human beings can so cavalierly, so insistently take for granted. In picture after picture, we see not only human erosion—people becoming worn and vulnerable—but the erosion of the American land: farmland devastated by the bad luck of a serious drought, but also by years and years of use that become abuse. It was as if the prodigal land had been deemed beyond injury or misfortune. But suddenly the parched land said no to a people, to a nation, and suddenly the roads that covered that land bore an unprecedented kind of traffic: human travail on the move.

But Lange and Taylor go further, give us more to think about than the tragedy of the dust bowl [having] become a major event in a nation already reeling from the collapse of its entire (manufacturing, banking) economy. Some of the pictures of California (the promised land!) tell us that new misfortunes, even catastrophes would soon enough follow what had taken place in Oklahoma and Texas and Kansas and Nebraska and the Dakotas. The lush Imperial Valley, where thousands came in hope of using their hands, their harvesting savvy, to pick crops and make a living, was already in the 1930s becoming a scene of litter, a place where the land had to bear a different kind of assault than that of a succession of plantings that aren't rotated, aren't planned in advance with consideration of what the earth needs as well as what it can enable. The debris, the junk that covers some of the California terrain was no doubt shown to us by Lange so that we could see how disorganized and bewildered and impoverished these would-be agricultural workers had become, see their down-and-out, even homeless lives: the bare earth all they had in the way of a place to settle, to be as families, at least for a while. Yet today we know how common such sights are across the nation—how those who live under far more comfortable, even affluent circumstances have their own ways of destroying one or another landscape, defacing fields, hills, and valleys that might otherwise be attractive to the eye, an aspect of nature untarnished.

These pictures remind us, yet again, that tragedies have a way of becoming contagious, that one of them can set in motion another, that the temptation to solve a problem quickly (let those people cross the country fast, and find much-needed work fast) can sometimes be costly indeed. There is something ever so desolate about the California of Lange's pictures—even though that state welcomed the people who flocked to it by providing jobs, and the hope that goes with work. Environmental problems to this day plague parts of the western states, problems that have to do with the way both land and water are used. Half a century ago, Lange and Taylor more than hinted at those problems, just as when they followed some of the South's black tenant farmers into the ghettos of a major city, Memphis, they gave us a peek at the urban crisis we would be having in a decade or two.

Also prophetic and important was the manner in which this project was done: informally, unpretentiously, inexpensively, with clear, lucid language and strong, direct, compelling photographs its instruments. For some of us, who still aim to learn from people out there in that so-called field, this particular piece of research stands out as a milestone: it offers us a guiding sense of what was (and presumably still is) possible—direct observation by people interested in learning firsthand from other people, without the mediation of statistics, theory, and endless elaborations of so-called methodology. Here were a man and a woman, a husband and a wife, who drove across our nation with paper, pen, and camera; who had no computers or questionnaires or "coding devices," no tape recorders, or movie cameras, no army of research assistants "trained" to obtain "data." Here were two individuals who would scorn that all-too-commonly upheld tenet of today's social-science research, the claim to be "value-free." They were, rather, a man and a woman of unashamed moral passion, of vigorous and proudly upheld subjectivity, anxious not to quantify or submit what they saw to conceptual assertion but to notice, to see and hear, and in so doing, to feel, then render so that others, too, would know in their hearts as well as their heads what it was that happened at a moment in American history, at a place on the American subcontinent. Here in Lange's photos, finally, the camera came into its own as a means of social and even economic and historical reflection. These pictures, in their powerfully unfolding drama, in their manner of arrangement and presentation and sequencing, in their narrative cogency and fluency, tell us so very much, offer us a gripping sense of where a social tragedy took place and how it shaped the lives of its victims. This is documentary study at its revelatory best—pictures and words joined together in a kind of nurturing interdependence that illustrates the old aphorism that the whole is greater than the sum of its parts.

American Exodus was not only a wonderfully sensitive, compellingly engaging documentary study; it challenged others to follow suit, to do their share in taking the measure, for good and bad, of our nation's twentieth-century fate. Dorothea Lange was an energetic ambitious photographer, but she also was a moral pilgrim of sorts, ever ready to give us a record of human experience that truly matters: our day-to-day struggles as members of a family, of a neighborhood, of a nation to make do, to take on life as best we can, no matter the obstacles we face. And so with Paul Taylor, a social scientist who dared pay a pastoral regard to his ordinary fellow citizens, even as he mobilized a broader kind of inquiry into the forces at work on them and on their nation. We can do no better these days than to look at their book, over half a century after it appeared, not only as an aspect of the past (a remarkable social record, an instance of careful collaborative inquiry), but as a summons to what might be done in the years ahead, what very much needs to be done: a humane and literate kind of social inquiry.

Speaking of such inquiry, Paul Taylor was quick to mention *Let Us Now Praise Famous Men* to Jane and me. He reminded us of Walker Evans's genius for careful, sometimes provocative cropping and editing of particular photographs—his ability to sequence his prints, look at their narrative momentum, and choose particular ones for presentation: the exactly memorable, summoning, kindling moments. Taylor made reference to Evans's photograph in *Let Us Now Praise Famous Men* that introduces one of the tenant farmers, a young man in overalls, his head slightly tilted to his right, his eyes (set in an unshaven face topped by curly hair) confronting the viewer head-on with an almost eerie combination of strength and pride on the one hand, and an unavoidable vulnerability on the other, as so many of us have felt [Fig. 9, p. 233]. That picture, now on the cover of the latest (1988) paperback edition of the book, signals to us the very point of the title, of the entire text as Agee conceived it: an ode to those hitherto unacknowledged, a salute to this man and others like him, this man whose fame has awaited a moral awakening of the kind this book hopes to inspire in us, just as the writer and photographer themselves were stirred from a certain slumber by all they witnessed during that Alabama time of theirs.

In the picture of this "famous man," as with certain of Lange's pictures, the viewer is given no room to wander, to be distracted. This is eye-to-eye engagement, a contrast to other possibilities available to Evans of the same man sitting at the same time in the same position. That farmer's daughter was actually sitting in a chair beside her father; one negative gives us a full-length portrait of him and her both, with the door and part of the side of their house and a portion of the porch also visible [Fig. 10, p. 234]. But Evans is struggling for an interiority, that of his subject and that of his subject's future viewer/visitor: let us not only praise this man, lift him to the ranks of the famous, but consider what might be going on within him, and let us, through the motions of our moral imagination, enter his life, try to understand it, and return with that understanding to our own, which is thereby altered. This is a tall order for a single picture, but then Evans and Agee were ambitious, as evidenced by their constant citation of the inadequacy of their project (vividly restless dreamers fearing the cold light of a morning).

Taylor also wanted us to look at a sequence of Evans's photographs of a tenant's daughter, bonneted, at work picking cotton. We who know the book remember her slouched, bent over the crops [Fig. 11, p. 235]. We don't see her

FIGURE [9]

face, don't really see any of *her;* she *is* her clothes, as if they were perched on an invisible person who is beyond our human approximations, who is of no apparent age or race. She is huddled over the fertile, flowering land to the point where she seems part of it, only barely above it, a lone assertion of our species and, too, a reminder of our incontestable dependence on the surrounding, the

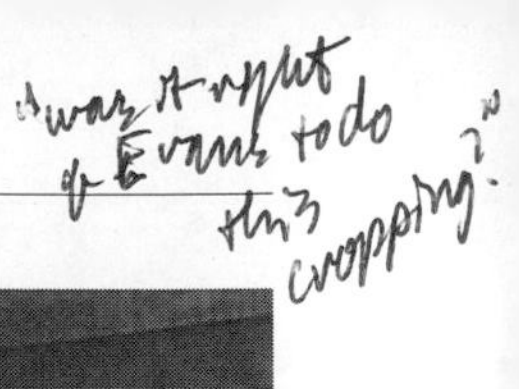

FIGURE [10]

enveloping world of plants and shrubs. Yet, other negatives taken of that same scene at that same time reveal the girl standing upright [Fig. 12, p. 236], looking in profile at the surrounding terrain [Fig. 13, p. 237], or hunched over a part of it that hasn't the abundance of crops that we see in the picture Evans chose to show us [Fig. 14, p. 238]. There is one photograph, taken from above [Fig. 15, p. 239], that shows only the girl's straw hat, immersed in the foliage—an "arty" picture, an "interesting" one, a pretty image. With the circularity of straw (another crop!) imposed, so to speak, on the cotton field, the girl becomes a mere bearer of that hat (only a hump of her is evident).

Evans resists the aesthetic temptations of that last picture and of others in the series; he picks and chooses his way through a narrative sequence that might be titled in various ways: Alabama child labor; a young harvester; a girl at work picking cotton; or, drawing on Rupert Vance's wonderfully literate 1930s work at the University of North Carolina, an instance of a white child's connection to the "cotton culture." A photographer is carving out his own declaration based on his own survey research. He wants us, finally, to face facelessness, to see a child who isn't looking at us or at the nearby terrain (despite the fact that he had pictures of the girl doing both), but whose eyes were watching a row of plants, and whose body, whose very being, seems scarcely above them, tied to them, merging with them.

FIGURE [11]

FIGURE [12]

FIGURE [13]

FIGURE [14]

FIGURE [15]

There is, to be sure, an appealing beauty to the picture Evans selected from this sequence for the book: a graceful curve to the body, an elegance, a consequence of a learned, relaxed capability to pick and pick, as I saw in a migrant worker I once knew, who tried to teach me how to harvest celery. As I watched him look carefully, then make this cut, then the next one with his knife—swiftly, adroitly, with seeming ease and authority and exactitude—I caught myself thinking of his dignity, his full knowledge of a particular scene, while at the same time I worried that I was being a romantic: I was struggling with my own obvious lack of skill by ennobling his hard, tough, ill-paid labor (as, arguably, Orwell did when he went down into those mines in 1936). And so, perhaps, with this picture of Evans: we attempt to contemplate people's strenuous exertions even as we try to rescue them, at least partially, from those exertions. A miner can have his nobility, or be seen in a noble light by an observer, and that migrant can exact from his terribly burdened life moments of great, knowing competence, and this girl whom Evans noticed so painstakingly can also have her times of agility, balance, suppleness, the mystery of a lithe, enshrouded form as it "works on a row." Or are we to think of her only as an example of exploited child labor? When, that is, does our empathy and compassion ironically rob those whom we want so hard to understand of their loveliness, however tough the circumstances of their life? (I recognize the serious dangers, here, of an aesthetic that becomes a moral escape, a shameful avoidance of a grim actuality, a viewer's flight of willful blindness—hence, I think, Evans's refusal to let us dote on that hat, with its "interesting" setting.)

Walker Evans, in his own way, addressed the broader question of documentary expression in a lecture at Yale on March 11, 1964. He was sixty-one then; he had spent a lifetime traveling with his camera, planning and then executing various photographic expeditions. At Yale he said this: "My thought is that the term 'documentary' is inexact, vague, and even grammatically weak, as used to describe a style in photography which happens to be my style. Further, that what I believe is really good in the so-called documentary approach in photography is the addition of lyricism. Further, that the lyric is usually produced unconsciously and even unintentionally and accidentally by the cameraman—and with certain exceptions. Further, that when the photographer presses for the heightened documentary, he more often than not misses it. . . . The real thing that I'm talking about has purity and a certain severity, rigor, simplicity, directness, clarity, and it is without artistic pretension in a self-conscious sense of the word. That's the base of it."

So much there to applaud, especially the descriptive words "inexact" and "vague" and "grammatically weak": the difficulty we have in doing justice to the range and variation of writing and photography and film that a given tradition embraces. The word "documentary" is indeed difficult to pin down; is intended, really, as mentioned earlier, to fill a large space abutted on all sides by more precise and established and powerful traditions: that of journalism or reportage, those of certain academic disciplines (sociology and anthropology in particular), and of late, a well-organized, structured approach to folklore and filmmaking (as opposed to an "unconscious" or "unintentional" or "accidental" approach)—university departments of "film studies" and "folklore studies." Evans's three adjectives are themselves meant to be scattershot, if not "inexact" and "vague"—a means of indicating a style, a manner of approach, or, in his friend Agee's phrase, "a way of seeing," and also a way of doing: the one who attempts documentary work as the willing, even eager beneficiary of luck and chance, the contingent that in a second can open the doors of a craftsman's imaginative life. Academics have their well-defined, carefully established, and ever so highly sanctioned (and supported) routines, procedures, requirements, "methodologies," their set language. Journalists are tied to the news closely or loosely. Nonfiction writing deals with the consideration of ideas and concepts, with ruminations and reflections of importance to a particular writer and his or her readers. Certain photographs follow suit, address *their* ideas and concepts: light, forms, the spatial arrangements of objects—lines, say, rather than lives. In contrast, even the word *documentarian* (never mind the nature of the work done) may be imprecise, hard to pin down, at times misleading—in fact, no "documents" need be gathered in the name of authenticity, in the name of moving from a suspect (to some) "oral history" to a history of affidavits and wills and letters, the older the better. But that is the way it goes—and there are advantages: no deadline of tomorrow for the morning edition, or three or four days for the Sunday one; no doctoral committee to drive one crazy with nit-picking scrutiny of a language already sanitized and watered-down and submitted to the test of departmental politics, a phenomenon that is surely a twentieth-century manifestation of original sin.

Instead, as Evans suggested, the doer of documentary work is out there in this world of five billion people, free (at least by the nature of his or her chosen manner of approach to people, places, events) to buckle down, to try to find a congenial, even inspiring take on things. Evans celebrates a lyricism, and defines aspects of it nicely: a directness and a lack of pretentiousness, a cleanness of presentation that he dares call severe and pure. It is a lyricism, be it noted, that proved worthy (in its expression by Evans) of companionship with Hart Crane's *The Bridge,* a lyricism that in general bridges the observer, the observed, and the third party, as it were, who is the second observer—a lyricism, Dr. Williams would insist, of "things," a broad rubric for him that included human beings, and a rubric meant to exclude only the rarefied, the insistently abstract. The document in mind (mind you) can for a while be hungrily, ecstatically abstract—the dreaming, the planning, the thinking out of a project—but down the line, somehow, in some way, we have to get to "the thing itself."

Here is Evans being ambitiously abstract, as well as impressively industrious, aspiring, enterprising: "Projects: New York Society in the 1930s. 1. national groups 2. types of the time (b. and wh.) 3. children in streets 4. chalk drawings 5. air views of the city 6. subway 7. ship reporter (this project get police cards)." He continues, "the art audience at galleries, people at bars, set of movie ticket takers, set of newsstand dealers, set of shop windows, the props of upper class set, public schools faces and life." Those notes were, appropriately enough, scribbled on the reverse side of a Bank of Manhattan blank check in New York City during 1934–35. Another series of notes: "the trades, the backyards of N.Y., Harlem, bartenders, interiors of all sorts—to be filed and classified." A letter to Roy Stryker of the FSA in 1934: "Still photography, of general sociological nature." The point was to dream, to wander from topic to topic, and then, finally, to find the specific place and time, so that the eyes were free to follow the reasons of heart and mind both: a lyrical sociology; a journalism of the muse; a dramatic storytelling adventure that attends a scene in order to capture its evident life, probe its secrets, and turn it over as whole and complicated and concrete and elusive as it is has been found to those of us who care to be interested.

In a handsomely generous and affecting tribute to his colleague, his friend, his soulmate, James Agee, written in 1960 for a fresh edition of *Let Us Now Praise Famous Men,* Evans describes James Agee in 1936 as one who "worked in what looked like a rush and a rage." He also refers, in that vein, to Agee's "resolute, private rebellion." I do not think Evans himself was immune to this virus—an utter impatience with, even outrage at a sometimes stuffy and often callous world. As I read Evans or Agee I think of a motley assortment of others who fit in to this odd, cranky crowd—Studs Terkel and Oscar Lewis and George Orwell and Dorothea Lange and Paul Taylor, to name again some whom I've been calling in witness. Once, as I tried to get down to the specifics, a documentary mind preparing for a task, I remembered Evans's comments on what he hoped to do on, of all places, New York City's subways:

> The choice of the subway as locale for these pictures was arrived at not simply because of any particular atmosphere or background having to do with the subway in itself—but because that is where the people of the city range themselves at all hours under the most constant conditions for the work in mind. The work does not care to be "Life in the Subway" and obviously does not "cover" that subject.
>
> These people are everybody. These pictures have been selected and arranged, of course, but the total result of the lineup has claim to some kind of chance-average.
>
> The gallery page is a lottery, that is, the selection that falls there is determined by no *parti pris* such as, say, "I hate women," or "women are dressed foolishly," or "———." It *is* an arrangement, of course, as is the rest of the book, but the forces determining it have to do not only with such considerations as page composition, tone of picture, inferential interest of picture or face in itself.
>
> Speculations from such a page of sixteen women's faces and hats remains then an open matter, the loose privilege of the reader, and

whoever chooses to decide from it that people are wonderful or that what America needs is a political revolution is at liberty to do so.

There he is, difficult and ungovernable for others, for his viewers and readers even, prepared to make substantial, maybe overwhelming demands on them. He'll have no truck with the most inviting and, alas, the most banal of titles for his work, even though one suspects that the abstraction "Life in the Subway" crossed his mind more than once as he thought about what he intended to do, its rationale, never mind its locale. He distances himself from all that is implied by the verb "cover," lest he be charged with the sin of inclusiveness, let alone that of a devouring topicality—as in a report or story that "covers" an issue by covering it with all sorts of facts, figures, opinions. Phrases like "chance-average" and "loose privilege" tell of the writer's venerable experience with both our language and this century's toll on our values. Who in the world today will settle for such informality, such a casual and relaxed attitude toward what is (or is not) an *average,* or a *privilege?* "Chance" and "loose" bespeak sipping whiskey in an armchair, with one of the big bands, Tommy Dorsey, maybe, playing "Whispering": a time before computer printouts arrived, or cocksure polls that have a plus or minus accuracy of—God knows what number. As for his concluding challenge (to himself, to all of us), it is one that laughs at ideology, that announces a sensibility contemptuous of singular interpretations, and that gives all of us splendid leeway to do as we damn please in what is volunteered unashamedly as an earnest, persistent, highly personal "visit" with some folks traveling underground.

There is evident discomfort in Evans's message, meant for himself above all; it never appeared in the foreword to the book showing his subway pictures. He wanted to define himself and his pictures so that they were not considered photojournalism, or part of yet another attempt to survey people or expose some (detrimental, damaging) aspect of their life. He was *there,* looking at men and women and children on their hurried way someplace. As the trains roared and sped, he presumably tried to catch hold of himself and others—literally as well as figuratively, a still moment in a quickly shifting scene of entrances and exits, a passing parade of technological and human activity. "I was pretty sure then, yes. I was sure that I was working in the documentary style. Yes, and I was doing social history, broadly speaking"—a cautious embrace at a point in a life's spectrum. But Evans would always qualify, circle around a purported professional location for himself, rather than hone in, dig in, *declare* without reservation. Here he is in a splendidly qualified and edifying further approach: "When you say 'documentary,' you have to have a sophisticated ear to receive that word. It should be documentary style, because documentary is police photography of a scene and a murder . . . that's a real document. You see, art is really useless, and a document has use. And therefore, art is never a document, but it can adopt that style. I do it. I'm called a documentary photographer. But that presupposes a quite subtle knowledge of this distinction."

A struggle there—to grasp, to adopt a style while reserving the artist's right of freedom to roam and select as he wishes. Others (in no way is this matter hierarchical) have their important and necessary obligations (the police photographer and, by extension, a host of people who work for or have joined a variety of institutions: newspapers, magazines, schools, universities). Evans's documentarian draws, in spirit, upon the earthy practicality of a police photographer, and also on the social and political indifference of an artist who, at a certain moment, has to be rid of all ideologies, even those he otherwise finds attractive, lest he become someone's parrot. The "style" he mentions here and elsewhere is nothing superficial; it refers to the connection an artist wants to have with, again, "human actuality," be it that of a police station, a subway, Alabama tenant farmers, Havana's 1930s street life—wherever it is that a Walker Evans imagines himself being, or ends up visiting. The rock-bottom issue is not only one's stated attitude toward "art" in general, but one's sense of oneself.

Once in a discussion at Dartmouth College in the 1970s, Evans took offense at questioners who wanted to know the mechanical details of his work, the kind of camera he used, and, beyond that, the way he developed and printed his photographs. He pointed out that what mattered to him was his intelligence, his taste, and his struggle for what such words imply and convey. Other photographers might have been eager to reply to such inquiries, men and women who are vitally interested in the technological possibilities of the machines they own and use, and who can get from them certain "effects": light or shadows amplified; appearances given new shape; the distortions, the "play" available to skilled men and women who, like Evans, are trying to be artists, photographic artists, but not artists and photographers in the "documentary style" or tradition, for which reality, however shaped and edited and narrated, has in some way to be an initial given. Hence the apprehension, the sorting of that reality in what Evans acknowledged to be a sociological manner, and hence his constantly moving presence in accordance with the demands of such a reality rather than those of a technological artistry, which certainly doesn't need central Alabama or the New York City subway for its expression, an artistry that can even confine itself to one room where the light arrives, moves about, and departs, all the while touching, in various ways, objects, human or inanimate.

William Carlos Williams was among Evans's admirers; he followed his work closely, wrote about it. He struggled, as Evans did, to be almost austere at times in his dispassionate insistence upon seeing many sides to whatever scene he was exploring—even as his big and generous heart could not help but press upon him as he sat at the typewriter, hence his gruff, tough moments followed by his fiery, exclamatory ones. In *Paterson* he struggled in that respect, struggled for a stance: the detached spectator, the informed but reserved onlooker as against the spy, the voyeur (and Evans, along with Agee, uses such imagery to indicate that side of himself: someone who has a lot at stake in what he's trying to do). Like Evans, Williams tried to come to grips with that word *documentary,* and made no bones about his belief that location and time mattered enormously: where one chose to stay and for how long, but also (he kept saying so in dozens of places and ways) the "language—and how it is used," by which he more broadly meant the relation of the watcher to the watched, of the one listening to those who fill his ears with words.

Williams was forever exploring in his mind the nature of a writer's, a photographer's, a filmmaker's dealings with those being called to what he once suggestively described as a "tentative alliance," one that might "fall apart at any minute." I asked for an explanation of that imagery (aware that in 1953, the Second World War and all the horror that preceded it, the pacts and agreements, the duplicities and betrayals, were still very much on his mind), and he was not loath to give it a try:

> When you're a doctor seeing a patient you're there by permission: the two of you have an agreement (or if it's a kid, the parents have signed you up, and the kid knows it). You can poke around; no other person in the world can poke around like that. You look and you listen and you poke some more, then you talk to yourself, you remember what you know and you compare notes with what you've seen in other patients (this silent talking, this recalling), and then you've made up your mind, so you start talking. Now, you're telling someone something, rather than asking; you're giving advice—orders, really. But the whole thing [the relationship] is based on that agreement: you can explore this body of mine, and you can ask me any damn thing you want, because that's who you are, a doctor, and that's who I am, a patient.
>
> Now, when I'm walking down the street there [in Paterson, where many of his patients lived] I'm trying to do another kind of "examination"—I'm still poking around, but I'm not doing it under the same terms. I'm hoping people will give me some access—talk with me and help me figure out what's going on around here [we were in Paterson]. I'm trying to look and listen, just as I do with the sick kids I see and their parents. I'm sizing up a place, a whole city, you could say: what is OK, what's working fine, and what's no good, and what "stinks out loud." A guy I know, I'll be standing there in the drugstore with him, and he's telling me "This positively stinks out loud," and I want to hear more. I'm excited, hearing him sound like he's Jeremiah's direct-line descendent. He can't do much more than sign his name. He has trouble reading the newspaper. He has to work to figure out those headlines. It's the radio that tells him everything. He hunkers down with it. He calls it his "friend" sometimes; [and] once I heard him call it his "source." Source of what, I wanted to know. "Everything," that's how specific he could get! "What, for instance?" I asked, and he said, "The Guiding Light," and "Vic and Sade" [two soap operas], and then he said "the local news," he keeps up with it, and if he had another life, he'd like to be a "radio

> guy," he called it—he meant an announcer, the one who gives people the news. Then, he said: "Only I'd like to go see what's happening out there, and I'd know the people, I'd really know them, before I'd say anything about them. If you talk about people on radio, you should know them, otherwise it's not fair!"
>
> I couldn't get him, what he said, out of my mind for a while. Days later, I'd think of him. It's not so easy to know people! I guess he'd find that out; he's ready to go try, in another life, if he could have it. But when I try to get him going more, about his own life, there's only so far he'll walk with me—and why should he? If you start thinking of yourself as a doctor examining a city, a diagnostician walking the streets, looking for people who can talk to you openly enough, so you can figure out what the illnesses are, the social illnesses, and what's "healthy" about it all—then you've got to *work* to get people to "sign up," to give you the trust you need for them to level with you, really level. Otherwise, you've got formality; you've got off-the-top-of-my-head stuff; you've got a quickie news story on that guy's radio, or the headline he struggles to make out. I feel like saying to him: save your energy, forget the damn headline and keep listening to that radio, if you can find something good on it, a big "if."

I've long felt that such "top-of-the head" ruminations, testy and splenetic, sometimes plaintive (if only it could be easier to learn what Williams so much wanted to learn about the "local pride" that was Paterson!) are themselves texts on documentary work for us to contemplate. Williams was anxious to connect his own thoughts to those of others, to let so-called ordinary people become his teachers, just as his patients all the time taught him. His profound distrust of all aestheticism ("The rest now run out after the rabbits") was prompted by his intuition that solipsistic art was not a suitable haven. He simply wasn't able to be indifferent to social reality in the ways that some of his poet friends found quite congenial. He knew the difficulties of apprehending that social reality, and, too, of finding the right words, the rhythms, the beat that would make his music somehow worthy of the music his ears picked up in Paterson: street music, tenement tunes, soul music and jazz and polkas and the tango and country music. He was always talking about the "American vein," which he tried to tap throughout his writing life—and to do so, he didn't only sit in his study and muse (though he wasn't at all averse to that kind of exploration). "Good luck to those who can keep their distance from the howl, the yell of things," he once said. Later, I'd wonder whether, by chewing out those writing colleagues every once in a while, he wasn't trying to exorcise his envy. But in the end he was who he was, and he more than settled for that existential fact. He built up, he wrote a *Paterson* that whispered and shouted, in good faith, stories of the chaste and bawdy Paterson, his witness to that city and its engagement with generations of needy seekers of all sorts: the words of honor spoken; the covenants abandoned; the people sold down the river; the victories won and lost; the folks who earned good dough, got a leg up; the folks who fell by the wayside. He gave us a chronicle, of course, but also a call to arms—and for him, the war was a struggle, against substantial odds, for a consciousness that isn't blunted and warped by the thousands of deceptions everywhere around. His version of Evans's "documentary style" was a vernacular not showily summoned out of a craving for distinction, but earned in the daily and various rounds of his several working lives (the doctor, the social observer, the historian and chronicler of the nearby, the poet and novelist and essayist, the painter even) whose simultaneity was a constant source of amazement to any of us lucky enough to catch sight of it all.

A precise definition is probably the last thing Walker Evans or William Carlos Williams would suggest for us today who want to consider, yet again, the nature of documentary work. Those two large spirits were unruly enough to scoff at the fantasy of control that informs a pretentiousness which won't allow for indefiniteness—that last word, for the documentarian, a necessity: the arm and leg room of exploration that has to take place, once one heeds the call, the refrain of "outside/outside myself/there is a world to explore," and the further instrumental refrain of "no ideas but in things." The one time I got Dr. Williams to consider the specific subject of "documentary research" or "documentary fieldwork," he laughed, and echoed Evans's wary refusal to get pinned down. He was more curt and gruff than, I suspect, Evans had ever desired to be, and so he dismissed the word documentary, in a way, by asking a rhetorical question, mimicking those who love to give themselves names, the more the better: "Would you want me to tell folks out there that I'm a documentary poet—and are you doing some documentary child psychiatry, now that you're visiting homes of people who haven't got the slightest interest in taking their kids to a clinic, and they don't need to?" He then laughed, to break the tension partially created by his remark, but also initiated by my floundering perplexity, and offered this, in a more gentle mode: "Lots of streets to walk, lots of ways to walk them"—a brief whistle, meant to signal the virtue of an elusive melody as about the best he could do.

To take Dr. Williams's hint, to remember the words of an Apocrypha rescued for our American century's time by James Agee and Walker Evans, let us praise the many "famous people" we can get to meet as we pursue a "documentary style," rather than keep trying to spell out authoritatively various essential characteristics; let the doing be a big part of the defining. Let us, that is, recount and depict, and thereby embody what we're aiming to do and, yes, to be. Let us think of those observers of their fellow human beings who have tried to hug hard what they also know can suddenly escape them, to their apprehending peril. Dr. Williams: "I'll be standing at the store counter talking to that loud-mouthed pest who is trying to con me into buying something stupid that I'll never need, and I should be enjoying the fun of hearing him out—what a *line!*—but instead I demolish him in my mind with *ideas,* ethnic and sociological and psychological, and pretty soon it's no fun for me, or for him either. I've forgotten him; he's disappeared under the withering fire of my clever thinking. I've left him for another ball game!"

To be less exhortative, more declarative, they are of many "sorts and conditions," documentarians (if that is what they want to be called—and we oughtn't be surprised if lots of people decline, say no to that word, maybe any word, any combination of words: "not the letter, but the spirit"). I think of writers or photographers or filmmakers, of musicologists who spend their time enraptured up Appalachian hollows or in Mississippi's Delta, of folklorists (Zora Neale Hurston was one) crazy for wonderfully wild stories told in odd and loony ways. I think of documentary work that is investigative or reportorial; that is muckraking; that is appreciative or fault-finding; that is pastoral or contemplative; that is prophetic or admonitory; that reaches for humor and irony, or is glad to be strictly deadpan and factually exuberant; that knows exactly where it is going and aims to take the rest of us along, or wants only to make an impression—with each of us defining its nature or intent. In a way, Orwell, in *Wigan Pier,* showed us the range of possibilities as he documented the life of the Brookers (and blasted them sky-high) and documented the life of certain miners (and put them on a tall pedestal), and, in between, wondered about the rest of us, himself and his buddies included: wondered about the way a study of others comes home to roost. In a way, as well, Williams was being more enlightening and helpful than a young listener of his comprehended when he jokingly referred to the documentary side of his prowling, roaming New Jersey patrol, and when he posed for me a consideration of how a clinician ought to think of the documentary work he is trying to do—home and school visits in which he talks with children who are of interest not because they have medical "problems," but because they are part of one or another larger (social or racial or national or economic) "problem." Journalists cover those children in their way; a documentarian will need to put in more time, and have a perspective at once broader and more detailed, one that is, maybe, a follow-up to the first, difficult, sometimes brave (and costly) forays of journalists.

How well, in that regard, I recall conversations with Ralph McGill of the Atlanta *Constitution* during the early years of the civil-rights struggle (1961–63). He had no small interest in the fate of the nine black students who initiated (high school) desegregation in Georgia's capital city during the autumn of 1961, even as my wife, Jane, and I were getting to know those black youths and their white classmates (Atlanta had managed to prevent the kind of riots that had plagued other Southern cities, such as Little Rock and New Orleans). The three of us would meet and talk, and from him, through his great storytelling generosity, Jane and I learned so very much. Often we discussed what Mr. McGill referred to as "the limits of journalism." He would remind us that "news" is the "commodity" his reporters go everywhere to pursue, their words worked into the "product" that gets sold on the streets and delivered to stores and homes. But those reporters (and photojournalists) are also great documentary teachers and scholars: they know so very well how to go meet people, talk with them, take pictures of them, right away take their measure, decide when and how to go further, look for others to question. They know how to make those utterly necessary first steps (find contacts, use them) that the rest of us can be slow in realizing will make all the difference in whether a particular project will unfold. They know, many of them, and they know well, how to pose the toughest, most demanding and scrutinizing questions, at times utterly necessary questions, and ones that naïfs such as I have certainly shirked entertaining, let alone asking. "How did you learn to do your work?" students ask me all the time. I reply: from the great reporters I was lucky to meet and observe, from Pat Watters of the Atlanta *Journal,* from Claude Sitton, the Southern correspondent of the *New York Times,* from the ubiquitous and sometimes riotous Maggie Long, who edited the *New South,* but called herself "an old newspaper hand," and from Dorothy Day, who edited the *Catholic Worker* when I first met her, but who had worked on journalistic assignments for newspapers for years (in the 1920s) before she turned her life so radically around upon her conversion to Catholicism, and who, as she often reminded us, was the daughter of a newspaperman and the sister of two of them.

Yet, as Mr. McGill sadly had to aver: "At a certain point we have to stop"—meaning that a documentary inquiry ends, in favor of the requirements of another documentary initiative. It is then, he explained, that "the magazine boys take over"—his way of referring to the greater amount of space magazines allow, but also, of course, to the more leisurely way of exercising Evans's "documentary style." We never got into specifics, but because of his comparison, I began to think of the essays I read in various magazines (including those published by newspapers) in a different way: began to see the relative degree to which the author turns to people other than himself or herself as fellow bearers of a story's burden, and the degree, as well, to which such people are allowed (encouraged) to teach us by giving of themselves. Today, I think of Truman Capote's *In Cold Blood,* of Ian Frazier's pieces, short and long, of Alec Wilkinson's efforts with migrants in Florida, of his remarkable *A Violent Act;* and I remember *The New Yorker* of William Shawn as very much, at times, given to a "documentary style." Among photographers we can go back to Matthew Brady and the devastation of war that he made a lasting part of our knowledge, if we care to remember; to Lewis Hine and those children through whose condition he aroused our moral sensibility (again, if we care to take notice); to, of course, the FSA men and women; and today, Wendy Ewald, with her many brilliantly ingenious, spiritual explorations of childhood, aided by the children to whom she gives cameras, and whose photographs and words she shares with us. Photographers Alex Harris and Eugene Richards and Susan Meiselas and Gilles Peress and Danny Lyon and Robert Frank and Thomas Roma and Helen Levitt and Lee Friedlander; filmmakers Robert Flaherty and Pare Lorentz and Fred Wiseman and Robert Young and Michael Roemer and Ken Burns and Buddy Squires—all of these men and women are deservedly famous in the way Agee and Evans meant to signify for their Alabama teachers, known to the world as tenant farmers: humble by various criteria, but learned in ways any documentary tradition worth its name would aim to detail, to corroborate.

At a certain point in his research on Gandhi's life, Erik H. Erikson became dissatisfied. He had read many books and had spent a long time talking with a variety of scholars, historians, and political scientists, not to mention his psychoanalytic colleagues. He had obtained access to various library collections; he had attended a number of conferences; he had reviewed, courtesy of microfilm, journalistic accounts of Gandhi's various deeds and evaluations of the significance of his life. Nevertheless, this would-be biographer felt himself at an impasse. Why? I had no answer, despite the fact that I was teaching in his course then, helping him run a seminar, and trying to write about him, even as he was "struggling" with Gandhi (the phrase he often used)—almost as if the two were personally at odds, I sometimes thought.

We are sitting in Erikson's Widener study and I am interested, at the moment, in his work on Luther (my favorite of all his writings). He doesn't want to talk about that; he wants to talk about Gandhi's moral virtues, and, just as important, his flaws, if not vices: "I don't know whether I can proceed without in some way having it out with him [Gandhi]—how he fasted so honorably, risked his life for a just and merciful and fair political settlement, how he developed a decent and civilized manner of protest [nonviolence], and yet how he behaved as a husband and a father." Eventually, Erikson would write his well-known "letter," a breakthrough moment both in *Gandhi's Truth* and in psychoanalytic and historical thinking generally: a direct confrontation, a "having it out" with the spirit (the psychological "remains") of a figure who has left the living yet will endure through the ages. I listen, nod, try to steer us back to the fifteenth century, to *Luther*'s contradictions—it is, after all, *my* interview that are we are conducting! Few of my attempted subtleties miss my teacher's notice. Why am I now so interested in *Luther?* Well, Erik, why are *you* now so interested in Gandhi? That is the "line" of our reasoning together: mutual irritation expressed through a reductionist assault, by implication, on one another's motives, all under the dubious protection our shared profession provides. Finally, Erikson tells me, in annoyance at someone *else,* what he'd recently heard said by a distinguished cultural critic (and political philosopher)—that his *Young Man Luther* was a "marvelous novel"! I am taken aback; I keep silent; I worry about what my face wants to do, smile; I worry about what my voice wants to say (that such words are a high compliment), for I feel sure he wouldn't agree. He can sense, though, that I don't share his apparent chagrin. He puts this to me: "What do *you* think?" Lord, *that* question, the endlessly recurrent one of the late-twentieth-century, psychoanalyzed American *haute bourgeoisie!* I gulp. I feel my lips holding on tight to one another. I feel the inquiring openness of those wide blue eyes of this almost awesome figure. I find myself glancing at that shock of white hair flowing backward. I plunge: "Erik, it's a high compliment." I pause. I know I need to amplify, but I'm not prepared to, I'm afraid to. I settle for two more words, "the highest." He stares back at me. His face is immobile. I plead silently for the descent of compassionate understanding upon both of us. Continued silence; seconds become hours. I'm ready to speak, though I don't really know what I'll say—a dangerous situation, people like Erikson and me have long known: random conversational thoughts are a grist for an all-too-familiar (these days) mill, a gradual presentation by the unconscious of various unsettling thoughts.

But suddenly, amid a still persisting silence, the great one's face yields a broad smile. I immediately return it without having any prior thought that I should or would. He ribs me: "I know why you said that." I then pour out my explanation: that "novel" is not a pejorative word, certainly. I then make a statement about the revelatory nature of stories, not unlike the one I have tried to write here and elsewhere. I remind him that no one can know for *sure* what "young man Luther" thought and felt; that his story has to do with speculations, with informed guesses as well as facts, all told persuasively if not convincingly; that imagination is at work in such an effort; and that sometimes, in those "gray areas" or moments, the imagination appeals to or invokes the imaginary—a Luther who becomes more in a writer's mind than he can possibly be with respect to anyone's records, recollections, or reports. I tell him about a question I once heard William Shawn ask of an about-to-be *New Yorker* writer: how would you like us to present this piece? What did Shawn mean? As a factual piece, a profile, or a short story? But, the writer said, it's about someone who was real, who lived! Yes, it certainly is, the distinguished, knowing editor acknowledges, but he could imagine it being presented, with a few narrative changes, as a *story,* with that "someone" as a character in it. Erikson now goes beyond smiles; he laughs heartily and tells me that I seem to be "enjoying all this," and he goes further: "Now, you see why I want to go to India and interview those people who knew Gandhi and worked with him! You see why I want you to show me how you use your tape recorder!"

He stops; it is my turn to laugh. I tell him he'll become a "field worker." He gets irritated, and justifiably so; he reminds me of his expeditions to Indian reservations (the Sioux, the Yurok) in the 1930s and 1940s, trips I well know to have been brave and resourceful (and, yes, imaginative) actions, given the prevailing psychoanalytic orthodoxy then settling in on his generation in the United States. I apologize. He tells me he isn't asking that of me; he wants us, rather, to discuss the nature of those trips, of his forthcoming "visit" to the Indian subcontinent. I call them, cautiously (following his lead), "field trips." He wonders about the adjectival addition of "anthropological." I demur. I say that these days any conversation with a child or adult on one of our Indian reservations gets connected to the discipline of anthropology—an outcome that needs its own kind of historical inquiry, because conversations by Erikson or anyone else (who isn't an anthropologist) in this country ought not be so reflexively regarded. We sit quietly thinking—one of the joys, always, with him: a capacity, a willingness to put aside mere chatter, to endure those lulls which, after all, sometimes fall for a good reason. Finally, he smiles, asks me this: "What would your friend Agee call those 'trips'—or the one I'm going on?"

I have been teaching Agee in my weekly section of Erikson's course, and I have introduced the professor to some of the more compelling passages of *Let Us Now Praise Famous Men.* I smile; we banter. I observe that I don't know what Agee would say, because he's so hard to pin down on such matters, even in connection with his own Alabama trip, but Erikson asks me to surmise. I reply that whatever Agee would say, it would be long, constantly modified, and perhaps hard to fathom without a good deal of effort. Erikson laughs, and tells me that I need to learn to "speak on behalf of Agee," whom I admire and whose values and work and thoughts interest me. No way, I say.

Now I feel him headed toward his own research, toward our earlier discussion, and we get there with the help of his jesting self-criticism, meant also to put more bluntly on the record a perception of mine, maybe even a felt criticism of mine with respect to his work: "You don't seem to want to do with Agee what I may do with Gandhi, and did with Luther: try to figure out what was more or less likely to have happened in someone's life, and then say it—with the knowledge on your part, and [on that of] your readers, that we're not talking about letters or diaries or conversations recalled by someone, but that it's someone today doing the best he can with what *is* available." I think and think, let his words sink in. I take a stab: I say yes, maybe so. But then I try to embrace what I've hitherto kept at arm's length. I use the word *documentary,* and say that in the 1930s that word had a common usage among certain photographers and filmmakers, including Agee's friend Walker Evans. Perhaps, I suggest, Agee, were he to be "sent back" here by his Maker, might oblige us with that word—might allow Erikson's search for a firsthand *documentary* exposure to Indians here, and now Indians abroad, in the hope that what he saw and heard and then described would, in sum, be informative.

He likes the word *documentary.* I've seen him savor English words before, he who spoke German as his native language for over two decades, and who learned to speak such excellent English and write a beautifully flowing, even graceful and spirited English prose. He looks the word up in his much-used Oxford dictionary. I tell him that a dictionary "doesn't always help." Quickly he replies, "What does?" I'm slow in replying: "A word can gradually emerge in its meaning—can fill a gap." "What gap?" We're on to an extended discussion now, one that anticipates by a long three decades these lectures, this book. We speak, especially, about "seeing for oneself," as he keeps putting it—the importance of "making a record that you the writer can believe, before you ask someone else to believe it." I remember that way of saying it, will keep going back to those words, will regard them as helpful, as greatly "clarifying" (a word Erik loved to use): the documentary tradition as a continually developing "record" that is made in so many ways, with different voices and visions, intents and concerns, and with each contributor, finally, needing to meet a personal test, the hurdle of *you,* the would-be narrator, trying to ascertain what you truly believe *is,* though needing to do so with an awareness of the confines of your particular capability—that is, of your warts and wants, your various limits, and, too, the limits imposed upon you by the world around you, the time allotted you (and the historical time fate has given you) for your life to unfold.

When Erikson returned from that voyage to India, he was full of new energy, excited by what he'd been told, what he'd witnessed. He loved being back in his Widener study, but as often happens to us when we have gone on a long and important and memorable journey, he was finding it hard to "settle down." He was full of memories of what he'd experienced; he was trying to do justice to those memories; and he was recounting them, fitting them into a narrative, one the rest of us would soon read; he was speaking of his "colleagues," now not professors in a big-shot university, but rather hitherto (for him) nameless, faceless fellow human beings who would soon become (for us readers) developed characters with something to put on "record." He was, indeed, doing documentary work. And so it goes, then—doing documentary work is a journey, and is a little more, too, a passage across boundaries (disciplines, occupational constraints, definitions, conventions all too influentially closed for traffic), a passage that can become a quest, even a pilgrimage, a movement toward the sacred truth enshrined not only on tablets of stone, but in the living hearts of those others whom we can hear, see, and get to understand. Thereby, we hope to be confirmed in our own humanity—the creature on this earth whose very nature it is to make just that kind of connection with others during the brief stay we are permitted here.

• • • • • • • • • • • •

QUESTIONS FOR A SECOND READING

1. Early in his essay, Coles refers to his students' discussions of documentary work. His students, he says, "emphasize the 'actuality' of the work—its responsibility to fact." They think of documentaries as "the familiar alternative of fiction, as though we were dealing in clear-cut opposites: if not the true as against the false, at least the real as against the imaginary" (p. 212). Coles says that such opposites don't "do justice" to what writers, photographers, and other documentary artists do when they work with "people's words, their music, gestures, movements, and overall appearance" to represent to others what they have seen, heard, and learned.

   So—what *is* the nature of documentary work? What *are* the issues, subtle rather than clear-cut, at the center of Coles's thinking? The essay could be said to be organized in five sections, each thinking through a different example: in the first, Coles talks about his own life and work, the second discusses the work of Dorothea Lange and Paul S. Taylor, the third the work of Walker

Evans and James Agee, the fourth tells a story about the physician-poet William Carlos Williams, and the fifth a story about psychologist Erik Erikson. As you reread, stop at the end of each section to write notes on what you think it is "about." What is Coles saying about documentary work? What are the issues? When you get to the end, stop to write briefly on the progression of the essay. What is its train of thought? its beginning, middle, and end?

2. Coles offers three interesting examples of artists cropping or choosing photographic images of working class life (the couple in the car, the father and daughter on the porch, the girl picking cotton). Go back to those images and the discussions around them. Be sure that you can represent the argument Coles is making about Lange or Evans and the choices they made in producing or selecting a final image. Then take time to think about alternative arguments. (Coles provides one example in his father's response to "Ditched, Stalled, and Stranded.") How might you argue for one of the discarded images? or against the close-up view? You should think that the choices made by these artists are at least potentially controversial. What are the issues? What is at stake?
3. Coles says that "in shaping an article or a book, the writer can add factors and variables in two directions: social and cultural and historical on the one hand, individual or idiosyncratic on the other" (p. 212). As you reread, see where and how this distinction is stated or implied in Coles's discussions of the various artists or projects he treats in the essay. What examples does he provide of work that is social/cultural/historical and what examples does he provide of work that is individual/idiosyncratic? And where does Coles stand on these two directions? Which does he prefer or promote? and on what grounds?
4. Coles's essay assumes some knowledge of Dorothea Lange, Walker Evans, and James Agee. One way to work on the essay, then, would be to read the excerpts from Lange and Taylor's *American Exodus* or Agee and Evans's *Let Us Now Praise Famous Men*. You could also look for other works by or on these figures. One strategy for rereading would be to reread Coles once you have a better understanding of the materials he works with. This allows you a better sense of *his* agenda and point of view, the shaping force of his imagination.

ASSIGNMENTS FOR WRITING

1. One of the striking things about Coles's essay is the way it expands the range of what might be considered "documentary work." There is nothing unusual in thinking about Lange, Evans, and Agee; it is striking, however, to think about them in relation to Coles's work as a child psychiatrist and to think, then, about William Carlos Williams and Erik Erikson. This essay brings together a range of materials in order to think about a common issue. What is the issue? How does Coles think about it by using and arranging these materials? Where does he come out at the end?

   Write an essay in which you represent this aspect of Coles's work as a writer in "The Tradition: Fact and Fiction." You will need to chart and summarize what he says. You will also need to think about how he does what he does. You could imagine that you are writing a review or writing a piece for a writing textbook or guidebook, one that wants to use Coles's essay as an example of how essays and essayists do their work.

2. It is possible to take Coles's essay as an invitation to do documentary work. The works he cites represent long-term projects and great commitments of time, energy, and spirit. One of the pleasures of being a student, however, is that you have the authority to try things out provisionally, tentatively, and on a smaller scale.

   This assignment has two parts. For the first part, create a written documentary in which you represent some aspect of another person or, to use the language of the essay, in which you are in pursuit of a moment of "human actuality." The text you create can include photographs, interviews, observation—whatever is available. The point is for you to feel what it is like to be responsible, as a writer, for representing someone else, his or her thoughts, words, and actions. To those who do it for a living, this is a deep and deeply fraught responsibility.

   Once you have completed your documentary (and perhaps once it has been read and evaluated by others), write a separate essay in which you use your work as a way of thinking back on and responding to Coles. Where and how, for example, did you serve as a "filter"? Where and how did you shape that material? What decisions did you have to make concerning foreground and background, the individual and idiosyncratic, or the social, cultural, and historical? What work would you need to do if you were to go back to this project and do an even better job with it? You could imagine this as a letter to Coles, a review of his book, or as a plan for future work of your own, perhaps the work of revising the documentary you have begun.

3. This assignment draws on the project outlined in the second of the "Questions for a Second Reading." Coles offers three examples of artists cropping or choosing photographic images of working class life (the couple in the car, the father and daughter on the porch, the girl picking cotton). These are relatively brief discussions, however, and these discussions do not engage with alternative points of view.

   Write an essay in which you begin with Coles's account of the images, summarizing what he says for someone who has not read the essay or who read it a while ago and won't take time to pick it up again. You will need to represent the photographs, their history, and the points that Coles is making. Then, you will need to engage and extend the discussion. Coles, for example, seems to take for granted that the decisions the artists made were good decisions. Were they? What is at stake in choosing one photograph over another or in cropping the image to remove context and to focus in on the individual face? What was at stake for Coles?

   And where and how might you enter this discussion? There should, in other words, be sections of your essay where you are speaking for Coles (and for Evans and Lange); there should also, however, be extended sections where you speak, thinking about the examples and engaging the issues raised by others.

4. "The Tradition: Fact and Fiction" is a chapter in Coles's book *Doing Documen-*

tary Work (1997). The final chapter in the book presents materials from courses he and his colleagues have taught at Duke University's Center for Documentary Studies. Here is a brief selection of books and films used in their courses (his book has a full account):

James Agee and Walker Evans, *Let Us Now Praise Famous Men* (1941)
Sherwood Anderson, *Home Town* (1940)
John Berger, *A Seventh Man: Migrant Workers in Europe* (1975)
Debbie Fleming Caffery, *Carry Me Home* (1990)
Bruce Chatwin, *In Patagonia* (1977)
Anton Chekhov, *The Island: A Journey to Sakhalin* (1895)
W. E. B. Du Bois, *The Philadelphia Negro* (1899)
George Eliot, *Scenes of Clerical Life* (1857)
Martín Espada, *City of Coughing and Dead Radiators* (1993)
Robert Flaherty, *Nanook of the North* (film) (1922)
Lee Freidlander, *The Jazz People of New Orleans* (1992)
Zora Neale Hurston, *Dust Tracks on a Road* (1942)
Dorothea Lange and Paul S. Taylor, *American Exodus* (1941)
Oscar Lewis, *The Children of Sanchez* (1961)
Henry Mayhew, *London Labour and the London Poor* (1851)
George Orwell, *The Road to Wigan Pier* (1958)
Studs Terkel, *Working* (1975)
William Carlos Williams, *Paterson* (1946)
Frederick Wiseman, *Titicut Follies* (film) (1967); *High School* (film) (1968); *Blind* (film) (1986); *Deaf* (film) (1986)

Choose one of these to use as the basis for an essay in which you apply Coles's notion that any account of the "real," any documentary, is filtered through an individual's imagination and point of view, and his sense that documentaries either favor the long view (with emphasis on social, cultural, and historical contexts) or the short view (with emphasis on the individual or the idiosyncratic). What is the evidence of the filtering process in the work you have studied? What are the consequences? Where and how might you use the work you have done to add to or to speak back to what Coles has to say in "The Tradition: Fact and Fiction"?

MAKING CONNECTIONS

1. In his essay, "The Tradition: Fact and Fiction," Robert Coles comments on the documentary photography done by Dorothea Lange and Walker Evans during the Great Depression of the 1930s. Coles is interested in the ways photographs are both documentary records and works of art and so disrupt any clear distinction between fact and fiction. In his comments on one of Evans's photographs, he says,

> But Evans is struggling for an interiority, that of his subject and that of his subject's future viewer/visitor: let us not only praise this man, lift him to the ranks of the famous, but consider what might be going on within him, and let us, through the motions of our moral imagination, enter his life, try to understand it, and return with that understanding to our own, which is thereby altered. (p. 232)

"This is a tall order for a single picture," he says, "but then Evans and Agee were ambitious. . . ."

When he speaks of the viewer, the viewer Evans is assuming in his photography, it is a viewer with a "moral imagination" who will do the work to "enter [the subject's] life, try to understand it, and return with that understanding" to his own life, a life which would, then, be altered.

Write an essay in which you read Coles's essay from the position of Marianne Hirsch's argument in "Projected Memory" (p. 261). Both have the goal of teaching us how to use the photographic record. How are they different? Both speak with an urgency about the necessity of paying attention to the records of the past and the ethical issues involved. Again, how are they different? And, finally, if they define two ways of approaching the photographic record, where do you locate yourself within these issues?

You should imagine that you are writing for someone who can understand the issues but who is familiar with neither of these sources. You will need to take care, in other words, to establish what the two authors say and to give a sense of what it is like to read their prose.

2. Both Robert Coles, in "The Tradition: Fact and Fiction," and W. J. T. Mitchell, in "The Photographic Essay" (p. 332) write about the genre of the photographic essay, and both take as a key text James Agee and Walker Evans's *Let Us Now Praise Famous Men*. You have the opportunity, then, to look at Coles's and Mitchell's primary source, to see what they selected and what they left out, to see the photographs and text in their original context. You can think about the logic (or desire) that led to their selections of exemplary material.

   Write an essay in which you elaborate the differences in Coles's and Mitchell's approaches to and accounts of this text. You can imagine that you are writing for a reader who has read none of the text at hand, so you will need to be careful in summary (perhaps reproducing some of the illustrations). What does each notice or choose to notice in the text? How are these decisions related to the larger projects of the two authors? to their underlying commitments and concerns? And, finally, where are you on the differences between the two? Would you align yourself with Coles or with Mitchell? From their example, is there a position you would define as your own or as an alternative?

3. In his chapter "The Tradition: Fact and Fiction," Robert Coles gives a detailed account of the photographs in *Let us Now Praise Famous Men* (p. 232). For this assignment, we'd like you to write an essay on *Let Us Now Praise Famous Men* that is your response to Coles. Perhaps the best way to do this is to write, first, about Evans's photographs on your own. The "Questions for a Second Reading" and the "Assignments for Writing" that accompany the excerpt from *Let Us Now Praise Famous Men* (p. 130) can provide a context and some help toward such an essay. For the sake of convenience, we'll reproduce the first writing assignment here:

   > Walker Evans's photographs stand at the head of the book *Let Us Now Praise Famous Men*, before the title page. There is no introduction; there are no captions; there is nothing to verbally prepare a reader or to establish a tie to the book that follows. They are just there, as though they could or should or must speak for themselves. (And James Agee's written text does not refer directly to the photographs. It doesn't gloss them or explain them or even describe them.)

> Write an essay about the photographs, about how you understand them (and the project they represent), and about their placement in the book. . . . Look back carefully through the photographs. Think of yourself as a reader reading the images, their presentation and their arrangement. What do they say? How are you expected to read them? or prepared to read them?

Once you have written out, in draft, your understanding of the photographs, read Coles's account. And write an essay in which you bring Coles's argument to bear on the work you have done with the photographs. What does he say? What does he say that you find useful? Where and how do you differ in approach or in conclusion? What might you make of these differences? (Or how, in your essay, might you define a relationship with an established scholar?)

In your essay, you should make it clear that Coles is serving *your* project. Your work is at the center. He is someone you are turning to after having developed (or in order to continue to develop) a position of your own. You need to be present in your essay as a scholar, in other words. Coles should not render you silent or make you disappear.

You should assume that your readers do not know (or remember) Coles's account of the photographs. You will need to represent his case. Your readers may know something about *Let Us Now Praise Famous Men*, but they don't have a copy handy. It would be useful, therefore, to work some of the images into the body of your essay.

Note: This assignment puts particular pressure on the first-person perspective of the essayist—you. You will need to write from your sense of the photographs and what might be said about them. It has been useful to our students to call attention to this from the very beginning. You might think of the "I" in your essay as a character, someone with a history, interests, a point of view, a style, someone of a particular age with a particular background in relation to photography, photographs, and Evans's subjects.

MARIANNE HIRSCH

MARIANNE HIRSCH (b. 1949) is the Parents Distinguished Research Professor in the Humanities at Dartmouth College, where she teaches French and comparative literature. You can trace the development of her scholarly interests through the titles of her books: Beyond the Single Vision: Henry James, Michel Butler, Uwe Johnson *(1981);* The Voyage In: Fictions of Female Development *(edited with Elizabeth Abel and Elizabeth Langland, 1983);* The Mother/Daughter Plot: Narrative, Psychoanalysis, and Feminism *(1989);* Conflicts in Feminism *(edited with Evelyn Fox Keller, 1990);* Family Frames: Photography, Narrative, and Postmemory *(1997); and* The Familial Gaze *(1999). Trained in literary theory and literary analysis, and with a particular interest in psychoanalysis and feminism, Hirsch turned her attention to the family and its representations. She was interested in the family as a concept, as a way of thinking and acting that arranges lives in the household and in society, and that has done so across time. Her work led her to everyday materials—to family records, letters, diaries, autobiographies, and photo albums. Like many trained in literary analysis, she has turned her methods and her attention to the materials of popular or everyday culture. The following essay, "Projected Memory: Holocaust Photographs in Personal and Public Fantasy," shows her interest in photography and memory—and in "postmemory," a term she coined to think about how memory is produced across generations.*

The essay was originally included in a collection titled Acts of Memory:

Cultural Recall in the Present *(edited by Mieke Bal, Jonathan Crewe, and Leo Spitzer, 1999). The argument of the book was that memory does not simply reside in individuals (stored in heads and hearts) or in institutional warehouses (libraries, museums, archives), but that memory is an active cultural project, one that represents our desire to link past and present. Or, as the editors note in the introduction, "This volume grew out of the authors' conviction that cultural recall is not merely something of which you happen to be a bearer but something that you actually* perform, *even if, in many instances, such acts are not consciously and willfully contrived."*

As you will see in the selection that follows, Marianne Hirsch is interested in "postmemory," memory that is not the product of direct or lived experience but that is produced by the stories and images that circulate from one generation to the next, evidenced in the ways children remember the memories of their parents. Her specific focus below is on how the children of Holocaust survivors remember the Holocaust; you could also think of the way today's generation of college freshmen "remember" the Vietnam War. This form of memory requires active participation—it must be an act of invention. Hirsch argues that it should also be a form of criticism (that is, a person needs to create the distance to know that what is remembered is invented). And, for its sources, it requires not only that which was heard at the dinner table but broader and more determined cultural productions—books, movies, magazines, television documentaries, and so on. Hirsch has written:

> *Postmemory is a powerful form of memory precisely because its connection to its object or source is mediated not through recollection but through an imaginative investment and creation. Postmemory characterizes the experience of those who grow up dominated by narratives that preceded their birth, whose own belated stories are evacuated by the stories of the previous generation, shaped by traumatic events that can be neither fully understood nor re-created. I have developed this notion in relation to children of Holocaust survivors, but I think it may usefully describe the second-generation memory of other cultural or collective traumatic events and experiences.*

And in a partially autobiographical essay, "Past Lives: Postmemories in Exile," Hirsch offers her own experience as a way of understanding this concept. Hirsch was born in Timisoara, Romania, in 1949, where her parents lived in exile from their native Czernowitz, once the capital of the Austrian Bukowina and annexed by the USSR in 1945. Czernowitz is a city she has never seen:

> *Still, the streets, buildings, and natural surroundings—the theater, restaurants, parks, rivers, and domestic settings of Czernowitz—none of which had I ever seen, heard, or smelled myself, occupy a monumental place in my childhood memories. All the while, as I was growing up hearing my parents' stories of life in Czernowitz before the war and the events during the wartime Russian and German occupations that culminated in their exile in 1945, I know that I would never see that place, and that my parents would never return there. I knew it not only because*

> *Czernowitz now belonged to the USSR and travel between there and Rumania was difficult; I knew it also from my parents' voice and demeanor, from the sense they projected that this world, their world, had been destroyed. . . . In our familial discourse, Czernowitz embodied the idea of home, of place, but to me it was, and would remain, out of reach.*

And, she continues, "The Czernowitz of my postmemory is an imaginary city, but that makes it no less present, no less vivid, and perhaps because of the constructed and deeply invested nature of memory itself, no less accurate."

The essay that follows is a wonderful and evocative piece of writing. It invites you (it teaches you) to look at a series of photographs and through them to think about how we think about the past as memory (rather than as history), whether those memories are our own or not.

Projected Memory: Holocaust Photographs in Personal and Public Fantasy

> I saw her wide-open eyes, and all of a sudden I knew: these eyes knew it all, they'd seen everything mine had, they knew infinitely more than anyone else in this country.
>
> –BINJAMIN WILKOMIRSKI

Past Lives: Three Photographs

> I. The photograph everyone knows: a boy in a peaked cap and knee-length socks, his hands raised. We do not know when it was taken. During the great extermination, in July or August 1942? Or during the Uprising in the ghetto in 1943? Or perhaps some other time. . . .
>
> It is hard to say if the boy is standing in a courtyard or outside a house entrance in a street. . . . To the right stand four Germans. . . . Two of their faces, three even in good reproductions, are clearly visible. I have pored over that photo for so long and so often that if I were now after forty-five years to meet one of those Germans in the street I'd identify him instantly.
>
> One of the Germans holds an automatic pistol under his arm, apparently aiming at the boy's back. . . . To the left there are several women, a few men, and about three children. All with their arms raised. . . . I have counted twenty-three people in this photo,

FIGURE [1]
From the *Stroop Report* on the destruction of the Warsaw ghetto.

> though the figures on the left are so huddled together that I may have miscounted: nineteen Jews and four Germans. . . .
>
> The boy in the center of the picture wears a short raincoat reaching just above his knees. His cap, tilted slightly askew, looks too big for him. Maybe it's his father's or his elder brother's? We have the boy's personal data: Artur Siematek, son of Leon and Sara née Dab, born in Łowicz. Artur is my contemporary: we were both born in 1935. We stand side by side, I in the photo taken on the high platform in Otwock. We may assume that both photographs were taken in the same month, mine a week or so earlier. We even seem to be wearing the same caps. Mine is of a lighter shade and also looks too big for my head. The boy is wearing knee-high socks, I am wearing white ankle socks. On the platform in Otwock I am smiling nicely. The boy's face—the photo was taken by an SS sergeant—betrays nothing.
>
> "You're tired," I say to Artur. "It must be very uncomfortable standing like that with your arms in the air. I know what we'll do. I'll lift my arms up now, and you put yours down. They may not notice. But wait, I've got a better idea. We'll both stand with our arms up."

The above is a passage from Jarosław Rymkiewicz's novel, originally published in Poland in 1988, *The Final Station: Umschlagplatz.*[1] Earlier in the novel, the narrator is perusing his family photo album with his sister. "'Look,' he says to his sister, 'that is Swider, in the summer of 1942. That is you on the swing near the house. Here we are standing on the beach by the river. And here I am on the platform at Otwock. Cap and tie. The same white socks. But I can't for the life of me remember the house where we spent our holidays that year.'

"'Nor can I,' says my sister reading the inscription our mother has made on the page with the photo that was taken of me complete with tie, cap, and white socks on the high platform at Otwock. 'Church fair in Otwock, July 19, 1942.'

"'Did you know,' I say, 'that in the summer of 1942 there was still a ghetto in Otwock?'" (23–24).

> II. In my house in Santiago there were certain photographs that kept me good company, that watched over me like a constant presence. There were photographs of my great-grandfather Isidoro, whom we named the chocolate-covered soldier because he was so beautiful and exquisite; also there was a photograph of my aunt Emma who sang arias and spoke French; and there was a small photograph that my grandfather José had given me in the summer of 1970. . . .
>
> Anne Frank's presence in that little photograph was always at my side during my childhood nightmares. I knew that Anne had written a diary and that she had perished in the concentration camps only months before the arrival of the Allied Forces. There was something in her face, in her aspect, and in her age that reminded me of myself. I imagined her playing with my sisters and reading fragments of her diary to us. . . .
>
> I began my dialogue with Anne Frank from a simultaneous desire to remember and to forget. I wanted to know more about that curious girl's face that for so long had occupied a place on the wall of my room. . . . I wanted to speak with Anne Frank from an almost obsessive desire to revive her memory and make her return and enter our daily lives.

This is a passage from the introduction to a book of poems by Marjorie Agosín entitled *Dear Anne Frank* and published in a bilingual edition in 1994.[2] In the poems the poet addresses Anne Frank directly, thus hoping to "mak[e] her part of our daily lives." "Dear Anne," the first poem begins, invoking the Anne behind the photograph that "disperses your thirteen shrouded years, your thick bewitching eyebrows." "Is it you in that photo? Is it you in that diary . . . ?" Agosín asks; "you seem the mere shadow of a fantasy that names you" (15).

Both of these texts, a novel written by a Polish man (a non-Jew) and a volume of poems written by a Latin American Jewish woman, are inspired and motivated by encounters with images that have become generally familiar,

FIGURE [2]
Past Lives. Color photograph, 30 × 36″.
© Lorie Novak, 1987.

perhaps even pervasive, in contemporary memory and discussion of the Holocaust. In both cases these are images of children. Indeed, if one had to name the visual images most frequently associated with the memory of the Holocaust, these two might well have been among them.

III. Perhaps a third image—an image of a slightly different character—can illuminate the interactions that emerge in these two passages and help me to articulate the issues they raise. It will allow me to explore how camera images mediate the private and the public memory of the Holocaust, how they generate a memorial aesthetic for the second and even for subsequent generations, and what happens when they become overly familiar and iconic. Also what happens—as is frequently the case—if they are images of children.

Past Lives is the work of the Jewish-American artist Lorie Novak dated 1987. It is a photograph of a composite projection onto an interior wall: in the foreground is a picture of the children in Izieu—the Jewish children hidden in a French orphanage in Izieu who were eventually found and deported by Klaus Barbie. Nineteen eighty-seven was the year of the Barbie trial; this photograph appeared in a *New York Times Magazine* article on the Barbie affair. In the middle ground is a picture of Ethel Rosenberg's face. She, a mother of two young sons, was convicted of atomic espionage and executed by electrocution together with her husband Julius Rosenberg. In the background of Novak's composite image is a photograph of a smiling woman holding a little girl who clutches her mother's dress and seems about to burst into tears. This is the photographer Lorie Novak as a young child held by her mother. Novak was born in 1954 and thus this image dates from the mid-1950s.

By allowing her own childhood picture literally to be overshadowed by two public images, Novak stages an uneasy confrontation of personal memory with public history. Visually representing, in the 1980s, the memory of growing up in the United States in the 1950s, Novak includes not only family images but also those figures that might have populated her own or her mother's daydreams and nightmares: Ethel Rosenberg, the mother executed by the state, who, in Novak's terms, looks "hauntingly maternal"[3] but who is incapable of protecting her children or herself, and the children of Izieu, unprotected child victims of Nazi genocide. Unlike Rymkiewicz's narrator, Novak is not the contemporary of the children in the image: she is, like Agosín, a member of the second generation, connected to the child victims of the Holocaust through an intergenerational act of adoption and identification. Her mother, though younger, is indeed a contemporary of Ethel Rosenberg. Together they trace the trajectory of memory from the first to the second generation.

What drama is being enacted in Novak's *Past Lives?* If it is a drama of childhood fear and the inability to trust, about the desires and disappointments of mother-child relationships, then it is also, clearly, a drama about the power of public history to crowd out personal story, about the shock of the knowledge of *this* history: the Holocaust and the cold war, state power and individual powerlessness. Lorie, the little girl in the picture, is, after all, the only child who looks sad or unhappy: the other children are smiling, confidently looking toward a future they were never to have. The child who lives is crowded out by the children who were killed, the mother who lives, by the mother who was executed; their lives must take their shape in relation to the murderous breaks in these other, past, lives.

In *Past Lives,* space and time are conflated to reveal memory's material presence. As projected and superimposed camera images, the children of Izieu, Ethel Rosenberg, the young Lorie and her young mother are *all* ghostly revenants, indexical traces of a past projected into the present, seen in the present as overlays of memory. As her childhood image bleeds into the picture of the murdered children, as the picture of her mother merges with the image of the mother who was executed, Novak enacts a very particular kind of confrontation between the adult artist looking back to her childhood, the child she is in the image, and the victims projected onto them. This triangulation of looking, figured by the superimposition of images from disparate moments of personal and public history, is in itself an act of memory—not individual but cultural memory. It reveals memory to be an act in the *present* on the part of a subject who constitutes herself by means of a series of identifications across temporal, spatial, and cultural divides. It reveals memory to be *cultural,* fantasy to be *social and political,* in the sense that the representation of one girl's childhood includes, as a part of her own experience, the history into which she was born, the figures that inhabited her public life and perhaps also the life of her imagination. The present self, the artist who constructs the work, encounters in the image the past self and the other selves—the child and maternal victims, related to her through a cultural act of identification and affiliation—that define that past self, shaping her imagination and constituting her memories.[4]

These affiliations mark the subject of these memories as a member of her generation and a witness of her particular historical moment: born after World War II, as a Jew, she represents herself as branded by the harrowing memory of Nazi genocide, a memory that gets reinterpreted, repeatedly, throughout the subsequent half-century. Her text, shaped by identification with the victims, invites her viewers to participate with her in a cultural act of remembrance. Photographic projections make this marking literal and material as the image of Novak's body is inscribed with the story of those other children. Losing their physical boundaries, they merge with one another. The use of familiar public images, moreover—the children of Izieu, Anne Frank, the boy from Warsaw—facilitates this participation, in that viewers will *remember* seeing them before. When Agosín describes Anne Frank's photographic presence in her childhood, her readers will likely remember seeing the same image during theirs: their respective memories will trigger one another. As readers, we can thus enter the network of looks established in Agosín's poem: we imagine Marjorie looking at Anne's picture, which is looking back at her and at us; at the same time, we look at our own earlier selves looking at Anne's photograph, or thinking about her story. The memorial circle is enlarged, allowing for shared memories and shared fantasies. As we look at Novak's image, the image looks back at us, through multiple layers of eyes; by means of the mutual reflection and projection that characterizes the act of looking, we enter its space, the visual space of postmemory. Let me try to explain this term.

Postmemory and "Heteropathic Identification"

I have been haunted by *Past Lives* since I first saw it. When I look at it I see myself both in the sad little girl who is clutching her mother's dress and in the smiling girl who, at the very left of the picture, is half outside its frame, looking to a space beyond. I look at that bare corner wall and at the ghostly figures emerging from its depths and I am propelled back into my childhood daydreams. The dreams and fantasies of a child of survivors of Nazi persecution during World War II growing up in Eastern Europe in the 1950s were dominated by The War: Where would I have been, then? How would I have acted? The door bell rings in the middle of the night, the Gestapo is at the door, what do I do? The imbalance of Novak's image speaks to me most forcefully: in remembering my childhood, I too feel as though I were crouching in the corner of a bare room populated by larger-than-life ghosts: my parents' younger selves during the war, and those who were children like me and who had to face dangers I tried hard to experience in my imagination. *Past Lives* describes the very quality of my memories of my childhood, memories crowded out by the memories of others: stronger, more weighty memories, more vivid and more real than any scenes I can conjure up from my own childhood. Thinking about my childhood, I retrieve their memories more readily than my own; their memories *are* my memories. And yet, Novak's image also invites us to resist this equation.

In *Past Lives* Novak begins to articulate the aesthetic strategies of tragic identification, projection, and mourning that specifically characterize the second-generation memory of the Holocaust—what I have called *postmemory*.[5] She stages, retrospectively, a moment of knowledge for the Jewish child growing up in the 1950s whose needs, desires, and cares fade out in relation to the stories that surround her, the traumatic memories that preceded her birth but nevertheless define her own life's narrative. Like Agosín who spends her childhood in Chile conversing with Anne Frank's picture, Novak in *Past Lives* inscribes herself, through projection and identification, into the subject position of the child of survivors.

I use the term *postmemory* to describe the relationship of children of survivors of cultural or collective trauma to the experiences of their parents, experiences that they "remember" only as the stories and images with which they grew up, but that are so powerful, so monumental, as to constitute memories in their own right. The term is meant to convey its temporal and qualitative difference from survivor memory, its secondary or second-generation memory quality, its basis in displacement, its belatedness. Postmemory is a powerful form of memory precisely because its connection to its object or source is mediated not through recollection but through projection, investment, and creation. That is not to say that survivor memory itself is unmediated, but that it is more directly connected to the past. Postmemory characterizes the experience of those who grow up dominated by narratives that preceded their birth, whose own belated stories are displaced by the stories of the previous generation, shaped by traumatic events that they can neither understand nor re-create.

Not themselves children of Holocaust survivors, Novak and Agosín nevertheless speak from the position of postmemory. And although Rymkiewicz's protagonist is a contemporary of the boy from Warsaw, he is rewriting his own past in light of the knowledge that at the time he did not have; as he revises his childhood story he must take on the Jewish memories of his contemporaries as well as his own Polish ones. As I conceive of it, postmemory is not an identity position, but a space of remembrance, more broadly available through cultural and public, and not merely individual and personal, acts of remembrance, identification, and projection. It is a question of adopting the traumatic experiences—and thus also the memories—of others as one's own, or, more precisely, as experiences one might oneself have had, and of inscribing them into one's own life story. It is a question of conceiving oneself as multiply interconnected with others of the same, of previous, and of subsequent generations, of the same and of other—proximate or distant—cultures and subcultures. It is a question, more specifically, of an *ethical* relation to the oppressed or persecuted other for which postmemory can serve as a model: as I can "remember" my parents' memories, I can also "remember" the suffering of others, of the boy who lived in the same town in the ghetto while I was vacationing, of the children who were my age and who were deported. These lines of relation and identification need to be theorized more closely, however: how the familial and intergenerational identification with my parents can extend to the identification among children of different generations and circumstances and also perhaps to other, less proximate groups. And how, more important, identification can resist appropriation and incorporation, resist annihilating the distance between self and other, the otherness of the other.

In her recent *Threshold of the Visible World,* Kaja Silverman (borrowing the term from Max Scheler [*The Nature of Sympathy,* 1923]) has termed this process "heteropathic memory" and "identification"—a way of aligning the "not-me" with the "me" without interiorizing it, or, in her terms, "introduc[ing] the 'not-me' into my memory reserve."[6] Through "discursively 'implanted' memories" the subject can "participate in the desires, struggles, and sufferings of the other"—particularly, in Silverman's examples, the culturally devalued and persecuted other (185). Thus the subject can engage in what Silverman calls "identification-at-a-distance": identification that does not interiorize the other within the self but that goes out of one's self and out of one's own cultural norms in order to align oneself, through displacement, with another. Heteropathic memory (feeling and suffering with the other) means, as I understand it, the ability to say, "It could have been me; it was me, also," and, *at the same time,* "but it was not me." Postmemory in my terms is a form of heteropathic memory in which the self and the other are more closely connected through familial or group relation, for example, through what it means to be Jewish, or Polish. While postmemory implies a temporal distance between the self and the other—like Agosín and Anne Frank—Silverman's heteropathic recollection could depend solely on spatial or cultural distance, and temporal coincidence (as for the two Polish boys, for instance). In both cases, an enormous distance must be bridged and, in the specific case of Holocaust memory, that distance *cannot* ultimately be bridged; the break between then and now, between the one who lived it and the one who did not, remains monumental and insurmountable, even as the heteropathic imagination struggles to overcome it.

Silverman's instrument of heteropathic recollection, like Lacan's vehicle of identification, is the look. Roland Barthes's distinction between *studium* and *punctum* dramatizes the relationship between these different forms of looking: while the *studium* inscribes the seen into the normative cultural script, the *punctum* finds in the image something so unfamiliar and unexpected that it acts like a "prick" or a "wound" interrupting any familiar relation to the visible world.[7] The productive look of heteropathic identification can see beyond "the given to be seen"; it can displace the incorporative, ingestive look of self-sameness and the familiar object it sees in favor of "an appetite for alterity" (181).

Camera images, particularly still photographs, are precisely the medium connecting first- and second-generation remembrance, memory and postmemory. Photographic images are stubborn survivors of death. We receive them, uncompromisingly, in the present tense. Inasmuch as they are instruments of memory, then, they expose its resolute but multilayered presentness. As objects of looking they lend themselves either to idiopathic *or* to heteropathic identification, to self-sameness *or* to displacement. Holocaust photographs, the leftovers and debris of a destroyed culture, made precious by the monumental losses they inscribe, certainly have the capacity to retain their radical otherness. The fragmentary sources and building blocks of the work of postmemory, they affirm the past's existence, its "having-been there," and, in their flat two-dimensionality, they also signal its insurmountable distance. In an image like *Past Lives,* however, so dependent on projection, these distances seem to disappear; within the image itself, past and present, self and other, appear to merge. In the form of projection, photographs can indeed lend themselves to the incorporative logic of narcissistic, idiopathic, looking. The challenge for the postmemorial artist is precisely to find the balance that allows the spectator to enter the image, to imagine the disaster, but that disallows an overappropriative identification that makes the distances disappear, creating too available, too easy an access to this particular past.

Images of Children

Why are such a large number of the archival images used in the texts documenting and memorializing the Holocaust images of children? The boy from Warsaw, for example, has appeared in numerous Holocaust films, novels, and poems; recently, he appears obsessively in advertising brochures for Holocaust histories, teaching aids, and books. The photograph is featured in both Alain Resnais's 1956 documentary *Night and Fog,* and Ingmar Bergman's

1966 film *Persona*, and, in 1990, it became the object of a documentary video (subtitled "a video about a photograph") entitled *Tsvi Nussbaum: A Boy from Warsaw.*[8] Made for Finnish and French television, the video is devoted to examining the contention of Holocaust survivor Tsvi Nussbaum that he is the boy with his hands up and that the picture was not taken in the Warsaw ghetto at all but in the "Aryan" part of Warsaw where he was hiding. Although he doesn't remember the moment depicted very clearly, he brings photographs of himself as a boy as proof of his identity with the boy in the picture; thus his story draws on the emblematic role that the image has come to play. Rymkiewicz, in contrast, identified the boy as Artur Siematek, showing that the photograph's status as document is as questionable as its symbolic role can be determinative.[9]

Of this so frequently invoked image, Lucy Dawidowicz writes in her book *The War against the Jews:* "in the deluded German mind, every Jewish man, woman, and child became a panoplied warrior of a vast Satanic fighting machine. The most concrete illustration of this delusion is the now familiar photograph taken from the collection attached to Stroop's report of the Warsaw ghetto uprising. It shows uniformed German SS men holding guns to a group of women and children; in the foreground is a frightened boy of about six, his hands up. This was the face of the enemy."[10] Yala Korwin's poem "The Little Boy with His Hands Up" also voices the enormously influential role of this photograph to shape the visual memory and transmission of the Holocaust:

> Your image will remain with us,
> and grow and grow
> to immense proportions,
> to haunt the callous world,
> to accuse it, with ever stronger voice
> in the name of the million
> youngsters
> who lie, pitiful ragdolls,
> their eyes forever closed.[11]

The image has become the consummate space of projection: while Rymkiewicz's narrator contends that "the boy's face . . . betrays nothing," and Dawidowicz describes him as "frightened," Korwin writes:

> your face contorted with fear,
> grown old with knowledge beyond your years.
> . . . .
> All the torments of this harassed crowd
> are written on your face.

But the boy from Warsaw is only one of numerous children displayed in the photographic discourses of memory and postmemory. Anne Frank's image and her story are utterly pervasive—this to the great distress of commentators like Bruno Bettelheim who find it problematic that this young girl's strangely hopeful story should for a generation have constituted the only encounter with the knowledge of the Holocaust, an encounter engendering the type of adolescent identification we see in Marjorie Agosín's book of poems.[12] Anne Frank, Agosín insists, "had a name, had a face, . . . she was not just one more anonymous story among the countless stories of the Holocaust" (6–7). But many other children's faces dominate postmemorial texts to similar effect. The image of Richieu, Art Spiegelman's "ghost brother" to whom the second volume of *Maus* is dedicated, for example, elicits a very specific kind of investment by Spiegelman's readers. Richieu's face at the beginning of this book of schematic cartoon drawings of mice and cats jumps out of the covers to haunt us with its strange lifelike presence. When we open *Maus II* we already know that Richieu was killed and his photograph, one of three in the two volumes of *Maus,* acts like a ghostly apparition, materially recalling Richieu's absence. Like many other Holocaust photographs, this image stubbornly survived not only its young subject but the intended destruction of an entire culture down to its very objects and artifacts.

Other images of children are more anonymous but, like the children of Izieu in Novak's work, they invite a very specific kind of spectatorial look, a particular form of investment; thus they can help us to understand the particular kind of subject taking shape in the act of postmemory. In his memorial installations, the French artist Christian Boltanski invariably uses archival images of children, usually school pictures from Jewish schools in Vienna and Berlin in the 1930s.[13] Boltanski rephotographs and enlarges individual faces, installs them on top of tin biscuit boxes, mounts them on the wall or shrouds them with sheets, illuminating each with a black desk lamp that creates a large circle of light at the center of each picture. The faces are stripped of individuality. Even though their indexical, referential, function reemerges through the use of the class photos of a population the majority of which certainly ended up in Hitler's death camps, the images themselves, separate from the identifying label, blown up to enormous proportions and thus depersonalized, become icons of untimely death, icons of mourning. The power of the installations is ensured by the fact that these are images of children, looking forward to lives they were never to have.

Why children? Lucy Dawidowicz provides one answer: images of children bring home the utter senselessness of Holocaust destruction. Who could see the enemy in the face of a child? Children, moreover, were particularly vulnerable in Hitler's Europe: in the entire Nazi-occupied territory of Europe only 11 percent of Jewish children survived and thus the faces of children signal the unforgiving ferocity of the Nazi death machine.[14] It does not matter whether the boy from Warsaw survived or not for us to feel that vulnerability; with statistics of such enormity, every child whose image we see is, at least metaphorically, one who perished. Boltanski's technique of enlargement and "anonymization" provides another answer. "For me it's very important to start with a real image," he says. "Then I blow it up to make it universal."[15] But images of children readily lend themselves to such universalization anyway. Culturally, at the end of the twentieth century, the figure of the "child" is an adult construction, the site of adult fantasy, fear, and desire. As recent controversies suggest, our culture has a great deal invested in the children's innocence and vulnerability—and at the same time, in their eroticism and knowledge. Less individualized, less marked by the particularities of identity, moreover, children invite multiple projections and identifications. Their photographic images elicit an affiliative and identificatory as well as a protective spectatorial look marked by these investments. No wonder that the identity of the boy from Warsaw is contested.

To describe more specifically the visual encounter with the child victim, and to sort out the types of identification—idiopathic or heteropathic, based on appropriation or displacement—that shape it, requires an analysis of the *visual* work involved in these identifications. I approach this analysis by way of a very revealing scene from the recent film *Hatred* by Australian director Mitzi Goldman.[16] This film uses interviews, archival footage, and montage shot largely in New York's Harlem, in Germany, and in the Middle East, to explore hatred as an emotion. It contains a number of scenes in which Goldman returns with her father to Dessau, the German city from which he fled as a Jew in 1939. Her position as the child of this survivor shapes her inquiry into hatred in numerous ways, but this determining subject position is most clearly revealed in a scene in which the voice-over asks "What do I know about the Holocaust?" In this recurring scene a white child (at one time a boy, another time a girl) watches archival film footage of Nazi horror; in a similar scene an Asian boy watches television footage of the Vietnam war. The archival images projected are, again, overfamiliar images seen in many films or displays on the Holocaust and on Vietnam: the records of the Allied soldiers taken on the liberation of the camps, and the journalistic footage taken in Vietnam during the war. The voice-over continues: "The horror that was fed to us as children, I buried beneath a tough exterior. It was ancient history, not my life."

The three children in Goldman's film are secondary witnesses of horror; they are witnesses not to the event but to its visual documentary records. In Goldman's scene the child on the screen—the child we see—is not the victim but the witness, looking not at an individualized child victim but at the anonymous victims of the horrors of human brutality and hatred. Still, it seems to me that this representation of the child witness can tell us a great deal about the visual encounter with the child victim. As we see the children watching, it appears as if the images are projected right onto them. Strangely, the children are chewing as they watch. Mitzi Goldman has spoken of her strange memories of the Jewish school she attended, where, on rainy days when they could not go outside at lunchtime, the children were shown films about the Holocaust.[17] The children on the screen *feed* on images of horror, they have to ingest them with lunch; even more graphically, they are marked by them, bodily, as "Jewish" or as "Vietnamese." They watch and, like the film's narrator, they "feed on" images that do and do not impact on their present lives. Looking at the children watching we see them and the images

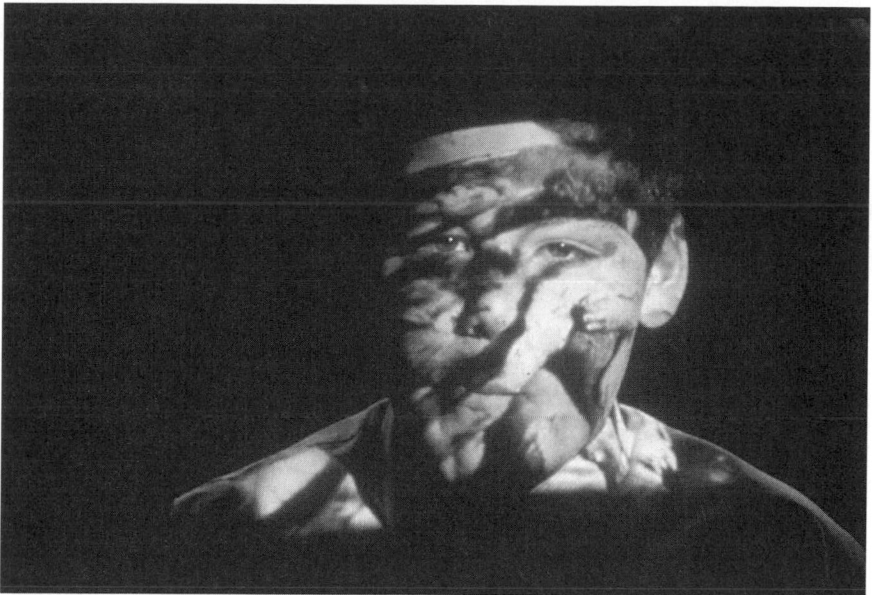

FIGURE [3]
Mitzi Goldman, *Hatred* (1996). Film still.

they see on the same plane; thus the child witness is merged with the victims she or he sees. More than just specularity, looking produces the coalescence of spectator and spectacle; the object of the look is inscribed not only on the retina but on the entire body of the looking subject.

As we look at the face of the child victim—Anne Frank, or the little boy from Warsaw—do we not also see there what that child saw? By encountering the child victim, we also, by implication, encounter the atrocities he has seen. In her poem, Yala Korwin describes this confrontation:

> All the torments of this harassed
> crowd
> are written on your face.
> In your dark eyes—a vision of horror.
> You have seen death already
> on the ghetto streets, haven't you?
> (*To Tell the Story* 75)

As the child victim merges with the child witness, as we begin to recognize their identity, we ourselves, as spectators looking at the child victim, become witnesses, child witnesses, in our own right. Thus we see from both the adult, retrospective and more knowing, vantage point and from the vantage point of the uncomprehending child "grown old with knowledge beyond your years" (Korwin, *To Tell the Story* 75).

It is my argument that the visual encounter with the child victim is a triangular one, that identification occurs in a triangular field of looking. The adult viewer sees the child victim through the eyes of his or her own child self. The poet Marjorie Agosín looks at Anne Frank's photo through the adolescent in Chile who had fantasized about conversing with Anne and had asked her to join in her games. The adult narrator of Rymkiewicz's *The Final Station* confronts the picture of the boy from Warsaw with the Polish boy who wears white kneesocks and does not know what the Jewish boy knows. When the artist Lorie Novak finds the picture of the children of Izieu in the *New York Times* she superimposes it on a picture of herself as a child: it is only through that distant subject position that she can encounter these children. And the director Mitzi Goldman takes her father back to Dessau but she can only do so by way of her own childhood experience of feeding on images of hatred. The adult viewer who is also an artist shares the child viewing position with her own audience, which also enters the image in the position of child witness. The present tense of the photograph is a layered present on which several pasts are projected; at the same time, however, the present never recedes. The adult also encounters the child (the other child and his/her own child self) both as a child, through identification, and from the protective vantage point of the adult-looking subject. Identificatory looking and protective looking coexist in uneasy balance.

The split viewing subject that is evoked by the image of the child victim—both adult and child—is emblematic of the subject of memory and of fantasy. In the act of memory as well as the act of fantasy the subject is simultaneously actor and spectator, adult and child; we act and, concurrently, we observe ourselves acting.[18] It is a process of projection backward in time; in that sense, it is also a process of transformation from adult to child that produces an identification between two children.

But in the particular case of postmemory and "heteropathic recollection" where the subject is not split just between past and present, adult and child, but also between self and other, the layers of recollection and the subjective topography are even more complicated. The adult subject of postmemory encounters the image of the child victim *as* the child witness, and thus the split subjectivity characterizing the structure of memory is triangulated. And that triangulation identifies postmemory as necessarily cultural. Identification is group or generational identification. The two children whose mutual look defines the field of vision I am trying to map here are linked culturally and not necessarily personally: Marjorie and Anne as Jews, Jarosław and Artur as Poles. But that connection is facilitated, if not actually produced, by their mutual status as children and by the child's openness to identification. Through photographic projection, moreover, distances diminish even more, identities blur. When two children "look" at one another in the process of photographic witnessing, the otherness that separates them is diminished to the point where recollection could easily slide into the idiopathic away from the heteropathic—where displacement gives way to interiorization and appropriation. The image of the child, even the image of the child victim of incomprehensible horror, displaces "the appetite for alterity" with an urge toward identity. This could be the effect of the "it could have been me" created specifically by the image of the child. In the present political climate that constructs the child as an unexamined emblem of vulnerability and innocence, the image of the child lends itself too easily to trivialization and stereotype. It can only exacerbate the effect of oversaturation with visual images that, as Geoffrey Hartman, Julia Kristeva, and others charge, have made us immune to their effect.[19] Under what circumstances, then, can the image of the child victim preserve its alterity and thus also its power?

(Im)Possible Witnessing

In his recent work on Holocaust memory, Dominick LaCapra has enjoined us to recognize the transferential elements that interfere with efforts at working through this traumatic past. He has distinguished between two memorial positions: acting out (melancholia) and working through (mourning). Acting out is based on tragic identification and the constitution of one's self as a surrogate victim. It is based on overidentification and repetition. Keeping the wounds open, it results in retraumatization. Working through, on the other hand, involves self-reflexivity, a determination of responsibility, some amount of distance. A goal and not an end, it is a process of evolution that is never fully accomplished—and therefore never free of some element of acting out: "Acting out may well be necessary and unavoidable in the wake of extreme trauma, especially for victims," LaCapra says in *Representing the Holocaust.* But for "the interviewer and the analyst" (and, one might add, for the postmemorial generation), LaCapra urges that "one . . . attempt to put oneself in the other's position without taking the other's place." He further suggests, "one component of the process is the attempt to elaborate a hybridized narrative that does not avoid analysis, . . . it requires the effort to achieve a critical distance on experience."[20]

If the image of the child victim places the artist, the scholar, or the historian into the space of the child witness, then it would seem to impede working through unless distancing devices are introduced that would discourage an appropriative identification. What is disturbing, however, is precisely the obsessive repetition of these images of children—in itself, examples of acting out and the compulsion to repeat. The image of the child victim, moreover, facilitates an identification in which the viewer can too easily become a surrogate victim. Most important, the easy identification with children, their virtually universal availability for projection, risks the blurring of important areas of difference and alterity: context, specificity, responsibility, history. This is especially true of the images I have discussed in this paper, images of children who are not visibly wounded or in pain. In this light, one might contrast the boy from Warsaw with other images of emaciated, dirty, visibly suffering children taken in the Warsaw ghetto, images that have never achieved the same kind of visual prominence as the little boy with his hands up.

And yet, depending on the context into which they are inscribed and the narrative that they produce, these obsessively repeated pictures can be vehicles of a heteropathic memory; they can maintain their alterity and become part of a "hybridized narrative that does not avoid analysis." Clearly, the images' use and meaning vary significantly with the context in which they are inscribed and ultimately it is that context that must be closely examined.

Thus some of the works I have included rely on specific distancing devices that allow for the triangulated looking, for the displacement that qualifies identification. The fact, for example, that Rymkiewicz describes the photos but does not reproduce them, creates some significant distance. The inclusion of Rosenberg's face in *Past Lives* introduces a third term between the child victim and the child witness, and refocuses the attention onto the two adults in the text. Similarly, the introduction of the Asian child in the scene from *Hatred* creates a space of reflection, a form of displacement and thus a mediated identification not necessarily based on ethnic or national identity.

I shall distinguish these different forms of identification more closely by way of another image and the context in which it mysteriously appears not once but twice. This is the picture of Holocaust survivor Menachem S. [p. 277], whose testimony was taken at the Yale Fortunoff Video Archive for Holocaust testimonies by the psychoanalyst Dori Laub. In separate chapters of their coauthored book *Testimony,* Shoshana Felman and Dori Laub refer to Menachem's moving story to illustrate the very different points they each try to make in their essays: Felman to explore how her class received the testimonies they read and watched; Laub to comment on the role of the listener or witness to testimony.[21] Strangely, both reproduce this photograph in their chapters but neither of them makes even the most cursory reference to it. What is the work performed by this image of the victim child in the work of memory performed by *Testimony?*

At the age of five, Menachem was smuggled out of a detention camp by his parents so that he might survive. In Laub's account, "his mother wrapped him up in a shawl and gave him a passport photograph of herself as a student. She told him to turn to the picture whenever he felt he needed to do so. His parents both promised him that they would come and find him and bring him home after the war" (*Testimony* 86). The little boy was sent into the streets alone; he went first to a brothel where he found shelter and later to several Polish families who took him in and helped him to survive. After the war, however, his reunion with his parents destroyed his coping mechanisms. As Laub says, "His mother does not look like the person in the photograph. His parents have come back as death camp survivors, haggard and emaciated, in striped uniforms, with teeth hanging loose in their gums" (88). The boy falls apart; he calls his parents Mr. and Mrs. and suffers from lifelong terrifying nightmares; only when he is able to tell his story in the testimonial

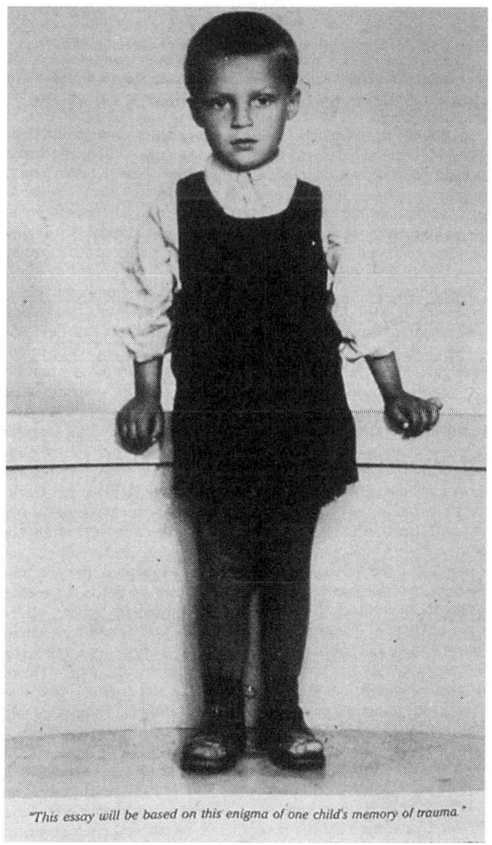

FIGURE [4]
Menachem S., age 4.

context, after a thirty-five-year silence, does he gain some possibility of working through his traumatic past.

Felman cites several of Menachem's own reflections: "The thing that troubles me right now is the following: if we don't deal with our feelings, if we don't understand our experience, what are we doing to our children? . . . Are we transferring our anxieties, our fears, our problems, to the generations to come? . . . We are talking here not only of *the lost generation* . . . this time we are dealing with *lost generations*" (46). For Felman's class "these reflections of the child survivor on the liberating, although frightening effects of his own rebirth to speech in the testimonial process . . . were meant to conclude the course with the very eloquence of life, with a striking, vivid and extreme *real example* of the *liberating, vital function of the testimony*" (47). Note the repetition of terms like "speech," and "eloquence": it is precisely language and the ability to speak that get lost in the class after the students watch Menachem's videotaped account. To address the "crisis" that her class was going through as they watched the video testimonies, Felman decides that "what was called for was for me to reassume authority as the teacher of the class, and bring the students back into significance" (48). (Again, note this term and note the strictly differentiated adult/child roles that are assumed.) To "bring the students back into significance," Felman gives a half-hour lecture, an address to her class. "I first *reread* to them an excerpt from Celan's 'Bremen Speech' about what happened to the act of speaking, and to language, after the Holocaust." Felman stresses to her students their own "loss of language" in the face of what they were encountering, their feeling that "language was somehow incommensurate with it" (50). She concludes the course with an invitation for students to write their own testimony of the class itself. Citing some of their reflections, she concludes that "the crisis, in effect had been worked through and overcome. . . . The written work the class had finally submitted turned out to be an amazingly articulate, reflective, and profound statement of the trauma they had gone through and of the significance of their own position as a witness" (52). By implication, they have resumed their adult status, in language, in a language commensurate with their experiences. They have been able to work through the trauma, as adults.

Felman's strong insistence on language as *the* means of working through the crisis of witnessing returns me to her inclusion of the child's photograph and her own rather remarkable silence about it. Clearly, this included photo is not the picture that is at the crux of Menachem's story: the ID picture of his mother he carried with him throughout his years as a hidden child. Menachem went into hiding in 1942 at age four; the picture is labeled "the end of 1944 (age 5)." It was taken during the war when Menachem was in hiding, when, according to his own narrative, he spent every evening gazing at his mother's photo. In his eyes, in his serious face, we can imagine seeing the reflection of that other, shadow, photograph and the simultaneous loss and presence it signaled. And, we can also see, as in the eyes of all child victims, the atrocities the child has already witnessed at the age of five. Perhaps this image is performing the same work in Felman's account that the video testimonies did in her class. In the formulation of one student: "until now and throughout the texts we have been studying . . . we have been talking (to borrow Mallarmé's terms) about the *'testimony of an accident.'* We have been *talking* about the accident—and here all of a sudden *the accident happened* in the class, happened *to* the class. An accident *passed through* the class" (50). In the midst of Felman's own "amazingly articulate, reflective, and profound" analysis in her chapter, the little boy's picture, we might say, is that "accident" that passes through the book, allowing the crisis to be communicated, if in a different register. And, as Laub's own account demonstrates, the image projects the viewer, the subject of "heteropathic" memory, into the position of the child witness and thus into speechlessness.

Laub's own essay, as he explains, "proceeds from my autobiographical awareness as a child survivor" (75). He shares with other child survivors a very peculiar ability to remember: "The events are remembered and seem to have been experienced in a way that was far beyond the capacity of recall in a young child of my age. . . . These memories are like discrete islands of precocious thinking and feel almost like the remembrances of another child, removed yet connected to me in a complex way" (76). The essay indeed goes on to tell the story of another child—Menachem S.—and to discuss his silence, his struggle with witnessing, so as to illustrate a larger point about the impossibility of telling, about the Holocaust as "an event without a witness."

In Laub's essay this same photo is labeled differently: "This essay will be based on this enigma of one child's memory of trauma" (77). Had we not seen this picture earlier in the book, we would not know that this is not a childhood picture of Laub himself; it is placed in the midst of his own story and not Menachem's at all. In fact, every time I look at the picture and its generalized caption, I have to remind myself that this is not a picture of Dori Laub; it is as if the identities of the two subjects of Laub's essay, Menachem S. and Laub himself, were projected or superimposed onto one another. The essay includes three more photographs: *Menachem S. and his mother, Krakow, 1940*; *Menachem S., 1942*; and *Colonel Dr. Menachem S., 1988*. The fact that the first image carries no name reinforces this blurring of identities between Dori Laub and Menachem S.

Laub's essay rides on another picture, the ID picture of the mother, in Laub's reading the necessary witness, which allowed the five-year-old to survive by standing in as a listener to his story. In the essay itself, however, the 1944 picture of the child victim Menachem S. is playing that very same role: it is the silent witness that allows the analyst Dori Laub to perform his articulate analysis but that, with the child's serious and sad eyes, undercuts that wisdom—a reminder of incomprehensible horror, a space in which to experience uncomprehending speechlessness in the midst of articulate analysis. This photograph, we might argue, is the ground of indirect and paradoxical witnessing in this "event without a witness."

In the ways in which it is reproduced, repeated, and/or discussed in *Testimony*, this image of the boy Menachem S. maintains its alterity, an alterity from which both Felman and Laub quite resolutely try to distance themselves in the very space of their identification. In the particular context in which they place it, in the distancing discourse of scholarly discussion in which they embed it, the image of the child victim stands in for all that cannot be—and perhaps should not be—worked through. This image *is* the accident that happened in the midst of all the talking and writing that can only screen its effect. It is the *other child,* in his irreducible otherness, the one who has not yet, who might never be able to, translate memory into speech. A reminder of unspeakability, a vehicle of infantilization, it may well be the best medium of postmemory and heteropathic identification, of cultural memorialization of a past whose vivid pain is receding more and more into the distance. In his own analysis of working through, Saul Friedlander explains why: "In fact, the numbing or distancing effect of intellectual work on the *Shoah* is unavoidable and necessary; the recurrence of strong emotional impact is also often unforeseeable and necessary. . . . But neither the protective numbing nor the disruptive emotion is entirely accessible to consciousness."[22] As my reading of Felman and Laub's texts suggests, in the right intertextual context, in the hybrid text, the image of the child victim can produce the disruptive emotion that prevents too easy a resolution of the work of mourning.

Two Endings

In a later scene from Mitzi Goldman's *Hatred,* an Israeli colonel—not Menachem S.—tells of a moment after his unit leveled a Palestinian household suspected of harboring terrorists. "Of course we had to destroy it," he says. When they are done, a little girl in a pink skirt walks out of the rubble, holding a doll. He describes her in such detail that we can visualize her face and dress and posture. "As a human being," the colonel concludes, "you see a small child and you think she can be your child. You cannot afford not to be a human being first." With his response—not identificatory, but protective—he elicits our sympathy, based on a shared humanity, on a universal identification with the image of the vulnerable child. Using the child as an alibi, the colonel erases his responsibility for the massacre that just occurred. He projects the image of the child between himself as agent and us as viewers, and it is the child who absorbs our attention. As a vehicle of an identificatory and protective look, the child screens out context, specificity, responsibility, agency. This scene contains all that is problematic about the pervasive use of the image of the child victim.

In her discussion of heteropathic memory, Kaja Silverman quotes a scene from Chris Marker's film *Sans Soleil:* "Who says that time heals all wounds? It would be better to say that time heals everything except wounds. With time the hurt of separation loses its real limits, with time the desired body will soon disappear, and if the desired body has already ceased to exist for the other then what remains is a wound, disembodied." Silverman adds: "If to remember is to provide the disembodied 'wound' with a psychic residence, then to remember other people's memories is to be wounded by their wounds" (*Threshold* 189). In the conclusion to his first essay in *Testimony,* Dori Laub speaks of the "hazards of listening" to the story of survivors, of becoming a secondary witness or the subject of heteropathic recollection. Those of us in the generation of postmemory watch survivors rebuild their lives; we watch them amass fortunes and erect castles. "Yet," says Laub, "in the center of this massive dedicated effort remains a danger, a nightmare, a fragility, a woundedness that defies all healing" (73). The image of the child witness, an image on which, figuratively at least, Laub projects his own childhood image, produces this woundedness in his writing and in our reading. It is a measure of the massive effort in which, as a culture, we have been engaged in the last half-century; to rebuild a world so massively destroyed without, however, denying the destruction or its wounds. The image of the child victim, which is also the image of the child witness, provides the disembodied wound of Holocaust destruction with a residence.[23]

NOTES

[1] Jarosław M. Rymkiewicz, *The Final Station: Umschlagplatz,* trans. Nina Taylor (New York: Farrar, Straus & Giroux, 1994), 324–26.

[2] Marjorie Agosín, *Dear Anne Frank,* trans. Richard Schaaf (Washington, D.C.: Azul Editions, 1994), 5–8. See also the new bilingual edition published by Brandeis University Press/University Press of New England (Hanover, N.H.: 1998).

[3] Artist talk, Hood Museum of Art, Dartmouth College, Hanover, New Hampshire, May 1996.

[4] For the definition of memory as an "act" see Pierre Janet, *Les Médications psychologiques* (1919–25; Paris: Société Pierre Janet, 1984, vol. 2), and the gloss on Janet's argument by Bessel A. van der Kolk and Otto van der Hart, "The Intrusive Past: The Flexibility of Memory and the Engraving of Trauma," in *Trauma: Explorations in Memory,* ed. Cathy Caruth (Baltimore: Johns Hopkins University Press, 1995).

[5] See Marianne Hirsch, *Family Frames: Photography, Narrative, and Postmemory* (Cambridge: Harvard University Press, 1997), esp. chaps. 1 and 6.

[6] Kaja Silverman, *The Threshold of the Visible World* (New York: Routledge, 1996), 185. Psychoanalytic theories of identification tend to stress its incorporative, appropriative logic based on idealization of the other. See in particular Diana Fuss's helpful discussion in *Identification Papers* (New York: Routledge, 1995). I appreciate Silverman's effort to theorize identification at a distance but what I find particularly helpful is her alignment, through the theorization of the look, of the structure of identification with the structure of memory, a process whereby we can "remember," through seeing, the memory of another.

[7] Roland Barthes, *Camera Lucida: Reflections on Photography,* trans. Richard Howard (New York: Hill and Wang, 1981). See Silverman's discussion of Barthes's terms, in *Threshold,* 181–85.

[8] Ilkaa Ahjopalo, dir., *Tsvi Nussbaum: A Boy from Warsaw* (1990), Ergo Media, Teaneck, N.J.

[9] The encounter between Rymkiewicz's narrator and Artur is in itself emblematic in Sidra DeKoven Ezrahi's "Representing Auschwitz," *History and Memory* 7, no. 2 (Fall–Winter 1996): 131.

[10] Lucy S. Dawidowicz, *The War Against the Jews: 1933–1945* (New York: Bantam, 1975), 166.

[11] Yala Korwin, *To Tell the Story: Poems of the Holocaust* (New York: Holocaust Library, 1987), 75. Other artists, writers, and critics have found this image equally inspiring. See especially the series of studies based on the photograph by painter Samuel Bak, which illustrates, yet again, the image's openness to identification. Samuel Bak, *Landscapes of Jewish Experience II* (Boston: Pucker Gallery, 1996). See also the long discussion of the image by Herman Rapaport in *Is There Truth in Art?* (Ithaca: Cornell University Press, 1997).

[12] Bruno Bettelheim, "The Ignored Lesson of Anne Frank," in *Surviving and Other Essays* (New York: Knopf, 1979).

[13] See Lynn Gumpert, *Christian Boltanski* (Paris: Flammarion, 1993). See also my own discussion of Boltanski's work in Hirsch, *Family Frames,* chap. 6.

[14] See Deboráh Dwork, *Children with a Star: Jewish Youth in Nazi Europe* (New Haven: Yale University Press, 1991), xxxiii. The most moving illustration of this is the monumental volume *French Children of the Holocaust: A Memorial,* ed. Susan Cohen, Howard Epstein, and Serge Klarsfeld, trans. Glorianne Depondt and Howard Epstein (New York: New York University Press, 1996), which lists the names of 11,400 deported French Jewish children and reproduces 2,500 of their photographs. The book, as the author writes in the introduction, is a "collective gravestone."

[15] Talk at the Institute for Contemporary Art, Boston, 25 January 1995.

[16] Mitzi Goldman, dir., *Hatred* (1996).

[17] Discussion following public showing of *Hatred* in Cape Town, South Africa, August 1996.

[18] On this split subject position, see Jean Laplanche and Jean-Bertrand Pontalis, "Fantasy and the Origins of Sexuality," in *Formation of Fantasy*, ed. Victor Burgin, James Donald, and Cora Kaplan (London: Routledge, 1989).

[19] See, among others, Julia Kristeva, "The Pain of Sorrow in the Modern World: The Works of Marguerite Duras," *PMLA* 102 (March 1987): 138–52, and Geoffrey Hartman, *The Longest Shadow: In the Aftermath of the Holocaust* (Bloomington: Indiana University Press, 1996), esp. "The Cinema Animal" and "Public Memory and Its Discontents."

[20] Dominick LaCapra, *Representing the Holocaust: History, Theory, Trauma* (Ithaca: Cornell University Press, 1994), 198–200. See Jacques Derrida's *Memoires, for Paul de Man*, trans. Cecile Lindsay, Jonathan Culler, Eduardo Cadava, and Peggy Kamuf (New York: Columbia University Press, 1988), for his reflections on the cannibalistic and appropriative modes of self/other relation that make mourning and identification after World War II impossible. See also Diana Fuss: "Trauma is another name for identification, the name we might give to the irrecoverable loss of a sense of human relatedness" (*Identification Papers*, 40).

[21] Shoshana Felman and Dori Laub, *Testimony: Crises of Witnessing in Literature, Psychoanalysis, and History* (New York: Routledge, 1992), chaps. 1 and 3.

[22] Saul Friedlander, "Trauma, Transference, and 'Working Through' in Writing the History of the *Shoah*," *History and Memory* 4 (1992): 51.

[23] I am grateful to the participants of the 1996 Dartmouth Humanities Institute on Cultural Memory and the Present for their ideas about cultural memory that have informed this argument and to audiences at the English Institute and the Comparative Literature Program at Dartmouth for their comments. Several colleagues have read earlier drafts of this paper and have made significant suggestions: Elizabeth Abel, Mieke Bal, Jonathan Crewe, Ivy Schweitzer, Leo Spitzer, Diana Taylor, Tom Trezise, Susanne Zantop. Mitzi Goldman and Lorie Novak have inspired this work with theirs; their encouragement is greatly appreciated.

• • • • • • • • • • • •

QUESTIONS FOR A SECOND READING

1. At one point Hirsch refers to the work that is required to enter the "visual space" of postmemory. As you reread, pay close attention to how she defines this work and pay close attention to how this work is demonstrated in her use of (her "readings" of) the photographs she includes as part of her text. What terms does she use to define this work? What are its goals? What is at stake?

   And then you might ask: Does she demonstrate in her practice (in her use of the photos) the goals she defines in her argument? And, finally, what might this essay on looking at images have to do with writing—that is, how might you extrapolate a writing lesson?

2. About two-thirds of the way through, Hirsch says, "It is my argument that the visual encounter with the child victim is a triangular one, that identification occurs in a triangular field of looking" (p. 274). This sentence may come

as a surprise (and perhaps is intended to), since the notion of a "triangular field" has not been front and center in the previous discussions. Keep this sentence in mind as you reread. How are you prepared to think about a "triangular field of looking"? And, as you read on, how are you being prepared for a "conclusion"?

3. The essay begins with three numbered sections (containing three images and two photographs). It concludes with two endings. The movement in the middle contains some surprising turns. The prose moves easily into first person. It relies heavily on images. This is not a conventional essay—introduction, body, conclusion. As you reread, pay close attention to the form of this essay—perhaps creating a chart or outline. Be prepared to use this to talk about the idea of the essay as it is represented in "Projected Memory."

4. The essay refers to a variety of sources: Rymkiewicz's novel, *The Final Station;* Marjorie Agosín's *Dear Anne Frank;* Art Spiegelman's *Maus* and *Maus II;* films by Resnais and Bergman (*Night and Fog* and *Persona*); a documentary, *Tsvi Nussbaum: A Boy from Warsaw;* a book of poetry by Yala Korwin; the *New York Times Magazine* article that included Lorie Novak's photograph *Past Lives;* a class taught by Shoshana Felman as reported in her book *Testimony*.

   There are others listed in the text and in the endnotes. Track one of these down and prepare a report for your class. What is it that would draw Hirsch to these examples (out of all the examples to represent the Holocaust)? Where and how is Hirsch's work suggested in them? How do you understand the work she did in bringing them into her essay?

ASSIGNMENTS FOR WRITING

1. The project of postmemory can be a writing project. In fact, to describe the individual's active engagement with the past that *is* postmemory, Hirsch uses metaphors of writing (or inscription): "It is a question of adopting the traumatic experiences—and thus also the memories—of others as one's own, or, more precisely, as experiences one might oneself have had, and of inscribing them into one's own life story. It is a question of conceiving oneself as multiply interconnected with others of the same, of previous, and of subsequent generations, of the same and of other—proximate or distant—cultures and subcultures" (p. 268).

   Use "Projected Memory" as an invitation to such a writing project, where you would write about a past that belongs to you but that is not yours. Hirsch is interested in stories of trauma and suffering. And there is, to be sure, much at stake (and much to be gained) by writing about the traumas that preoccupy us as a culture. You should not, however, feel that you must write about a traumatic past. You should write about what you have at hand—connections to the past through family, neighborhood, or (as Hirsch says) "group relation"—and as those memories can be prompted, assisted, and mediated by some documentary or photographic record (as in the case of the photos in "Projected Memory" and the story of Anne Frank for Rymkiewicz and Agosín). The past that you are tied to need not necessarily have national or international significance. The importance is that you can identify yourself with this past and with these memories (and that you can inscribe them into your own life story).

Since we are using Hirsch to invite you to write about the past, it is important to note where and how she identifies the problems that accompany such a task. It comes in the distinction she makes between "idiopathic" and "heteropathic" identification; her concern is cliché, sentimentality, a too-easy identification with that which is beyond you, even incomprehensible. She says,

> The challenge for the postmemorial artist is precisely to find the balance that allows the spectator [the reader] to enter the image, to imagine the disaster, but that disallows an overappropriate identification that makes the distances disappear, creating too available, too easy an access to this particular past. (p. 269)

2. In a sense, we have all been asked to remember the Holocaust. Its images, stories, reminders, words are regularly present in what we see, read, and hear. Our culture and European culture continue to rework and remember the attempt to exterminate the Jews in World War II. Choose an example that you remember or that you would like to know more about—a film or television show, an image, a work of art, a work of literature—and bring it under the sway of Hirsch's essay. You should assume that your readers are not familiar with Hirsch and her work and, even if they are familiar with your example, that they will need reminders.

   Once you establish Hirsch's work as your frame of reference, you will need to bring your example into the discussion. And your effort should be to do this in your voice and from your point of view. You want to show that you can use Hirsch's terms and bring her argument to bear; you also want to show that you have something to add to the discussion.

3. The essay begins with three numbered sections (containing three images and two photographs). It concludes with two endings. The movement in the middle contains some surprising turns. The prose moves easily into first person. It relies heavily on images. This is not a textbook essay.

   Reread the essay paying particular attention to its form and style, to what Hirsch is *doing* as well as what she is saying. While there is certainly an argument *in* Hirsch's essay, your concern should be with the argument represented *by* the essay, an argument about writing and scholarship and the relation of academic work to its potential audiences. Write an essay in which you discuss "Projected Memory" as a writing project. What might you learn from it as a writer? What might you learn from it about professors and about the academy? (You should assume that your readers have not read the essay; you can assume that they are students, like you, in a position to learn something about writing.)

4. As the title indicates, Hirsch's essay is about "projected memory" and it is about "Holocaust photographs in personal and public fantasy." It is not presented in the style of thesis, example, and conclusion. There is neither a conventional introduction nor a conventional summation. The arguments and demonstrations in between are rich, varied, and complicated.

   What, so far as you are concerned, is this essay about? And how does it speak to you—to your interests and concerns and projects and to your education? Write an essay, perhaps in the genre of a review, in which you present "Projected Memory: Holocaust Photographs in Personal and Public Fantasy" to those who have not yet read it. You will need to take care to give a thorough and accurate account of what Hirsch says and does. You should also establish your position in relation to the essay, discussing where and how you found it useful or interesting.

MAKING CONNECTIONS

1. According to Hirsch, Lorie Novak *"stages an uneasy confrontation of personal memory with public history."* Hirsch studies, writes about (and stages) such confrontations herself. The phrase is an apt one to use to describe the work of Edward Said and Jean Mohr in "States" (p. 378), an essay where image and text provide the occasion to connect "intimate memory and contemporary social reality." Said and Mohr, too, could be said to stage an uneasy confrontation of personal memory with public history.

   The project of postmemory, as defined by Hirsch, can be a writing project. In fact, to describe the individual's active engagement with the past that *is* postmemory, Hirsch uses metaphors of writing: "It is a question of adopting the traumatic experiences—and thus also the memories—of others as one's own, or, more precisely, as experiences one might oneself have had, and of inscribing them into one's own life story. It is a question of conceiving oneself as multiply interconnected with others of the same, or previous, and of subsequence generations, of the same and of other—proximate or distant—cultures and subcultures" (p. 268).

   Said speaks directly of the writing project in *After the Last Sky.* In the introduction, he says of the book,

   > Its style and method—the interplay of text and photos, the mixture of genres, modes, styles—do not tell a consecutive story, nor do they constitute a political essay. Since the main features of our present existence are dispossession, dispersion, and yet also a kind of power incommensurate with our stateless exile, I believe that essentially unconventional, hybrid, and fragmentary forms of expression should be used to represent us. What I have quite consciously designed, then, is an alternative mode of expression to the one usually encountered in the media, the works of social science, in popular fiction.

   Write an essay in which you consider Hirsch's "Projected Memory" through the lens provided by Said and Mohr's work in "States," with particular attention to differences. How do they each create, invoke, and value memory? What is the role of writing—or, what lessons can a writer draw from each? If you were to undertake such a project, whose example would you find most useful, whose most compelling? You will need to establish Said and Mohr's essay as an introduction and a point of reference. You will need to establish what they say and what they do and how they might talk about a project like Hirsch's. And then you will need to turn with care to the text of "Projected Memory."

2. In his essay, "The Tradition: Fact and Fiction," Robert Coles (p. 212) comments on the documentary photography done by Dorothea Lange and

Walker Evans during the Great Depression of the 1930s. Coles is interested in the ways photographs are both documentary records and works of art and so disrupt any clear distinction between fact and fiction. In his comments on one of Evans's photographs, he says,

> But Evans is struggling for an interiority, that of his subject and that of his subject's future viewer/visitor: let us not only praise this man, lift him to the ranks of the famous, but consider what might be going on within him, and let us, through the motions of our moral imagination, enter his life, try to understand it, and return with that understanding to our own, which is thereby altered. (p. 232)

"This is a tall order for a single picture," he says, "but then Evans and Agee were ambitious. . . ."

When he speaks of the viewer, the viewer Evans is assuming in his photography, it is a viewer with a "moral imagination" who will do the work to "enter [the subject's] life, try to understand it, and return with that understanding" to his own life, a life which would, then, be altered.

Write an essay in which you read Coles's essay from the position of Hirsch's argument. Both have the goal of teaching us how to use the photographic record. How are they different? Both speak with an urgency about the necessity of paying attention to the records of the past and the ethical issues involved. Again, how are they different? And, finally, if they define two ways of approaching the photographic record, where do you locate yourself within these issues?

You should imagine that you are writing for someone who can understand the issues but who is familiar with neither of these sources. You will need to take care, in other words, to establish what the two authors say and to give a sense of what it is like to read their prose.

3. While there are fewer photographs in "Projected Memory" than, say, in *Let Us Now Praise Famous Men,* the photographs are important to the work; you can't read the essay without taking time to study them. We should assume they were carefully chosen and carefully arranged, that this essay is, in fact, an example of a "photographic essay." Reread "Projected Memory" to think about the staging, the placement, and use of the photographs. Choose examples you can use to think about the various relationships of image to word and word to image.

   When you are done, reread W. J. T. Mitchell's "The Photographic Essay: Four Case Studies" (p. 332), and read it with the thought that "Projected Memory" might serve as a fifth case study. You should assume that you are writing for an audience familiar with neither text. You will, then, need to take care to present each, its key terms, examples, and arguments. And you should use Mitchell to think about Hirsch and her project. How might Mitchell classify "Projected Memory" in his account of the "dialectic of exchange and resistance between photography and language"? Where might he place "Projected Memory" in relation to the other four case studies? Both Hirsch and Mitchell express an urgency in their discussion of how we use and understand images. Are there connections? Is this urgency something you might share?

DOROTHEA LANGE
and
PAUL S. TAYLOR

DOROTHEA LANGE (1895–1965) began her career as a freelance and portrait photographer in San Francisco. One of her projects, prompted by the change in the social landscape during the Great Depression, was a series of photographs of people, including the poor and homeless, on the streets of her city. Paul S. Taylor (1895–1984) was a labor economist and a professor at the University of California at Berkeley; he had committed his work to the social problems created by (and behind) the Depression. In 1934, he was preparing an article on the San Francisco General Strike. He had seen some of Lange's street photos and asked if he could use them. They began to work together, including fieldwork that included meeting, interviewing, and photographing laborers and migrants; in 1935, they were married.

Their commitment to President Franklin D. Roosevelt's New Deal policies, and their work documenting the problems of poverty, led them to government work sponsored by the Resettlement Agency (later the Farm Security Administration, or FSA). That work, directed by Roy Striker, head of the photography unit, had the goal of bringing the reality of rural poverty into the homes of urban Americans, with the object of creating a national sense of crisis and providing visual evidence of the changes in rural life brought about by the Depression, the Dust Bowl, and farm mechanization. Striker said, "We are going to have to turn new devices, the movie and the still pictures and other things . . . to tell the rest of the world that there is a lower third [and] that they are human beings like the rest of us. . . ." The unflinching, heads-on, grim black-and-white style of photography that we associate with photographic "realism" was a product of the work of this era.

Taylor was a social scientist and his concern was to interview farm workers, including those who had lost their farms and who were on the road looking for work. His method was to let the people speak, to record their words, and to bring those words and those lives into the context of broad social, historical, and economic analysis. Taylor saw in Lange's photography images that could speak with power and eloquence. Her work, he said, was "professional research work . . . not to be confused with mere taking of pictures." Lange, too, made personal contact with the people she was photographing, asking them questions, taking time to converse, and carefully recording what was said. Lange saw in Taylor's fieldwork a way of providing a context for her photos and began to regularly accompany her photographs with captions.

After four years of fieldwork (usually in the summers), with particular attention to the migration of displaced farm workers hoping to find jobs in California, Lange and Taylor decided to begin work on the book that would become An American Exodus: A Record of Human Erosion. *Lange had been frustrated by the use of her photographs, usually one at a time as an "illustration" of a text over which she had no control. She wanted to present her work in a series and, with Taylor, began to plan a book in which photographs would not be simple illustrations but part of a complicated text, one that presented a story, evidence, research, and argument. As they say in the "Foreword,"*

> *This is neither a book of photographs nor an illustrated book, in the traditional sense. Its particular form is the result of our use of techniques in proportions and relations designed to convey understanding easily, clearly, and vividly. We use the camera as a tool of research. Upon a tripod of photographs, captions, and text we rest themes evolved out of long observations in the field.*

The book was published in 1940. It is divided into six sections, titled: "Old South," "Plantation Under the Machine," "Midcontinent," "Plains," "Dust Bowl," and "Last West." In the selection that follows, we have included the "Foreword," the first two sections, and the brief coda, titled "Directions."

When it first appeared, An American Exodus *was read, reviewed, and promoted under the shadow of John Steinbeck's* The Grapes of Wrath. *(Steinbeck's novel, published in 1939, achieved enormous success and was soon followed by the equally successful John Ford film adaptation, released in the same month* An American Exodus *hit the bookstores.) In a letter to their publisher, Lange and Taylor said:*

> *You may or may not wish, in promoting our book, to call attention to the fact that it has been in preparation long before the appearance of either* Grapes of Wrath *or* Factories in the Field. *We are not regretful that these two books have been published immediately before our own, and are drawing so much attention to portions of our theme. . . . Our book is not a follow-up of these books. It documents independently a nation-wide condition of which the California situation is an aggravated part. It en-*

ables an enlarged audience of readers to answer for themselves, by examining the photographic evidence, whether or not what they read and hear of the migrants is true.

Lange us considered one of the great photographers of her era, and An American Exodus *is both an important modernist text and a crucial document in the history of the Depression. During the war, Lange worked for the U.S. War Relocation Agency in San Francisco and for the Office of War Information. Later she was a staff photographer for* Life *magazine and, with Taylor, she worked as a freelance photographer on U.S. aid assignments in Asia, South America, and the Middle East. Her work is available in a number of collections, including* Dorothea Lange: Photographs of a Lifetime *(1996),* The Photographs of Dorothea Lange *(1996),* Photographing the Second Gold Rush: Dorothea Lange and the East Bay at War, *1941–1945 (1995), and* Dorothea Lange: Farm Security Administration Photographs, 1935–1939, *with writings by Paul S. Taylor (1980). Taylor's publications include* Mexican Labor in the United States *(1928),* Spanish-Mexican Peasant Community: Arandas in Jalisco *(1933), and* American-Mexican Frontier: Nueces County, Texas *(1934).*

Foreword

Exodus from the land is not new. Since the Middle Ages in Europe an unending stream of rural folk has fed the growth of cities and furnished manpower for rising manufactures. In America throughout our national history people have migrated in a double stream. One current, itself a part of the 500-year old stream of Europe, has drawn off surplus population from land already settled in order to urbanize and industrialize the United States. The other current, described a century ago by the Frenchman de Toqueville, has moved steadily westward with "the solemnity of a providential event . . . like a deluge of men rising unabatedly, and daily driven onward by the hand of God." Its goal was a piece of unoccupied domain for each family to assure a living through tillage of the soil.

The generation of our fathers saw the end of the western frontier of free land. And it is now a full decade since the doors of our factories were open wide to boys from the farms. Indeed, in the face of industrial collapse in 1929 millions of Americans sought refuge in recoil to the land from which they had sprung. . . . Now our people are leaving the soil again. They are being expelled of powerful forces of man and of Nature. They crowd into cities and towns near the plantations. Once more great numbers of landseekers trek west.

This contemporary exodus is our theme. It attains its most dramatic form on the deltas, the prairies, and the plains of the South, and in the tide of people which moves to the Pacific Coast. But this time the cities and are already burdened with unemployed, and opportunity upon the land is sharply restricted.

This is neither a book of photographs nor an illustrated book, in the traditional sense. Its particular form is the result of our use of techniques in proportions and relations designed to convey understanding easily, clearly, and vividly. We use the camera as a tool of research. Upon a tripod of photographs, captions, and text we rest themes evolved out of long observations in the field. We adhere to the standards of documentary photography as we have conceived them. Quotations which accompany photographs report what the persons photographed said, not what we think might be their unspoken thoughts. Where there are no people, and no other source is indicated, the quotation comes from persons whom we met in the field.

We show you what is happening in selected regions of limited area. Something is lost by this method, for it fails to show fully the wide extent and the many variations of rural changes which we describe. But we believe that the gain in sharpness of focus reveals better the nature of the changes themselves.

In this work of collaboration it is not easy nor perhaps important to weigh the separate contributions of each author. Those distinctions which are clearest arise from the fact that this rural scene was viewed together by a photographer and a social scientist. All photographs, with the few exceptions indicated, were taken by Dorothea Lange. Responsibility for the text rests with Paul Taylor. Beyond that, our work is a product of cooperation in every aspect from the form of the whole to the least detail of arrangement or phrase.

Our work has produced the book, but in the situations which we describe are living participants who can speak. Many whom we met in the field vaguely regarded conversation with us as an opportunity to tell what they are up against to their government and to their countrymen at large. So far as possible we have let them speak to you face to face. Here we pass on what we have seen and learned from many miles of countryside of the shocks which are unsettling them.

DOROTHEA LANGE
PAUL SCHUSTER TAYLOR

Berkeley, California
August 1, 1939

Old South

THE EMPIRE OF COTTON
NOW STRETCHES FROM THE ATLANTIC TO THE PACIFIC

HOE CULTURE

Alabama, 1937

ONE MULE, SINGLE PLOW

"The South is an agricultural area in the midst of an industrialized nation."
– RUPERT B. VANCE

Eutah, Alabama. July 1, 1937

"The South is poor, the land is poor,
the only crop is cotton, the houses are without paint,
weeds crowd up to the door, the tenants are illclad. . . ."
– RUPERT B. VANCE

Alabama, 1937

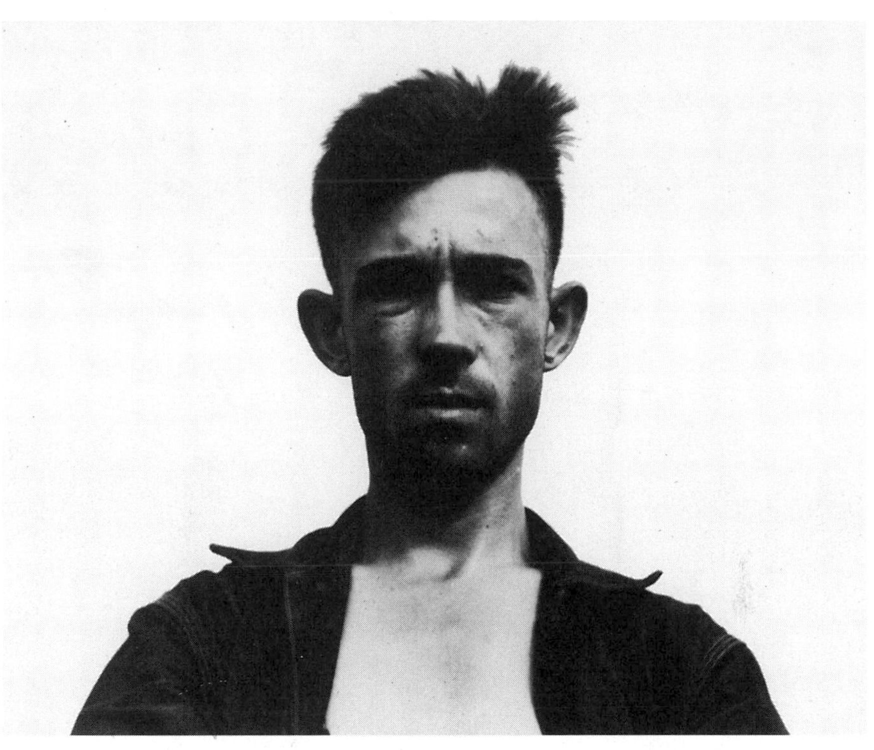

YOUNG SHARECROPPER ON $5 A MONTH "FURNISH"

"Hit's a hard get-by. The land's just fit fer to hold the world together. We think the landlord ought to let the government have this land and build it up, but he's got money and he don't believe in that way. Between Buck Creek and Whitewater Creek nobody can make a living."

NEIGHBOR: *"A piece of meat in the house would like to scare these children of mine to death."*

Macon County, Georgia. July 16, 1937

Couple, Born in Slavery

"I remember when the Yankees come through, a whole passel of 'em, hollerin', and told the Negroes you're free. But they didn't get nothin' 'cause we had carried the best horses and mules over to the gulley."

Plantation with 28 families abandoned in 1924 after the boll weevil struck.

Greene County, Georgia. July 20, 1937

AGRICULTURAL LADDER

"The Committee's examination of the agricultural ladder has indicated . . . an increasing tendency for the rungs of the ladder to become bars—forcing imprisonment in a fixed social status from which it is increasingly difficult to escape."

–*PRESIDENT'S COMMITTEE ON FARM TENANCY. 1937*

"The collapse of the plantation system, rendered inevitable by its exploitaiton of land and labor, leaves in its wake depleted soil, shoddy livestock, inadequate farm equipment, crude agricultural practices, crippled institutions, a defeated and impoverished people."
– Arthur F. Raper

Lower Piedmont, Greene County, Georgia. July 1937

Old South

Although we have nearly forgotten it, the spread across the South of a vigorous rural structure which we now call a problem was itself the product of a machine invented barely five generations ago. Planted by the earliest English settlements in America, cotton served little more than the domestic uses of households throughout the colonial era. Not until the slow, laborious, hand method of separating closely-adhering lint from cottonseed could be mechanized, was commercial production feasible.

In 1793 the Yankee Whitney invented the saw gin. The effect was immediate. Cotton production doubled in four years and increased eight-fold during the decade ending in 1804. There were no limits to the expanding market, for inventions in Great Britain were revolutionizing the textile industry and beginning to clothe the world in machine-made cotton cloth. In America slavery became more profitable.

In the Piedmont from Georgia to Virginia men grew more cotton. By 1825 planters and their slaves were beginning to settle Alabama, the Lower Mississippi, the Red River Valley in Louisiana, and western Tennessee. By 1860 the center of gravity of southern cotton production already had moved west along the Black Belt in Alabama on to the delta lands of the Mississippi, and the fringes of the Cotton Belt lay across Arkansas and eastern Texas.

As the planters advanced westward through the forests they established the basic characteristics of the Cotton Belt. They settled on the choicest lands of the South. They reared a landed aristocracy. They developed a one-crop economy and laid the southern foundations of a sectionalism which split the nation in the War between the States.

On the ruins of War the sharecropper replaced the slave. Neither planter nor laborer could readily command credit. So the propertyless freedman took his pay in a share of the crop instead of wages, and he mortgaged that share for the advances of subsistence "furnished" him by the planter while the crop matured. Thus, despite scattered protests by southern farmers in the late sixties that the sharecrop system was "a ruinous one to the interests of the country and its labor" it became riveted on the South.

Rural property in cotton is no longer a problem of race. After the War white workers began to engage in the production of cotton which previously they had shunned. Today after less than three generations white sharecroppers are almost equal in number to black sharecroppers, and as tenants they outnumber the colored by nearly two to one.

Nor does exhaustion of the soil distinguish the color of its victims. As in the North the pioneers were wasteful of the land. Even before the War a southern Congressman complained of Alabama "fields once fertile, now unfenced, abandoned and covered with those evil harbingers, fox-tail and broomsedge. . . . Indeed, a country in its infancy, where, fifty years ago, scarce a forest tree had been felled by the axe of the pioneer, is already exhibiting the painful signs of senility and decay apparent in Virginia and the Carolinas." Erosion, boll weevil, lost markets have forced plantation mansions into decay and left undernourished families on impoverished land.

The rural problems of the lower strata in the South are deeply rooted in the past. They have developed in the society created by cotton. They focus largely on masses of poor or propertyless workers, white and black, using simple methods of production in the fields, with little opportunity to rise.

Plantation Under the Machine

DELTA OF THE MISSISSIPPI

"Cotton obsessed, Negro obsessed, and flood ridden, it is the deepest South, the heart of Dixie, America's super-plantation belt. The Delta . . . consists of a series of basins of rivers . . . in Arkansas . . . in Mississippi . . . in Louisiana . . . Together with the alluvial lands of this great river, these basins form the Delta.

– *RUPERT B. VANCE*

Cotton plantation in Arkansas Delta.

August 1938

"Nowhere are ante bellum conditions so nearly preserved as in the Yazoo Delta."
– *Rupert B. Vance*

Yazoo Delta, Mississippi. August 1938

The Delta is the most concentrated cotton-growing section of the deep South. Land holdings are large, and on each 12 to 15 acres of this crop lives a tenant or sharecropper family. The countryside was deliberately populated densely in order to make available on the plantation itself enough hands to meet peak requirements for hand pickers at harvest.

Pulaski County in the Arkansas Bottoms. June 1938

Mechanization Is Invading the Delta with Development of the Pneumatic-tired, All-purpose Tractor

On this plantation only 30 families remain to work at day labor where 160 sharecropper families lived on the land. Twenty-two tractors and 13 four-row cultivators have replaced 130 families.

Near Greenville, Mississippi. June 1937

New and Old Elements in the Landscape

Tractor and plantation cabin.

Arkansas Delta. August 1938

Old Forms Remain, but They are Changed at the Core

Day labor family on a plantation; formerly sharecroppers.

On U.S. 61. Arkansas Delta. Saturday afternoon, August 1938

Cotton workers, swept from the land, fill the towns. From crowded slums they are daily drawn back to the plantations to hoe and to pick cotton in seasons when they are needed. At the bridgehead, 5 a.m., bound for a day's work on the Arkansas Delta. Wages 90 cents to $1.25 a day.

Memphis, Tennessee. June 1937

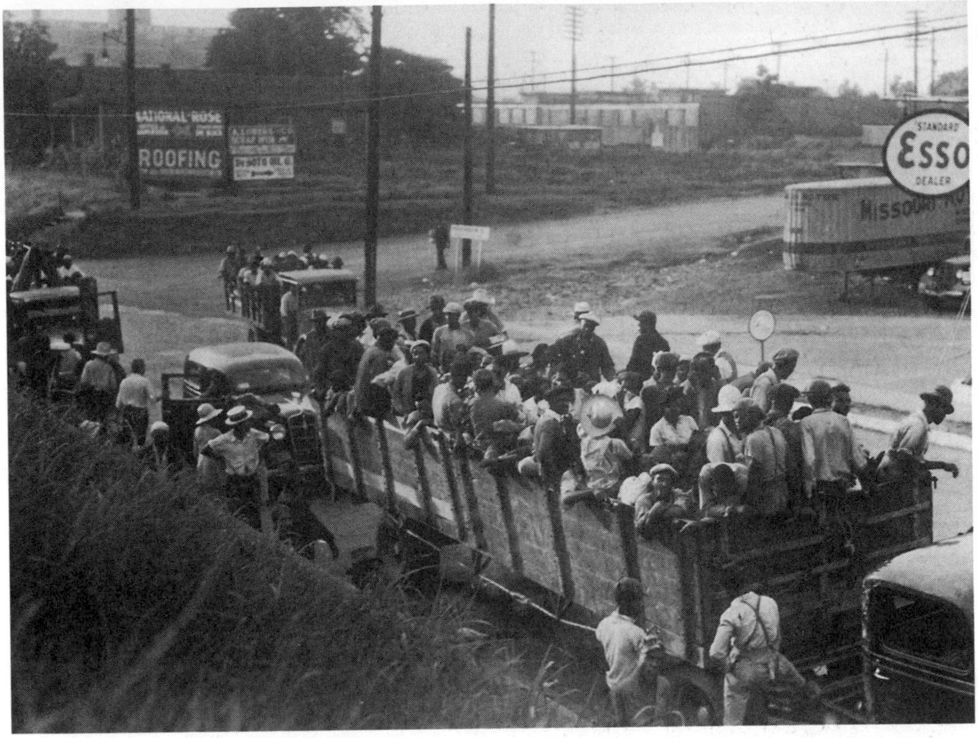
ROOFING
STANDARD
ESSO
DEALER

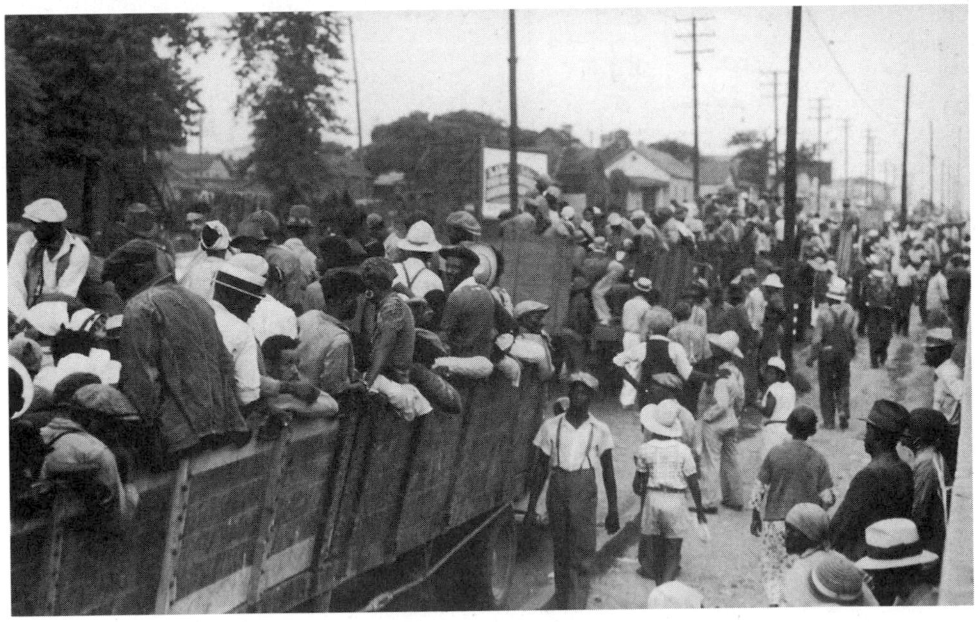

LINE-UP OF NEGRO UNEMPLOYED
AT THE STATE EMPLOYMENT SERVICE

Memphis, Tennessee. June 1938

Abandoned Tenant Cabin in the Mississippi Delta. 1937

"They ain't nothin' but day labor . . .
Right smart empty houses on that place . . .
Heap of 'em go far places."

AN AGRICULTURAL EXPERIMENT STATION RECOMMENDS—

"Making Cotton Cheaper"
"CAN PRESENT PRODUCTION COSTS BE REDUCED?"

"From 30 to 50 percent of present Delta farm labor must ultimately be replaced by machinery if plantations are to escape foreclosure. . . .

Putting labor on a cash or day basis will increase its efficiency 50 to 100 percent.

As cultivating machinery is improved, more hoeing can be eliminated by cross plowing. Cotton-chopping machines will also assist. . . .

Soap box orators may decry cotton pickers, tractors, two- and four-mule machinery but they and other modern farm machines are just as essential to farmers who expect to earn decent livings and fair returns on investments as are linotypes to printers, compressed air and concrete-mixing machines to contractors, modern spinning and weaving machines to textile manufacturers, or modern equipment to other American industries. . . . It is not up to American farms to absorb, even at pauper wages, either the labor released from modernized industry or non-essential farm labor replaced by the economical use of adapted farm machines."

Bulletin 298. Delta Experiment Station. 1932

Hoers going back to work after lunch on a Mississippi Delta plantation.
Part of day-labor gang hauled by truck out of Clarksdale.

June 1937

MORE MEN THAN JOBS AT THE BRIDGEHEAD LABOR MARKET

*"They come off the plantations 'cause they ain't got nothin' to do. . . .
They come to town and they* still *got nothin' to do."*

Memphis, Tennessee. June 1938

"The country's in an uproar now—it's in bad shape. The people's all leaving the farm. You can't get anything for your work, and everything you buy costs high. Do you reckon I'd be out on the highway if I had it good at home?"

On U.S. 80 near El Paso. June 1938

THE QUESTION ARISES—

"I say: A rollin' stone gathers no moss.
He says: A settin' hen never gets fat.
I say to him: Better stay here where people know us.
We'd have to sell our team and maybe we'd be left flatfooted.
I know about 15 families from Senath that's gone to California.
Some of 'em made out and some of 'em didn't."

Southeast Missouri. August 7, 1938

FAMILY COMING FROM TOWN ON SATURDAY AFTERNOON.
DELTA OF THE MISSISSIPPI

Southeast Missouri. August 1938

Plantations of the Delta are coming under the machine. The sharecropper system is collapsing at its advance, and croppers are being cut from the land. In protest, hundreds of families—white and black victims of its devastation—left their cabins in January 1939 to camp along 150 miles of open road.

Highway U.S. 61 in southeast Missouri.

Plantation Under the Machine

On the alluvial lands of the Mississippi River and its tributaries the plantation system reached its fullest development. By 1810 in the cotton parishes of the Louisiana delta slaves already were 55 to 63 percent of the total population. By 1840 in Bolivar and Issaquena counties of the Yazoo-Mississippi delta where settlement was retarded by floods, 72 percent of the population were slaves. At the outbreak of the War between the States 89 percent of the total population in that area were slaves, a population approached in the Cotton Belt only across the river in delta parishes of Louisiana.

Not only did the proportion of slave to free population approximate nine to one in sections of the delta, but the concentration of slaves held by each cotton plantation was the highest in the South. In 1860 when the average holding of slaves ranged from 17 to 47 in the older upland cotton areas of the Southeast, from 10 to 49 in upland areas of Alabama and Mississippi, and from 16 to 29 in upland regions west of the River, the average reached 55 in the Yazoo delta, 117 in Concordia Parish of the Louisiana delta, 118 in Issaquena County, Mississippi, and 125 in Rapides Parish in the Arkansas Valley.

Since Emancipation large plantations have survived more vigorously in the delta than anywhere in the Cotton Belt, with sharecropping and tenancy substituted for slavery as their foundation. Today about 85 percent of the farm land is operated in plantations; the largest in the world is in Bolivar County. In county after county of the delta in Mississippi and Louisiana the colored farm population still outnumbers the white by four and five to one, and even more. Only on the alluvial lands of southeast Missouri and adjacent

Arkansas delta where cotton production developed late after the Civil War do whites on the land outnumber the blacks.

Methods of producing cotton have remained primitive in the delta. One Negro behind one mule drawing a simple cultivator down long rows is still the common sight. Hoeing and picking are by hand as they were in 1793. Many hands are needed for chopping in late Spring and many more are needed for picking in early Fall. But plowing, planting, and cultivating require few workers, and between seasons and in winter there is idleness. To meet the heavy seasonal demands the plantations were drenched with laborers, and large families were encouraged. Then, since labor was ample, cheap, and must be supported anyway, there was slight incentive for more progressive methods of tillage.

But a series of changes during the 1930's is dealing the old system a series of heavy blows—a collapse in the price of cotton, the plow-up of cotton and curtailment of acreage to stiffen prices with government checks to farm operators who cooperate, a national program of public relief, and finally, perfection of the all-purpose, row-crop tractor. Faced with bankruptcy and loss of their plantations, landlords have begun to question the paternalism which since slavery has laid upon them the responsibility of caring for their people from one crop to the next. Under economic pressure they are yeilding, and relief makes it easier to yield. More and more they throw the care of their workers between crops upon the public, and let their people drift to the towns. Mechanization accelerates the process, for one man with tractor and four-row tillage equipment can do the work of eight mules and eight Negroes.

The record of power farming in cutting cotton workers from the land is already impressive. A pattern of mobile labor is developing. The landless cotton worker's year is being divided into occasional employment by the day on the plantations between May and December, and virtual idleness on relief in the towns from December to May.

This problem, originating in the South, is national in its repercussions. In January 1939 more than a thousand persons, white and black, encamped in the open along the highways of southeastern Missouri and the Arkansas delta in protest against the changes on the plantations of which they are the victims. Already whites from this section are picking cotton in Arizona and peas in California. Negroes in small numbers follow the well-worn channels cut by earlier migrations to the North. No tide of blacks has yet started west.

Heard in the Delta, 1937

State Official, Memphis:

"Modern efficiency has hit the farms like everywhere else. Since the twenties the banks and loan companies have more and more been interested in the plantations. The banks, loan companies, and business men figure costs on the farms. They say, 'Why maintain a nigger the year around when they need him only a few months?' It's simpler to let 'em go and cut down overhead. They buy tractors, and the tenants and croppers come to the cities and we put them on relief. More and more they drive them into town and then want them back only for day labor."

NEGRO EX-CROPPER, NOW TRACTOR DRIVER AT $1.50 A DAY, ARKANSAS DELTA:

"Most every farm—most every big farm—in this country has tractors on it. For the owners hit's good, but for the tenants this is much worser."

PLANTER WHO USES TRACTORS AND DAY LABOR, ISSAQUENA COUNTY:

"There were 34 tenant families on this plantation until 1935. Now I have 11 families all on day labor. When they get organized the way they are starting to organize a union up in Arkansas, they won't be no more tenants unless they reduce their shares from halves to thirds. They'll use tractors."

TOWN NEGRO, GREENVILLE, MISSISSIPPI:

"Tractors are against the black man. Every time you kill a mule you kill a black man. You've heard about the machine picker? That's against the black man too."

OFFICIAL OF TENANT FARMER'S UNION:

"The causes of the present situation are mechanization and large-scale ownership, the government checks, and relief. The big farmers are changing to day labor. Then they don't have to feed their families. They can bring labor from town to work by the day, and they can collect the entire government rental themselves. The AAA contract says the landowner can't cut his tenants to day labor, but after the contract is signed they *put* them on day labor. That's what started the union—the fight to get half of the check."

SHARECROPPER:

"These things are a pressin' on us in the State of Mississippi."

• • •

Directions

Some readers will ask, "If these are the conditions, why do you not tell us what is being done to meet them, and what ought we to do?" The question is fair and deserves a candid reply.

Measures to relieve some acute distress have been taken, but beyond these little is done. In southern areas which families are leaving, government work projects (WPA) and loans to farmers for rehabilitation retard the exodus. Yet as 1939 opened, unknown numbers were leaving farm and plantation for towns nearby, and in May and June needy people, principally from rural sections, were being counted entering California at the rate of six thousand a month.

What these people want who have long made their living from the land is not relief. They want a chance for self-support. Yet often they are driven to relief. In areas of emigration direct relief is inadequate. Rates of from $4 to $12 per month per case which prevail are plainly insufficient from any point of view. And neither direct relief nor work relief are now administered selectively. We need administration which will distinguish between those who because of age or other reason should be anchored at home, and those younger families with strength and resilience, but facing blank futures, who should be released with some aid to find opportunity elsewhere.

In areas of destination general relief is makeshift and uncertain. Needy migrants fall afoul of settlement laws which make "residence" in state and county the requisite to receive help. States and counties vie with each other in their efforts to shed responsibility. As an inevitable expedient federal relief grants, largely of clothing and food, are given through the Farm Security Administration to sustain farm families who falter in this no man's land between the laws. We need comprehensive congressional action. We need federal aid to the states for general assistance as we now give federal aid for the aged, blind, and dependent children. This is necessary to diminish relief differentials between states of origin and states of destination, to equalize responsibility between them, and to care more surely and decently for families who seek opportunity by migration.

We do not yet know the magnitude of the problems we face in any of the areas where they are most pressing. The count of the influx over the California border is more than a clue to volume of movement, but there is no count of movement westward into other states, eastward through Arizona, southeastward into Florida, or northward to the cities. By the end of 1939 the results of studies under the Bureau of Agricultural Economics will furnish statistics of the migration to California, Oregon, Washington, and Idaho. But we must wait until 1941 for what the census can tell of this cleaning the land of people and filling the towns of the South.

Although we cannot now give figures for the dimensions of our problem, we do know that many hundreds of thousands of people already are caught in the toils of rural change, and that more hundreds of thousands face common fates. We know that continued or recurring agricultural depression or drought threatens the precarious foothold of many who still cling to the land. We know that more tractors were sold in 1937 than were in use on all farms in the country in 1920, and read in our magazines of more and better machines soon to reach market. By their very efficiency and advantage to some Americans on the land they spell tragedy for others. Surely the urgency of a national effort of first magnitude is not concealed by our lack of statistics.

What direction shall action take? It is plain that with advances in agricultural techniques the country requires fewer farmers rather than more. Probably nine-tenths of the commercial production of agriculture at this time is supplied by well under half of the nation's farms. Mechanization accentuates this. Further, the income of agriculture is not great enough to support more people adequately. About 21 percent of our gainfully employed workers are engaged in agriculture, but they received less than 9 percent of the national income in 1938. We do not believe, therefore, that more small subsistence farms afford suitable solution for those who are displaced from either agriculture or industry. The advance of the machine should not, and probably cannot be halted, but we do not favor denying participation in the advantages of a machine-produced standard of living to more farmers for subsistence.

The great reservoirs which the Reclamation Service is building in the West have given hope to some that upon their completion a new, if brief, era of homesteading will return. But the capacity of these projects to absorb settlers is limited. The Columbia Basin alone will ultimately irrigate 1,200,000 acres of land, or half the total of land to be irrigated by all of the Reclamation projects of the West. None of it will be ready for several years and the process of settlement will stretch out for a full generation. The United States Commissioner of Reclamation dashed effectively the hopes that new irrigation will resettle the refugees to the West when as early as January 1938 he said, "The Columbia Basin project, if it were finished at this time, would provide homes for less than half of the farm families already driven by drought from the Great Plains alone."

The real opportunity for large-scale absorption of the displaced must lie in the direction of industrial expansion, not in crowding them back onto the land where already they are surplus. Industrial expansion alone offers hope of permanently raising agricultural income to high levels and of employing at good standards the population produced but unneeded on the farms.

Awaiting industrial expansion, then, must those who are leaving the farms in tragedy be left to wander as day laborers on the face of the land, supported only by the mercy of relief? We do not think so. We believe that a number of measures can be taken to ameliorate their situation. Some of them already are under way, inaugurated by both public and private agencies. Something has been done by both growers and government to establish decent camps for migratory workers, especially in California, but only the beginning has been made. These shelters afford a basis upon which are built health, morale, and fitness for the exercise of citizenship under their new conditions.

Extensive construction of housing for agricultural workers in the good lands can also help those who are adrift in the country or crowded into the towns and intermittently drawn back to work on the land. For housing is not only shelter, but properly designed and coordinated with cooperative dairy, garden, and poultry production, it can be the source of income to supplement wages, an anchor of stability to families, and the foundation of a better community life.

One of the most serious and tragic aspects of the life of those who are loosened from the land is their ostracism from the communities in which they live and work. Nothing but good can result from the breakdown of the social barriers which are erected against them. The means of doing this are simple, and very human. We leave their details to the initiative and common humanity of the growers, to the members of small churches, to members of baseball teams, to teachers in the schools, and others who live in the communities where migrant people work.

In our concern over the visible and acute distress of dislocated people, we must not lose sight of the permanent farming organization which is being laid down. This grave question arises: After the sweep of mechanization, how shall our best land be used—our southern plains, prairies, deltas, and our irrigated valleys of the West? Shall factory agriculture—our modern latifundia—prevail with its absentee owners, managers, day laborers, landless migrants, and recurrent strife? Or shall other patterns be sought for the relation of man to the land?

A very old American ideal, crystallized in the Homestead Act of 1862, holds that our land shall be farmed by working owners. But history has made serious inroads on this ideal. By 1935 tenancy had risen to 42 percent of all farms, and stood above 60 percent in many of the cotton states. Wage labor, standing at 26 percent of all persons gainfully employed in agriculture in 1930, reached 53 percent in Arizona and 57 percent in California. In order to preserve what we can of a national ideal, new patterns, we believe, must be developed.

Associations of tenants and small farmers for joint purchase of machinery, large-scale corporate farms under competent management with the working farmers for stockholders, and cooperative farms, are developments in the right direction. These devices conserve both the economies of machinery and organization and those elements of our national ideal which require security and a full share of the benefits for those who still till the soil. They can be aided not only by the government agencies which administer farm purchase and tenancy legislation, but also by private processors and others who now finance farm production.

In many places the old American family-size farm will long remain. But where it does not survive under the shock of change, new ways must be found if we are not to be confronted more and more with an organization of farm production which is harsh and already widespread. Our national effort must be well-planned, its support must be broadly based, and it must be long-sustained.

. . . We are now witnessing the outbreak of European war. Both agriculture and industry in this country will be stimulated. This may appear to some like a life preserver thrown to the displaced. But the acceleration of agriculture will be felt most in those very forms which now are displacing and limiting the opportunities of our people. Mechanization and industrialization on the land will spread. The false prosperity of war is no solution to the problems we describe. It is more likely to aggravate them.

• • • • • • • • • • • •

QUESTIONS FOR A SECOND READING

1. Lange and Taylor's "Foreword" includes the following account of method in preparing and assembling the photographs and the written text for their book:

   > This is neither a book of photographs nor an illustrated book, in the traditional sense. Its particular form is the result of our use of techniques in proportions and relations designed to convey understanding easily, clearly, and vividly. (p. 290)

   As you reread, see how you might identify, chart, and evaluate their "use of techniques in proportions and relations designed to convey understanding easily, clearly, and vividly." What are these techniques? Where do you see them? How would you describe them? What forms of understanding do they provide? What don't they provide?

2. Lange and Taylor's "Foreword" includes the following account of method in preparing and assembling the photographs and in writing the text for their book:

   > This is neither a book of photographs nor an illustrated book, in the traditional sense. Its particular form is the result of our use of techniques in proportions and relations designed to convey understanding easily, clearly, and vividly. We use the camera as a tool of research. Upon a tripod of photographs, captions, and text we rest themes evolved out of long observations in the field. We adhere to the standards of documentary photography as we have conceived them. Quotations which accompany photographs report what the persons photographed said, not what we think might be their unspoken thoughts. Where there are no people, and no other source is indicated, the quotation comes from persons whom we met in the field. (p. 290)

   As you reread, pay particular attention to the photographs and their captions. Lange and Taylor refer to their fieldwork: "Upon a tripod of photographs, captions, and text we rest themes evolved out of long observations in the field." What evidence can you see of the force of fieldwork on the photographs, their selection, presentation, and arrangement? What expertise would have chosen *these* shots from all the possible shots available? What expertise would have focused or cropped the shot in just this way? How do you understand "the standards of documentary photography" as Lange and Taylor have conceived them?

3. This question leads from the one that precedes it and draws on the terms in the long block quotation from the "Foreword" cited above.

   Lange and Taylor speak of their preparation in advance of the book. The prior research allowed the authors to develop themes, "themes evolved out of long observations in the field." What would you take to be the "themes" that organized this project? And, finally, how do you understand the relationship of caption to photograph (and to theme)? Some captions seem to have a direct fit; some are more askew or ironic or discontinuous. What information or guidance are you given? In what ways are you being taught to read a photograph, to speak for it, or to understand what it represents?

4. There are two extended blocks of prose: "Old South" and "Plantation Under the Machine." As you reread, think about these two as pieces of writing; they mark the places where writing takes over, performs, does *its* work in service of the project. Who speaks in these passages? What is the voice, the point of view, the investment or commitment to the people and places in the photographic images? How would you describe this style of writing? Is there an argument— and, if so, what is it? How does it proceed? And how do you understand the force of these sections in relation to the force of the photographs?

5. In the "Foreword" to *An American Exodus,* Lange and Taylor say:

   > We show you what is happening in selected regions of limited area. Something is lost by this method, for it fails to show fully the wide extent and the many variations of rural changes which we describe. But we believe that the gain in sharpness of focus reveals better the nature of the changes themselves. (p. 290)

   The "Foreword" refers to "sharpness of focus" as opposed to the "wide extent" and the "many variations" of the changes they document in rural Southern life and labor in the United States in the 1930s. As you reread, keep these terms in mind. Where do you most see the lack of the "wide" and "varied"? Where do you see its pull—or a gesture in that direction? And where would you find the best examples of the gains that are achieved through a "sharpness of focus"? Where do you find the best examples of the losses?

6. Rupert B. Vance appears several times in the captions. He becomes a character in the story that unfolds. As you reread, how do you imagine his character? And the role he plays in the story of the Old South and the change in agricultural practices? This should be supplemented, however, with research on Vance. You can get basic information off the Internet, but it would be useful as well to read some of his work. On the basis of this research, how do you now understand the role he plays and the force of his words in relation to the general project of *An American Exodus?*

7. It is hard to find Paul Taylor in this work. He doesn't announce himself anywhere in the writing. Who *is* Paul Taylor? You can get basic information off the Internet, but it would be useful as well to read some of his work. On the basis of this research, how do you now understand the role he plays and the force of his words in relation to the general project of *An American Exodus?*

ASSIGNMENTS FOR WRITING

1. The "Foreword" includes the following account of method in preparing and assembling the photographs and in writing the text for *An American Exodus:*

   > This is neither a book of photographs nor an illustrated book, in the traditional sense. Its particular form is the result of our use of techniques in proportions and relations designed to convey understanding easily, clearly, and vividly. We use the camera as a tool of research. Upon a tripod of photographs, captions, and text we rest themes evolved out of long observations in the field. We adhere to the standards of documentary photography as we have conceived them. Quotations which accompany photographs report what the persons photographed said, not what we think might be their unspoken thoughts. Where there are no people, and no other source is indicated, the quotation comes from persons whom we met in the field.

> We show you what is happening in selected regions of limited area. Something is lost by this method, for it fails to show fully the wide extent and the many variations of rural changes which we describe. But we believe that the gain in sharpness of focus reveals better the nature of the changes themselves. (p. 290)

The preceding "Questions for a Second Reading" can be helpful in thinking about this passage and about Lange and Taylor's project in general.

Write an essay that presents Lange and Taylor's project *as* a project. You will need to consider, then, not only what these selections say, but how they say what they say, and why the basic elements (photograph, caption, and text) are prepared and assembled as they are.

To prepare for this essay, you will need to reread with a particular attention to the images (particularly the way they are selected and arranged) and to the relationship between words and images. "Upon a tripod of photographs, captions, and text we rest themes evolved out of long observations in the field." How do these three elements work together: photographs, captions, and text? What demands do they put upon a reader? How do they teach the reader to read a photograph, to speak for it, or to understand what it represents? What decisions did Lange and Taylor seem to be making in preparing and assembling each element?

You should assume that you are writing for a reader who is familiar with Lange and Taylor but who has not read the work lately and who does not have a copy of the book at hand. You will need to provide examples (including examples of images). You'll need to put them in context, and you will need to teach your reader to understand them as you do.

2. In the "Foreword," Lange and Taylor say:

> We show you what is happening in selected regions of limited area. Something is lost by this method, for it fails to show fully the wide extent and the many variations of rural changes which we describe. But we believe that the gain in sharpness of focus reveals better the nature of the changes themselves. (p. 290)

"Sharpness of focus." "[W]e believe that the gain in sharpness of focus reveals better the nature of the changes themselves." Write an essay in which you consider this term *sharpness of focus* as it might provide access to Lange and Taylor's project. Your goal should be to describe their project and to think about its availability to readers like you, readers at this point in time (a time far more saturated with words and images).

What do you see that constitutes Lange and Taylor's concern for a sharpness of focus, particularly as the term relates not only to images but to images and texts? What, as you understand their concern, is lost with a sharp focus? What is gained? And write as well from your own point of view as a reader of this text. How might you describe your experience as a reader—your experience as a reader of words and images, your access to the world these words and images represent? What metaphor might you provide? Can you think of a similar project from your own point in time that you could use as a point of reference—one that works to provide "sharpness of focus"?

3. One of the oddest features of "Old South" and "Plantation Under the Ma-

chine" is the relationship between the photographs and the captions. It is clear that Taylor (if, in fact, he was the one to provide these) was careful, even scrupulous, in thinking about whose words (and what words) should accompany the photographic images:

> Quotations which accompany photographs report what the persons photographed said, not what we think might be their unspoken thoughts. Where there are no people, and no other source is indicated, the quotation comes from persons whom we met in the field (p. 290).

There is a logic, or a "grammar," to the selection and arrangement of the captions. The decisions were rule-governed, in others words; the captions were not added thoughtlessly or randomly.

Write an essay in which you consider this logic. Work closely with a representative set of four or five photographs. You will want to consider what Lange and Taylor say in the "Foreword," but you should also consider what is "said" by the example of their work. What they *do,* their practice, may provide information above and beyond what they say they do. And, finally, you should write from your perspective as a reader—what do they do for *you?* How do you understand the principles at work and the effectiveness of those principles? If there is a theory of captioning here, what is it? Whose interests does it serve? What is at stake in the limits and boundaries it draws? What would be the cost of violating these principles?

MAKING CONNECTIONS

1. James Agee and Walker Evans's *Let Us Now Praise Famous Men* (1941) (p. 22) and Dorothea Lange and Paul Taylor's *An American Exodus: A Record of Human Erosion* (1939) were conceived as projects at about the same time. They participate in the same documentary tradition and, as texts, they are in indirect conversation with each other. Both express a strong commitment to the Southern poor; both are aware of the dangers inherent in their projects, dangers that include exploitation and paternalism, relatively wealthy white Northern intellectuals profiting by retailing the images and stories of ex-slaves, tenant farmers, and sharecroppers. But the work of each is also very different, as the excerpts we've included in this textbook will show.

   Write an essay that presents and explores the significant differences. You will need to pick and choose. You will need to carefully select and present your examples. You will need to limit yourself to the differences that seem to you to be most significant or interesting. You should aim for an extended discussion of one or two rather than a catalog account of everything. And you should assume that the differences represent decisions made about appropriate method and form, that the work is different because of different approaches to the problems of representing rural scenes to an audience that would otherwise be ignorant of them.

2. In John Berger's "Appearances" (p. 175) and in Roland Barthes's excerpt from *Camera Lucida* (p. 140), the authors give an extended demonstration of how they "read" and value photographs. There is a personal urgency in each

discussion. Each author, that is, is working out something important; each provides an example of research driven by interest and desire. And both authors, it seems safe to say, are offering lessons. They are urging action. They are not just filing a report. Both "Appearances" and *Camera Lucida* are available to teach others how to read and value photographs; both offer methods, justification, motive, examples. Barthes resists "studium" (what he is supposed to see) and courts "punctum" (what he insists on seeing); Berger values "expressive photographs," photographs that allow him to elaborate not only narrative but ideas.

Choose one of the photographs from "Old South" or "Plantation Under the Machine" and write two brief accounts of it—one in the method and style of John Berger, one in the method and style of Roland Barthes. With these as key examples, write an essay in which you talk about the documentary tradition as represented by Lange and Taylor, and the more contemporary projects of Berger and Barthes. What are the goals of each? the political or social ambitions? the pleasures or abuses? What is at stake for them? What is at stake for you, and for students of your generation now living in the twenty-first century, in choosing one as a guide or model?

3. Lange and Taylor's "Foreword" includes the following account of method in preparing and assembling the photographs and in writing the text for their book:

> This is neither a book of photographs nor an illustrated book, in the traditional sense. Its particular form is the result of our use of techniques in proportions and relations designed to convey understanding easily, clearly, and vividly. We use the camera as a tool of research. Upon a tripod of photographs, captions, and text we rest themes evolved out of long observations in the field. We adhere to the standards of documentary photography as we have conceived them. Quotations which accompany photographs report what the persons photographed said, not what we think might be their unspoken thoughts. Where there are no people, and no other source is indicated, the quotation comes from persons whom we met in the field. (p. 290)

The preceding "Questions for a Second Reading" can be helpful in thinking about this passage.

To prepare for this essay, you will need to reread the selections from Lange and Taylor, paying particular attention to the relationship between words and images. "Upon a tripod of photographs, captions, and text we rest themes evolved out of long observations in the field." How do these three elements work together? What demands do they put upon a reader? How do they teach the reader to read a photograph, to speak for it, or to understand what it represents? What decisions did Lange and Taylor seem to be making in preparing and assembling photographs, captions, and text? (If there is time, you might use these questions as prompts for a first draft of an essay on the relationship between words and images in "Old South" and "Plantation Under the Machine.")

When you are done, reread W. J. T. Mitchell's "The Photographic Essay: Four Case Studies" (p. 332), and read it with the thought that Lange and Taylor's work might serve as a fifth case study. You should assume that you are writing for an audience familiar with neither text. You will, then, need to take care to present each, its key terms, examples, and arguments. How might Mitchell classify the work of Lange and Taylor in his account of the "dialectic of exchange and resistance between photography and language"? Where would he place their work in relation to the other four case studies? Lange and Taylor, like Mitchell, express an urgency in their discussion of how we use and understand images. Are there connections? Is this urgency something you might share?

W. J. T. MITCHELL

W. J. T. MITCHELL (b. 1941) is Gaylord Donnelley Distinguished Service Professor of English and Art History at the University of Chicago. His books include Iconology *(1987),* Blake's Composite Art *(1978),* The Language of Images *(1980),* Against Theory *(1985),* Art and the Public Sphere *(1993),* Landscape and Power *(1994), and* The Last Dinosaur Book: The Life and Times of a Cultural Icon *(1998). He is the editor of one of the leading journals in the humanities,* Critical Inquiry, *and has received fellowships from the Guggenheim Foundation, the National Endowment for the Humanities, the Rockefeller Foundation, and the American Philosophical Society. Mitchell's career as a scholar and teacher is distinguished not only by its productivity and wide-reaching influence (his work, for example, is read beyond his discipline and outside the academy) but also for the ways it has brought together subjects usually treated as separate: literature and art, words and pictures, language and vision.*

The following selection is taken from his 1994 prize-winning book, Picture Theory. Picture Theory *is a massive, brilliant, and controversial book whose goal is to examine the interaction of words and images, verbal and visual representations, in a variety of media, including literature, painting, advertising, and film. It not only describes these interactions but traces their linkages to issues of knowledge, power, value, and human interest. (The following selection looks at the hybrid medium of the photographic essay.)*

Picture Theory *brings together the materials and arguments of seminars Mitchell taught at the University of Chicago, seminars with titles like "Image and Text" and "Verbal and Visual Representation." His book is not, he says, so much a textbook as a "pedagogical primer or prompt-book for classroom experiments," experiments that would bring together the study of literature and the study of visual art under the general category of "representation." For Mitchell, this urgently needed form of study should be central to the undergraduate curriculum.*

Here is Mitchell in the introduction to Picture Theory:

> *W. E. B. Du Bois said "the problem of the Twentieth Century is the problem of the color-line." As we move into an era in which "color" and "line" (and the identities they designate) have become potently manipulable elements in pervasive technologies of simulation and mass mediation, we may find that the problem of the twenty-first century is the problem of the image. Certainly I would not be the first to suggest that we live in a culture dominated by pictures, visual simulations, stereotypes, illusions, copies, reproductions, imitations, and fantasies. Anxieties about the power of visual culture are not just the province of critical intellectuals. Everyone knows that television is bad for you and that its badness has something to do with the passivity and fixation of the spectator. But then people have always known, at least since Moses denounced the Golden Calf, that images were dangerous, that they can captivate the onlooker and steal the soul. . . . What we need is a critique of visual culture that is alert to the power of images for good and evil and that is capable of discriminating the variety and historical specificity of their uses.*

Mitchell's work is a contribution to that effort. A key word in Picture Theory, *one you will find in the chapter below, is "ekphrasis." Ekphrasis was originally used to name a minor literary genre, poems written about paintings; for Mitchell the term stands for the more general topic of "the verbal representation of visual representation" (words standing for images) and the human desire across time to believe that words can make us see or that they can give voice to (articulate, explain) something which is beyond or outside of language. In the chapter that follows, Mitchell looks at four "classic" texts of photojournalism to consider what is at stake in representing the world through picture and paragraph, and what is at stake in the arguments over which medium (photography or writing) can best make the claim to represent reality most truly, completely, or powerfully. Rather than choosing a side, Mitchell opens up the debate as a significant and useful contestation. His goal is to provide a practical example of how to think through particular texts, like a book of photojournalism, to larger questions of how we know what we know about the world, how we come to value what we value, and how power operates both through us and on us.*

The Photographic Essay: Four Case Studies

Three questions:

1. *What is the relation of photography and language?*
2. *Why does it matter what this relation is?*
3. *How are these questions focused in the medium known as the "photographic essay"?*

Three answers:

1. *Photography is and is not a language; language also is and is not a "photography."*
2. *The relation of photography and language is a principal site of struggle for value and power in contemporary representations of reality; it is the place where images and words find and lose their conscience, their aesthetic and ethical identity.*
3. *The photographic essay is the dramatization of these questions in an emergent form of mixed, composite art.*

What follows is an attempt to connect these questions and answers.

Photography and Language

> The totality of this relationship is perhaps best indicated by saying that appearances constitute a half-language.
>
> –JOHN BERGER,
> *Another Way of Telling*

The relationship of photography and language admits of two basic descriptions, fundamentally antithetical. The first stresses photography's difference from language, characterizing it as a "message without a code," a purely objective transcript of visual reality.[1] The second turns photography into a language, or stresses its absorption by language in actual usage. This latter view is currently in favor with sophisticated commentators on photography. It is getting increasingly hard to find anyone who will defend the view (variously labeled "positivist," "naturalistic," or "superstitious and naive") that photographs have a special causal and structural relationship with the reality that they represent. Perhaps this is due to the dominance of linguistic and semiotic models in the human sciences or to the skepticism, relativism, and conventionalism which dominates the world of advanced literary criticism. Whatever the reason, the dominant view of photography is now the kind articulated by Victor Burgin when he notes that "we rarely see a photograph *in use* which is not accompanied by language" and goes on to claim that the rare exceptions only confirm the domination of photography by language: "even the uncaptioned 'art' photograph," argues Burgin, "is invaded by language in the very moment it is looked at: in memory, in association, snatches of words and images continually intermingle and exchange one for the other."[2] Indeed, Burgin carries his argument well beyond looking at photography to "looking" as such, deriding the "naive idea of purely retinal vision," unaccompanied by language, a view which he associates with "an error of even greater consequence: that ubiquitous belief in 'the visual' as a realm of experience totally separated from, indeed antithetical to, 'the verbal'" (p. 53). Burgin traces "the idea that there are two quite distinct forms of communication, words and images" from the neoplatonic faith in a "divine language of things, richer than the language of words" to Ernst Gombrich's modern defense of the "natural" and "nonconventional" status of the photograph. "Today," concludes Burgin, "such relics are obstructing our view of photography" (p. 70).

What is it that troubles me about this conclusion? It isn't that I disagree with the claim that "language" (in some form) usually enters the experience of viewing photography or of viewing anything else. And it isn't the questioning of a reified distinction between words and images, verbal and visual representation; there seems no doubt that these different media interact with one another at numerous levels in cognition, consciousness, and communication. What troubles me, I suppose, is the confidence of tone, the assurance that we are able "today" to cast off certain "relics" that have mystified us for over two thousand years in favor of, presumably, a clear, unobstructed view of the matter. I'm especially struck by the figure of the "relic" as an obstructive image in contrast to the unobstructed view, since this is precisely the opposition which has (superstitiously) differentiated photography from more traditional forms of imagery and which formerly differentiated perspectival representation from "pre-scientific" modes of pictorial representation. Burgin's conclusions, in other words, are built upon a figurative opposition ("today/yesterday"; "clear view/obstructive relic") he has already dismissed as erroneous in its application to photography and vision. This return of an inconvenient figure suggests, at a minimum, that the relics are not quite so easily disposed of.

I'm also troubled by Burgin's confidence that "our view" can so easily be cleared up. Who is the "we" that has this "view"? It is implicitly divided between those who have overcome their superstitions about photography and those naifs who have not. "Our view" of photography is, in other words, far from homogeneous, but is the site of a struggle between the enlightened and the superstitious, moderns and ancients, perhaps even "moderns" and "postmoderns." Symptoms of this struggle emerge in Burgin's rhetoric when he speaks of the photograph as "invaded by language" (p. 51); what he seems not to consider is that this invasion might well provoke a resistance or that there might be some value at stake in such a resistance, some real motive for a defence of the nonlinguistic character of the photograph. Burgin seems content to affirm the "fluidity" (p. 52) of the relation between photography and language and to treat photography as "a complex of exchanges between the verbal and the visual" (p. 58).

But why should we suppose this model of free and fluid "exchanges" between photography and language to be true or desirable? How do we account for the stubbornness of the naive, superstitious view of photography? What could possibly motivate the persistence in erroneous beliefs about the radical difference between images and words and the special status of photography? Are these mistaken beliefs simply conceptual errors, like mistakes in arithmetic? Or are they more on the order of ideological beliefs, convictions that resist change by ordinary means of persuasion and demonstration? What if it were the case that the "relics" which "obstruct" our view of photography also *constitute* that view? What if the only adequate formulation of the relation of photography and language was a paradox: photography both is and is not a language?

This, I take it, is what lies at the heart of what Roland Barthes calls "the photographic paradox," "the co-existence of two messages, the one without a code (the photographic analogue), the other with a code (the 'art,' or the treatment, or the 'writing,' or the rhetoric of the photograph)."[3] Barthes works through a number of strategies to clarify and rationalize this paradox. The most familiar is the division of the photographic "message" into "denotation" and "connotation," the former associated with the "mythical," nonverbal status of the photograph "in the perfection and plenitude of its analogy," the latter with the readability and textuality of the photograph. Barthes sometimes writes as if he believes that this division of the photographic message into "planes" or "levels" may solve the paradox:

> how, then, can the photograph be at once 'objective' and 'invested,' natural and cultural? It is through an understanding of the mode of imbrication of denoted and connoted messages that it may one day be possible to reply to that question. (p. 20)

But his more characteristic gesture is to reject easy answers predicated on a model of "free exchange" of verbal and visual messages, connoted or denoted "levels": "structurally," he notes, "the paradox is clearly not the collusion of a denoted message and a connoted message . . . it is that the connoted (or coded) message develops on the basis of a message *without a code*" (p. 19). To put the matter more fully: one connotation always present in the photograph is that it is a pure denotation; that is simply what it means to recognize it as a photograph rather than some other sort of image. Conversely, the denotation of a photograph, what we take it to represent, is never free from what we take it to mean. The simplest snapshot of a bride and groom at a wedding is an inextricably woven network of denotation and connotation: we cannot divide it into "levels" which distinguish it as a "pure" reference to John and Mary, or a man and a woman, as opposed to its "connotations" of festivity. Connotation goes all the way down to roots of the photograph, to the motives for its production, to the selection of its subject matter, to the choice of angles and lighting. Similarly, "pure denotation" reaches all the way up to the most textually "readable" features of the photograph: the photograph is "read" *as if it were* the trace of an event, a "relic" of an occasion as laden with aura and mystery as the bride's garter or her fading bouquet. The distinction between connotation and denotation does not resolve the paradox of photography; it only allows us to restate it more fully.

Barthes emphasizes this point when he suggests that the "structural paradox" of photography "coincides with an ethical paradox: when one wants to be 'neutral,' 'objective,' one strives to copy reality meticulously, as though the analogical were a factor of resistance against the investment of values" (pp. 19–20). The "value" of photography resides precisely in its freedom from "values," just as, in cognitive terms, its principal connotation or "coded" implication is that it is pure denotation, without a code. The persistence of these paradoxes suggests that the "mode of imbrication" or overlapping between photography and language is best understood, not as a structural matter of "levels" or as a fluid exchange, but (to use Barthes's term) as a site of "resistance." This is not to suggest that resistance is always successful or that "collusion" and "exchange" between photography and language is impossible or automatically undesirable. It is to say that the exchanges which seem to make photography just another language, an adjunct or supplement to language, make no sense without an understanding of the resistance they overcome. What we need to explore now is the nature of this resistance and the values which have motivated it.

The Photographic Essay

> The immediate instruments are two: the motionless camera and the printed word.
>
> –JAMES AGEE,
> *Let Us Now Praise Famous Men*[4]

The ideal place to study the interaction of photography and language is in that subgenre (or is it a medium within the medium?) of photography known as the "photographic essay." The classic examples of this form (Jacob Riis's *How the Other Half Lives,* Margaret Bourke-White and Erskine Caldwell's *You Have Seen Their Faces*) give us a literal conjunction of photographs and text—usually united by a documentary purpose, often political, journalistic, sometimes scientific (sociology). There is an argument by Eugene Smith that the photographic series or sequence, even without text, can be regarded as a photo-essay,[5] and there are distinguished examples of such works (Robert Frank's *The Americans*).[6] I want to concentrate, however, on the kinds of photographic essays which contain strong textual elements, where the text is most definitely an "invasive" and even domineering element. I also want to focus on the sort of photo-essay whose text is concerned, not just with the subject matter in common between the two media, but with the way in which the media address that subject matter. Early in Jacob Riis's *How the Other Half Lives* he describes an incident in which his flash powder almost set a tenement on fire. This event is not represented in the photographs: what we see, instead, are scenes of tenement squalor in which dazed subjects (who have often been roused from their sleep) are displayed in passive bedazzlement under the harsh illumination of Riis's flash powder [Figure 1]. Riis's textual anecdote reflects on the scene of production of his images, characterizing and criticizing the photographer's own competence, perhaps even his ethics. We might say that Riis allows his text to subvert his images, call them into question. A better argument would be that the text "enables" the images (and their subjects) to take on a kind of independence and humanity that would be unavailable under an economy of straightforward "exchange" between photographer and writer. The photographs may be "evidence" for propositions quite at odds with the official uses that Riis wants to put them. The beholder, in turn, is presented with an uncomfortable question: is the political, epistemological power of these images (their "shock" value) a justification for the violence that accompanies their production? (Riis worked as a jour-

FIGURE [1]
Jacob Riis, *Lodgers in Bayard St. Tenement . . .*
Page spread from *How the Other Half Lives* (1890). Photo reproduced courtesy of the Museum of the City of New York.

nalist in close collaboration with the police; many of these photos were taken during nighttime raids; these are, in a real sense, surveillance photographs; they also had a profound effect on reform efforts in the New York slums.) Riis's joining of an inconvenient, disruptive text foregrounds this dilemma, draws us into it. A resistance arises in the text-photo relation; we move less easily, less quickly from reading to seeing. Admittedly, this resistance is exceptional in Riis, whose general practice is to assume a straightforward exchange of information between text and image. But its emergence even in this relatively homogeneous photo-essay alerts us to its possibility, its effect and motivations.

Another way to state this dilemma is as a tension between the claims of the ethical and the political, the aesthetic and the rhetorical. Photo-essays have been, by and large, the product of progressive, liberal consciences, associated with political reform and leftist causes. But the best of them, I want to suggest, do not treat photography or language simply as instruments in the service of a cause or an institution. Nor are they content to advertise the fine moral or artistic sensitivities of their producers. The problem is to mediate these disparate claims, to make the instrumentality of both writing and photography and their interactions serve the highest interests of "the cause" by subjecting it to criticism while advancing its banner. Agee distinguishes between the "immediate instruments" of the photo-essay, "the still camera and the printed word," and the "governing instrument—which is also one of the centers of the subject—[which] is individual, anti-authoritative human consciousness" (p. xiv). The production of the photo-essay, the actual labor that goes into it, should not be, in Agee's view, simply an instrumental application of media to politics, ideology, or any other subject matter. The "taking" of human subjects by a photographer (or a writer) is a concrete social encounter, often between a damaged, victimized, and powerless individual and a relatively privileged observer, often acting as the "eye of power," the agent of some social, political, or journalistic institution. The "use" of this person as instrumental subject matter in a code of photographic messages is exactly what links the political aim with the ethical, creating exchanges and resistances at the level of value that do not concern the photographer alone, but which reflect back on the writer's (relatively invisible) relation to the subject as well and on the exchanges between writer and photographer.[7]

One last question about the genre: why should it be called the "photographic *essay*"? Why not the photo novel or lyric or narrative or just the "photo text"? There are, of course, examples of all these forms: Wright Morris has used his photographs to illustrate his fiction; Paul Strand and Nancy Newhall link photographs with lyric poems in *Time in New England;* Jan Baetens has analyzed the emergent French genre of the "photographic novel." What warrant is there for thinking of the "photo-essay" as an especially privileged model for the conjunction of photography and language? One reason is simply the dominance of the essay as the textual form that conventionally accompanies photography in magazines and newspapers. But there are, I think, some more fundamental reasons for a decorum that seems to link the photograph with the essay in the way that history painting was linked to the epic or landscape painting to the lyric poem. The first is the presumption of a common referential reality: not "realism" but "reality," nonfictionality, even "scientificity" are the generic connotations that link the essay with the photograph.[8] The second is the intimate fellowship between the informal or personal essay, with its emphasis on a private "point of view," memory, and autobiography, and photography's mythic status as a kind of materialized memory trace imbedded in the context of personal associations and private "perspectives." Third, there is the root sense of the essay as a partial, incomplete "attempt," an effort to get as much of the truth about something into its brief compass as the limits of space and writerly ingenuity will allow. Photographs, similarly, seem necessarily incomplete in their imposition of a frame that can never include everything that was there to be, as we say, "taken." The generic incompleteness of the informal literary essay becomes an especially crucial feature of the photographic essay's relations of image and text. The text of the photo-essay typically discloses a certain reserve or modesty in its claims to "speak for" or interpret the images; like the photograph, it admits its inability to appropriate everything that was there to be taken and tries to let the photographs speak for themselves or "look back" at the viewer.

In the remainder of this essay I want to examine four photo-essays that, in various ways, foreground the dialectic of exchange and resistance between photography and language, the things that make it possible (and sometimes impossible) to "read" the pictures, or to "see" the text illustrated in them. I will limit myself to four main examples: the first, Agee and Evans's *Let Us Now Praise Famous Men,* generally acknowledged as a "classic" (and a modernist) prototype for the genre, will be used mainly to lay out the principles of the form. The other three, exemplifying more recent and perhaps "postmodern" strategies (Roland Barthes's *Camera Lucida,* Malek Alloula's *The Colonial Harem,* and Edward Said and Jean Mohr's *After the Last Sky*), will be analyzed in increasing detail to show the encounter of principles with practice. The basic questions to be addressed with each of these works are the same: what relationship between photography and writing do they articulate? What tropes of differentiation govern the division of labor between photographer and writer, image and text, the viewer and the reader?

Spy and Counter-spy: Let Us Now Praise Famous Men

> Who are you who will read these words and study these photographs, and through what cause, by what chance and for what purpose, and by what right do you qualify to, and what will you do about it.
>
> —JAMES AGEE

The central formal requirements of the photographic essay are memorably expressed in James Agee's introduction to *Let Us Now Praise Famous*

Men: "The photographs are not illustrative. They and the text are coequal, mutually independent, and fully collaborative" (p. xv). These three requirements—equality, independence, and collaboration—are not simply given by putting any text together with any set of photographs, and they are not so easily reconcilable. Independence and collaboration, for instance, are values that may work at cross-purposes, and a "co-equality" of photography and writing is easier to stipulate than it is to achieve or even to imagine. Agee notes, for instance, that "the impotence of the reader's eye" (p. xv) will probably lead to an underestimation of Evans's photographs; it is not hard to imagine a deafness or illiteracy underestimating the text as well—a fate that actually befell *Let Us Now Praise Famous Men* when it reached the editors of *Fortune* magazine, who had commissioned it.[9] Agee's generic requirements are not only imperatives for the producers of an art form that seems highly problematic, they are also prescriptions for a highly alert reader/viewer that may not yet exist, that may in fact have to be created.

It is easy enough to see how *Famous Men* satisfies the requirements of independence and co-equality. The photographs are completely separate, not only from Agee's text, but from any of the most minimal textual features that conventionally accompany a photo-essay: no captions, legends, dates, names, locations, or even numbers are provided to assist a "reading" of the photographs. Even a relatively "pure" photographic essay like Robert Frank's *The Americans* provides captions telling the subject and the location. Frank's opening image, for instance, of shadowy figures at the window of a flag-draped building [Figure 2, p. 340], is accompanied by the caption "Parade—Hoboken, New Jersey" which immediately gives us informational location not provided by the photograph and names a subject which it does not represent. Evans allows us no such clues or access to his photographs. If we have studied Agee's text at some length, we may surmise that the opening photograph is of Chester Bowles, and we may think we can identify three different tenant families in Evans's pictures based on their descriptions in Agee's text, but all of these connections must be excavated; none of them are unequivocally given by any "key" that links text to images. The location of Evans's photos at the front of the volume is an even more aggressive declaration of photographic independence. In contrast to the standard practices of interweaving photos with text or placing them in a middle or concluding section where they can appear in the context provided by the text, Evans and Agee force us to confront the photographs without context, before we have had a chance to see a preface, table of contents, or even a title page. When we do finally reach the contents, we learn that we are already in "Book Two" and that the photographs are the "Book One," which we have already "read."

The "co-equality" of photos and text is, in one sense, a direct consequence of their independence, each medium being given a "book" of its own, each equally free of admixture with the other—Evans providing photos without text, Agee a text without photos. But equality is further suggested by the feeling that Evans's photos really do constitute, in W. Eugene Smith's phrase, an

FIGURE [2]
Robert Frank, *Parade—Hoboken, New Jersey* (1955–1956), from *The Americans* (1958). Copyright © Robert Frank. Courtesy, Pace/MacGill Gallery, New York.

"essay" in their own right.[10] The sequence of Evans's photos does not tell a story but suggests rather a procession of general "topics" epitomized by specific figures—after the anomalous opening figure [Figure 3, p. 341] whose rumpled sport coat suggests a wealth and class somewhat above those of the tenant farmers, a survey of representative figures: Father [Figure 4, p. 342], Mother [Figure 5, p. 343], Bedroom [Figure 6, p. 344], House [Figure 7, p. 345], and Children (Girl-Boy-Girl) of descending ages [Figures 8, 9, 10, pp. 346–348].[11] It is possible to construct a master-narrative if we insist on one. Agee provides one some eighty pages later if we are alert to it: "a man and a woman are drawn together upon a bed and there is a child and there are children" (p. 55). We can even give these figures proper names: George and Annie Mae Gudger, their house, their children. But these text-image "exchanges" are not *given* to us by either the text or the images; if anything, the organization of the volume makes this difficult; it resists the straightforward collaboration of photo and text. And this resistance is not overcome by repeated readings and viewings, as if a secret code linking the photos to the text were there to be deciphered. When all the "proper" names and places are identified, we are reminded that these are fictional names: the Gudgers, Rickettses, and Woodses do not exist by those names. We may feel we "know" them through Evans's images, through Agee's intimate meditations on their lives, but we never do, and we never will.

FIGURE [3]
Walker Evans, photograph from *Let Us Now Praise Famous Men* (1939) by James Agee and Walker Evans.
Photograph courtesy of the Library of Congress.

What is the meaning of this blockage between photo and text? One answer would be to link it with the aesthetics of a Greenbergian modernism, a search for the "purity" of each medium, uncontaminated by the mixing of pictorial and verbal codes. Evans's photos are like aggressively untitled abstract paint-

FIGURE [4]
Walker Evans, photograph from *Let Us Now Praise Famous Men* (1939) by James Agee and Walker Evans. Photograph courtesy of the Library of Congress.

ings, bereft of names, reference, and "literary" elements. They force us back onto the formal and material features of the images in themselves. The portrait of Annie Mae Gudger [see Figure 5, p. 343], for instance, becomes a

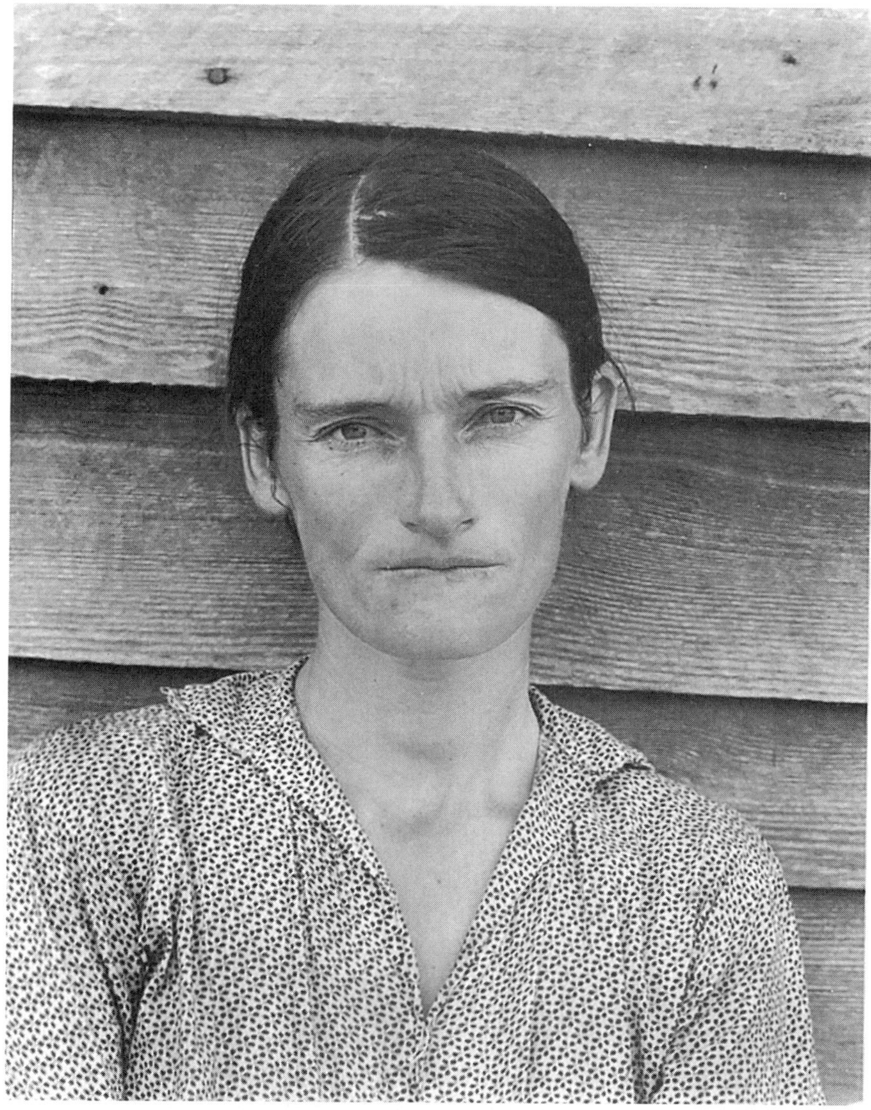

FIGURE [5]
Walker Evans, *Annie Mae Gudger,* photograph from *Let Us Now Praise Famous Men* (1939) by James Agee and Walker Evans.
© Copyright, Estate of Walker Evans.

purely formal study of flatness and worn, "graven" surfaces: the lines of her face, the weathered grain of the boards, the faded dress, the taut strands of her hair, the gravity of her expression all merge into a visual complex that is hauntingly beautiful and enigmatic. She becomes an "icon," arguably the

FIGURE [6]
Walker Evans, photograph from *Let Us Now Praise Famous Men* (1939) by James Agee and Walker Evans.
Photograph courtesy of the Library of Congress.

most famous of all the anonymous men and women captured by Evans's camera, a pure aesthetic object, liberated from contingency and circumstance into a space of pure contemplation, the Mona Lisa of the Depression.

There is something deeply disturbing, even disagreeable, about this (unavoidable) aestheticizing response to what after all is a real person in desperately impoverished circumstances. Why should we have a right to look on this woman and find her fatigue, pain, and anxiety beautiful? What gives us the right to look upon her, as if we were God's spies? These questions are, of course, exactly the sorts of hectoring challenges Agee's text constantly confronts us with; they are also the questions that Evans's photos force on us when he shows us the tenant farmers as beautiful, formal studies filled with mystery, dignity, and presence. We cannot feel easy with our aesthetic appreciation of Annie Mae Gudger any more than we can pronounce her true name. Her beauty, like her identity, is held in reserve from us, at a distance: she looks back at us, withholding unreadable secrets. She asks as many questions of us as we of her: "who are you who will read these words and study these photographs?"

FIGURE [7]
Walker Evans, photograph from *Let Us Now Praise Famous Men* (1939) by James Agee and Walker Evans.
Photograph courtesy of the Library of Congress.

The aestheticizing separation of Evans's images from Agee's text is not, then, simply a formal characteristic but an ethical strategy, a way of preventing easy access to the world they represent. I call this an "ethical" strategy because it may well have been counterproductive for any political aims. The collaboration of Erskine Caldwell and Margaret Bourke-White in the representation of tenant farmers provides an instructive comparison. *You Have Seen Their Faces* offers unimpeded exchange between photos and text: Bourke-White's images interweave with Caldwell's essay; each photo is accompanied by a "legend" locating the shot and a "quotation" by the central figure. Consider *Hamilton, Alabama*/"We manage to get along" [Figure 11, p. 349].[12] The photograph restates the legend in its pictorial code, creating with its low-angle viewpoint and wide-angle lens an impression of monumentality and strength (note especially how large the figure's hands are made to seem). This sort of rhetorical reinforcement and repetition is by far the more conventional arrangement of the photo-essay, and it may explain the enormous popular success of *You Have Seen Their Faces.*

It also illustrates vividly the kind of rhetorical relation of photo and text

FIGURE [8]
Walker Evans, photograph from *Let Us Now Praise Famous Men* (1939) by James Agee and Walker Evans.
Photograph courtesy of the Library of Congress.

that Evans and Agee were resisting. This is not to say that Evans and Agee are "unrhetorical," but that their "collaboration" is governed by a rhetoric of resistance rather than one of exchange and cooperation. Their images and words are "fully collaborative" in the project of subverting what they saw as a false and facile collaboration with governmental and journalistic institutions (the Farm Security Administration, *Fortune* magazine).[13] The blockage between photo and text is, in effect, a sabotaging of an effective surveillance and propaganda apparatus, one which creates easily manipulable images and narratives to support political agendas. Agee and Evans may well have agreed with many of the reformist political aims of Caldwell and Bourke-White and the institutions they represented: where they parted company is on what might be called the "ethics of espionage." Agee repeatedly characterizes himself and Evans as "spies": Agee is "a spy, traveling as a journalist"; Evans "a counter-spy, traveling as a photographer" (p. xxii). The "independence" of their collaboration is the strict condition for this spy/counter-spy relation; it is their way of keeping each other honest, playing the role of "conscience" to one another. Evans exemplifies for Agee the ruthless violence of

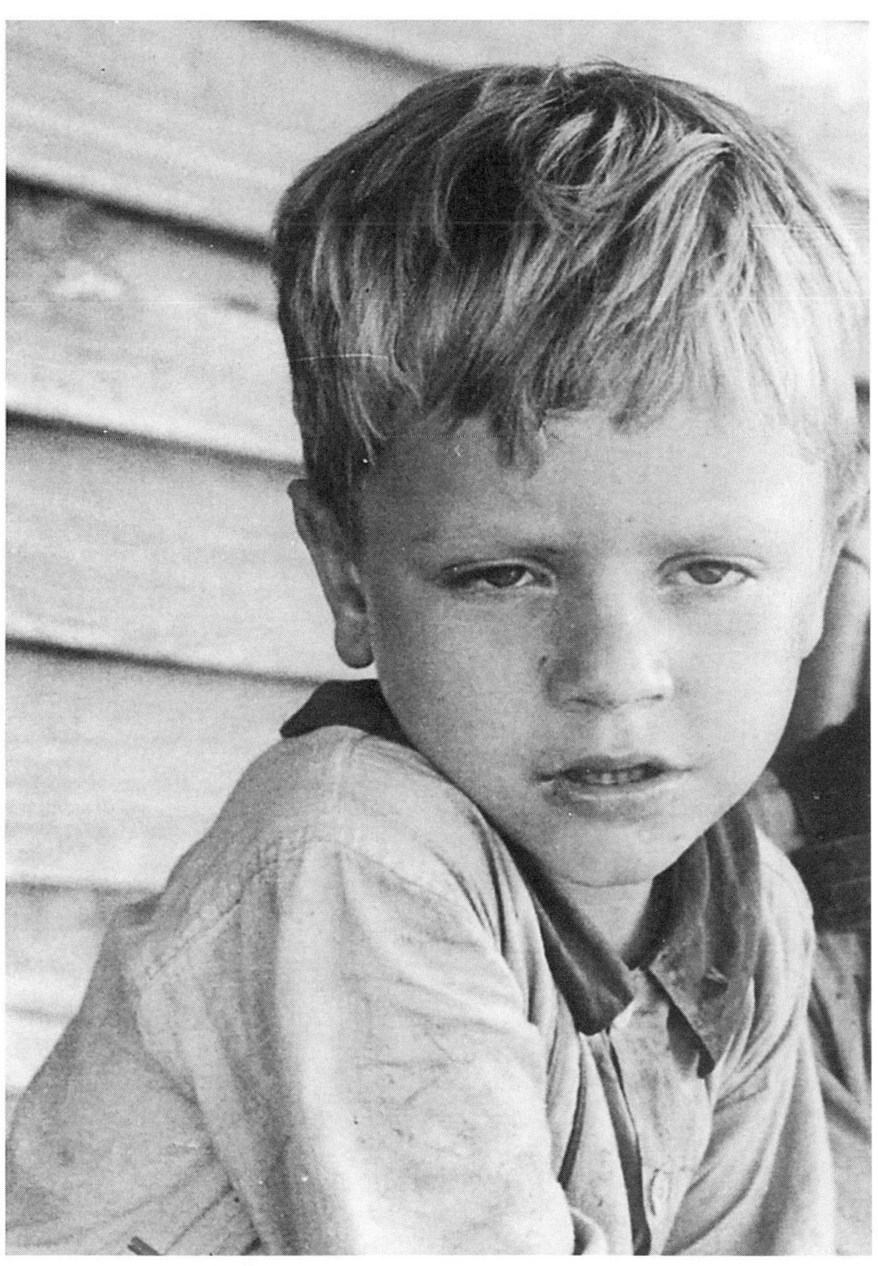

FIGURE [9]
Walker Evans, photograph from *Let Us Now Praise Famous Men* (1939) by James Agee and Walker Evans. Photograph courtesy of the Library of Congress.

FIGURE [10]
Walker Evans, photograph from *Let Us Now Praise Famous Men* (1939) by James Agee and Walker Evans. Photograph courtesy of the Library of Congress.

FIGURE [11]
Margaret Bourke-White, *HAMILTON, ALABAMA. "We manage to get along."*
From *You Have Seen Their Faces,* by Erskine Caldwell and Margaret Bourke-White.
Courtesy of the Estate of Margaret Bourke-White.

their work and the possibility of doing it with some sort of honor. The visibility of the photographic apparatus brings their espionage out into the open, and Agee admires the openness of Evans at work, his willingness to let his human subjects pose themselves, stage their own images in all their dignity and vulnerability, rather than treating them as material for pictorial self-expression. Agee, for his part, is all self-expression, as if the objectivity and restraint of Evans's work had to be countered by the fullest subjectivity and copiousness of confession. This division of labor is not just an ethics of production affecting the work of the writer and photographer;[14] it is, in a very real sense, an ethics of form imposed on the reader/viewer in the structural division of the photos and text. Our labor as beholders is as divided as that of Agee and Evans, and we find ourselves drawn, as they were, into a vortex of collaboration and resistance.[15]

Labyrinth and Thread: Camera Lucida

A labyrinthine man never seeks the truth, but only his Ariadne.
–NIETZSCHE
(quoted by Barthes)[16]

The strong, "agonistic" form of the photographic essay tends, as we have seen, to be as concerned with the nature of photography, writing, and the relation of the two, as with its represented subject matter (tenant farming, New York tenements, migrant workers, etc.). But most essays on photography (including this one) are not "photographic essays" in the sense I am giving the term here. Walter Benjamin's "A Short History of Photography" is not a photographic essay for the obvious reason that it is not illustrated. But even if it were, the photos would only be there to illustrate the text; they would not have the independence or co-equality that permits collaboration in a truly composite form.

One of the few "essays on photography" that approaches the status of a photographic essay is Barthes's *Camera Lucida.* The "independence" and "co-equality" of the photographs in Barthes's text is achieved, not by grouping them in a separate "book" where their own syntactical relations may emerge, but by a consistent subversion of the textual strategies that tend to incorporate photographs as "illustrative" or evidentiary examples. We open *Camera Lucida* to a frontispiece [Figure 12, p. 351], a color polaroid by Daniel Boudinet that never receives any commentary in the text. The only words of Barthes that might be applied to it are equivocal or negative ("Polaroid? Fun, but disappointing, except when a great photographer is involved" [p. 9]; "I am not very fond of Color . . . color is a coating applied *later on* to the original truth of the black-and-white photograph . . . an artifice, a cosmetic (like the kind used to paint corpses)" (p. 81). Are we to suppose, then, that Barthes simply "likes" this photograph and admires Boudinet's art? These criteria are continually subverted in Barthes's text by his seemingly capricious prefer-

FIGURE [12]
Daniel Boudinet, *Polaroid, 1979,* in Roland Barthes, *Camera Lucida* (1981).

ences, his refusal to assent to canonized masterpieces and masters: "there are moments when I detest Photographs: what have I to do with Atget's old tree trunks, with Pierre Boucher's nudes, with Germain Krull's double exposures (to cite only the old names)?" (p. 16). The Boudinet polaroid stands independent of Barthes's text: the best "reading" we can get it is perhaps simply as an emblem of the unreadability of photography, its occupation of a site forever prior to and outside Barthes's text. The photo presents an image of a veiled, intimate *boudoir,* simultaneously erotic and funereal, its tantalizingly partial revelation of light gleaming through the cleavage in the curtains like the secret at the center of a labyrinth. Barthes tells us that "it is a mistake to associate Photography . . . with the notion of a dark passage *(camera obscura).* It is *camera lucida* that we should say" (p. 106). But the darkened chamber of Barthes's frontispiece refuses to illustrate his text. If there is a *camera lucida* in this image it resides beyond the curtains of this scene, or perhaps in the luminous opening at its center, an evocation of the camera's aperture.[17]

Most of the other photographs in Barthes's text seem, at first glance, purely illustrative, but a closer reading subverts this impression. Barthes's commentaries are doggedly resistant to the rhetoric of the *"studium,"* the "rational intermediary of an ethical or political culture" (p. 26) that allows photographs to be "read" or that would allow a scientific theory of the photograph to emerge. Instead, Barthes emphasizes what he calls the *"punctum,"* the stray, pointed detail that "pricks" or "wounds" him. These details (a necklace, bad teeth, folded arms, dirt streets) are accidental, uncoded, nameless features that open the photograph metonymically onto a contingent realm of memory and subjectivity: "it is what I add to the photograph and *what is nonetheless already there*" (p. 55), what is more often remembered about a photograph than what is seen in its actual presence.[18] The effect of this rhetoric is to render Barthes's text almost useless as a semiological theory of photography, while making it indispensable *to* such a theory. By insisting on his own personal experiences of photographs, by accepting the naive, primitive "astonishment," "magic," and "madness" of photography, Barthes makes his own experience the raw material of experimental data for a theory—a data, however, that is filled with consciousness of a skepticism about the theories that will be brought to it.[19]

The photograph that is of most importance to Barthes's text, a "private" picture of his mother taken in a glassed-in conservatory or "Winter Garden" when she was five years old, is not reproduced. "Something like the essence of the Photograph," says Barthes, "floated in this particular picture." If "all the world's photographs formed a Labyrinth, I knew at the center of this Labyrinth I should find nothing but this sole picture" (p. 73). But Barthes cannot take us into the center of the labyrinth except blindfolded, by ekphrasis, leading us with the thread of language. Barthes "cannot reproduce" the photograph of his mother because it "would be nothing but an indifferent picture" for anyone else. In its place he inserts a photograph by Nadar of *The Artist's Mother (or Wife)* [Figure 13, p. 353], which one "no one knows for certain" (p. 70).[20] This photograph receives only the most minimal, even banal commentary ("one of the loveliest photographs in the world" [p. 70]) and an equally banal caption which pretends to be quoted from the text, but (charac-

FIGURE [13]
Nadar, *The Artist's Mother (or Wife)* (n.d.), in Roland Barthes, *Camera Lucida* (1981).

teristically) is misquoted or constructed especially for this image: "'Who do you think is the world's greatest photographer?' 'Nadar'" (p. 68). Barthes's substitution of this maternal image for his own mother launches him into a series of increasingly general associative substitutions: this photograph becomes "*the* Photograph" becomes "*the* Image"; Barthes's mother becomes "The Artist's Mother" becomes "*the* Mother." The link between "Image" and "Mother" is then summarized as a universal cultural complex which has been reproduced in the particularity of Barthes's own experience of photography:

> Judaism rejected the image in order to protect itself from the risk of worshipping the Mother. . . . Although growing up in a religion-without-images where the Mother is not worshipped (Protestantism) but doubtless formed culturally by Catholic art, when I confronted the Winter Garden photograph I gave myself up to the Image, to the Image-Repertoire. (pp. 74–75)

Barthes is not a photographer; he made none of the photographs in his book, his only responsibility being to collect and arrange them within his text. He therefore has no collaborator in the usual sense. His collaborator is "Photography" itself, exemplified by an apparently miscellaneous collection of images, some private and personal, most the work of recognized masters from Niepce to Stieglitz to Mapplethorpe and Avedon.[21] "All the world's photographs" are treated by Barthes as a labyrinth whose unrepresentable center conceals the Mother, *his* mother. A mother who, like the subjects of all photographs, "is dead and . . . is going to die" (p. 95) unites all the photographs in Barthes's text, endowing them with the independent unity that enables them to look back at us while withholding their secrets. The Nadar portrait, its maternal figure gazing abstractedly out of the photo, mouth discreetly covered by the rose she kisses, is the closest we come to an emblem of this self-possession and reserve.

The relation of the photographs to Barthes's text is, then, that of labyrinth and thread, the "maternal image-repertoire" and the umbilical cord of language. His role as a writer is not to master the photos, but to surrender himself as captivated observer, as naive subject of the idolatrous magic of images. The whole project is an attempt to suspend the appropriate "scientific" and "professional" discourse of photography in order to cultivate photography's resistance to language, allowing the photographs to "speak" their own language—not "its usual blah-blah: 'Technique,' 'Reality,' 'Reportage,' 'Art,' etc." but making "the image speak in silence" (p. 55). Barthes dismisses, therefore, much "sophisticated" commentary on photography, his own included:

> It is the fashion, nowadays, among Photography's commentators (sociologists and semiologists), to seize upon a semantic relativity: no "reality" (great scorn for the "realists" who do not see that the photograph is always coded) . . . the photograph, they say, is not an *analogon* of the world; what it represents is fabricated, because

> the photographic optic is subject to Albertian perspective (entirely historical) and because the inscription on the picture makes a three-dimensional object into a two-dimensional effigy. (p. 88)

Barthes declares this argument "futile," not just because photographs, like all images, are "analogical" in their coded structure, but because realism must be located in a different place: "the realists do not take the photograph for a 'copy' of reality, but for an emanation of *past reality:* a *magic,* not an art." This lost "magic" of photography, based in its naive realist stage (also its place in modernism), is what Barthes's text attempts to recover and why it must seem to efface itself, "give itself up to" its photographs, even as it weaves them into a labyrinth of theory and desire, science and autobiography.[22]

Voyeurism and Exorcism: The Colonial Harem

> It is as if the postcard photographer had been entrusted with a social mission: *put the collective phantasm into images.* He is the first to benefit from what he accomplishes through the delegation of power. The true voyeurism is that of the colonial society as a whole.
>
> –MALEK ALLOULA

The "magic" of photography can be the occasion of mystification as well as ecstasy, a point that is made by Malek Alloula's photographic essay on French colonial postcards of Algerian women.[23] Alloula dedicates his book to Barthes and adopts his basic vocabulary for the description of photographic magic, but he inverts Barthes's textual strategies in order to confront a body of images that exercised a detestable, pernicious magic over the representation of Algeria:

> What I read on these cards does not leave me indifferent. It demonstrates to me, were that still necessary, the desolate poverty of a gaze that I myself, as an Algerian, must have been the object of at some moment in my personal history. Among us, we believe in the nefarious effects of the evil eye (the evil gaze). We conjure them with our hand spread out like a fan. I close my hand back upon a pen to write *my* exorcism: *this text.* (p. 5)

There is no nostalgia here for a lost "primitive" or "realist" stage; there is no room for the "*punctum*" or ecstatic "wound" Barthes locates in the accidental detail. There is only the massive trauma of the "degrading fantasm" legitimating itself under the sign of photographic "reality." These photographs exclude all the "accidents" Barthes associates with the subversive "white magic" of the image. They stage for the voyeuristic French consumer the fantasy of "Oriental" luxury, lust, and indolence, as the unveiled "booty" before the colonial gaze. The critical text is counter-magic, a contrary incantation, repetitiously intoning its execrations on the filthy European pornographers with their ethnographic alibis.

Alloula's text fulfills the three conditions of the photographic essay in a quite unsuspected manner: his text is obviously independent of the images, that independence a direct result of Algeria's revolutionary independence of the French empire (Barbara Harlow's introduction places the book quite explicitly in the framework of Pontecorvo's film, *The Battle of Algiers*). There is "equality" of text and image in at least two senses. First, the text offers a point-by-point critical refutation of the implicit "argument" of the images. Second, it attempts to realize a contrary visual image or "staring back" into the face of the predatory colonial gaze. Alloula's text presents itself as a kind of substitute for a body of photographs that should have been taken, but never were:

> A reading of the sort that I propose to undertake would be entirely superfluous if there existed photographic traces of the gaze of the colonized upon the colonizer. In their absence, that is, in the absence of a confrontation of opposed gazes, I attempt here . . . to return this immense postcard to its sender. (p. 5)

Finally, there is "collaboration" in the sense that the postcards must be reproduced along with the text and thus forced to collaborate in their own deconstruction, their own "unveiling," much as the *algérienne* were forced to collaborate in the misrepresentation of Algerian women and their images forced to collaborate in a false textualizing—their insertion into a staged fantasy of exotic sexuality and unveiling, the colonial "chit-chat" (full of crude jokes) written on their backs, the colonial seal stamped across their faces, canceling the postage and their independent existence in one stroke.

Alloula's project is clearly beset on every side by contradictory impulses, the most evident being the necessity of reproducing the offending postcards in a book which may look to the casual observer like a coffee-table "collector's item" of exactly the sort he denounces. Occasional "classics" and "masterpieces" emerge, even in a pornographic genre:

> It is on "accomplishments" of this sort that a lucrative business of card collecting has been built and continues to thrive. It is also by means of this type of "accomplishment" that the occultation of meaning is effected, the meaning of the postcard that is of interest to us here. (p. 118)

"Aestheticization," far from being an antidote to the pornographic, is seen as an extension of it, a continuing cover-up of evil under the sign of beauty and rarity. This problem was also confronted by Agee, who dreaded the notion that his collaboration with Evans would be mystified by notions of special expertise or authority, chief among these the authority of the "artist": "the authors," he said, "are trying to deal with it not as journalists, sociologists, politicians, entertainers, humanitarians, priests, or artists, but seriously" (p. xv). "Seriousness" here means something quite antithetical to the notion of a canonical "classic" stamped with "aesthetic merit" and implies a sense of temporary, tactical intervention in an immediate human problem, not a claim on the indefinite future. That is why Agee wanted to print *Let Us Now Praise Famous Men* on newspaper stock. When told that "the pages would crumble to dust in a few years," he said, "that might not be a bad idea" (Stott, p. 264).

Let us add, then, to the generic criteria of the photographic essay a notion of seriousness which is frequently construed in anti-aesthetic terms, as a confrontation with the immediate, the local and limited, with the unbeautiful, the impoverished, the ephemeral, in a form that regards itself as simultaneously *indispensable* and *disposable.* The text of Alloula's *The Colonial Harem* sometimes reads as if it wanted to shred or incinerate the offending postcards it reproduces so well, to disfigure the pornographic beauty of the colonized women. But that would be, like most shreddings of historical documents, only a cover-up that would guarantee historical amnesia and a return of the repressed. Although Alloula can never quite say this, one feels that his essay is not simply a polemic against the French evil, but a tacit confession and purgation. Alloula reproduces the offending images, not just to aggressively "return an immense postcard to its sender," but to repossess and redeem those images, to "exorcise" an ideological spell that captivated mothers, wives, and sisters, as well as the "male society" that "no longer exists" (p. 122) in the colonial gaze. The rescue of women is an overcoming of impotence; the text asserts its manhood by freeing the images from the evil eye.

Barthes found the secret of photography in an image of his prepubescent mother at the center of a labyrinth. His text is the thread that takes us toward that center, a ritual surrender to the maternal image-repertoire. Alloula drives us out of the mystified labyrinth constructed by European representations of Arab women. He avenges the prostitution not only of the Mother, but of Photography itself, seeking to reverse the pornographic process.

What are we left with? Are the images redeemed, and if so, in what terms and for what sort of observer? How do we see, for instance, the final photograph of the book [Figure 14, p. 358], which Alloula only mentions in passing, and whose symmetry approaches abstraction, reminiscent of an art nouveau fantasy? Can an American observer, in particular, see these photographs as anything more than quaint, archaic pornography, hauntingly beautiful relics of a lost colonial era, "collector's items" for a coffee-table book? I don't have a simple answer to this question, but my first impulse is to register a feeling of *impotence* in the face of these women, whose beauty is now mixed with danger, whose nakedness now becomes a veil that has always excluded me from the labyrinth of their world.[24] I feel exiled from what I want to know, to understand, or (more precisely) what I want to acknowledge and to be acknowledged by. In particular, Alloula's text forces these acknowledgments from me: that I cannot read these photographs; that any narrative I might have brought to them is now shattered; that the labyrinth of photography, of the maternal image-repertoire, defies penetration and colonization by any textual system, including Malek Alloula's. The photographs,

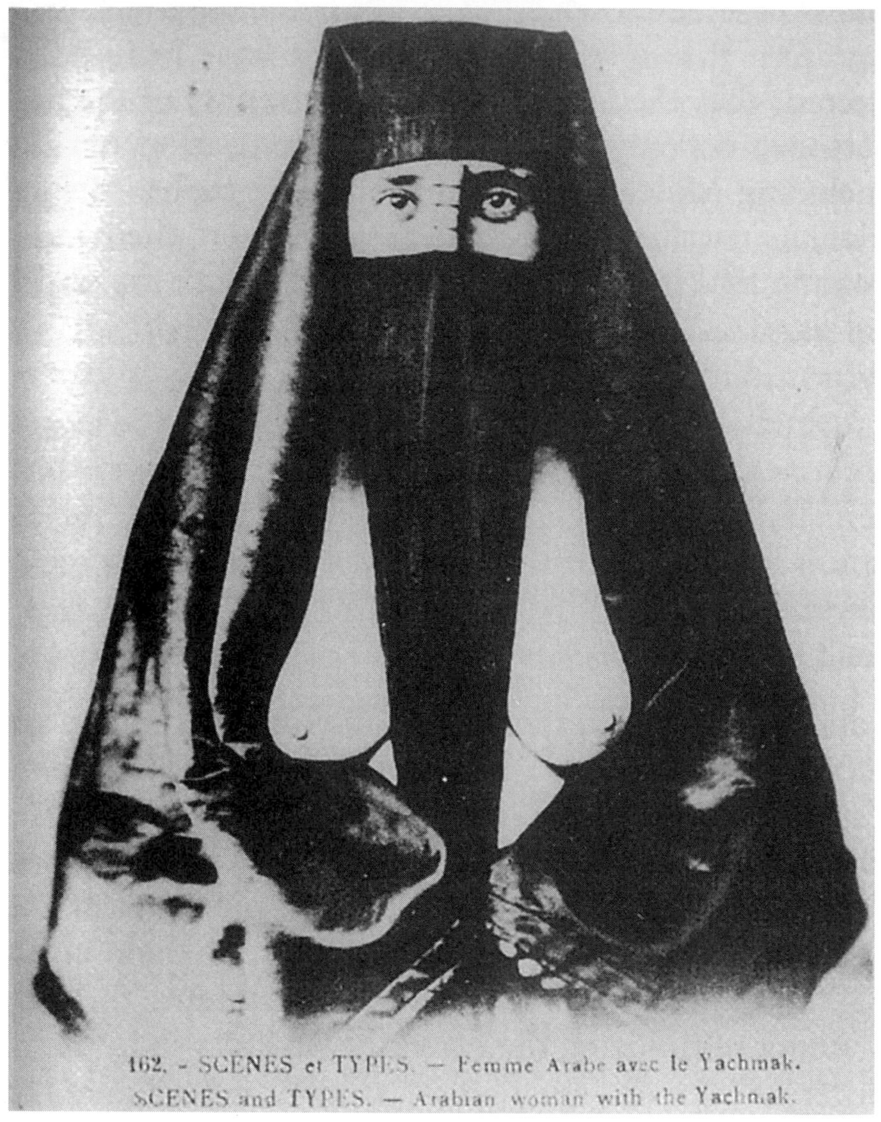

FIGURE [14]
Scenes and Types: Arabian woman with the Yachmak (n.d.), from *The Colonial Harem* (1986) by Malek Alloula, translated by Myrna and Wlad Godzich (French edition, 1981; English edition, Minneapolis: University of Minnesota Press, 1986).

so long exchanged, circulated, inscribed, and traded, now assert their independence and equality, looking at us as they collaborate in the undoing of the colonial gaze.

Exile and Return: After the Last Sky

But I am the exile
Seal me with your eyes.
–Mahmoud Darwish

Feelings of exile and impotence in the face of the imperial image are the explicit subject of Edward Said and Jean Mohr's photographic essay on the Palestinians. But instead of the aggressive "return of the repressed" in the form of degraded, pornographic images, *After the Last Sky*[25] projects a new set of images, self-representations of the colonized and dispossessed subjects, representations of their views of the colonizers: "our intention was to show Palestinians through Palestinian eyes without minimizing the extent to which even to themselves they feel different" (p. 6). The text is (as in *Camera Lucida*) a thread leading the writer and his readers back into the labyrinth of otherness and the self-estrangement of exile. Its task is to see that the "photographs are not" seen as "the exhibition of a foreign specimen" (p. 162), without, on the other hand, simply domesticating them. Said's text is not, then, like Alloula's, a scourge to drive Western eyes out the labyrinth. If Alloula treats the collaboration of text and image as a violent, coercive confrontation, Said and Mohr create a dialogical relation of text and image that is collaborative in the classic (that is, modernist) sense articulated by Agee and Evans, a cooperative endeavor by two like-minded and highly talented professionals, writer and photographer.

The results of this "positive" collaboration are anything but straightforward. The independence of text and image is not asserted directly, as in Agee and Evans, by a strict physical separation. Said and Mohr follow something closer to the mode of *Camera Lucida*'s dialectical, intertwined relation of photos and essay, a complex of exchange and resistance.[26] Writer and photographer both refuse the stereotyped division of labor that would produce a "text with illustrations" or an "album with captions." Said's text oscillates between supplementary relations to the images (commentary, meditations, reflections on photography) and "independent" material (the history of the Palestinians, autobiographical anecdotes, political criticism). Mohr's photographs oscillate between "illustrative" relations (pictures of boys lifting weights, for instance, document the "cult of physical strength" Said describes among Palestinian males) and "independent" statements that receive no direct commentary in the text, or play some kind of ironic counterpoint to it. An example: Said's discussion of his father's lifelong attempt to escape memories and material mementos of Jerusalem is juxtaposed (on the facing page) with an image that conveys just the opposite message and which receives no commentary, only a minimal caption: "the former mayor of Jerusalem and his wife, in exile in Jordan" [Figure 15, p. 360]. Behind them a photographic mural of the Mosque of Omar in Jerusalem occupies the entire wall of their living room. The collaboration of image and text here is not simply one of mutual support. It conveys

FIGURE [15]
Jean Mohr, *Mayor of Jerusalem,* page spread from *After the Last Sky,* by Edward W. Said. Copyright © 1986 by Edward W. Said. Reprinted by permission of Pantheon Books, a division of Random House, Inc.

the anxiety and ambivalence of the exile whose memories and mementos, the tokens of personal and national identity, may "seem . . . like encumbrances" (p. 14). The mural seems to tell us that the former mayor and his wife *cherish* these encumbrances, but their faces do not suggest that this in any way reduces their weight.

The relation of photographs and writing in *After the Last Sky* is consistently governed by the dialectic of *exile* and its overcoming, a double relation of estrangement and re-unification. If, as Said claims, "exile is a series of portraits without names, without context" (p. 12), return is figured in the attachment of names to photographs, contexts to images. But "return" is never quite so simple: sometimes the names are lost, unrecoverable; too often the attachment of text to an image can seem arbitrary, unsatisfactory. Neither pole in the dialectic of exile is univocally coded: estrangement is both imposed from without by historical circumstance and from within by the painfulness of memory, the will to forget and shed the "encumbrance" of Palestinian identity. "Re-unification," similarly, is the utopian object of desire and yet an object of potential aversion in its utopian impracticality. "Homecoming," says Said, "is out of the question. You learn to transform the mechanics of loss into a constantly postponed metaphysics of return" (p. 150). Where does the exile go "after the last sky" has clouded over, after Beirut, Cairo, Amman, the West Bank have failed to provide a home? What attitude do the physically exiled Palestinians take to the "exiles at home," the "present absentees" who live in "The Interior," inside Israel? The ambivalence expressed in these questions is also inscribed in the delicate, intricate, and precarious relations of text and image—the inside and outside, as it were, of this book.

The casual "Outsider," the beholder who takes this simply as an album of photographs, will have no difficulty grasping the major polemical point of the book, which is to counter the usual visual representation of Palestinians as menacing figures with *kaffiyas* and ski-masks. Anonymous "terrorists" are displaced by a set of visual facts that everyone knows in theory, but rarely acknowledges in practice—that Palestinians are also women, children, businessmen, teachers, farmers, poets, shepherds, and auto mechanics. That the representation of Palestinians as ordinary human beings, "capturable" by ordinary, domestic sorts of snapshots, should be in itself remarkable is a measure of how extraordinarily limited the normal image of the Palestinian is. There is an acceptable "icon" of the Palestinian, as Said puts it, and the images in *After the Last Sky*—domestic, peaceful, ordinary—do not fit this decorum, as anyone will find who attempts to insert this book among the other photographic texts that adorn the typical coffee-table.

The history of this particular set of photographs suggests that this decorum is not simply natural or empirical but has to be reinforced by the most stringent prohibitions. Jean Mohr was commissioned to take the pictures for an exhibition at the International Conference on the Question of Palestine held by the United Nations in Geneva in 1983. "The official response," as Said notes

> was puzzling. . . . You can hang them up, we were told, but no writing can be displayed with them. No legends, no explanations. A compromise was finally negotiated whereby the name of the

> country or place (Jordan, Syria, West Bank, Gaza) could be affixed to the much-enlarged photographs, but not one word more. (p. 3)

The precise motives for this bureaucratic "prohibition on writing" never become clear. Said speculates that the various Arab states who participated in the conference (Israel and the United States did not) found the Palestinian cause "useful up to a point—for attacking Israel, for railing against Zionism, imperialism, and the United States," but the notion of considering the Palestinians *as a people* (that is, with a story, a text, an argument) was unacceptable. The prohibition on writing was perhaps a way of keeping these disturbing images from taking on an even more disturbing voice. Context, narrative, historical circumstances, identities, and places were repressed in favor of what might be seen as a parody of the abstract and "modernist" space of visual exhibition: minimal captions, no "legends," pure visual display without reference or representation. Exile is a series of photographs without texts.

After the Last Sky, then, is a violation of a double prohibition against a certain kind of image (nonbellicose, nonsublime) and against a writing joined to these images. This might seem an excessively formalistic point. But Said notes that "most literary critics . . . focus on what is said in Palestinian writing . . . [its] sociological and political meaning. But it is the *form* that should be looked at" (p. 38). This "form" is not something distinct from content; it *is* the content in its most material, particular sense, the specific places it carves out as the site of Palestinian existence. As such, it resists the reduction of the Palestinian question to a political issue, insisting on the ethical as well as aesthetic relation of text and image. The collaboration of photographer and writer in *After the Last Sky* cannot be seen, then, simply as corrective to the prohibition which segregates the Palestinian image from the Palestinian text. This collaboration is also embedded in a complex field of heterogeneities that can never quite be accommodated to traditional dialectical forms of aesthetic unity. We don't find a Coleridgean "multeity in unity" in this book, but something more like a multeity of glimpses of unity, seen as if through a pair of spectacles, one lens of which is shattered. (This image, drawn from one of the most striking photographs in the book, is one I will return to later.)

The two lenses of this book are writing and photography, neither understood abstractly or generically but as constructions of specific histories, places, and displacements. The photographer, a German born in Geneva, naturalized as a Swiss citizen in 1939, has had concrete experience of intra-European exile. The writer is a Palestinian Christian born in Jerusalem, exiled to Lebanon, Egypt, the United States. From one point of view the writer is the insider, the clear, intact lens who can represent through his own experience a focused image of "the Palestinian"; the photographer is the alien, unable to speak the languages of Palestine or Israel, "seeing" only the mute, inarticulate fragments of lives that the camera allows (thus, many of the people in

Mohr's photographs are anonymous, unidentified, and photography redoubles the exile of image from referent). From another point of view, the photographer is the clear, intact lens. His Swiss neutrality allows him what was denied to the writer in the 1980s, the freedom to travel throughout Israel and the West Bank, to go "inside" Palestine and represent it with the transparent accuracy of photography. The writer is the alien, the outsider, estranged from a land he dimly remembers as a child, a land in which he would have been, as an urbane, Christian intellectual, estranged from the rural, local culture of the Palestinian masses. The writer acknowledges that he himself is the "cracked lens," unable to see, quite literally, the native country he longs for except in fragmentary glimpses provided by others.

The divisions of labor we have traced between writer and photographer—spy and counter-spy, thread and labyrinth, voyeur and exorcist—are consistently undermined by the tightly woven collaboration of *After the Last Sky.* But there is one vestige of traditional divisions of labor in the way Said's meditations on gender difference suggest the collaboration of a male text with a body of female images. Like Barthes, Said installs Woman at the center of the photographic matrix. The section of the book called "Interiors" (concerned with Palestinians who live inside Israel, with domestic spaces and the theme of privacy) is mainly devoted to images of women. Said also follows Barthes in finding that the primal scene of the photograph involves his mother. A British customs official rips up her passport, destroying her legal identity and (presumably) her photographic image in the same gesture. Like Alloula, Said is vindicating the disfigured image of his mother; like Barthes, he is trying to re-assemble the fragments of her identity. But he also portrays the women as the real preservers of this identity, associated with "the land" and the idea of home, portrayed as clinging irrationally, stubbornly, to "memories, title deeds, and legal claims" (p. 81). The women are also the keepers of images in the Palestinian interior, the ones who hang up too many pictures too high on the walls, who save the photograph albums and mementos that may encumber the male Palestinian who wants to travel light. (Recall that Said's father "spent his life trying to escape these objects" [p. 14].) Yet Said acknowledges a "crucial absence of women" (p. 77) in the representation of Palestinians. The official icon is one of "automatic manhood," the macho terrorist who may feel himself both goaded and reproached by the "protracted discipline" (p. 79) of women's work.

Like Barthes, Said wants to preserve the feminine mystique of the image, its difference from the male writer's "articulate discourse" (p. 79). Thus, it sometimes seems as if he would prefer to leave the female images unidentified and therefore mysterious. Like Barthes, he does not reproduce an image of his mother, but substitutes an image of an elderly woman, generalized as an emblem—"a face, I thought when I first saw it, of our life at home" (p. 84). But six months later Said is reminded by his sister that this woman [Figure 16, p. 364] is actually a distant relative whom he met in the forties and fifties, a reminder that produces mixed emotions:

FIGURE [16]
Jean Mohr, *Amman, 1984. Mrs. Farraj.* In *After the Last Sky,* by Edward W. Said. Copyright © 1986 by Edward W. Said. Reprinted by permission of Pantheon Books, a division of Random House, Inc.

> As soon as I recognized Mrs. Farraj, the suggested intimacy of the photograph's surface gave way to an explicitness with few secrets. She is a real person—Palestinian—with a real history at the interior of ours. But I do not know whether the photograph can, or does, say things as they really are. Something has been lost. But the representation is all we have. (p. 84)

The uncharacteristic awkwardness of Said's writing here is, I think, a tacit acknowledgment of his ambivalence toward the associative complex, Woman/Image/Home, a confession of his complicity in the sentimentalizing of women and of the lost pastoral homeland that fixates the imagination of the Palestinian male.[27] His candor about this ambivalence, his recognition that the photographic image has a life beyond the discursive, political uses he would make of it, allows the photograph to "look back" at him and us and assert the independence we associate with the strong form of the photo-essay. The poetic secrecy and intimacy he had hoped to find in this image is replaced by a prosaic familiarity and openness.

Jean Mohr provides Said with a striking emblem of his own ambivalence in a photograph which comes closer than any other in this book to supplying a portrait of the writer. Once again, the photo is an unidentified portrait, exiled from its referent, an image of an "elderly Palestinian villager" with a bro-

FIGURE [17]
Jean Mohr, *Elderly Palestinian Villager. Ramallah, 1984.* In *After the Last Sky,* by Edward W. Said. Copyright © 1986 by Edward W. Said. Reprinted by permission of Pantheon Books, a division of Random House, Inc.

ken lens in his glasses [Figure 17]. The photograph reminds Said of Rafik Halabi, "a Palestinian-Druze-Israeli" whose book, *The West Bank Story,* is highly critical of Israeli occupation, but "who writes from the viewpoint of a loyal Israeli" who served in the army and "subscribes to Zionism." Said finds Halabi's position impossibly contradictory. Either he is "deluded" or "up to some elaborate rhetorical game" which Said does not understand. Either way, "the result is a book that runs on two completely different tracks" (p. 127). It occurs to Said, of course, that there is something of himself, and perhaps of his own book, in this image: "Perhaps I am only describing *my* inability to order things coherently, sequentially, logically, and perhaps the difficulties of resolution I have discerned in Halabi's book and in the old man with broken glasses are mine, not theirs" (p. 130). First, the image is a double portrait of the Other as Insider, "a symbol, I said to myself, of some duality in our life that won't go away—refugees and terrorists, victims and victimizers, and so on" (p. 128). Not a bad reading, but Said is unhappy with it, as he is generally with emblematic readings that reduce the photograph to convenient verbal formulas. The man's face is "strong and gentle," the "blotch is on the lens, not in him" (p. 128). He has agreed to be photographed this way, so he can watch the camera and exert some control over his own image.

The resulting visual field (both for the wearer of the glasses and the beholder), Said notes, will always disclose a "small disturbance," a "curiously balanced imbalance" which is "very similar to the textual imbalance in Halabi's book" and, clearly, in Said and Mohr's. The Palestinians, a people without a geographic center and with only the most fragile cultural and historical identity have "no one central image," no "dominant theory," no "coherent discourse"; they are "without a center. Atonal" (p. 129). At moments like this, one glimpses Said's allegiance to the musical aesthetics of modernism, to that combination of pessimism and formalism we associate with Adorno. Said's composite, decentered, shifting, imbalanced collaboration with Mohr is nonetheless a shapely, congruent, and formal creation, a material embodiment of the reality he wants to represent, built out of a refusal to simplify, to sentimentalize or settle for polemic. Both writer and photographer could see themselves in this anonymous portrait, itself in exile from its subject: exile is indeed "a series of portraits without names, without contexts" (p. 12). But if photographs sundered from texts portray exile, photographs *with* text are images of return, sites of reconciliation, accommodation, acknowledgment. The delicate balancing act of a book "on two different tracks" may be a rhetorical game Said does not understand even as he is compelled to play it, but then he remarks that Palestinians sometimes "puzzle even ourselves" (p. 53).

The "central image" of the Palestinians is, for the moment, a double vision of just this sort—secular, rational, yet deeply involved in the emotions of victimage—figures in a rhetoric of paranoia which constructs them as the enemy of the victims of the Holocaust or as mere pawns in geopolitical schemes. Said and Mohr cannot be content, therefore, with a propaganda piece to "pretty up the image" of the Palestinians; they must work as well for an *internally directed* representation and critique, chiding not only the Arab and Israeli and Big Power interests, but the Palestinians themselves, Said included. The Palestinians' failings—their pursuit of inappropriate revolutionary models such as Cuba and Algeria, their impatient, macho romanticism, their failure to organize properly with the "protracted discipline" of women, their lack of a coherent history—are all part of the picture. The idea of the book, then, is ultimately to help bring the Palestinians into existence for themselves as much as for others; it is that most ambitious of books, a nation-making text.

Texts that make nations are, of course, what we call "classics," the worst fate (according to Agee) that can befall a book. It was a fate that befell *Let Us Now Praise Famous Men* after a period of neglect and misunderstanding. Our understanding of the thirties, particularly the Depression, is often seen as a product of Evans's and Agee's collaboration, and it helped to form an image of a nation in poverty, presented with dignity, sympathy, and truth. But Evans and Agee could never hope, as Said and Mohr do, to address the people they represent, to help bring them into being as a people. Whether this book fulfills such a hope is a question that will be settled beyond its pages: "there is no completely coherent discourse adequate to us, and I doubt whether at this point, if someone could fashion such a discourse, we could be adequate for it" (p. 129). It is at such moments of inadequacy, perhaps, that a mixed, hybrid discourse like that of the photographic essay emerges as a historical necessity.

Insofar as my own remarks here have been essays toward the definition of a genre or a medium, an attempt to articulate the formal principles of the photographic essay, they might be seen as a betrayal of the anti-aesthetic, anticanonical experimentalism of this form. Why attempt to "classicize" by classifying and formalizing a medium that is so young and unpredictable? The photographic essay occupies a strange conceptual space in our understanding of representation, a place where "form" seems both indispensable and disposable. On the one hand, it seems to participate in what Stanley Cavell has described as the tendency of "modernist painting" to "break down the concept of genre altogether,"[28] as if the medium were not given naturally, but had to be re-invented, re-evaluated in each new instance; this is the tendency I've associated with the mutual "resistance" of photography and writing, the insistence on the distinctive character of each medium, the search for a "purity" of approach that is both aesthetic and ethical. On the other hand, the roots of the photo-essay in documentary journalism, newspapers, magazines, and the whole ensemble of visual-verbal interactions in mass media connect it to popular forms of communication that seem quite antithetical to modernism in their freedom of exchange between image and text and their material ephemerality. Perhaps this is just a way of placing the photographic essay at the crossroads between modernism and postmodernism, understanding it as a form in which the resistance to image-text exchange is (in contrast to painting) most crucial precisely because it has the most to over- come.[29] If this crossroads occupies a real place in our cultural history, it is one we cannot leave unmapped. To take literally the antiformalist rhetoric of the photographic essay would be to empty it of its specific, historical materiality as a representational practice and to neglect those labors of love in which we are enjoined to collaborate.

NOTES

[1] The phrase "message without a code" is from Roland Barthes's essay, "The Photographic Message," in *Image/Music/Text,* translated by Stephen Heath (New York: Hill and Wang, 1977), p. 19. I am grateful to David Antin and Alan Trachtenberg for their many intelligent suggestions and questions about an earlier version of this essay.

[2] Victor Burgin, "Seeing Sense," in *The End of Art Theory: Criticism and Post-Modernity* (Atlantic Highlands, NJ: Humanities Press, 1986), p. 51; further page references will be cited in the text.

[3] Roland Barthes, "The Photographic Message," in *Image/Music/Text,* p. 19; further page references will be cited in the text.

[4] James Agee and Walker Evans, *Let Us Now Praise Famous Men* (originally published, 1939; New York: Houghton Mifflin, 1980), p. xiv; further page references will be cited in the text.

[5] See Tom Moran, *The Photo Essay: Paul Fusco and Will McBride,* in the Masters of Contemporary Photography series (Los Angeles, CA: Alskog, Inc., 1974). Eugene Smith's re-

marks on the genre of the photo-essay were made in conversation with the editors of this book and appear on pages 14–15.

[6] Robert Frank, *The Americans* (1st edition, 1959; rev. and enlarged ed., New York: Grossman Publishers, 1969). Frank's book is not entirely free of text, however. All the photographs are accompanied by brief captions, usually a designation of subject, time, or location, and there is an introduction by Jack Kerouac that emphasizes the implicit verbal coding of Frank's photographs: "What a poem this is, what poems can be written about this book of pictures some day by some young new writer . . ." (p. iii).

[7] For an excellent account of the way writers address the ethical issues of "approach to the subject" made visible by the photographic apparatus in action, see Carol Schloss, *In Visible Light: Photography and the American Writer: 1840–1940* (New York: Oxford University Press, 1987), p. 11.

[8] Recall the classic photo-essays based in scientific discourse such as geological surveys (Timothy O'Sullivan, for instance) and sociological studies (the work of Dorothea Lange and Paul Taylor). The modern discipline of art history is inconceivable without the illustrated slide lecture and the photographic reproduction of images. Any discourse that relies on the accurate mechanical reproduction of visual evidence engages with photography at some point.

[9] For a good account of the reception of Agee and Evans's work, see William Stott, *Documentary Expression and Thirties America* (New York: Oxford University Press, 1973), pp. 261–66.

[10] Eugene Smith argues that photojournalists tend to work within narrative conventions, producing "picture stories": "that's a form of its own, not an essay" (*The Photo Essay,* p. 15).

[11] This "topical" and nonnarrative format persists throughout the sequence of Evans's photos. The photos are divided into three sections, the first concentrating on the Gudgers and Woodses, the second on the Rickettses, and the third on the towns in their neighborhood.

[12] The reader who supposes that these quotations have some documentary authenticity, or even an expressive relation to the photographic subject, should heed Bourke-White's opening note: "the legends under the pictures are intended to express the authors' own conceptions of the sentiments of the individuals portrayed; they do not pretend to reproduce the actual sentiments of these persons." The candor of this admission is somewhat offset by the persistent fiction of the "quotation" throughout the text. This manipulation of verbal material is quite in keeping with Bourke-White's penchant for re-arranging the objects in the sharecroppers' households to conform with her own aesthetic tastes.

[13] Jefferson Hunter's book, *Image and Word: The Interaction of Twentieth Century Photographs and Texts* (Cambridge, MA: Harvard University Press, 1987) notes this resistance but sees it merely as an "affront" to convention that made *Famous Men* "unsuccessful in 1941" and "uninfluential now" on the practice of photo-text collaboration. Hunter takes the "stylistic consistency" of Bourke-White and Caldwell as a model for the way "collaborative efforts succeed" (p. 79).

[14] For an excellent account of what I'm calling an "ethics of production," see Carol Schloss's chapter on Agee and Evans in her *In Visible Light.*

[15] I use the word "vortex" here to echo Agee's allusions to the Blakean vortex and to the presence of Blake as a presiding genius in *Famous Men.* I do not know how familiar Agee was with Blake's work as a composite artist, but if he knew the illuminated books, he must have been struck by the oft-remarked independence of Blake's engravings from his texts, an independence which is coupled, of course, with the most intimate collaboration. For more on Blakean text-image relations, see my *Blake's Composite Art* (Princeton, NJ: Princeton University Press, 1977), and chapter 4 above.

[16] Roland Barthes, *Camera Lucida* (French original, 1981; New York: Hill and Wang, 1981), p. 73; further page references will be cited in the text.

[17] The *camera lucida,* as Barthes knew, is not properly translated as a "light room" in op-

position to a "dark room." It is "the name of that apparatus, anterior to Photography, which permitted drawing an object through a prism, one eye on the model, the other on the paper" (p. 106). The opening in the curtains, as optical aperture, plays precisely this role.

18 "I may know better a photograph I remember than a photograph I am looking at, as if direct vision oriented its language wrongly, engaging it in an effort of description which will always miss its point of effect, the *punctum*" (p. 53). The opposition between *studium* and *punctum* is coordinated, in Barthes's discussion, with related distinctions between the public and the private, the professional and the amateur. The captions further reinforce what Barthes calls "the two ways of the Photograph," dividing themselves into a scholarly, bibliographic identification of photographer, subject, date, etc. and an italicized quotation registering Barthes's personal response, the *punctum*. This practice of double captioning is, I think, a pervasive convention in photographic essays, often signaled by hyphenation (as in Robert Frank's *The Americans*), or contrasting type-styles (as in *You Have Seen Their Faces*): *Hamilton, Alabama*/ "We manage to get along."

19 Victor Burgin regards the antiscientific rhetoric of *Camera Lucida* with dismay: "The passage in *Camera Lucida* where Barthes lambasts the scientist of the sign (his own other self) has become widely quoted amongst precisely the sorts of critics Barthes opposed" ("Re-reading *Camera Lucida*," in *The End of Art Theory*, p. 91). Burgin's reduction of this to a straightforward political clash ignores the fact that the "sorts of critics" Barthes "opposed" included *himself*, and this opposition is precisely what gives his criticism ethical and political force.

20 Joel Snyder informs me that these identifications are confused. The photograph was taken by Paul Nadar, the artist's son, and is of his mother, Nadar's wife. Given the use Barthes makes of the photograph, the confusion of father and son, wife and mother, is hardly surprising. The manifest uncertainty of the caption and its misquotation of Barthes's own text suggest that Barthes was deliberately attaching a confused "legend" to this photo.

21 The twenty-five European and American photos in *Camera Lucida* range from journalism to art photos to personal family photographs and include examples of "old masters" (the "first photograph"—by Niepce; Charles Clifford, "The Alhambra"; G. W. Wilson, "Queen Victoria") from the nineteenth century as well as twentieth-century works. The effort is clearly to suggest "Photography" in its full range without making any effort to be comprehensive or systematic.

22 This respect for the "naive realism" of photography is also a crucial feature of Agee's text. Agee notes "how much slower white people are to catch on than negroes, who understand the meaning of a camera, a weapon, a stealer of images and souls, a gun, an evil eye" (p. 362).

23 Malek Alloula, *The Colonial Harem*, translated by Myrna and Wlad Godzich (French edition, 1981; English edition, Minneapolis: University of Minnesota Press, 1986); further page references will be cited in the text.

24 This impotence is perhaps nothing more than the familiar liberal guilt of the white male American becoming conscious of complicity in the ethos of imperialism. But it is also a more personal reaction which stems from a not altogether pleasant failure to react "properly" to the pornographic image, a failure which I can't take credit for as a matter of moral uprightness (morality, I suspect, only enters in when the proper reaction is there to be resisted). I had registered this feeling at the first perusal of the photographs in *The Colonial Harem*. Needless to say, a sensation of the uncanny attended my reading of the final paragraph of Alloula's text: "Voyeurism turns into an obsessive neurosis. The great erotic dream, ebbing from the sad faces of the wage earners in the poses, lets appear, in the flotsam perpetuated by the postcard, another figure: that of *impotence*" (p. 122).

25 Edward Said and Jean Mohr, *After the Last Sky* (London: Pantheon, 1986); further page references will be cited in the text.

26 Mohr's earlier collaborations with John Berger are clearly an important precedent also. See especially *The Seventh Man* (originally published, Penguin, 1975; London: Writers and Readers, 1982), a photographic essay on migrant workers in Europe.

[27] "I can see the women everywhere in Palestinian life, and I see how they exist between the syrupy sentimentalism of roles we ascribe to them (mothers, virgins, martyrs) and the annoyance, even dislike that their unassimilated strength provokes in our warily politicized, automatic manhood" (p. 77).

[28] Stanley Cavell, *The World Viewed: Reflections on the Ontology of Film*, enlarged edition (Cambridge, MA: Harvard University Press, 1979), p. 106.

[29] I say "in contrast to painting" because the emancipation of painting from language, or at least the rhetoric of emancipation, has dominated the sophisticated understanding of painting for most of this century. For a fuller version of this argument, see chapter 7. . . .

• • • • • • • • • • • •

QUESTIONS FOR A SECOND READING

1. Mitchell's essay is very straightforward and helpful in its structure. It opens with three questions and three answers. These are followed by six sections. The first two raise issues and questions related to photography and language and to the medium of the "photographic essay"; the last four present the case studies, the readings of particular texts from the point of view of the issues and questions raised at the opening. With all of this assistance, "The Photographic Essay" is still not easy to read. The arguments are subtle (and in some cases counterintuitive), and they refer constantly to other books and ideas, to a conversation among scholars and artists with a long history and, at times, a specialized vocabulary.

   As you reread, let the structure of the essay organize your work. When you finish the first two sections, stop to summarize and restate the argument. Underline or write down the key terms and questions. Mitchell, for example, alludes to naive and sophisticated responses to photos. What are they? What is Mitchell's position?

   The "case studies" work with books that you may not have seen or read and may not have at hand. And yet they require you to know something about them. Mitchell, in other words, must provide summary, example, and illustration as part of his discussion. After each of the case studies, stop, go back, and be ready to provide an account of the book at the center of each case study. Who wrote it? What is its project? And then be ready to provide an account of Mitchell's discussion. What use is Mitchell making of this book? What point? How does it serve his project?

2. This is an essay written by a scholar, a specialist in literature, art history, critical theory, and cultural studies. The specialized terms he uses are drawn from these fields of study. Sometimes he uses them as though they were familiar; in other cases he locates them in relation to a particular text and author. As you reread, underline or create a list of those terms that seem significant and particular to Mitchell's project, terms like "code," "trope," "dialectical," "figurative," "non-linguistic," "modernism," and "post-modernism." As an exercise, create a glossary of terms for use by other readers of this text. From their use and context, or (as a last resort) from other sources you can find, prepare defi-

nitions of these terms. Or, better yet, write summary sentences about "The Photographic Essay" that put these terms to work.

3. At the end of the second section, Mitchell says, "In the remainder of this essay I want to examine four photo-essays that, in various ways, foreground the dialectic of exchange and resistance between photography and language, the things that make it possible (and sometimes impossible) to 'read' the pictures, or to 'see' the text illustrated in them." As you reread, locate and mark those moments in the four case studies where Mitchell foregrounds "the dialectic of exchange and resistance between photography and language." What are the examples? How do the texts differ? Why, for Mitchell, is this interesting or important?

4. There are four books that serve as central examples to Mitchell's study: *Let Us Now Praise Famous Men,* James Agee and Walker Evans; *Camera Lucida,* Roland Barthes; *The Colonial Harem,* Malek Alloula; and *After the Last Sky,* Edward Said and Jean Mohr. Jacob Riis's *How the Other Half Lives* also provides an important illustration in the second section of the essay. Go to the library to study one of these texts. Find one or two examples you can copy and bring to class to extend or challenge Mitchell's discussion of that text. Be sure to bring words as well as images.

ASSIGNMENTS FOR WRITING

1. To introduce the four case studies in "The Photographic Essay," Mitchell says, "I want to examine four photo-essays that, in various ways, foreground the dialectic of exchange and resistance between photography and language." For this assignment, work closely with the four case studies to bring forward what remains implied in Mitchell's text, the *differences* in the four cases. What *are* the "various ways" they foreground the dialectic of exchange and resistance between photography and language? What position does Mitchell seem to take on the value or achievement of each of the four books? What seems to you to be the significant or interesting differences? Mitchell's essay is designed to prepare you to be a reader of the photographic essay. From the examples Mitchell gives, what sorts of books would you be hoping to find?

   You should imagine that you are writing for someone who has not read "The Photographic Essay." You will need, then, to be sure to represent and summarize the text. (See the first "Question for a Second Reading.") The point of the summary, however, is to define a position from which you can begin to do your work. And, to repeat what was said above, your work is to bring forward what Mitchell does not foreground—his sense of the differences between the four cases and the implication or value of those differences. And, in relation to what you see in Mitchell, your job is to articulate your own position on the range, importance, and possibility of the genre of the photo-essay.

2. These four books provide the central examples for Mitchell's study: *Let Us Now Praise Famous Men,* James Agee and Walker Evans; *Camera Lucida,* Roland Barthes; *The Colonial Harem,* Malek Alloula; and *After the Last Sky,* Ed-

ward Said and Jean Mohr. Jacob Riis's *How the Other Half Lives* also provides an important illustration in the second section of the essay. Go to the library to study one of these texts. Or, find an example of a "photographic essay" that you could put alongside Mitchell's examples.

For this assignment, take up Mitchell's project by extending his work in "The Photographic Essay" and considering new or additional examples. You should assume that you are writing for a reader who is familiar with Mitchell's essay (but who does not have the book open on his or her desk). Your work is to put Mitchell to the test—to extend, test, and perhaps challenge or qualify his account of the genre. As with his project, the basic questions are these: What relationship between photography and writing do these examples articulate? What tropes of differentiation govern the division of labor between photographer and writer, image and text, the viewer and the reader?

3. In the introduction to *Picture Theory,* Mitchell says,

> What we need is a critique of visual culture that is alert to the power of images for good and evil and that is capable of discriminating the variety and historical specificity of their uses.

One way to think about the "variety and historical specificity" of the use of images is to look at the examples Mitchell provides in this chapter, examples of writers using images as the subjects of their writing, but also the example of his own use and "reading" of those images.

At times, Mitchell is quick to include us in his ways of reading. In response to the Walker Evans photograph of Annie Mae Gudger, he says:

> There is something deeply disturbing, even disagreeable, about this (unavoidable) aestheticizing response to what after all is a real person in desperately impoverished circumstances. Why should we have a right to look on this woman and find her fatigue, pain, and anxiety beautiful? (p. 344)

His readers are written into the "we" of such sentences. At times he highlights the "reading" represented by the writer of the photo-essay, as he does, for example, in his account of Roland Barthes's use of Nadar's *The Artist's Mother (or Wife).* And at times he singles himself out as an individual case, as, for example, when he says of the postcard image of the "Arabian Woman with the Yachmak":

> Can an American observer, in particular, see these photographs as anything more than quaint, archaic pornography, hauntingly beautiful relics of a lost colonial era, "collector's items" for a coffee-table book? I don't have a simple answer to this question, but my first impulse is to register a feeling of *impotence* in the face of these women, whose beauty is now mixed with danger, whose nakedness now becomes a veil that has always excluded me from the labyrinth of their world. (p. 357)

Write an essay in which you present a close reading of Mitchell's text, looking specifically at the ways it figures (or represents) readers reading. What variety of readings does he chart? Where and how are they historically specific? What lessons are there to be learned from these examples? What does Mitchell seem to be saying about appropriate ways of reading? What about you—what's your position?

MAKING CONNECTIONS

1. *After the Last Sky: Palestinian Lives* is one of the central "cases" in W. J. T. Mitchell's "The Photographic Essay: Four Case Studies." Mitchell's essay examines the "dialectic of exchange and resistance that make it possible (and sometimes impossible) to 'read' the pictures, or to 'see' the text illustrated in them."

   Before reading Mitchell, take time to work on Edward Said and Jean Mohr's "States" (p. 378) and to write a draft addressing the relationship of image to text. (The first of the "Questions for a Second Reading" provides a way of preparing for this.)

   Once you have worked through the opening three paragraphs, reread the essay with an eye to the accumulating relationships between image and text. Is there a pattern? Do any stand out for their force, variety, innovation?

   Once you've written that draft, read Mitchell and bring his analysis into the conversation. You will want to refer to the general frame and the terms of his argument and to the specific discussion of images in *After the Last Sky.* What does Mitchell bring to the essay? How would you define his expertise? What do you see that he doesn't? How might you define your position or point of view in relation to his?

2. Both Robert Coles, in "The Tradition: Fact and Fiction" (p. 212), and W. J. T. Mitchell, in "The Photographic Essay," write about the genre of the photographic essay, and both take as a key text James Agee and Walker Evan's *Let Us Now Praise Famous Men.* You have the opportunity, then, to look at Coles's and Mitchell's primary source, to see what they selected and what they left out, to see the photographs and text in their original context. You can think about the logic (or desire) that led to their selections of exemplary material.

   Write an essay in which you elaborate the differences in Coles's and Mitchell's approaches to and accounts of this text. You can imagine that you are writing for a reader who has read none of the text at hand, so you will need to be careful in summary (perhaps reproducing some of the illustrations). What does each notice or choose to notice in the text? How are these decisions related to the larger projects of the two authors? to their underlying commitments and concerns? And, finally, where are you on the differences between the two? Would you align yourself with Coles or with Mitchell? From their example, is there a position you would define as your own or as an alternative?

3. Reread John Berger's "Appearances" as a photographic essay (p. 175). There are photographs in "Appearances" that are directly acknowledged in the text. Not all the photographs get equal time, however. And there are photographs without direct acknowledgment. We should assume they were carefully chosen and carefully arranged, that this essay is, in fact, an example the genre Mitchell had in mind when he was working on "The Photographic Essay." Take time to reread "Appearances" to think about the staging, the placement, and the use of the photographs. Choose examples you can use to think about the various relationships of image to word and word to image.

   When you are done, reread W. J. T. Mitchell's "The Photographic Essay: Four Case Studies," and read it with the thought that "Appearances" might serve as a fifth case study. You should assume that you are writing for an audience familiar with neither text. You will, then, need to take care to present each, its key terms, examples, and arguments. And you should use Mitchell to think about Berger and his project. How might Mitchell classify "Appearances" in his account of the "dialectic of exchange and resistance between photography and language"? Where might he place "Appearances" in relation to the other four case studies? Both Barthes and Mitchell express an urgency in their discussion of how we use and understand images. Are there connections? Is this urgency something you might share?

4. The "Foreword" to Dorothea Lange and Paul S. Taylor's *An American Exodus* includes the following account of method in preparing and assembling the photographs and in writing the text for their book:

   > This is neither a book of photographs nor an illustrated book, in the traditional sense. Its particular form is the result of our use of techniques in proportions and relations designed to convey understanding easily, clearly, and vividly. We use the camera as a tool of research. Upon a tripod of photographs, captions, and text we rest themes evolved out of long observations in the field. We adhere to the standards of documentary photography as we have conceived them. Quotations which accompany photographs report what the persons photographed said, not what we think might be their unspoken thoughts. Where there are no people, and no other source is indicated, the quotation comes from persons whom we met in the field (p. 290)

   (The "Questions for a Second Reading" for Lange and Taylor on pp. 324–25 can be helpful in thinking about this passage.)

   To prepare for this essay, you will need to reread the selections from Lange and Taylor with a particular attention to the relationship between words and images. "Upon a tripod of photographs, captions, and text we rest themes evolved out of long observations in the field." How do these three elements work together? What demands do they put upon a reader? How do they teach the reader to read a photograph, to speak for it, or to understand what it represents? What decisions did Lange and Taylor seem to be making in preparing and assembling photographs, captions, and text? (If there is time, you might use these questions as prompts for a first draft of an essay on the relation between words and images in "Old South" and "Plantation Under the Machine.")

   When you are done, reread W. J. T. Mitchell's "The Photographic Essay: Four Case Studies," and read it with the thought that Lange and Taylor's work might serve as a fifth case study. You should assume that you are writing for an audience familiar with neither text. You will, then, need to take care to present each, its key terms, examples, and arguments. How might Mitchell classify the work of Lange and Taylor in his account of the "dialectic of exchange and resistance between photography and language"? Where would he place their work in relation to the other four case studies? Lange and Taylor, like Mitchell, express an urgency in their discussion of how we use and understand images. Are there connections? Is this urgency something you might share?

EDWARD SAID
and
JEAN MOHR

EDWARD SAID (b. 1935) is one of the world's most distinguished literary critics and scholars, distinguished (among other things) for his insistence on the connectedness of art and politics, literature and history. As he argues in his influential essay "The World, the Text, the Critic,"

> *Texts have ways of existing, both theoretical and practical, that even in their most rarefied form are always enmeshed in circumstance, time, place, and society—in short, they are in the world, and hence worldly. The same is doubtless true of the critic, as reader and as writer.*

Said (pronounced "sigh-eed") has been a "worldly" reader and writer and the selection that follows is a case in point. It is part of his long-term engagement with the history and politics of the Middle East, particularly of the people we refer to as Palestinians. His critical efforts, perhaps best represented by his most influential book, Orientalism *(1978), examine the ways the West has represented and understood the East ("They cannot represent themselves; they must be represented"), demonstrating how Western journalists, writers, artists, and scholars have created and preserved a view of Eastern cultures as mysterious, dangerous, unchanging, and inferior.*

Said was born in Jerusalem, in what was at that time Palestine, to parents who were members of the Christian Palestinian community. In 1947, as the United Nations was establishing Israel as a Jewish state, his family fled to Cairo. In the introduction to After the Last Sky: Palestinian Lives *(1986), the book from which the following selection was taken, he says,*

> *I was twelve, with the limited awareness and memory of a relatively sheltered boy. By the mid-spring of 1948 my extended family in its entirety had departed, evicted from Palestine along with almost a million other Palestinians. This was the* nakba, *or catastrophe, which heralded the destruction of our society and our dispossession as a people.*

Said was educated in English-speaking schools in Cairo and Massachusetts; he completed his undergraduate training at Princeton and received his Ph.D. from Harvard in 1964. Since 1963 he has been a member of the English department at Columbia University in New York. In the 1970s, he began writing to a broad public on the situation of the Palestinians; from 1977 to 1991 he served on the Palestinian National Council, an exile government. In 1991 he split from the Palestinian Liberation Organization (PLO) over its Gulf War policy (Yasir Arafat's support of Saddam Hussein) and, as he says, for "what I considered to be its new defeatism."

The peculiar and distinctive project represented by After the Last Sky *began in the 1980s, in the midst of this political engagement. "In 1983," Said writes in the introduction,*

> *while I was serving as a consultant to the United Nations for its International Conference on the Question of Palestine (ICQP), I suggested that photographs of Palestinians be hung in the entrance hall to the main conference site in Geneva. I had of course known and admired Mohr's work with John Berger, and I recommended that he be commissioned to photograph some of the principal locales of Palestinian life. Given the initial enthusiasm for the idea, Mohr left on a special UN-sponsored trip to the Near East. The photographs he brought back were indeed wonderful; the official response, however, was puzzling and, to someone with a taste for irony, exquisite. You can hang them up, we were told, but no writing can be displayed with them.*

In response to a UN mandate, Said had also commissioned twenty studies for the participants at the conference. Of the twenty, only three were accepted as "official documents." The others were rejected "because one after another Arab state objected to this or that principle, this or that insinuation, this or that putative injury to its sovereignty." And yet, Said argues, the complex experience, history, and identity of the people known as Palestinians remained virtually unknown, particularly in the West (and in the United States). To most, Said says, "Palestinians are visible principally as fighters, terrorists, and lawless pariahs." When Jean Mohr, the photographer, told a friend that he was preparing an exhibition on the Palestinians, the friend responded, "Don't you think the subject's a bit dated? *Look, I've taken photographs of Palestinians too, especially in the refugee camps . . . it's really sad! But these days, who's interested in people who eat off the ground with their hands? And then there's all that terrorism . . . I'd have thought you'd be better off using your energy and capabilities on something more worthwhile."*

For both Said and Mohr, these rejections provided the motive for After the Last

Sky. *Said's account, from the book's introduction, is worth quoting at length for how well it represents the problems of writing:*

> *Let us use photographs and a text, we said to each other, to say something that hasn't been said about Palestinians. Yet the problem of writing about and representing—in all senses of the word—Palestinians in some fresh way is part of a much larger problem. For it is not as if no one speaks about or portrays the Palestinians. The difficulty is that everyone, including the Palestinians themselves, speaks a very great deal. A huge body of literature has grown up, most of it polemical, accusatory, denunciatory. At this point, no one writing about Palestine—and indeed, no one going to Palestine—starts from scratch: We have all been there before, whether by reading about it, experiencing its millennial presence and power, or actually living there for periods of time. It is a terribly crowded place, almost too crowded for what it is asked to be by way of history or interpretation of history.*

The resulting book is quite a remarkable document. The photos are not the photos of a glossy coffee-table book and yet they are compelling and memorable. The prose at times leads to the photos; at times it follows as meditation or explanation, an effort to get things right—"things like exile, dispossession, habits of expression, internal and external landscapes, stubbornness, poignancy, and heroism." It is a writing with pictures, not a writing to which photos were later added. Said had, in fact, been unable to return to Israel/Palestine for several years. As part of this project, he had hoped to be able to take a trip to the West Bank and Gaza in order to see beyond Mohr's photographs, but such a trip proved to be unsafe and impossible—both Arab and Israeli officials had reason to treat him with suspicion. The book was written in exile; the photos, memories, books, and newspapers, these were the only vehicles of return.

After the Last Sky *is, Said wrote in 1999, "an unreconciled book, in which the contradictions and antinomies of our lives and experiences remain as they are, assembled neither (I hope) into neat wholes nor into sentimental ruminations about the past. Fragments, memories, disjointed scenes, intimate particulars." The Palestinians, Said wrote in the introduction, fall between classifications. "We are at once too recently formed and too variously experienced to be a population of articulate exiles with a completely systematic vision and too voluble and trouble making to be simply a pathetic mass of refugees." And he adds, "The whole point of this book is to engage this difficulty, to deny the habitually simple, even harmful representations of Palestinians, and to replace them with something more capable of capturing the complex reality of their experience."*

Furthermore, he says, "just as Jean Mohr and I, a Swiss and a Palestinian, collaborated in the process, we would like you—Palestinians, Europeans, Americans, Africans, Latin Americans, Asians—to do so also." This is both an invitation and a challenge. While there is much to learn about the Palestinians, the people and their history, the opening moment in the collaborative project is to learn to look and to read in the service of a complex and nuanced act of understanding.

Said is the author of many books and collections, including Joseph Conrad and the Fiction of Autobiography *(1966),* Beginnings: Intention and Method *(1975),* Orientalism *(1978),* The Question of Palestine *(1979),* Covering Islam: How the Media and the Experts Determine How We See the Rest of the World *(1981),* Blaming the Victims *(1988),* Musical Elaborations *(1991),* Culture and Imperialism *(1993),* The Politics of Dispossession: The Struggle for Palestinian Self-Determination, 1989–1994 *(1994),* Representations of the Intellectual *(1994),* Peace and Its Discontents: Essays on Palestine in the Middle East Peace Process *(1995),* Out of Place: A Memoir *(2000),* The End of the Peace Process: Oslo and After *(2001), and* Mona Hatoum: The Entire World as a Foreign Land *(2001).*

Jean Mohr has worked as a photographer for UNESCO, the World Health Organization, and the International Red Cross. He has collaborated on four books with John Berger, Ways of Seeing *(1972),* A Seventh Man *(1975),* Another Way of Telling *(1982), and* A Fortunate Man *(1967).*

States

Caught in a meager, anonymous space outside a drab Arab city, outside a refugee camp, outside the crushing time of one disaster after another, a wedding party stands, surprised, sad, slightly uncomfortable [p. 379]. Palestinians—the telltale mixture of styles and attitudes is so evidently theirs—near Tripoli in northern Lebanon. A few months after this picture was taken their camp was ravaged by intra-Palestinian fighting. Cutting across the wedding party's path here is the ever-present Mercedes, emblazoned with its extra mark of authenticity, the proud *D* for *Deutschland.* A rare luxury in the West, the Mercedes—usually secondhand and smuggled in—is the commonest of cars in the Levant. It has become what horse, mule, and camel were, and then much more. Universal taxi, it is a symbol of modern technology domesticated, of the intrusion of the West into traditional life, of illicit trade. More important, the Mercedes is the all-purpose conveyance, something one uses for everything—funerals, weddings, births, proud display, leaving home, coming home, fixing, stealing, reselling, running away in, hiding in. But because Palestinians have no state of their own to shield them, the Mercedes, its provenance and destination obscure, seems like an intruder, a delegate of the forces that both dislocate and hem them in. "The earth is closing on us, pushing us through the last passage," writes the poet Mahmoud Darwish.

The paradox of mobility and insecurity. Wherever we Palestinians are, we are not in our Palestine, which no longer exists. You travel, from one end of the Arab world to the other, in Europe, Africa, the Americas, Australia, and there you find Palestinians like yourself who, like yourself, are subject to special laws, a special status, the markings of a force and violence not yours. Ex-

TRIPOLI, BADAWI CAMP. MAY 1983

iles at home as well as abroad, Palestinians also still inhabit the territory of former Palestine (Israel, the West Bank, Gaza), in sadly reduced circumstances. They are either "the Arabs of Judea and Samaria," or, in Israel, "non-Jews." Some are referred to as "present absentees." In Arab countries, except for Jordan, they are given special cards identifying them as "Palestinian refugees," and even where they are respectable engineers, teachers, business people, or technicians, they know that in the eyes of their host country they will always be aliens. Inevitably, photographs of Palestinians today include this fact and make it visible.

Memory adds to the unrelieved intensity of Palestinian exile. Palestine is central to the cultures of Islam, Christianity, and Judaism; Orient and Occident have turned it into a legend. There is no forgetting it, no way of overlooking it. The world news is often full of what has happened in Palestine-Israel, the latest Middle East crisis, the most recent Palestinian exploits. The sights, wares, and monuments of Palestine are the objects of commerce, war, pilgrimage, cults, the subjects of literature, art, song, fantasy. East and West, their high and their commercial cultures, have descended on Palestine. Bride and groom wear the ill-fitting nuptial costumes of Europe, yet behind and around them are the clothes and objects of their native land, natural

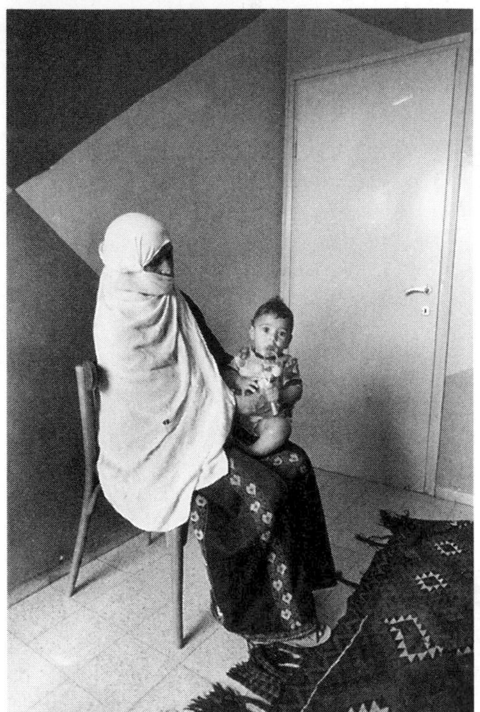

TEL SHEVA, 1979
A village of settled nomads near Bersheeba. Some years ago, these people still lived in a tent, under the desert sky. The carpet on the ground is the only reminder of that earlier period.

to their friends and attendants. The happiness of the occasion is at odds with their lot as refugees with nowhere to go. The children playing nearby contrast starkly with the unappealing surroundings; the new husband's large workman's hands clash with his wife's delicate, obscuring white. When we cross from Palestine into other territories, even if we find ourselves decently in new places, the old ones loom behind us as tangible and unreal as reproduced memory or absent causes for our present state.

Sometimes the poignancy of resettlement stands out like bold script imposed on faint pencil traces. The fit between body and new setting is not good. The angles are wrong. Lines supposed to decorate a wall instead form an imperfectly assembled box in which we have been put. We perch on chairs uncertain whether to address or evade our interlocutor. This child is held out, and yet also held in. Men and women re-express the unattractiveness around them: The angle made across her face by the woman's robe duplicates the ghastly wall pattern, the man's crossed feet repeat and contradict the outward thrust of the chair leg. He seems unsettled, poised for departure. Now what? Now where? All at once it is our transience and impermanence that our visibility expresses, for we can be seen as figures forced to push on to another house, village, or region. Just as we once were taken from one "habitat" to a new one, we can be moved again.

Exile is a series of portraits without names, without contexts. Images that are largely unexplained, nameless, mute. I look at them without precise anecdotal knowledge, but their realistic exactness nevertheless makes a deeper impression than mere information. I cannot reach the actual people who were photographed, except through a European photographer who saw them for me. And I imagine that he, in turn, spoke to them through an interpreter. The one thing I know for sure, however, is that they treated him politely but as someone who came from, or perhaps acted at the direction of, those who put them where they so miserably are. There was the embarrassment of people uncertain why they were being looked at and recorded. Powerless to stop it.

When A. Z.'s father was dying, he called his children, one of whom is married to my sister, into his room for a last family gathering. A frail, very old man from Haifa, he had spent his last thirty-four years in Beirut in a state of agitated disbelief at the loss of his house and property. Now he murmured to his children the final faltering words of a penniless, helpless patriarch. "Hold on to the keys and the deed," he told them, pointing to a battered suitcase near his bed, a repository of the family estate salvaged from Palestine when Haifa's Arabs were expelled. These intimate mementos of a past irrevocably lost circulate among us, like the genealogies and fables of a wandering singer of tales. Photographs, dresses, objects severed from their original locale, the rituals of speech and custom: Much reproduced, enlarged, thematized, embroidered, and passed around, they are strands in the web of affiliations we Palestinians use to tie ourselves to our identity and to each other.

Sometimes these objects, heavy with memory—albums, rosary beads, shawls, little boxes—seem to me like encumbrances. We carry them about, hang them up on every new set of walls we shelter in, reflect lovingly on them. Then we do not notice the bitterness, but it continues and grows nonetheless. Nor do we acknowledge the frozen immobility of our attitudes. In the end the past owns us. My father spent his life trying to escape these objects, "Jerusalem" chief among them—the actual place as much as its reproduced and manufactured self. Born in Jerusalem, as were his parents, grandparents, and all his family back in time to a distant vanishing point, he was a child of the Old City who traded with tourists in bits of the true cross and crowns of thorn. Yet he hated the place; for him, he often said, it meant death. Little of it remained with him except a fragmentary story or two, an odd coin or medal, one photograph of his father on horseback, and two small rugs. I never even saw a picture of my grandmother's face. But as he grew older, he reverted to old Jerusalemite expressions that I did not understand, never having heard them during the years of my youth.

AMMAN, 1984
A visit to the former mayor of Jerusalem and his wife, in exile in Jordan.

Identity—who we are, where we come from, what we are—is difficult to maintain in exile. Most other people take their identity for granted. Not the Palestinian, who is required to show proofs of identity more or less constantly. It is not only that we are regarded as terrorists, but that our existence as native Arab inhabitants of Palestine, with primordial rights there (and not elsewhere), is either denied or challenged. And there is more. Such as it is,

RAMALLAH, 1979
An everyday street scene, banal and reassuring. And yet, the tension is constant. A passing military jeep, a flying stone—the incident, the drama, can occur at any moment.

our existence is linked negatively to encomiums about Israel's democracy, achievements, excitement; in much Western rhetoric we have slipped into the place occupied by Nazis and anti-Semites; collectively, we can aspire to little except political anonymity and resettlement; we are known for no actual achievement, no characteristic worthy of esteem, except the effrontery of disrupting Middle East peace. Some Israeli settlers on the West Bank say: "The Palestinians can stay here, with no rights, as resident aliens." Other Israelis are less kind. We have no known Einsteins, no Chagall, no Freud or Rubinstein to protect us with a legacy of glorious achievements. We have had no Holocaust to protect us with the world's compassion. We are "other," and opposite, a flaw in the geometry of resettlement and exodus. Silence and discretion veil the hurt, slow the body searches, soothe the sting of loss.

A zone of recollected pleasure surrounds the few unchanged spots of Palestinian life in Palestine. The foodsellers and peddlers—itinerant vendors of cakes or corn—are still there for the casual eye to see, and they still provoke the appetite. They seem to travel not only from place to place, but from an earlier time to the present, carrying with them the same clientele—the young girls and boys, the homeward-bound cyclist, the loitering student or clerk—now as then. We buy their wares with the same surreptitiously found change (who can remember the unit? was it a piaster? fils? shilling?) spent on the same meager object, neither especially good nor especially well prepared. The luxurious pleasure of tasting the vendor's *simsim,* the round sesame cakes dipped in that tangy mixture of thyme and sumac, or his *durra,* boiled corn sprayed with salt,

surpasses the mere act of eating and opens before us the altogether agreeable taste of food not connected with meals, with nourishment, with routine. But what a distance now actually separates me from the concreteness of that life. How easily traveled the photographs make it seem, and how possible to suspend the barriers keeping me from the scenes they portray.

For the land is further away than it has ever been. Born in Jerusalem in late 1935, I left mandatory Palestine permanently at the end of 1947. In the spring of 1948, my last cousin evacuated our family's house in West Jerusalem; Martin Buber subsequently lived there till his death, I have been told. I grew up in Egypt, then came to the United States as a student. In 1966 I visited Ramallah, part of the Jordanian West Bank, for a family wedding. My father, who was to die five years later, accompanied my sister and me. Since our visit, all the members of my family have resettled—in Jordan, in Lebanon, in the United States, and in Europe. As far as I know, I have no relatives who still live in what was once Palestine. Wars, revolutions, civil struggles have changed the countries I have lived in—Lebanon, Jordan, Egypt—beyond recognition. Until thirty-five years ago I could travel from Cairo to Beirut overland, through territories held or in other ways controlled by rival colonial powers. Now, although my mother lives in Beirut, I have not visited her since the Israeli invasion of 1982: Palestinians are no longer welcome there. The fact is that today I can neither return to the places of my youth, nor voyage freely in the countries and places that mean the most to me, nor feel safe from arrest or violence even in the countries I used to frequent but whose governments and policies have changed radically in recent times. There is little that is more unpleasant for me these days than the customs and police check upon entering an Arab country.

Consider the tremendous upheavals since 1948 each of which effectively destroyed the ecology of our previous existence. When I was born, we in Palestine felt ourselves to be part of a small community, presided over by the majority community and one or another of the outside powers holding sway over the territory. My family and I, for example, were members of a tiny Protestant group within a much larger Greek Orthodox Christian minority, within the larger Sunni Islam majority; the important outside power was Britain, with its great rival France a close second. But then after World War II Britain and France lost their hold, and for the first time we directly confronted the colonial legacy—inept rulers, divided populations, conflicting promises made to resident Arabs and mostly European Jews with incompatible claims. In 1948 Israel was established; Palestine was destroyed, and the great Palestinian dispossession began. In 1956 Egypt was invaded by Britain, France, and Israel, causing what was left of the large Levantine communities there (Italian, Greek, Jewish, Armenian, Syrian) to leave. The rise of Abdel Nasser fired all Arabs—especially Palestinians—with the hope of a revived Arab nationalism, but after the union of Syria with Egypt failed in 1961, the Arab cold war, as it has been called, began in earnest; Saudi Arabia versus Egypt, Jordan versus Syria, Syria versus Iraq. . . . A new population of refugees, migrant workers, and traveling political parties crisscrossed the Arab world. We Palestinians immersed ourselves in the politics of Baathism in Syria and Iraq, of Nasserism in Egypt, of the Arab Nationalist Movement in Lebanon.

The 1967 war was followed shortly after by the Arab oil boom. For the first time, Palestinian nationalism arose as an independent force in the Middle East. Never did our future seem more hopeful. In time, however, our appearance on the political scene stimulated, if it did not actually cause, a great many less healthy phenomena: fundamentalist Islam, Maronite nationalism, Jewish zealotry. The new consumer culture, the computerized economy, further exacerbated the startling disparities in the Arab world between rich and poor, old and new, privileged and disinherited. Then, starting in 1975, the Lebanese civil war pitted the various Lebanese sects, the Palestinians, and a number of Arab and foreign powers against each other. Beirut was destroyed as the intellectual and political nerve center of Arab life; for us, it was the end of our only important, relatively independent center of Palestinian nationalism, with the Palestinian Liberation Organization at its heart. Anwar Sadat recognized Israel, and Camp David further dismantled the region's alliances and disrupted its balance. After the Iranian revolution in 1979 came the Iran-Iraq war. Israel's 1982 invasion of Lebanon put more Palestinians on the move, as the massacres in the Palestinian refugee camps of Sabra and Shatila reduced the community still further. By the end of 1983, Palestinians were fighting each other, and Syria and Libya were directly involved, supporting Palestinian dissidents against PLO loyalists. With the irony typical of our political fate, however, in mid-1985 we were united together in Sabra and Shatila to fight off a hostile Shi'ite militia patronized by Syria.

The stability of geography and the continuity of land—these have completely disappeared from my life and the life of all Palestinians. If we are not stopped at borders, or herded into new camps, or denied reentry and residence, or barred from travel from one place to another, more of our land is taken, our lives are interfered with arbitrarily, our voices are prevented from reaching each other, our identity is confined to frightened little islands in an inhospitable environment of superior military force sanitized by the clinical jargon of pure administration. On the West Bank and in Gaza we confront several Zionist "master plans"—which, according to Meron Benvenisti, ex-deputy mayor of Jerusalem, are "explicitly sectarian." He continues:

> The criteria established to determine priorities of settlement regions are "*interconnection* [*havirah*] between existing Jewish areas for the creation of [Jewish] settlement continuity" and "*separation* [*hayitz*] to restrict uncontrolled Arab settlement and the prevention of Arab settlement blocs"; "*scarcity* [*hesech*] refers to areas devoid of Jewish settlement." In these criteria "pure planning and political planning elements are included."
>
> (*The West Bank Data Project: A Survey of Israeli Policies*)

Continuity for *them,* the dominant population; discontinuity for *us,* the dispossessed and dispersed.

The circle is completed, though, when we Palestinians acknowledge that much the same thesis is adhered to by Arab and other states where sizable Palestinian communities exist. There too we are in dispersed camps, regions, quarters, zones; but unlike their Israeli counterparts, these places are not the scientific product of "pure planning" or "political planning." The Baqa'a camp in Amman, the Palestinian quarter of Hawaly in Kuwait, are simply there.

All forms of Palestinian activity, all attempts at unity, are suspect. On the West Bank and Gaza, "development" (the systematic strengthening of Palestinian economic and social life) is forbidden, whereas "improvement" is tolerated so long as there isn't too much of it; so long as it doesn't become development. The colors of the Palestinian flag are outlawed by Israeli military law; Fathi Gabin of Gaza, an artist, was given a six-month prison sentence for using black, green, red, and white in one of his works. An exhibit of Palestinian culture at al-Najah University in Nablus earned the school a four-month closing. Since our history is forbidden, narratives are rare; the story of origins, of home, of nation is underground. When it appears it is broken, often wayward and meandering in the extreme, always coded, usually in outrageous forms—mock-epics, satires, sardonic parables, absurd rituals—that make little sense to an outsider. Thus Palestinian life is scattered, discontinuous, marked by the artificial and imposed arrangements of interrupted or

TYRE, SOUTH LEBANON, 1983
Bourj el-Shemali camp. The car bears witness to a drama, circumstances unknown.
The flowers: the month of May, it is spring. The children:
wearing smart clothes, almost certainly donated by a charity.
They are refugees—the children of refugees.

BEDOUIN ENCAMPMENT NEAR BERSHEEBA, 1979.

confined space, by the dislocations and unsynchronized rhythms of disturbed time. Across our children's lives, in the open fields in which they play, lie the ruins of war, of a borrowed or imported industrial technology, of cast-off or abandoned forms. How odd the conjuncture, and yet for Palestinians, how fitting. For where no straight line leads from home to birthplace to school to maturity, all events are accidents, all progress is a digression, all residence is exile. We linger in nondescript places, neither here nor there; we peer through windows without glass, ride conveyances without movement or power. Resourcefulness and receptivity are the attitudes that serve best.

The difference between the new generation of Palestinians and that of 1948 is striking. Our parents bore on their faces the marks of disaster uncomprehended. Suddenly their past had been interrupted, their society obliterated, their existence radically impoverished. Refugees, all of them. Our children know no such past. Cars are equally for riding or, ruined, for playing in. Everything around them seems expendable, impermanent, unstable, especially where—as in Lebanon—Palestinian communities have been disastrously depleted or destroyed, where much of their life is undocumented, where they themselves are uncounted.

No Palestinian census exists. There is no line that can be drawn from one Palestinian to another that does not seem to interfere with the political designs of one or another state. While all of us live among "normal" people, people with complete lives, they seem to us hopelessly out of reach, with their countries, their familial continuity, their societies intact. How does a Palestinian father tell his son and daughter that Lebanon (Egypt, Syria, Jordan, New York) is where we are, but not where we are *from?* How does a mother confirm her intimate recollections of childhood in Palestine to her children, now that the facts, the places, even the names, are no longer allowed to exist?

So we borrow and we patch things together. Palestinians retain the inflections of Jaffa, of Hebron, of Jerusalem and other cities left behind, even as their dialect becomes that of Beirut, Detroit, or Paris. I have found out much more about Palestine and met many more Palestinians than I ever did, or perhaps could have, in pre-1948 Palestine. For a long time I thought that this was so because I was a child then, somewhat sheltered, a member of a minority. But my experience is confirmed by my oldest and closest Palestinian friend, Ibrahim Abu-Lughod. Although he was more in and of pre-1948 Palestine—because older, more conscious and active—than I ever was, he too says that he is much more in contact with Palestinians today than when he was in Palestine. He writes, "Thanks to modern technological progress, Palestinian families, and Palestinian society as a whole, have been able to forge very numerous human, social, and political links. By getting on a plane I can see the majority of my friends. It's because of this that our family has remained unified. I see all the members of my family at least once or twice a year. Being in Jaffa, I could never have seen relatives who lived in Gaza, for example." But Ibrahim does not celebrate this sociability: "I constantly expe-

GAZA, 1979
Refugee camp. A boy of unknown age.

rience the sense that something is missing for me. To compensate for this lack, I multiply and intensify human contacts."

Over the missing "something" are superimposed new realities. Plane travel and phone conversations nourish and connect the fortunate; the symbols of a universal pop culture enshroud the vulnerable.

There can be no orderly sequence of time. You see it in our children who seem to have skipped a phase of growth or, more alarming, achieved an out-of-season maturity in one part of their body or mind while the rest remains childlike. None of us can forget the whispers and occasional proclamations that our children are "the population factor"—to be feared, and hence to be

TEL SHEVA, 1979
A group portrait, taken at the request of the children.

deported—or constitute special targets for death. I heard it said in Lebanon that Palestinian children in particular should be killed because each of them is a potential terrorist. Kill them before they kill you.

How rich our mutability, how easily we change (and are changed) from one thing to another, how unstable our place—and all because of the missing foundation of our existence, the lost ground of our origin, the broken link with

BERSHEEBA, 1979
Near a Bedouin encampment, a little kitchen garden—and its scarecrow of bits and pieces.

our land and our past. There are no Palestinians. Who are the Palestinians? "The inhabitants of Judea and Samaria." Non-Jews. Terrorists. Troublemakers. DPs.° Refugees. Names on a card. Numbers on a list. Praised in speeches—*el pueblo palestino, il popolo palestino, le peuple palestinien*—but treated as interruptions, intermittent presences. Gone from Jordan in 1970, now from Lebanon.

None of these departures and arrivals is clean, definitive. Some of us leave, others stay behind. Remnants, new arrivals, old residents. Two great images encapsulate our unresolved existence. One is the identity card (passport, travel document, laissez-passer), which is never Palestinian but always something else; it is the subject of our national poem, Mahmoud Darwish's "Bitaqit Hawia": "Record! I am an Arab / Without a name—without title / patient in a country / with people enraged." And the second is Emil Habiby's invention the Pessoptimist (*al-mutasha 'il*), the protagonist of a disorderly and ingenious work of Kafkaesque fiction, which has become a kind of national epic. The Pessoptimist is being half here, half not here, part historical creature, part mythological invention, hopeful and hopeless, everyone's favorite obsession and scapegoat. Is Habiby's character fiction, or does his extravagant fantasy only begin to approximate the real? Is he a made-up figure or the true essence of our existence? Is Habiby's jamming-together of words—*mutafa'il*

DPs Displaced persons or displaced people. [Editor's note]

and *mutasha'im* into *mutasha'il,* which repeats the Palestinian habit of combining opposites like *la* ("no") and *na'am* ("yes") into *la'am*—a way of obliterating distinctions that do not apply to us, yet must be integrated into our lives?

Emil Habiby is a craggy, uncompromisingly complex, and fearsomely ironic man from Haifa, son of a Christian family, Communist party stalwart, longtime Knesset member, journalist, editor. His novel about the Pessoptimist (whose first name, incidentally, is Said) is chaotic because it mixes time, characters, and places; fiction, allegory, history, and flat statement, without any thread to guide the reader through its complexities. It is the best work of Palestinian writing yet produced, precisely because the most seemingly disorganized and ironic. In it we encounter characters whose names are of particular significance to Palestinians: The name of Yuaad, the work's female lead, means "it shall be repeated," a reference to the string of defeats that mark our history, and the fatalistic formulae that color our discourse. One of the other characters is Isam al-Bathanjani—Isam the Eggplant, a lawyer who is not very helpful to Said but who keeps turning up just the same. So it is with eggplants in Palestine. My family—my father in particular—has always been attached to eggplants from Battir, and during the many years since any of us had Battiri eggplants the seal of approval on good eggplants was that "they're almost as good as the Battiris."

Today when I recall the tiresome paeans to Battiris, or when in London and Paris I see the same Jaffa oranges or Gaza vegetables grown in the *bayarat* ("orchards") and fields of my youth, but now marketed by Israeli export companies, the contrast between the inarticulate rich *thereness* of what we once knew and the systematic export of the produce into the hungry mouths of Europe strikes me with its unkind political message. The land and the peasants are bound together through work whose products seem always to have meant something to other people, to have been destined for consumption elsewhere. This observation holds force not just because the Carmel boxes and the carefully wrapped eggplants are emblems of the power that rules the sprawling fertility and enduring human labor of Palestine, but also because the discontinuity between me, out here, and the actuality there is so much more compelling now than my receding memories and experiences of Palestine.

Another, far more unusual, item concerning this vegetable appears in an article by Avigdor Feldman, "The New Order of the Military Government: State of Israel Against the Eggplant," which appeared in the journal *Koteret Rashit,* August 24, 1983. Laws 1015 and 1039, Feldman reports, stipulate that any Arab on the West Bank and Gaza who owns land must get written permission from the military governor before planting either a new vegetable—for example, an eggplant—or fruit tree. Failure to get permission risks one the destruction of the tree or vegetable plus one year's imprisonment.

Exile again. The facts of my birth are so distant and strange as to be about someone I've heard of rather than someone I know. Nazareth—my mother's town. Jerusalem—my father's. The pictures I see display the same produce,

GAZA, 1979
Farm using refugee labor.

presented in the same carelessly plentiful way, in the same rough wooden cases. The same people walk by, looking at the same posters and trinkets, concealing the same secrets, searching for the same profits, pleasures, and goals. The same as what? There is little that I can truly remember about Jerusalem and Nazareth, little that is specific, little that has the irreducible durability of tactile, visual, or auditory memories that concede nothing to time, little—and this is the "same" I referred to—that is not confused with pictures I have seen or scenes I have glimpsed elsewhere in the Arab world.

Palestine is exile, dispossession, the inaccurate memories of one place slipping into vague memories of another, a confused recovery of general wares, passive presences scattered around in the Arab environment. The story of Palestine cannot be told smoothly. Instead, the past, like the present, offers only occurrences and coincidences. Random. The man enters a quiet alley where he will pass cucumbers on his right, tomatoes on his left; a priest walks down the stairs, the boy dashes off, satchel under arm, other boys loiter, shopkeepers look out for business; carrying an airline bag, a man advances past a display of trinkets, a young man disappears around the corner, two boys idle aimlessly. Tomatoes, watermelons, arcades, cucumbers, posters, people, eggplants—not simply there, but represented by photographs as being there—saturated with meaning and memory, and still very far away. Look more closely and think through these possibilities: The poster is about Egypt. The trinkets are made in Korea or Hong Kong. The scenes are surveyed, enclosed,

NAZARETH, 1979
Portrait of Om Kalsoum.

JERUSALEM, 1979
A snapshot.

JERUSALEM, 1979
A snapshot.

OLD CITY OF JERUSALEM, 1984
A tourist shop. Customers are rare. Will they be American, Swiss, or Israeli?

and surrounded by Israelis. European and Japanese tourists have more access to Jerusalem and Nazareth than I do. Slowly, our lives—like Palestine itself—dissolve into something else. We can't hold to the center for long.

• • •

JERUSALEM, 1979.

Exile. At a recent conference in America featuring a "dialogue" between Israeli and Palestinian intellectuals with reconciliation high on the agenda, a man rises from the audience to pose a question. "I am a Palestinian, a peasant. Look at my hands. I was kicked out in 1948 and went to Lebanon. Then I was driven out, and went to Africa. Then to Europe. Then to here. Today [he pulls out an envelope] I received a paper telling me to leave this country. Would one of you scholars tell me please: Where am I supposed to go now?" No one had anything to tell him. He was an embarrassment, and I have no idea what in fact he did, what became of him. My shame.

The Palestinian's claims on Israel are generally unacknowledged, much less seen as directly connected to the founding of the state. On the Arabs there is an ambivalent Palestinian claim, recognized in Arab countries by countless words, gestures, threats, and promises. Palestine, after all, is the centerpiece of Arab nationalism. No Arab leader since World War II has failed to make Palestine a symbol of his country's nationalist foreign policy. Yet, despite the avowals, we have no way of knowing really how they—all the "theys"—feel about us. Our history has cost every one of our friends a great deal. It has gone on too long.

Let Ghassan Kanafani's novella *Men in the Sun* stand for the fear we have that unless we press "them" they will allow us to disappear, and the equal worry that if we press them they will either decry our hectoring presence, and quash it in their states, or turn us into easy symbols of their nationalism. Three refugees concealed in the belly of a tanker truck are being transported illegally across the border into Kuwait. As the driver converses with the guards, the men (Palestinians) die of suffocation—in the sun, forgotten. It is not the driver's forgetfulness that nags at him. It is their silence. "Why didn't you knock on the sides of the tank? Why didn't you bang the sides of the tank? Why? Why? Why?" Our fear to press.

The Palestinians as commodity. Producing ourselves much as the *masabih*, lamps, tapestries, baskets, embroideries, mother-of-pearl trinkets are produced. We turn ourselves into objects not for sale, but for scrutiny. People ask us, as if looking into an exhibit case, "What is it you Palestinians want?"—as if we can put our demands into a single neat phrase. All of us speak of *awdah*, "return," but do we mean that literally, or do we mean "we must restore ourselves to ourselves"? The latter is the real point, I think, although I know many Palestinians who want their houses and their way of life back, exactly. But is there any place that fits us, together with our accumulated memories and experiences?

Do we exist? What proof do we have?

The further we get from the Palestine of our past, the more precarious our status, the more disrupted our being, the more intermittent our presence. When did we become "a people"? When did we stop being one? Or are we in the process of becoming one? What do those big questions have to do with our intimate relationships with each other and with others? We frequently end our letters with the mottoes "Palestinian love" or "Palestinian kisses." Are there really such things as Palestinian intimacy and embraces, or are they simply intimacy and embraces, experiences common to everyone, neither politically significant nor particular to a nation or a people?

The politics of such a question gets very close to our central dilemma: We all know that we are Arabs, and yet the concept, not to say the lived actuality, of Arabism—once the creed and the discourse of a proud Arab nation, free of imperialism, united, respected, powerful—is fast disappearing, cut up into the cautious defensiveness of relatively provincial Arab states, each with its own traditions—partly invented, partly real—each with its own nationality and restricted identity. In addition, Palestine has been replaced by an Israel whose aggressive sense of itself as the state of the Jewish people fuels the exclusivity of a national identity won and maintained to a great extent at our expense. We are not Jews, we have no place there except as resident aliens, we are outsiders. In the Arab states we are in a different position. There we are Arabs, but it is the process of nationalization that excludes us: Egypt is for and by Egyptians, Iraq is for and by Iraqis, in ways that cannot include Palestinians whose intense national revival is a separate phenomenon. Thus we are the same as other Arabs, and yet different. We cannot exist except as Arabs, even though "the Arabs" exist otherwise as Lebanese, Jordanians, Moroccans, Kuwaitis, and so forth.

Add to this the problems we have of sustaining ourselves as a collective unit and you then get a sense of how *abstract*, how very solitary and unique, we tend to feel.

VILLAGE OF RAMAH, GALILEE, 1979
A secular high school with students from thirty-six neighboring villages.

Strip off the occasional assertiveness and stridency of the Palestinian stance and you may catch sight of a much more fugitive, but ultimately quite beautifully representative and subtle, sense of identity. It speaks in languages not yet fully formed, in settings not completely constituted, like the shy glance of a child holding her father's knee while she curiously and tentatively examines the stranger who photographs her. Her look conjures up the unappreciated fact of birth, that sudden, unprepared-for depositing of a small bundle of self on the fields of the Levant after which comes the trajectory of dispossession, military and political violence, and that constant, mysterious entanglement with monotheistic religion at its most profound—the Christian Incarnation and Resurrection, the Ascension to heaven of the Prophet Mohammed, the Covenant of Yahweh with his people—that is knotted definitively in Jerusalem, center of the world, *locus classicus* of Palestine, Israel, and Paradise.

A secular world of fatigue and miraculously renewed energies, the world of American cigarettes and an unending stream of small papers pulled out of miscellaneous notebooks or "blocnotes," written on with disposable pens, messages of things wanted, of people missing, of requests to the bureaucracy. The Palestinian predicament: finding an "official" place for yourself in a system that makes no allowances for you, which means endlessly improvising solutions for the problem of finding a missing loved one, of planning a trip, of entering a school, on whatever bit of paper is at hand. Constructed and deconstructed, ephemera are what we negotiate with, since we authorize no part of the world and only influence increasingly small bits of it. In any case, we keep going.

The striking thing about Palestinian prose and prose fiction is its formal instability: Our literature in a certain very narrow sense *is* the elusive, resistant reality it tries so often to represent. Most literary critics in Israel and the West focus on what is said in Palestinian writing, who is described, what the plot and contents deliver, their sociological and political meaning. But it is *form* that should be looked at. Particularly in fiction, the struggle to achieve form expresses the writer's efforts to construct a coherent scene, a narrative that might overcome the almost metaphysical impossibility of representing the present. A typical Palestinian work will always be concerned with this peculiar problem, which is at once a problem of plot and an enactment of the writer's enterprise. In Kanafani's *Men in the Sun* much of the action takes place on the dusty streets of an Iraqi town where three Palestinian men must petition, plead, and bargain with "specialists" to smuggle them across the border into Kuwait. Impelled by exile and dislocation, the Palestinians need to carve a path for themselves in existence, which for them is by no means a given or stable reality. Like the history of the lands they left, their lives seem interrupted just before they could come to maturity and satisfaction; thus each man leaves behind family and responsibilities, to whose exigencies he must answer—unsuccessfully—here in the present. Kanafani's very

AMMAN, 1984
Pediatric clinic.

SIDON, SOUTH LEBANON, 1983
A refugee writes out a message destined for her husband,
a prisoner in the camp at Ansar.

SIDON, SOUTH LEBANON, 1983
Camp at Ein el-Hilwé. Time passes: destruction, reconstruction, redestruction.

sentences express instability and fluctuation—the present tense is subject to echoes from the past, verbs of sight give way to verbs of sound or smell, and one sense interweaves with another—in an effort to defend against the harsh present and to protect some particularly cherished fragment of the past. Thus, the precarious actuality of these men in the sun reproduces the precarious status of the writer, each echoing the other.

Our characteristic mode, then, is not a narrative, in which scenes take place *seriatim,* but rather broken narratives, fragmentary compositions, and self-consciously staged testimonials, in which the narrative voice keeps stumbling over itself, its obligations, and its limitations.

Each Palestinian structure presents itself as a potential ruin. The theme of the formerly proud family house (village, city, camp) now wrecked, left behind, or owned by someone else, turns up everywhere in our literature and cultural heritage. Each new house is a substitute, supplanted in turn by yet another substitute. The names of these places extend all the way from the private (my friend Mohammed Tarbush expatiates nobly on the beauties of Beit Natif, a village near Bethlehem that was wiped out of existence by Israeli bulldozers in 1948; his widowed mother now lives in Jarash, Jordan, he in Paris) to the official, or institutionalized, sites of ruin—Deir Yassin, Tel el-Zaatar, Birim and Ikrit, Ein el-Hilwé, Sabra, Shatila, and more. Even "Palestine" itself is such a place and, curiously, already appears as a subject of elegy in journalism, essays, and literature of the early twentieth century. In the works of Halim Nassar, Ezzat Darwaza, Khallil Beidas, and Aref el-Aref, Palestine's destruction is predicted.

All cultures spin out a dialectic of self and other, the subject "I" who is native, authentic, at home, and the object "it" or "you," who is foreign, perhaps threatening, different, out there. From this dialectic comes the series of heroes and monsters, founding fathers and barbarians, prized masterpieces and despised opponents that express a culture from its deepest sense of national self-identity to its refined patriotism, and finally to its coarse jingoism, xenophobia, and exclusivist bias. For Palestinian culture, the odd thing is that its own identity is more frequently than not perceived as "other." "Palestine" is so charged with significance for others that Palestinians cannot perceive it as intimately theirs without a simultaneous sense of its urgent importance for others as well. "Ours" but not yet fully "ours." Before 1948, Palestine had a central agonistic meaning both for Arab nationalism and for the Zionist movement. After 1948, the parts of Palestine still inhabited by Arabs took on the additional label of the "non-Jewish" part of the Jewish state. Even a picture of an Arab town—like Nazareth where my mother was born and grew up—may express this alienating perspective. Because it is taken from outside Nazareth (in fact, from Upper Nazareth, a totally Jewish addition to the town, built on the surrounding hills), the photograph renders Palestine as "other." I never knew Nazareth, so this is my only image of it, an image of the "other," from the "outside," Upper Nazareth.

Thus the insider becomes the outsider. Not only have the interpositions between us and Palestine grown more formidable over time, but, to make matters worse, most of us pass our lives separated from each other. Yet we live in comradely communication despite the barriers. Today the Palestinian genius expresses itself in crossings-over, in clearing hurdles, activities that do not lessen the alienation, discontinuity, and dispossession, but that dramatize and clarify them instead. We have remained; in the words of Tawfik Zayyad's famous poem, "The Twenty Impossibles," it would be easier "to catch fried fish in the Milky Way, / to plow the sea, / to teach the alligator speech" than to make us leave. To the Israelis, whose incomparable military and political power dominates us, we are at the periphery, the image that will not go away. Every assertion of our nonexistence, every attempt to spirit us away, every new effort to prove that we were never really there, simply raises the question of why so much denial of, and such energy expended on, what was not there? Could it be that even as alien outsiders we dog their military might with our obdurate moral claim, our insistence (like that of Bartleby the Scrivener) that "we would prefer not to," not to leave, not to abandon Palestine forever?

The proof of whatever small success we have had is not that we have regained a homeland, or acquired a new one; rather, it is that some Israelis have admitted the possibility of sharing a common space with us, in Pales-

ARAB NAZARETH, 1979
Viewed from Upper Nazareth.

tine. The proposed modes of such a sharing are adventurous and utopian in the present context of hostility between Arabs and Jews, but on an intellectual level they are actual, and to some of us—on both sides—they make sense. Most Palestinians have their own special instance of the Israeli who reached out across the barricade most humanly. For some it is the intrepid Israeli lawyer defending Palestinian political prisoners, or trying to prevent land expropriations and collective punishment; for others it is—the testimony of Salah Ta'amari, leader of the Palestinian prisoners rounded up during the Israeli invasion and put in the Ansar prison camp, comes to mind—an Israeli in a position of authority (prison guard or army officer) who prevented some atrocity or showed some clear sign of humanity and fellow feeling. For my part, removed from the terrible pressures of the scene, I think of all the Israeli (or non-Israeli) Jews whose articulate witness to the injustice of their people against mine has marked out a communal territory. The result has usually been a friendship whose depth is directly proportional to the admiration I feel for their tenacity of conscience and belief in the face of the most slanderous attacks. Surely few have equaled the courage and principle of Israel Shahak, of Leah Tsemal and Felicia Langer, of Noam Chomsky, of Izzy Stone, of Elmer Berger, of Matti Peled, of so many others who stood up bravely during the events in Lebanon.

There are few opportunities for us Palestinians, or us Palestinians *and* Israelis, to learn anything about the world we live in that is *not* touched by, in-

TYRE, SOUTH LEBANON, 1983
Rashidyé camp: A local official collects messages from the relations of refugees for the International Red Cross.

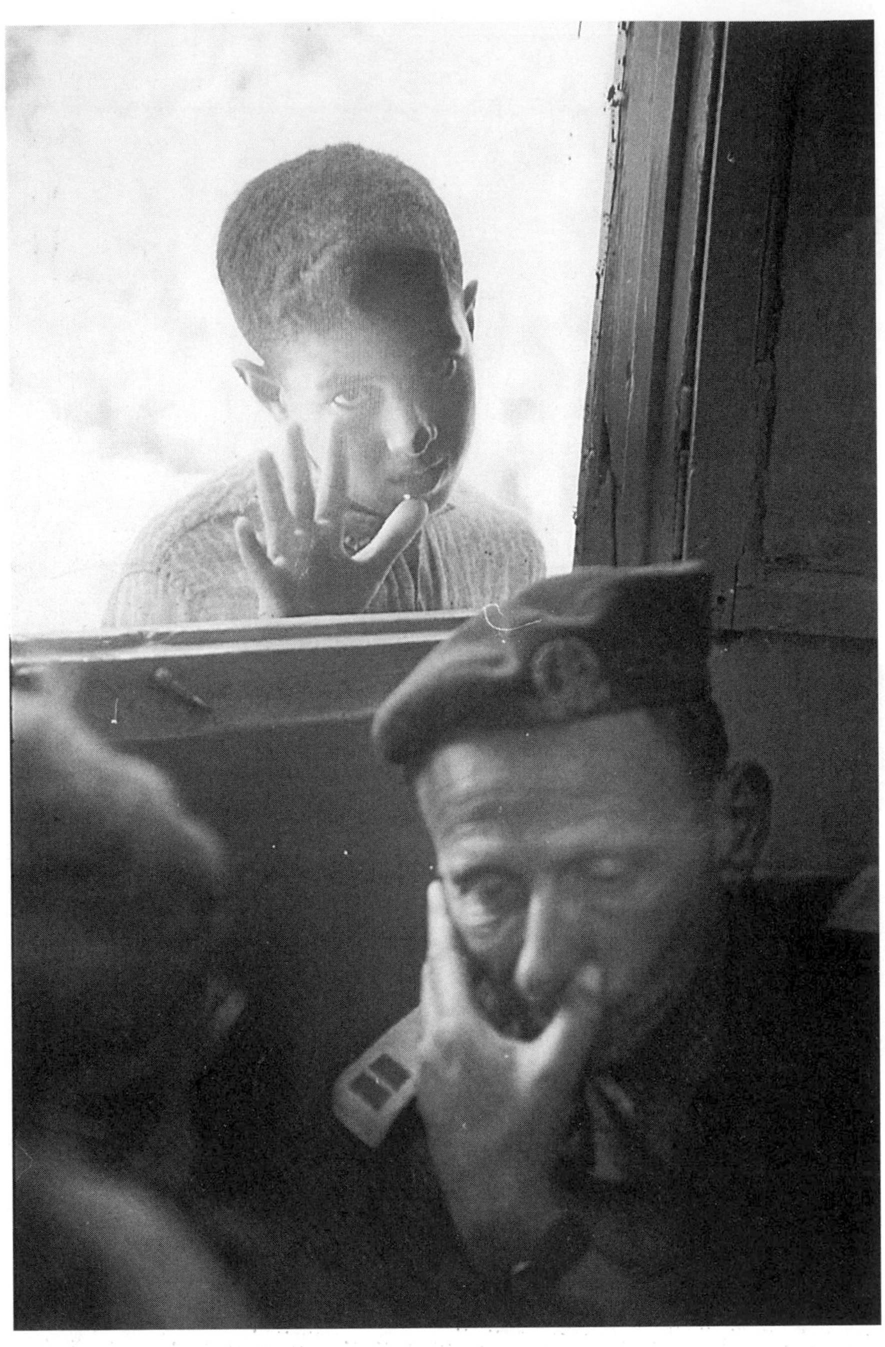

KALANDIA (NEAR RAMALLAH), 1967
A few days after the end of the June War:
in the foreground, an Israeli officer, lost in thought.
Behind the window, a young villager.

JERUSALEM, 1979
A dialogue between left-wing Israeli and Arab intellectuals.

deed soaked in, the hostilities of our struggle. And if it isn't the Palestinian-Zionist struggle, there are the pressures of religion, of every conceivable ideology, of family, peers, and compatriots, each of them bearing down upon us, pushing, kneading, prodding every one of us from childhood to maturity.

In such an environment, learning itself is a chancy, hybrid activity, laced with the unresolvable antitheses of our age. The child is full of the curious hope and undirected energy that attract the curatorial powers of both church and state. Fortunately, here the spirit of the creative urge in all human activity asserts itself—neither church nor state can ultimately exhaust, or control, the possibilities latent in the classroom, playground, or family. An orderly row of chairs and tables, a disciplined recitation circle in a Catholic school with a nun in charge, are also places for the absorption of more knowledge and experience than authorities impart—places where the child explores here and there, his/her mind and body wandering in space and time despite the constraints in each. In a school where the teacher is a devout Muslim, the child's propensity for disturbing or opposing the schemes of knowledge and discipline causes him/her to leave the table, disrupt the pattern, seek unthought-of possibilities. The tension between teachers and students remains, but better the tension than the peace of passivity, or the unresisting assent to authority.

The pressures of the here and now require an answer to the Palestinian crisis here and now. Whereas our interlocutors, our "others"—the Arab states, the United States, the USSR, Israel, our friends and enemies—have the

NAZARETH, 1979
A municipal kindergarten, looked after by nuns.

AMMAN, 1984
Camp at Baqa'a, one of the oldest in Jordan.
The YWCA looks after some of the kindergartens.

luxury of a state in which institutions do their work undisturbed by the question of existence-or-not, we lead our lives under a sword of Damocles, whose dry rhetorical form is the query "When are you Palestinians going to accept a solution?"—the implication being that if we don't, we'll disappear. This, then, is our midnight hour.

It is difficult to know how much the often stated, tediously reiterated worries about us, which include endless lectures on the need for a clear Palestinian statement of the desire for peace (as if we controlled the decisive factors!), are malicious provocation and how much genuine, if sympathetic, ignorance. I don't think any of us reacts as impatiently to such things as we did, say, five years ago. True, our collective situation is more precarious now than it was, but I detect a general turning inward among Palestinians, as if many of us feel the need to consolidate and collect the shards of Palestinian life still present and available to us. This is not quietism at all, nor is it resignation. Rather, it springs from the natural impulse to stand back when the headlong rush of events gets to be too much, perhaps, for us to savor life as life, to reflect at some distance from politics on where we came from and where we are, to regrasp, revise, recomprehend the tumultuous experiences at whose center, quite without our consent, we have been made to stand.

Jean Mohr's photograph of a small but clearly formed human group surrounded by a dense and layered reality expresses very well what we experi-

JERUSALEM, 1984.

ence during that detachment from an ideologically saturated world. This image of four people seen at a distance near Ramallah, in the middle of and yet separated from thick foliage, stairs, several tiers of terraces and houses, a lone electricity pole off to the right, is for me a private, crystallized, almost Proustian evocation of Palestine. Memory: During the summer of 1942—I was six—we rented a house in Ramallah. My father, I recall, was ill with high blood pressure and recovering from a nervous breakdown. I remember him as withdrawn and constantly smoking. My mother took me to a variety show at the local Friends school. During the second half I left the hall to go to the toilet, but for reasons I could not (and still do not) grasp, the boy-scout usher would not let me back in. I recall with ever-renewed poignancy the sudden sense of distance I experienced from what was familiar and pleasant—my mother, friends, the show; all at once the rift introduced into the cozy life I led taught me the meaning of separation, of solitude, and of anguished boredom. There was nothing to do but wait, although my mother did appear a little later to find out what had happened to me. We left immediately, but not before I furtively took a quick look back through the door window at the lighted stage. The telescoped vision of small figures assembled in a detached space has remained with me for over forty years, and it reappears in the adjusted and transformed center of Jean's 1983 picture. I never ventured anywhere near that part of Ramallah again. I would no more know it than I would the precise place of this photo; and yet I am sure it would be familiar, the way this one immediately seemed.

My private past is inscribed on the surface of this peaceful but somehow brooding pastoral scene in the contemporary West Bank. I am not the only one surveying the scene. There is the child on the left who looks on. There are also the Swiss photographer, compassionate, curious, silent, and of course the ever-present Israeli security services, who hold the West Bank and its population in the vise of occupation. As for those terraces and multiple levels: Do they serve the activities of daily life or are they the haunted stairs of a prison which, like Piranesi's, lead nowhere, confining their human captives? The dense mass of leaves, right and left, lend their bulk to the frame, but they too impinge on the slender life they surround, like memory or a history too complex to be sorted out, bigger than its subject, richer than any consciousness one might have of it.

The power grid recalls the Mercedes in Tripoli. Unassimilated, its modernity and power have been felt with considerable strength in our lives here and there throughout the Third World. Another childhood memory: Driving through the Sinai from Egypt into Palestine, we would see the row of telephone and electricity pylons partnering the empty macadamized road that cut through an even emptier desert. Who are they, I would ask myself. What do they think when we are not here? When we stopped to stretch our legs, I would go up to a pole and look at its dull brown surface for some sign of life, identity, or awareness. Once I marked one with my initials EWS, hoping to find it again on the trip back. All of them looked exactly the same as we

NEAR SENJEL, A VILLAGE BETWEEN RAMALLAH AND NABLUS, 1979.

hurtled by. We never stopped. I never drove there again, nor can I now. Futile efforts to register my presence on the scene.

Intimate memory and contemporary social reality seem connected by the little passage between the child, absorbed in his private, silent sphere, and the three older people, who are the public world of adults, work, and community. It is a vacant, somewhat tenuously maintained space, however; sandy, pebbly, and weedy. All the force in the photograph moves dramatically from trees left to trees right, from the visible enclave of domesticity (stairs, houses, terrace) to the unseen larger world of power and authority beyond. I wonder whether the four people are in fact connected, or whether as a group they simply happen to be in the way of unseen forces totally indifferent to the dwelling and living space these people inhabit. This is also, then, a photograph of latent, of impending desolation, and once again I am depressed by the transience of Palestinian life, its vulnerability and all too easy dislocation. But another movement, another feeling, asserts itself in response, set in motion by the two strikingly marked openings in the buildings, openings that suggest rich, cool interiors which outsiders cannot penetrate. Let us enter.

• • • • • • • • • • • •

QUESTIONS FOR A SECOND READING

1. The first three paragraphs provide a "reading" of the opening photograph, "Tripoli, Badawi camp, May 1983." Or, to put it another way, the writing evolves from and is in response to that photograph. As you reread these paragraphs, pay close attention to what Said is doing, to what he notices, to what prompts or requires commentary. How would you describe and explain the writing that follows? What is he doing with the photo? What is he doing as a writer? What is he doing for a reader? (How does he position a reader?)

   It might be useful to begin by thinking about what he is *not* doing. It is not, for example, the presentation one might expect in a slide show on travel in Lebanon. Nor is it the kind of presentation one might expect while seeing the slides of family or friends, or slides in an art history or art appreciation class.

   Once you have worked through the opening three paragraphs, reread the essay paying attention to Said's work with all the photographs. Is there a pattern? Do any of the commentaries stand out for their force, variety, innovation?

2. Here is another passage from the introduction to *After the Last Sky:*

   > Its style and method—the interplay of text and photos, the mixture of genres, modes, styles—do not tell a consecutive story, nor do they constitute a political essay. Since the main features of our present existence are dispossession, dispersion, and yet also a kind of power incommensurate with our stateless exile, I believe that essentially unconventional, hybrid, and fragmentary forms of expression should be used to represent us. What I have quite consciously designed, then, is an alternative mode of expression to the one usually encountered in the media, in works of social science, in popular fiction.

   And later:

   > The multifaceted vision is essential to any representation of us. Stateless, dispossessed, de-centered, we are frequently unable either to speak the "truth" of our experience or to make it heard. We do not usually control the images that represent us; we have been confined to spaces designed to reduce or stunt us; and we have often been distorted by pressures and powers that have been too much for us. An additional problem is that our language, Arabic, is unfamiliar in the West and belongs to a tradition and civilization usually both misunderstood and maligned. Everything we write about ourselves, therefore, is an interpretive translation—of our language, our experience, our senses of self and others.

   And from "States":

   > The striking thing about Palestinian prose and prose fiction is its formal instability: Our literature in a certain very narrow sense *is* the elusive, resistant reality it tries so often to represent. Most literary critics in Israel and the West focus on what is said in Palestinian writing, who is described, what the plot and contents deliver, their sociological and political meaning. But it is *form* that should be looked at. Particularly in fiction, the struggle to achieve form expresses the writer's efforts to construct a coherent scene, a narrative that might overcome the almost metaphysical impossibility of representing the present. (p. 401)

   As you reread, think about form—organization, arrangement, and genre.

What *is* the order of the writing in this essay? (We will call it an "essay" for lack of a better term.) How might you diagram or explain its organization? By what principle(s) is it ordered and arranged? The essay shifts genres—memoir, history, argument. It is, as Said says, "hybrid." What surprises are there? or disappointments? How might you describe the writer's strategy as he works on his audience, on readers? And, finally, do you find Said's explanation sufficient or useful—does the experience of exile produce its own inevitable style of report and representation?

3. The essay is filled with references to people (including writers), places, and events that are, most likely, foreign to you. Choose one that seems interesting or important, worth devoting time to research. Of course the Internet will be a resource, but you should also use the library, if only to become aware of the different opportunities and materials it provides. Compile a report of the additional information; be prepared to discuss how the research has served or changed your position as a reader of "States."

4. The final chapter of *After the Last Sky* ends with this:

> I would like to think, though, that such a book not only tells the reader about us, but in some way also reads the reader. I would like to think that we are not just the people seen or looked at in these photographs: We are also looking at our observers.

Read back through Said's essay by looking at the photos with this reversal in mind—looking in order to see yourself as the one who is being looked at, as the one observed. How are you positioned by the photographer, Jean Mohr? How are you positioned by the person in the scene, always acknowledging your presence? What are you being told?

Once you have read through the photographs, reread the essay itself, with a similar question in mind. This time, however, look for evidence of how Said positions you, defines you, invents you as a presence in the scene.

ASSIGNMENTS FOR WRITING

1. Compose a similar project, a Said-like reading of a set of photos. These can be photos prepared for the occasion (by you or a colleague); they could also be photos already available. Whatever their source, they should represent people and places, a history and/or geography that you know well, that you know to be complex and contradictory, and that you know will not be easily or readily understood by others, both the group for whom you will be writing (most usefully the members of your class) and readers more generally. You must begin with a sense that the photos cannot speak for themselves; you must speak for them.

   In preparation, you should reread closely to come to a careful understanding of Said's project. (The first and second "Questions for a Second Reading" should be useful for this.) To prepare a document that is Said-like (one that shows your understanding of what Said is doing), you will need to have an expert's sense of how to write from and to photographs, and you will need to consider questions of form—of order, arrangement, and genre.

2. While "States" does not present itself as polemical writing—an argument in

defense of Palestinian rights, an argument designed to locate blame or propose national or international policy—it is, still, writing with a purpose. It has an argument, it has a particular project in mind, and it wants something to happen.

Write an essay that represents the argument or the project of "States" for someone who has not read it. You will need, in other words, to establish a context and to summarize. You should also work from passages (and images)—that is, you will want to give your reader a sense of the text, its key terms and language. And write about "States" as though it has something to do with you.

Your essay is not just summary, in other words, but summary in service of statement, response, or extension. As you are invited to think about the Palestinians, or about exile more generally, or about the texts and images that are commonly available, what do you think? What do you have to add?

3. The final chapter of *After the Last Sky* ends with this:

> I would like to think, though, that such a book not only tells the reader about us, but in some way also reads the reader. I would like to think that we are not just the people seen or looked at in these photographs: We are also looking at our observers.

The fourth question in "Questions for a Second Reading" sets a strategy for rereading with this passage in mind—looking in order to see yourself as the one who is being looked at, as the one observed. Write an essay in which you think this through by referring specifically to images and to text. How are you positioned? By whom and to what end?

MAKING CONNECTIONS

1. Edward Said talks about the formal problems in the writing of "States" (and for more on this, see the second of the "Questions for a Second Reading"):

> The striking thing about Palestinian prose and prose fiction is its formal instability: Our literature in a certain very narrow sense *is* the elusive, resistant reality it tries so often to represent. Most literary critics in Israel and the West focus on what is said in Palestinian writing, who is described, what the plot and contents deliver, their sociological and political meaning. But it is *form* that should be looked at. Particularly in fiction, the struggle to achieve form expresses the writer's efforts to construct a coherent scene, a narrative that might overcome the almost metaphysical impossibility of representing the present. (p. 401)

And here is a similar discussion from the introduction to *After the Last Sky:*

> The multifaceted vision is essential to any representation of us. Stateless, dispossessed, de-centered, we are frequently unable either to speak the "truth" of our experience or to make it heard. We do not usually control the images that represent us; we have been confined to spaces designed to reduce or stunt us; and we have often been distorted by pressures and powers that have been too much for us. An additional problem is that our language, Arabic, is unfamiliar in the West and belongs to a tradition and civilization usually both misunderstood and maligned. Everything we write about ourselves, therefore, is an interpretive translation—of our language, our experience, our senses of self and others.

Edward Said's sense of his project as a writing project, a writing project requiring formal experimentation, is similar to James Agee's in *Let Us Now Praise Famous Men* (p. 22). Reread Agee. You can turn to what he says about the project in the "Preface" and "Preamble," but you should certainly also turn to the example of the prose that follows. What is he doing at the level of the sentence? What is he doing beyond the sentence? How does this prose serve his "nominal" subject? How does it define or represent a "real" subject?

Write an essay in which you consider these two writing projects: Said's in "States" and Agee's in *Let Us Now Praise Famous Men.* The formal experimentation in each is said by the writers to be fundamental, necessary, a product of the distance between a particular world of experience and the available modes of representation. In what ways are the essays similar? In what ways are they different? Where and how is a reader (where and how are you) positioned in each? What is the position of the writer? How is that defined? What does one need to learn to be the ideal reader of each text? As a writer, which example do you find most useful or compelling?

2. *After the Last Sky: Palestinian Lives* is one of the central "cases" in W. J. T. Mitchell's "The Photographic Essay: Four Case Studies"(p. 332). Mitchell's essay examines the "dialectic of exchange and resistance that make it possible (and sometimes impossible) to 'read' the pictures, or to 'see' the text illustrated in them."

   Before reading Mitchell, take time to work on "States" and to write a draft addressing the relationship of image to text. (The first of the "Questions for a Second Reading" provides a way of preparing for this.)

   Once you have worked through the opening three paragraphs, reread the essay with an eye to the accumulating relationships between image and text. Is there a pattern? Do any stand out for their force, variety, innovation?

   Once you've written that draft, read Mitchell and bring his analysis into the conversation. You will want to refer to the general frame and the terms of his argument and to the specific discussion of images in *After the Last Sky.* What does Mitchell bring to the essay? How would you define his expertise? What do you see that he doesn't? How might you define your position or point of view in relation to his?

3. Jean Mohr's collaboration with John Berger was important to Said, particularly in the 1975 book *A Seventh Man,* a photographic essay on migrant workers in Europe. You'll need to use the library or the bookstore for this assignment. Find a copy of *A Seventh Man* and write an essay on what you think it was in Mohr's work, and in his collaboration with Berger, that was most compelling to Said.

4. Both John Berger, in "Appearances" (p. 175), and Edward Said, in "States," are concerned with how photographs might be used to yield ideas, to produce understanding. Write an essay in which you work closely with an example from each writer, one in which he is providing a written account of a photograph. In what context are they providing this "reading" of a photograph? How, that is, do they understand the goal and importance of their work? And what is represented in the act, in the writing? How might the writing be seen to work between image and idea in the service of understanding?

   It would probably be best to assume that your readers are not familiar with the work of either Berger or Said. You will need to provide an introduction; you will need to take care to introduce their projects and your interest in them.

Assignment Sequences

WORKING WITH ASSIGNMENT SEQUENCES

THE ASSIGNMENT SEQUENCES that follow are different from the single writing assignments at the end of each essay. The single writing assignments are designed to give you a way back into the works you have read. They define the way you, the reader, can work on an essay by writing about it—testing its assumptions, probing its examples, applying its way of thinking to a new setting or to new material. A single assignment might ask you to read what Robert Coles has to say about documentary work and then, as a writer, to use Coles's terms and methods to analyze a documentary project. The single assignments are designed to demonstrate how a student might work on an essay, particularly an essay that is long or complex, and they are designed to show how pieces that might seem daunting are open, manageable, and managed best by writing.

The assignment sequences have a similar function, but with one important difference. Instead of writing one paper, or working on one or two selections from the book, you will be writing several essays and reading several selections. Your work will be sequential as well as cumulative. The work you do on Coles, for example, will give you a way of beginning with John Berger, or Roland Barthes. It will give you an angle of vision. You won't be a newcomer to such discussions. Your previous reading will make the new essay rich with association. Passages or examples will jump out, as if magnetized, and demand your attention. And by reading these essays in context, you will see each writer as a single voice in a larger discussion. Neither Coles, nor Berger, nor Barthes, after all, has had the last word on the subject of photography. It is not as though, by working on one of the essays, you have wrapped the subject up, ready to be put on the shelf.

The sequences are designed, then, so that you will be working not only on essays but on a subject, like the documentary tradition (or the relationship between words and images), a subject that can be examined, probed, and understood through the various frames provided by your reading. Each essay becomes a way of seeing a problem or a subject; it becomes a tool for thinking, an example of how a mind might work, a way of using language to make a subject rich and alive. In the assignment sequences, your reading is not random. Each sequence provides a set of readings that can be pulled together into a single project.

The sequences allow you to participate in an extended academic project, one with several texts and several weeks' worth of writing. You are not just adding one essay to another (Coles + Berger = ?) but trying out an approach to a subject by revising it, looking at new examples, hearing what someone else has to say, and beginning again to take a position of your own. Projects like these take time. It is not at all uncommon for professional writers to devote weeks or even months to a single essay, and the essay they write marks not the end of their thinking on the subject, but only one stage. Similarly, when readers are working on a project, the pieces they read accumulate on their desks and in their minds and become part of an extended conversation with several speakers, each voice offering a point of view on a subject, a new set of examples, or a new way of talking that resonates with echoes from earlier reading.

A student may read many books, take several courses, write many papers; ideally each experience becomes part of something larger, an education. The work of understanding, in other words, requires time and repeated effort. The power that comes from understanding cannot be acquired quickly—by reading one essay or working for a few hours. A student, finally, is a person who choreographs such experiences, not someone who passes one test only to move on to another. And the assignment sequences are designed to reproduce, although in a condensed period of time, the rhythm and texture of academic life. They invite you to try on its characteristic ways of seeing, thinking, and writing. The work you do in one week will not be lost when it has bearing on the work you do in the next. If an essay by Robert Coles has value for you, it is not because you proved to a teacher that you read it, but because you have put it to work and made it a part of your vocabulary as a student.

Working with a Sequence

Here is what you can expect as you work with a sequence. You begin by working with a single essay. You will need to read each piece twice, the second time with the "Questions for a Second Reading" and the assignment sequence in mind. Before rereading the selection, in other words, you should read through the assignments to get a sense of where you will be headed. And you should read the questions at the end of each selection. (You can use those questions to help frame questions of your own.) The purpose of all these questions, in a sense, is to prepare the text to speak—to bring it to life and insist that it respond to your attention, answer your questions. If you think of the authors as people you can talk to, if you think of their pages as occasions for dialogue (as places where you get to ask questions and insist on responses)—if you prepare your return to those pages in these ways, you are opening up the essays or stories (not closing them down or finishing them off) and creating a scene where you get to step forward as a performer.

While each sequence moves from selection to selection in *Ways of Reading Words and Images,* the most significant movement in the sequence is defined by the essays you write. Your essays provide the other major text for the course. In fact, when we teach these sequences, we seldom have any discussion of the assigned readings before our students have had a chance to write. When we talk as a group about Coles's "The Tradition: Fact or Fiction," for example, we begin by reproducing one or two student essays, handing them out to the class, and using them as the basis for discussion. We want to start, in other words, by looking at ways of reading Coles's essay—not at his essay alone.

The essays you write for each assignment in a sequence might be thought of as work-in-progress. Your instructor will tell you the degree to which each essay should be finished—that is, the degree to which it should be revised and copyedited and worked into a finished performance. In our classes, most writing assignments go through at least one revision. After we have had a chance to see a draft (or after a draft has been seen by others in the class), and after we have had some discussion of sample student essays we ask students to read the assigned essay or story one more time and to rework their essays to bring their work one step further—not necessarily to finish the essays (as though there would be nothing else to say) but to finish up this stage in their work and to feel their achievement in a way a writer simply cannot the first time through. Each assignment, then, really functions as two assignments in the schedule for the course. As a consequence, we don't "cover" as many essays in a semester as students might in another class. But coverage is not our goal. In a sense, we are teaching our students how to read slowly and closely, to return to a text rather than set it aside, to take the time to reread and rewrite and to reflect on what these activities entail. Some of these sequences, then, contain more readings or more writing assignments than you can address in a quarter or semester. Different courses work at different paces. It is important, however, to preserve time for rereading and rewriting. The sequences were written with the assumption that they would be revised to meet the needs of teachers, students, and programs. As you look at your syllabus, you may find, then, that reading or writing assignments have been changed, added, or dropped.

You will be writing papers that can be thought of as single essays. But you will also be working on a project, something bigger than its individual parts. From the perspective of the project, each piece you write is part of a larger body of work that evolves over the term. You might think of each sequence as a revision exercise, where the revision looks forward to what comes next as well as backward to what you have done. This form of revision asks you to do more than complete a single paper; it invites you to resee a subject or reimagine what you might say about it from a new point of view. You should feel free, then, to draw on your earlier essays when you work on one of the later assignments. There is every reason for you to reuse ideas, phrases, sentences, even paragraphs as your work builds from one week to the next. The advantage of work-in-progress is that you are not starting over completely every time you sit down to write. You've been over this territory before. You've developed some expertise in your subject. There is a body of work behind you.

Most of the sequences bring together several essays from the text and ask you to imagine them as an extended conversation, one with several speakers. The assignments are designed to give you a voice in the conversation as well, to allow you to speak in turn and to take your place in the company of other writers. This is the final purpose of the assignment sequence: after several weeks' work on the essays and on the subject that draws them together, you will begin to establish your own point of view. You will develop a position from which you can speak with authority, drawing strength from the work you have done as well as from your familiarity with the people who surround you.

This book brings together some of the most powerful voices of our culture. They speak in a manner that asks for response. The assignments at the end of each selection and, with a wider range of reference, the assignment sequences here at the end of the book demonstrate that there is no reason for a student, in such company, to remain silent.

SEQUENCE ONE

The Documentary Tradition

James Agee and Walker Evans
Dorothea Lange and Paul S. Taylor
Robert Coles
W. J. T. Mitchell

DOCUMENTARY WORK has traditionally combined words and images in an attempt to capture and bring forward areas of the world (or areas of human experience) that would otherwise remain hidden from view. The impulse is thought to be generous and politically progressive—that is, those doing documentary work have assumed that by providing accounts of, for example, the conditions of poverty, this knowledge would lead those with money and power to act to ameliorate those conditions.

This sequence is designed to introduce you to two key texts in the documentary tradition: James Agee and Walker Evans's *Let Us Now Praise Famous Men* and Dorothea Lange and Paul S. Taylor's *An American Exodus*. The opening assignments provide occasions to work closely with the photographs, learning to "read" them as texts, and to think about the relationship of words and images in the general project of each book. Assignments 6 and 7 turn to the work of two distinguished scholars, Robert Coles and W. J. T. Mitchell, both of whom have significant interest in both the history and the future of documentary work. The final assignment asks you to establish a position of your own in relation to Agee and Evans, Lange and Taylor, and the arguments of these two scholars—Coles and Mitchell.

• • • • • • • • • • • •

ASSIGNMENT 1

The Photographs of Walker Evans [Agee and Evans]

Walker Evans's photographs stand at the head of the book *Let Us Now Praise Famous Men*, before the title page. There is no introduction; there are no captions; there is nothing to verbally prepare a reader or to establish a tie to the book that follows. They are just there, as though they could or should or must speak for themselves. (And James Agee's written text does not refer directly to the photographs. It doesn't gloss them or explain them or even describe them).

Write an essay about the photographs, about how you understand them (and the project they represent), and about their placement in the book. The questions we asked earlier in the "Questions for a Second Reading" (p. 130) can serve here. Look back carefully through the photographs. Think of yourself as a reader reading the images, their presentation, and their arrangement. What do they say? How are you expected to read them? or prepared to read them?

If it is appropriate to turn this assignment into a larger research project, you might also look to see what Walker Evans has said about these photographs and, in general, about his work as a photographer.

Note: This assignment puts particular pressure on the first-person perspective of the essayist—you. You will need to write from your sense of the photographs and what might be said about them. It has been useful to our students to call attention to this from the very beginning. You might think of the "I" in your essay as a character, someone with a history, interests, a point of view, a style, someone of a particular age with a particular background in relation to photography, photographs, and Evans's subjects. And you might want to distinguish between your responses and others that you can imagine. It might become appropriate to acknowledge, in other words, that not everyone can, will, or should see these photographs the way you do.

• • • • • • • • • • • •

ASSIGNMENT 2

Let Us Now Praise Famous Men [Agee and Evans]

James Agee's written text does not refer directly to the photographs. It doesn't gloss them or explain them or even describe them. He does, however, refer to Evans, to photographs, and to photography in the "Preface" and the "Preamble." He says, for example, "The photographs are not illustrative. They, and the text, are coequal, mutually independent, and fully collaborative" (p. 87).

Write an essay in which you explain your understanding of the relationship between one of the photographs and a section of the text. You should be sure to provide examples and a close discussion of both photograph and text as part of the body of your essay. Think of yourself as providing a lesson to others in how one might best read these examples and, through them, the book. While you should certainly consider what Agee says about the project in the "Preface" and "Preamble," (pp. 86 and 96), you should not feel limited by or tied to his account.

• • • • • • • • • • • •

ASSIGNMENT 3

The Photographs of Dorothea Lange [Lange and Taylor]

The "Foreword" to *An American Exodus* includes the following account of method in preparing and assembling the photographs and the written text for the book:

> This is neither a book of photographs nor an illustrated book, in the traditional sense. Its particular form is the result of our use of techniques in proportions and relations designed to convey understanding easily, clearly, and vividly. We use the camera as a tool of research. (p. 290)

Lange and Taylor go on to say:

> We show you what is happening in selected regions of limited area. Something is lost by this method, for it fails to show fully the wide extent and the many variations of rural changes which we describe. But we believe that the gain in sharpness of focus reveals better the nature of the changes themselves. (p. 290)

"Sharpness of focus" is opposed to "wide extent" and "many variations." "Techniques in proportions and relations designed to convey understanding easily, clearly, and vividly define a method." As you reread, keep these terms in mind. Where do you most see the lack of the "wide" and "varied"? Where do you see its pull—or a gesture in that direction? And where would you find the best examples of the gains that are achieved through a "sharpness of focus"?

How might you identify, chart, and evaluate their "use of techniques in proportions and relations designed to convey understanding easily, clearly, and vividly"? What are these techniques? Where do you see them? How would you describe them? What forms of understanding do they provide? What don't they provide?

Lange was particularly concerned with the arrangement of the photographs, the sequence and the story it told or the argument it represented. How might you account for and describe the order of the images?

Write an essay in which you discuss the photographs and the work they do in providing focus, proportion, and relation in order to produce understanding. How, that is, does Lange teach a viewer to read them?

• • • • • • • • • • • •

ASSIGNMENT 4

Photographs, Captions, and Text [Lange and Taylor]

Here, in fuller form, is Lange and Taylor's account of their methods in preparing and assembling the photographs and in writing the text for *An American Exodus*:

> This is neither a book of photographs nor an illustrated book, in the traditional sense. Its particular form is the result of our use of techniques in proportions and relations designed to convey understanding easily, clearly, and vividly. We use the camera as a tool of research. Upon a tripod of photographs, captions, and text we rest themes evolved out of long observations in the field. We adhere to the standards of documentary photography as we have conceived them. Quotations which accompany photographs report what the persons photographed said, not what we think might be their unspoken

> thoughts. Where there are no people, and no other source is indicated, the quotation comes from persons whom we met in the field.
>
> We show you what is happening in selected regions of limited area. Something is lost by this method, for it fails to show fully the wide extent and the many variations of rural changes which we describe. But we believe that the gain in sharpness of focus reveals better the nature of the changes themselves. (p. 290)

Write an essay that presents Lange and Taylor's project *as* a project. You will need to consider, then, not only what these selections say, but how they say what they say, and why the basic elements (photograph, caption, and text) are prepared and assembled as they are.

To prepare for this essay, you must reread with a particular attention to the images (note the way they are selected and arranged) and to the relationship between words and images. "Upon a tripod of photographs, captions, and text we rest themes evolved out of long observations in the field." How do these three elements work together: photographs, captions, and text? What demands do they put upon a reader? How do they teach the reader to read a photograph, to speak for it, or to understand what it represents? What decisions did Lange and Taylor seem to be making in preparing and assembling each element?

• • • • • • • • • • • •

ASSIGNMENT 5

Documentary Projects
[Agee and Evans, Lange and Taylor]

James Agee and Walker Evans's *Let Us Now Praise Famous Men* (1941) and Dorothea Lange and Paul S. Taylor's *An American Exodus: A Record of Human Erosion* (1939) were conceived as projects at about the same time. They participate in the same documentary tradition and, as texts, they are in indirect conversation with each other. Both express a strong commitment to the Southern poor; both are aware of the dangers inherent in their projects, dangers that include exploitation and paternalism, relatively wealthy white Northern intellectuals profiting by retailing the images and stories of ex-slaves, tenant farmers, and sharecroppers. But the work of each is also very different, as the excerpts we've included in this textbook will show.

Write an essay that presents and explores the significant differences. You will need to pick and choose. You will need to carefully select and present your examples. You will need to limit yourself to the differences that seem to you to be most significant or interesting. You should aim for an extended discussion of one or two rather than a catalog account of everything. And you should assume that the differences represent decisions made about appropriate method and form, that the work is different because of different approaches to the problems of representing rural scenes to an audience that would otherwise be ignorant of them.

• • • • • • • • • • • •

ASSIGNMENT 6

"The Tradition" [Coles, Agee and Evans, Lange and Taylor]

In his essay, "The Tradition: Fact and Fiction," Robert Coles gives a detailed account of the photographs in *Let Us Now Praise Famous Men* and in *An American Exodus*. Write an essay in which you bring Coles's argument to bear on the work you have done with the photographs in these books. What does he say? What does he say that you find useful? Where and how do you differ in approach or in conclusion? What might you make of these differences? (Or how, in your essay, might you define a relationship with an established scholar?)

In your essay, you should make it clear that Coles is serving *your* project. In fact, this essay could be thought of as a revision of your earlier written work on Agee and Evans and Lange and Taylor. Your sense of the primary sources should remain at the center. Coles is someone you are turning to after having developed (or in order to continue to develop) a position of your own. You need to be present in your essay as a scholar, in other words. Coles should not render you silent or make you disappear.

• • • • • • • • • • • •

ASSIGNMENT 7

The Photographic Essay [Mitchell, Agee and Evans, Lange and Taylor]

In W. J. T. Mitchell's, "The Photographic Essay: Four Case Studies," one of those case studies is *Let Us Now Praise Famous Men*. Reread Mitchell's essay, and read it with the thought that Lange and Taylor's work might serve as the fifth case in his sequence of case studies. With Agee and Evans, you should take care to be prepared to represent Mitchell's argument and to be able to manipulate his key terms. And as you reread, you should think about how Mitchell might classify the work of Lange and Taylor in his account of the "dialectic of exchange and resistance between photography and language." Where would he place their work in relation to the other four case studies?

Write an essay in which you bring Mitchell's arguments to bear on the work you have done with the photographs in these books. What does he say? What does he say that you find useful? Where and how do you differ in approach or in conclusion? What might you make of these differences? (Or how, in your essay, might you define a relationship with an established scholar?) Again, in your essay, you should make it clear that Mitchell is serving *your* project. In fact, this essay could be thought of as a revision of your earlier written work on Agee and Evans and on Lange and Taylor.

• • • • • • • • • • • •

ASSIGNMENT 8

The Uses of Scholarship [Coles, Mitchell]

Both Robert Coles, in "The Tradition: Fact and Fiction," and W. J. T. Mitchell, in "The Photographic Essay," write about the genre of the photographic essay, and both take as key texts two books that are excerpted in *Ways of Readings Words and Images*: James Agee and Walker Evans's *Let Us Now Praise Famous Men* and Dorothea Lange and Paul S. Taylor's, *An American Exodus*. You have had the opportunity to look at Coles's and Mitchell's primary sources, to see what they selected and what they left out, to see the photographs and text in their original context. You can think about the logic (or desire) that led to their selections of exemplary material.

Write an essay in which you elaborate on the differences in Coles's and Mitchell's approaches to and accounts of these texts. You can imagine that you are writing for a reader who has read none of the texts at hand, so you will need to be careful in summary (perhaps reproducing some of the illustrations). What does each notice or choose to notice in the texts? How are these decisions related to the larger projects of the two authors? To their underlying commitments and concerns? And, finally, where are you on the differences between the two? Would you align yourself with Coles or with Mitchell? From their example, is there a position you would define as your own or as an alternative?

SEQUENCE TWO
Fact and Fiction (?)

Robert Coles

Dorothea Lange and Paul S. Taylor

James Agee and Walker Evans

John Berger

Roland Barthes

Edward Said and Jean Mohr

ONE OF DOROTHEA LANGE'S most well-known images is the photograph titled "Couple, Born in Slavery" (p. 296). Is that image "true"? Is it propaganda? Can it speak for itself? Can we trust it? Does it need words to provide meaning and context? These are the questions that occupy the writers of the essays in this sequence, and they are, then, the questions to which this sequence turns your attention, so that you can join the conversation.

The first two assignments ask you to work with Robert Coles's essay "The Tradition: Fact and Fiction." Coles provides one way of framing the issue. The next two assignments ask you to look carefully at the work of two of his key figures, Dorothea Lange and Walker Evans. The fourth and fifth and sixth assignments turn to two other theorists, Roland Barthes and John Berger, and to a more contemporary photographic essay, one by Edward Said (the writer) and Jean Mohr (the photographer). The final assignments ask you to carry out a project of your own, one with a commitment to the values underlying documentary work.

• • • • • • • • • • • •

ASSIGNMENT 1

Human Actuality [Coles]

> So often in our discussions of documentary work my students . . . emphasize the "actuality" of the work—its responsibility to fact. They commonly pose for themselves the familiar alternative of fiction, as though we were dealing in clear-cut opposites: if not the true as against the false, at least the real as against the imaginary. But such opposites or alternatives don't quite do justice either conceptually or pragmatically to the aspect of "human actuality" that has to do with the vocational life of writers, photographers, folklorists, musicologists, and filmmakers, those who are trying to engage with people's words, their music, gestures, movements, and overall appearance and then let others know what they have learned. (p. 212)

Coles says that his students don't get it—or don't quite get it. They take the work of writers, photographers, and other documentary workers, and they understand them in terms of the familiar categories of "fact"or "fiction," "real" or "imaginary." So, what is the alternative?

Write an essay in which you summarize Coles's argument and in which you present it to someone who has not read the text. We would invite you to see your summary as strategic. You are trying to get down on paper what Coles is saying because you want to respond to it. One way to begin to find an opening, a place where you, too, can speak, is by working closely with his examples, particularly those of photographers focusing, cropping, and selecting as they prepare images of rural, working life (the couple in the car, the father and daughter on the porch, the girl picking cotton). As you work with those images (or others of your choosing) and the discussion that surrounds them, take time to think about alternative arguments. (Coles provides one example in his father's response to "Ditched, Stalled, and Stranded.") How might you argue for one of the discarded images? or against the "close-up view"? How might you argue with the way Coles values the images he values? In every case, in the case of the photographers, the writers, and Coles, individuals are making choices and making judgments. You can make choices, too.

• • • • • • • • • • • •

ASSIGNMENT 2

Proportions and Relations; Sharpness of Focus [Lange and Taylor]

> This is neither a book of photographs nor an illustrated book, in the traditional sense. Its particular form is the result of our use of techniques in proportions and relations designed to convey understanding easily, clearly, and vividly. We use the camera as a tool of research. Upon a tripod of photographs, captions, and text we rest themes evolved out of long observations in the field. We adhere to the standards of documentary photography as we have conceived them. Quotations which accompany photographs report what the persons photographed said, not what we think might be their unspoken thoughts. Where there are no people, and no other source is indicated, the quotation comes from persons whom we met in the field.
>
> We show you what is happening in selected regions of limited area. Something is lost by this method, for it fails to show fully the wide extent and the many variations of rural changes which we describe. But we believe that the gain in sharpness of focus reveals better the nature of the changes themselves. (p. 290)

The passages above come from the "Foreword" to Lange and Taylor's *An American Exodus*. It refers to "sharpness of focus" as opposed to the "wide extent" and the "many variations" of the changes they document in rural, Southern life and labor in the United States in the 1930s. It speaks of "techniques in proportions and relations designed to convey understanding easily, clearly, and vividly."

Write an essay that presents Lange and Taylor's project *as* a project. You will need to consider, then, not only what these selections say, but how they say what they say, and why the basic elements (photograph, caption, and text) are prepared and assembled as they are.

To prepare for this essay, you will need to reread giving particular attention to the images (particularly the way they are selected and arranged) and to the relationship between words and images. "Upon a tripod of photographs, captions, and text we rest themes evolved out of long observations in the field." How do these three elements work together: photographs, captions, and text? What demands do they put on a reader? How do they teach the reader to read a photograph, to speak for it, or to understand what it represents? What decisions did Lange and Taylor seem to be making in preparing and assembling each element? And what might those decisions have to do with Coles's concern for "human actuality"?

• • • • • • • • • • • •

ASSIGNMENT 3

The Impotence of the Reader's Eye [Agee and Evans]

> The photographs are not illustrative. They, and the text, are coequal, mutually independent, and fully collaborative. By their fewness, and by the impotence of the reader's eye, this will be misunderstood by most of that minority which does not wholly ignore it. In the interests, however, of the history and future of photography, that risk seems irrelevant, and this flat statement necessary. (p. 87)

Walker Evans's photographs stand at the head of the book *Let Us Now Praise Famous Men*, before the title page. There is no introduction; there are no captions; there is nothing to verbally prepare a reader or to establish a tie to the book that follows. They are just there, as though they could or should or must speak for themselves. (And James Agee's written text does not refer directly to the photographs. It doesn't gloss them or explain them or even describe them).

Write an essay about the photographs, about how you understand them (and the project they represent), and about their placement in the book. Look back carefully through the photographs—as a reader reading the images, their presentation and their arrangement. What do they say? How are you expected to read them? or prepared to read them?

Once you have written out, in draft, your understanding of the photographs, go back to Coles's account. Write an essay in which you bring Coles's argument to bear on the work you have done with the photographs. What does he say? What does he say that you find useful? Where and how do you differ in approach or in conclusion? What might you make of these differences? (Or how, in your essay, might you define a relationship with an established scholar?)

In your essay, you should make it clear that Coles is serving *your* project. Your work is at the center. He is someone you are turning to after having developed (or in order to continue to develop) a position of your own. You need to be present in your essay as a scholar, in other words. Coles should not render you silent or make you disappear.

You should assume that your readers do not know (or remember) Coles's account of the photographs. You will need to present his case. Your readers may know something about *Let Us Now Praise Famous Men*, but they don't have a copy handy. It would be useful, therefore, to work some of the images into the body of your essay.

Note: This assignment puts particular pressure on the first-person perspective of the essayist—you. You will need to write from your sense of the photographs and what might be said about them. It has been useful to our students to call attention to this from the very beginning. You might think of the "I" in your essay as a character, someone with a history, interests, a point of view, a style, someone of a particular age with a particular background in relation to photography, photographs, and Evans's subjects.

• • • • • • • • • • • •

ASSIGNMENT 4

Citing the Real [Berger]

> An instant photographed can only acquire meaning insofar as the viewer can read into it a duration extending beyond itself. When we find a photograph meaningful, we are lending it a past and a future. (p. 178)

Berger uses metaphors of reading and writing to explain how photographs express (or can be made to express) meaning. He writes that "photographs quote from appearances" (p. 193). He says that the longer the quotation, the greater the possibilities for the extension of meaning. Photographs that constitute a shorter quotation, then, don't offer as much for viewers to "read" or "give reason to." Photographs are treated as texts. The photograph of the long quotation, he says, makes ideas possible, ideas that are discontinuous with the content of the photograph. "A photograph which achieves expressiveness thus works dialectically: it preserves the particularity of the event recorded, and it chooses an instant when the correspondences of the particular appearances articulate a general idea" (p. 200).

This is a difficult argument. His demonstration of the expressiveness of certain photographs is achieved in his own writing. As you prepare to summarize Berger's argument, you might look at his written account of "Boy Sleeping," "Friends," "Lovers," or, with a significant difference, "A Red Hussar Leaving, June 1919, Budapest."

For this assignment, choose two public photographs, photographs for which you do not have any personal connections. Use these to test his claims and to try out his style. Write about each, using his writing as a model. And from these exercises, write an essay in which you present, test, and extend Berger's argument. How might Berger account for their "length," the "extension" of meaning they allow? How would he value this? And what about you? How would you explain what you have done? How might you explain its value to you and to people like you, people of your generation? And what might his work (and his values) have to do with Coles's concern for "human actuality"?

• • • • • • • • • • • •

ASSIGNMENT 5

Studium *and* Punctum [Barthes]

> Hence the detail which interests me is not, or at least not strictly, intentional, and probably must not be so; it occurs in the field of the photographed thing like a supplement that is at once inevitable and delightful; it does not necessarily attest to the photographer's art; it says only that the photographer was there, or else, still more simply, that he could *not* photograph the partial object at the same time as the total object. . . . " (p. 160)

Working with "public photographs" (not family photos, in other words), present them through your deployment of Barthes's terms *studium* and *punctum.* You can choose photographs from a book or a collection; you can work with photographs in this textbook (and you can draw some, but not all, from Barthes's essay). You can use his discussions of photographs as models for your own.

Write an essay in which you discuss these photographs in order to think about (and to think with) Barthes's example in *Camera Lucida.* You should take plenty of time to work through your discussions of the photographs. You will need to set this up as a project. Where do these terms come from—*studium* and *punctum*? What interests you in trying them out? Can they possibly serve a documentary project as imagined by Coles? What values are represented here? What commitments to "human actuality"?

• • • • • • • • • • • •

ASSIGNMENT 6

Style and Convention [Said and Mohr]

> Its style and method—the interplay of text and photos, the mixture of genres, modes, styles—do not tell a consecutive story, nor do they constitute a political essay. Since the main features of our present existence are dispossession, dispersion, and yet also a kind of power incommensurate with our stateless exile, I believe that essentially unconventional, hybrid, and fragmentary forms of expression should be used to represent us. What I have quite consciously designed, then, is an alternative mode of expression to

> the one usually encountered in the media, in works of social science, in popular fiction.
>
> –EDWARD SAID
> "Introduction" to *After the Last Sky*

The first three paragraphs of Edward Said's "States" provide a "reading" of the opening photograph, "Tripoli, Badawi camp, May 1983." Or, to put it another way, the writing evolves from and is in response to that photograph. As you reread these paragraphs, pay close attention to what Said is doing, to what he notices, to what prompts or requires commentary. How would you describe and explain the relationship of word to image? What is he doing as a writer? What is he doing for a reader? (How does he position a reader in relation to the image?)

It might be useful to begin by thinking about what he is *not* doing. It is not, for example, the presentation one might expect in a slide show on travel in Lebanon. He is not providing captions. It is not, then, the presentation familiar in magazines like *National Geographic*.

Once you have worked through the opening three paragraphs, read the essay paying particular attention to Said's work with all of the photographs. Is there a pattern? Are there variations? Can you develop a theory of his use of words and images? Do any of the commentaries stand out for their force, eloquence, or innovation? Write an essay in which you present, with a careful use of examples (including visual examples), your sense of Said's project as he provides words to images. How does Said understand a writer's responsibility to his subject, his reader, "human actuality"?

• • • • • • • • • • • •

ASSIGNMENT 7

Doing Documentary Work [Coles]

It is possible to take Coles's essay as an invitation to do documentary work. The works he cites represent long-term projects and great commitments of time, energy, and spirit. One of the pleasures of being a student, however, is that you have the authority to try things out provisionally, tentatively, and on a smaller scale.

This assignment has two parts. For the first part, create a written documentary in which you represent some aspect of another person or, to use the language of the essay, in which you are in pursuit of a moment of "human actuality." The text you create can include photographs, interviews, observation—whatever is available. The point is for you to feel what it is like to be responsible, as a writer, for representing someone else, his or her thoughts, words, and actions. To those who do it for a living, this is a deep and deeply fraught responsibility.

Once you have completed your documentary (and perhaps once it has been read and evaluated by others), write a separate essay in which you use your work as a way of thinking back on and responding to Coles. Where and how, for example, did you serve as a "filter"? Where and how did you shape that material? What decisions did you have to make concerning foreground and background, the individual and idiosyncratic, or the social, cultural, and historical? What work would you need to do if you were to go back to this project and do an even better job with it? You could imagine this as a letter to Coles, a review of his book, or as a plan for future work of your own, perhaps the work of revising the documentary you have begun.

SEQUENCE THREE

Memory, Image, and Text

Marianne Hirsch
James Agee and Walker Evans
Edward Said and Jean Mohr

IN THE DOCUMENTARY TRADITION, it is not uncommon to find words and photographs linked together, as though the two could somehow get closer to the truth, to the real world they represent, than either one alone. And yet it is often the case that the juxtaposition of words and images only serves to call each into question. The images are revealed as unable to speak for themselves. The words speak of the need for interpretation; and they often seem incomplete, distracting, unreliable, or distant. This sequence is designed to focus attention on the instability of image and text, as represented in practice and in commentary. The sequence begins with Marianne Hirsch's essay "Projected Memory: Holocaust Photographs in Personal and Public Fantasy." Hirsch provides the opening terms for the difficult relationship of spectator to photograph and of word to image. The second and third assignments bring James Agee, Walker Evans, and *Let Us Now Praise Famous Men* into the mix. The concerns here are not memory but the distant present, the use of words and images to bring an understanding of the rural poor to a relatively comfortable urban reading public. The fourth turns to the work of Edward Said and Jean Mohr. Said writes from and about images of Palestinian people and places. He provides both practice and theory, the work with image, history, and memory and a commentary on such a project. The final assignment is a large-scale revision, the occasion for you to bring together the work you have done on previous papers and to stake out a final (if tentative) position of your own.

• • • • • • • • • • • •

ASSIGNMENT 1

Photographs in Personal and Public Fantasy [Hirsch]

As the title indicates, Hirsch's essay is about "projected memory" and it is about "Holocaust photographs in personal and public fantasy." It is not presented in the style of thesis, example, and conclusion. There is neither a conventional introduction nor a conventional summation. The arguments and demonstrations in between are rich, varied, and complicated.

What, so far as you are concerned, is this essay about? And how does it speak to you—to your interests and concerns and projects and to your education? Write an essay, perhaps in the genre of a review, in which you present "Projected Memory: Holocaust Photographs in Personal and Public Fantasy" to those who have not yet read it. You will need to take care to give a thorough and accurate account of what Hirsch says and does. You should also establish your position in relation to the essay, discussing where and how you found it useful or interesting.

• • • • • • • • • • • •

ASSIGNMENT 2

Image and Text [Agee and Evans]

Walker Evans's photographs stand at the head of the book *Let Us Now Praise Famous Men,* before the title page. There is no introduction; there are no captions; there is nothing to verbally prepare a reader or to establish a tie to the book that follows. They are just there, as though they could or should or must speak for themselves.

James Agee's written text does not refer directly to the photographs. It doesn't gloss them or explain them or even describe them. He does, however, refer to Evans, to photographs and to photography in the "Preface" and the "Preamble" (pp. 86 and 96).

Write an essay in which you explain your understanding of the relationship between the photographs and the text. In doing so, you are providing a lesson to others in how one might best read this book (or the excerpts in *Ways of Reading Words and Images*). You should certainly consider what Agee says in the frontmatter. You should not be limited by or tied to his account, however.

Note: For this assignment, it might be best to assume that your reader is not yet familiar with Agee and Evans and *Let Us Now Praise Famous Men*. You will need to provide some introduction and context. For the written text, you will need to provide summary, paraphrase, and quotation. You should certainly feel free to reproduce images in the body of your essay.

• • • • • • • • • • • •

ASSIGNMENT 3

The Cruel Radiance of What Is
[Agee and Evans, Hirsch]

In "Projected Memory," Marianne Hirsch writes about the past as it is defined by (created by) photographs and our use of them. It is a cautionary essay; it is about the proper uses of the past, about how to understand the power and presence of photographs. Agee writes about photographs and the present. It, too, is full of cautions. Here, from the "Preamble," is a statement of particular urgency:

> For in the immediate world, everything is to be discerned, for him who can discern it, and centrally and simply, without either dissection into science, or digestion into art, but with the whole of consciousness, seeking to perceive it as it stands: so that the aspect of a street in sunlight can roar in the heart of itself as a symphony, perhaps as no symphony can: and all of consciousness is shifted from the imagined, the revisive, to the effort to perceive simply the cruel radiance of what is.
>
> This is why the camera seems to me, next to unassisted and weaponless consciousness, the central instrument of our time; and is why in turn I feel such rage at its misuse: which has spread so nearly universal a corruption of sight that I know of less than a dozen alive whose eyes I can trust even so much as my own." (p. 98)

Write an essay that works with these two selections and their possible uses for you (and people like you) at this point in time, a time filled with photographic images. What does each say about photography? What do they say about the dangers and powers in photographic images and our uses of them? What do they show or enact in their writing about these images? And where are you with these lessons? What makes sense to you?

You should feel free to draw from your earlier papers.

• • • • • • • • • • • •

ASSIGNMENT 4

Alternate Modes of Expression
[Hirsch, Said and Mohr]

According to Hirsch, Lorie Novak "stages an uneasy confrontation of personal memory with public history." Hirsch studies, writes about (and stages) such confrontations herself. The phrase is an apt one to use to describe the work of Edward Said and Jean Mohr in "States," an essay where image and text provide the occasion to connect "intimate memory and contemporary social reality." Said and Mohr, too, could be said to stage an uneasy confrontation of personal memory with public history.

The project of postmemory, as defined by Hirsch, can be a writing project. In fact, to describe the individual's active engagement with the past that *is* postmemory, Hirsch uses metaphors of writing: "It is a question of adopting the traumatic experiences—and thus also the memories—of others as one's own, or, more precisely, as experiences one might oneself have had, and of inscribing them into one's own life story. It is a question of conceiving oneself as multiply interconnected with others of the same, or previous, and of subsequent generations; of the same and of other—proximate or distant—cultures and subcultures" (p. 268).

Said speaks directly of the writing project in *After the Last Sky*. In the "Introduction," he says of the book,

> Its style and method—the interplay of text and photos, the mixture of genres, modes, styles—do not tell a consecutive story, nor do they constitute a political essay. Since the main features of our present existence are dispossession, dispersion, and yet also a kind of power incommensurate with our stateless exile, I believe that essentially unconventional, hybrid, and fragmentary forms of expression should be used to represent us. What I have quite consciously designed, then, is an alternative mode of expression to the one usually encountered in the media, the works of social science, in popular fiction.

Write an essay in which you consider Said and Mohr's "States" through the lens provided by Hirsch's "Projected Memory," with particular attention to differences. How do they each create, invoke, and value memory? What is the role of writing—or, what lessons can a writer draw from each? If you were to undertake such a project, whose example would you find most useful, whose most compelling?

• • • • • • • • • • • •

ASSIGNMENT 5

Thinking Back [Hirsch, Agee and Evans, Said and Mohr]

In all of the work you have read for this sequence, photographs have prompted pages and pages of writing—a troubled, difficult writing, writing that is not simply caption or introduction or even commentary. The writing has its own force and agenda. To prepare for this writing assignment, work back through each of these selections looking for interesting and representative passages that can be placed next to the photographs and that can be used to talk about the achieved relation between words and images.

With these examples as your primary material, write an essay that examines the different ways Hirsch, Said and Mohr, and Agee and Evans understand their projects, their relationship to the images, to their subject, to their audience, and to history—to the broad set of political concerns that are served by each project. And consider what their projects and their concerns might have to do with you and with people like you—people of your generation, perhaps, or students at college or university.

SEQUENCE FOUR

Words and Images

W. J. T. Mitchell
James Agee and Walker Evans
Roland Barthes
Edward Said and Jean Mohr

IN THE INTRODUCTION to his book *Picture Theory*, W. J. T. Mitchell says, "What we need is a critique of visual culture that is alert to the power of images for good and evil and that is capable of discriminating the variety and historical specificity of their uses." He refers to his book as a "pedagogical primer or prompt-book for classroom experiments," experiments that would bring together the study of literature and the study of visual art under the general category of "representation."

The sequence of assignments below focus on the question of representation. In what ways can words and images provide us access to the "real world," to particular people or places, to history or the grounding social facts of our lives? Mitchell provides the frame for this process of inquiry. The first assignment is intended to give you a starting point, a way of representing your sense of what he says and why. The remaining assignments work through his sources, three of the four "case studies" alluded to in his title. Each articulates a concern for word and image; each is a "case" for Mitchell. Each can provide a prompt for you as you begin to organize your own parallel study, one informed by Mitchell but not consumed (or contained or overwhelmed) by his. The final assignment is a general revision, a final account of what Mitchell understands to be at stake and at risk and a final account of your position on words, images, and the problems of representation.

• • • • • • • • • • • •

ASSIGNMENT 1

The Photographic Essay [Mitchell]

Write an essay in which you present Mitchell's argument in "The Photographic Essay: Four Case Studies" to someone who has not yet read the text. This is a complicated task, since the argument is long and complicated, and it has its shifts and turns. You will need to give a sense of his argument and its key terms and phrases. You will need to give a sense of the progress of his essay, where it begins and ends, and a sense of his examples and what he does with them.

We would invite you to think of this summary as strategic. You are trying to get down on paper what Mitchell is saying because you want to respond to it—if not now, then later. (How to respond? You can imagine yourself in conversation with Mitchell. You can respond as a reader, describing the experience of working through the text. You can extend his argument, or challenge it. You can turn from his concerns to yours—you, too, are surrounded by words and images.)

In a summary, much of the time you will be speaking for Mitchell. Be sure, however, that there are sentences or paragraphs or sections in your essay that you can point to as yours, where you are speaking, too.

• • • • • • • • • • • •

ASSIGNMENT 2

A Writing Experiment [Mitchell, Agee and Evans]

Walker Evans's photographs stand at the head of the book *Let Us Now Praise Famous Men,* before the title page. There is no introduction; there are no captions; there is nothing to verbally prepare a reader or to establish a tie to the book that follows. They are just there, as though they could or should or must speak for themselves. (And James Agee's written text does not refer directly to the photographs. It doesn't gloss them or explain them or even describe them.) Agee does, however, refer to Evans, to photographs and to photography in the "Preface" and the "Preamble." He says, for example,

"The photographs are not illustrative. They, and the text, are coequal, mutually independent, and fully collaborative" (p. 87).

Write an essay in which you explain your understanding of the relationship between one of the photographs and a section of the text. You should be sure to provide these as a part of the body of your essay. Think of yourself as providing a lesson to others in how one might best read these examples and, through them, the book. While you should certainly consider what Agee says about the project in the "Preface" and "Preamble," you should not feel limited by or tied to his account.

And, perhaps in a revision, see where and how Mitchell might appear in your essay. You shouldn't begin with him, you should begin with your own impressions, concerns, and ideas. But you are not working alone. Mitchell is there too (whether you want him to be or not!). At some point (or points) in your essay, you should acknowledge what he has to say, his angle of vision, his argument, his key terms.

• • • • • • • • • • • •

ASSIGNMENT 3

Studium *and* Punctum: *Roland Barthes and the Photographic Image* [Barthes, Mitchell]

Barthes's discussion of photography in *Camera Lucida* relies on the distinction he makes between *studium* and *punctum*. We'd like you to see if you can put these terms to work. Gather two or three "public photographs" (not family photos, in other words) and present them through your deployment of Barthes's terms *studium* and *punctum*. You can choose photographs from a book or a collection; you can work with photographs in this textbook. If you do work with photographs in this textbook, you can draw some, but not all, from Barthes's essay).

Write an essay in which you discuss these photographs in order to think about (and to think with) Barthes's example in *Camera Lucida*. You will need to set this up as a project. Where do these terms come from—*studium* and *punctum?* What interests you in trying them out? You should take plenty of time to work through your discussions of the photographs. And, in the end, you should talk about the exercise and what you can conclude from it.

As you move from Barthes's world to your own, for example, how useful is this distinction (*studium* and *punctum*)? As you look at a newspaper or a magazine or still images on television or a computer screen, or at "art" photographs in a book or a museum, how useful is it? As you think about new technologies (digital cameras, computer editing), does the argument need to be revised?

• • • • • • • • • • • •

ASSIGNMENT 4

Reading Mitchell Reading Barthes [Mitchell, Barthes]

Camera Lucida is one of the "case studies" in W. J. T. Mitchell's "The Photographic Essay: Four Case Studies." (Mitchell's key examples, the missing photograph of Barthes's mother and the photograph "The Artist's Mother," both fall in the second half of the book and so are not in the excerpt included here.)

For this assignment, we'd like you to write an essay on Barthes that represents your response to Mitchell. Perhaps the best way to do this is to, first, establish a position of your own. Take time to reread *Camera Lucida* to think about the staging, the placement, and the use of the photographs. Choose examples you can use to think about the various relationships of image to word and word to image, and begin to write, in draft form, your thoughts.

Once you have written out, in draft, your understanding of the relationship of photographs to text, reread Mitchell's account. And write an essay in which you bring Mitchell's argument to bear on the work you have done. What does Mitchell say? What does he say that you find useful? Where and how do you differ in approach or in conclusion? (Or how, in your essay, might you define a relationship with an established scholar?)

Note: This assignment puts particular pressure on the first-person perspective of the essayist—you. It has been useful to our students to call attention to this from the very beginning. You might think of the "I" in your essay as a character, someone with a history, interests, a point of view, a style, someone of a particular age with a particular background in relation to photography and photographs.

ASSIGNMENT 5

The Interplay of Text and Photo: Edward Said and Jean Mohr [Said and Mohr]

The first three paragraphs of Edward Said and Jean Mohr's essay "States" provide a "reading" of the opening photograph, "Tripoli, Badawi camp, May 1983." Or, to put it another way, the writing evolves from and is in response to that photograph. As you reread these paragraphs, pay close attention to what Said is doing, to what he notices, to what prompts or requires commentary. How would you describe and explain the relationship of word to image? What is he doing as a writer? What is he doing for a reader? (How does he position a reader in relation to the image?)

It might be useful to begin by thinking about what he is *not* doing. It is not, for example, the presentation one might expect in a slide show on travel in Lebanon. He is not providing captions. It is not, then, the presentation familiar in magazines like *National Geographic*.

Once you have worked through the opening three paragraphs, read the essay paying particular attention to Said's work with all of the photographs. Is there a pattern? Are there variations? Can you develop a theory of his use of words and images? Do any of the commentaries stand out for their force, eloquence, or innovation? Write an essay in which you present, with a careful use of examples (including visual examples), your sense of Said's project as he provides words to images.

ASSIGNMENT 6

Reading Mitchell Reading Said and Mohr [Mitchell, Said and Mohr]

After the Last Sky: Palestinian Lives is one of the central "cases" in W. J. T. Mitchell's "The Photographic Essay: Four Case Studies." Mitchell's essay examines the "dialectic of exchange and resistance that make it possible (and sometimes impossible) to 'read' the pictures or to 'see' the text illustrated in them." You have thought carefully about Said and Mohr and their project. What does Mitchell bring to the essay? How might you define his expertise? What concerns of yours does he not share? How might you match his concerns for words and images with those concerns expressed by Said (both in what Said says and what Said does)? How might you define your position or point of view in relation to his?

• • • • • • • • • • • •

ASSIGNMENT 7

A Final Revision [Mitchell, Agee and Evans, Barthes, Said and Mohr]

To introduce the four case studies in "The Photographic Essay," Mitchell says, "I want to examine four photo-essays that, in various ways, foreground the dialectic of exchange and resistance between photography and language." For this assignment, work closely with the four case studies to bring forward what remains implied in Mitchell's text, the *differences* in the four cases. What *are* the "various ways" they foreground the dialectic of exchange and resistance between photography and language? What position does Mitchell seem to take on the value or achievement of each of the four books? What seems to you to be the significant or interesting differences? Mitchell's essay is designed to prepare you to be a reader of the photographic essay. From the examples Mitchell gives, what sorts of books would you be hoping to find?

You should imagine that you are writing for someone who has not read "The Photographic Essay." You will need, then, to be sure to represent and summarize the text. (See the first "Question for a Second Reading" on p. 370.) The point of the summary, however, is to define a position from which you can begin to do your work. And, to repeat what was said above, your work is to bring forward what Mitchell does not foreground—his sense of the differences between the four cases and the implication or value of those differences. And, in relation to what you see in Mitchell, your job is to articulate your own position on the range, importance, and possibility of the genre of the photo-essay. This essay should draw heavily on what you have written throughout this sequence of assignments.

SEQUENCE FIVE
Writing Projects

Edward Said and Jean Mohr
James Agee and Walker Evans
Marianne Hirsch
Roland Barthes
John Berger

THE PURPOSE of this sequence is to invite you to work closely with pieces of writing that call attention to themselves as writing, that make visible writing as a problem, a fundamental problem of representation and understanding. The seven assignments that follow bring together writing projects that rely heavily on images. The opening assignments direct your work with those readings. While you will be writing separate essays, you can choose to work on related subject matter. (The projects can become pieces of something larger, in other words.) Connecting the essays is not necessary, however. (Some students, in fact, have found this to be a burden.) The final assignment asks you to revise and to reflect on the work you have done. This sequence is perhaps too long for many courses. It is possible to pick and choose from assignments 1 through 6.

• • • • • • • • • • • •

ASSIGNMENT 1

Words and Images [Said and Mohr]

The first three paragraphs of Edward Said and Jean Mohr's essay "States" provide a "reading" of the opening photograph, "Tripoli, Badawi camp, May 1983." Or, to put it another way, the writing evolves from and is in response to that photograph. As a way of preparing for this assignment, reread these paragraphs and pay close attention to what Said is doing, to what he notices, to what prompts or requires commentary. How would you describe and explain the writing that follows? What is he doing with the photo? What is he doing as a writer? What is he doing for a reader? (How does he position a reader?)

It might be useful to begin by thinking about what he is *not* doing. It is not, for example, the presentation one might expect in a slide show on travel in Lebanon. Nor is it the kind of presentation one might expect while seeing the slides of family or friends, or slides in an art history or art appreciation class.

Once you have worked through the opening three paragraphs, reread the essay paying attention to Said's work with all the photographs. Is there a pattern? Do any of the commentaries stand out for their force, variety, innovation?

For this assignment, compose a similar project, a Said-like reading of a set of photos. These can be photos prepared for the occasion (by you or a colleague); they could also be photos already available. Whatever their source, they should represent people and places, a history and/or geography that you know well, that you know to be complex and contradictory, and that you know will not be easily or readily understood by others, both the group for whom you will be writing (most usefully the members of your class) and readers more generally.

You must begin with a sense that the photos cannot speak for themselves—you must speak for them.

• • • • • • • • • • • •

ASSIGNMENT 2

An Experiment in Style [Agee]

Agee's prose style is odd and distinctive. (By some standards, it is not standard English.) Here is a representative passage:

> Burt half-woke, whimpering before he was awake, an inarticulated soprano speaking through not quite weeping in complaint to his mother as before a sure jury of some fright of dream: the bed creaked and I heard her bare feet slow, the shuffling soles, and her voice, not whispering but stifled and gentle, Go to sleep now, git awn back to sleep, they aint nothin agoin to pester ye, git awn back to sleep, in that cadence of strength and sheltering comfort which anneals all fence of language and surpasses music; and George's grouched, sleepy voice, and hers to him, no words audible; and the shuffling; and a twisting in beds, and grumbling of weak springs; and the whimpering sinking, and expired; and the sound of breathing, strong, not sleeping, now, slowed, shifted across into sleep, now, steadier; and now, long, long, drawn off as lightest lithest edge of bow, thinner, thinner, a thread, a filament; nothing: and once more that silence wherein more deep than starlight this home is foundered. (p. 108)

You can work with this passage or choose one of your own—one that interests you and that you feel is representative of Agee's prose style. There are three parts to this exercise:

a. Be prepared to read your passage aloud and to discuss what the language *does*—not what it says, but what it does as an act of attention or as a way of recording experience or as a way of organizing a reader's time and understanding. Agee says, in the "Preface," "The text was written with reading aloud in mind. . . it is suggested that the reader attend with his ear to what he takes off the page: for variations of tone, pace, shape, and dynamics are here particularly unavailable to the eye alone, and with their loss, a good deal of meaning escapes" (p. 87).
b. Write a similar passage, one that describes a moment you observe or recall.
c. And write a paragraph of commentary on what you have done. What now, now that you have done this work from the inside, would you say that this way of writing allows a writer to *do?*

• • • • • • • • • • • •

ASSIGNMENT 3

A Curious Piece of Work [Agee and Evans]

In the "Preface," Agee refers to *Let Us Now Praise Famous Men* as a "curious piece of work." To prepare for this assignment, you will need to have a close and precise sense of just what that work is. The "Questions for a Second Reading" (p. 130) are designed to assist you in developing that sense.

With that preparation, prepare a similar project, a miniversion of the work of Agee and Evans. You will need a set of photographs. They could be yours or ones you gather from other sources (including the sources in this textbook). To be most in line with Agee and Evans, they should be photographs of a place, a people, a way of life and/or work that you urgently feel the need to make present to others. You will need to gather photographs, and you will need to prepare a written text.

You could think of this as a strict imitation, where you are arranging and selecting (perhaps taking) photographs in the manner of Walker Evans, and where you are writing prose in the style of Agee. Or you could think of this as a homage, or a response, or an argument, or a way of entering the conversation. You offering your work, as appropriate to your experience and place in time, as an engaged response to theirs.

It would be useful to prepare a brief "Preface" to your project.

• • • • • • • • • • • •

ASSIGNMENT 4

Memory as Image and Text [Hirsch]

The project of postmemory can be a writing project. In fact, to describe the individual's active engagement with the past that *is* postmemory, Hirsch uses metaphors of writing (or inscription): "It is a question of adopting the traumatic experiences—and thus also the memories—of others as one's own, or, more precisely, as experiences one might oneself have had, and of inscribing them into one's own life story. It is a question of conceiving oneself as multiply interconnected with others of the same, of previous, and of subsequent generations, of the same and of other—proximate or distant—cultures and subcultures" (p. 268).

Use "Projected Memory" as an invitation to such a writing project, where you would write about a past that belongs to you but that is not yours. Hirsch is interested in stories of trauma and suffering. And there is, to be sure, much at stake (and much to be gained) by writing about the traumas that preoccupy us as a culture. You should not, however, feel that you must write about a traumatic past. You should write about what you have at hand—connections to the past through family, neighborhood, or (as Hirsch says) "group relation"—and as those memories can be prompted, assisted, and mediated by some documentary or photographic record (as in the case of the photos in "Projected Memory" and the story of Anne Frank for Rymkiewicz and Agosín). The past that you are tied to need not necessarily have national or international significance. The importance is that you can identify yourself with this past and with these memories (and that you can inscribe them into your own life story).

Since we are using Hirsch to invite you to write about the past, it is important to note where and how she identifies the problems that accompany such a task. It comes in the distinction she make between "idiopathic" and "heteropathic" identification; her concern is cliché, sentimentality, a too-easy identification with that which is beyond you, even incomprehensible. She says,

> The challenge for the postmemorial artist is precisely to find the balance that allows the spectator [the reader] to enter the image, to imagine the disaster, but that disallows an overappropriate identification that makes the distances disappear, creating too available, too easy an access to this particular past. (p. 269).

• • • • • • • • • • • •

ASSIGNMENT 5

Organizing Principles [Barthes]

The selection we've provided from *Camera Lucida* is made up of numbered sections. These define a unit of writing that is larger than the paragraph and smaller than the essay. (What name might you give to this unit?) Choose one of these sections that seems characteristic and fun and write one of your own in imitation. Try to capture its form, method, structure of thought, energy, style. You can provide your own photographs or you can work with Barthes's. When you are done, take time to think about what this form of writing allows you to do. If possible, take time to share these thoughts with others in your class.

With this as preparation, prepare a Barthes-like essay that is made up of three or four of these numbered sections.

• • • • • • • • • • • •

ASSIGNMENT 6

Expressive Writing [Berger]

In "Appearances," John Berger provides written accounts of several photographs. They are presented with care and detail and with a predictable pattern: "A mother with her child is staring intently at a soldier. Perhaps they are speaking" (p. 186); or, "A young man is asleep at the table in a public place, perhaps a café. The expression on his face, his character, the way the light and shade dissolve him and his clothes, his open shirt and the newspaper on the table, his health and his fatigue, the time of night: all these are visibly present in this event and are particular" (p. 200).

The "expressiveness" of certain photographs is represented in the writing. For this assignment, choose two public photographs, photographs to which you do not have any personal connections. Write about each, using Berger's writing as a model, and use these passages as central examples in an essay designed to present, test, and extend his argument. This is the sort of thing Berger would do. How might he account for their "length," the "extension" of meaning they allow? How would he value this? And what about you? How would you explain what you have done? How might you explain its value to you and to people like you, people of your generation?

• • • • • • • • • • • •

ASSIGNMENT 7

Commentary [Said and Mohr, Agee and Evans, Hirsch, Barthes, Berger]

This is the final assignment in the sequence. It is the occasion for you to revise and reflect on the assignments on which you have worked. Gather the writing you have prepared into a folder. These may be chapters in a linked piece; they may be separate pieces collected as part of a more general project on writing and representation.

Write a brief essay in which you comment on the work you have done, perhaps on its reception by others in your class, and through it to your work as a writer in relation to the work of Said and Mohr, Agee and Evans, Hirsch, Barthes, and Berger.

You could think of this essay as a kind of introduction or afterword to the work in your folder. Or you could think of it as a plan for revision. You could also think of it as the occasion to write about the relationship of this kind of writing to the world you imagine outside this classroom—the world of work, the rest of the curriculum, the community, the circle of family, lovers, and friends.

(Acknowledgments continued from p. iv)

James Agee and Walker Evans, excerpts from *Let Us Now Praise Famous Men: Three Tenant Families.* Copyright 1939, 1940 by James Agee. Copyright 1941 by James Agee and Walker Evans. Copyright renewed © 1969 by Mia Fritsch Agee and Walker Evans. Copyright © 1960 by Walker Evans. Copyright renewed © 1988 by John T. Hill, executor of the estate of Walker Evans. Reprinted with the permission of Houghton Mifflin Company. All rights reserved. ***Photo credits:*** pp. 22, 23, 24, 25, 27, 28, 29, 35, 36, 37, 43, 44, 45, 53, 54, 55, 57, 60, 65, 72, 73, 74, 75, 79: Library of Congress; pp. 26, 30, 31, 32, 33, 34, 39, 40, 41, 42, 43, 46, 47, 49, 50, 51, 52, 56, 58, 59, 61, 62, 63, 64, 67, 68, 69, 70, 71, 76, 77, 78, 80, 81, 82, 83, 84, 85: Harry Ransom Humanities Research Center, The University of Texas at Austin.

Roland Barthes, excerpt from *Camera Lucida: Reflections on Photography,* translated by Richard Howard. Copyright © 1981 by Farrar, Straus & Giroux, LLC. Reprinted with the permission of Farrar, Straus & Giroux, LLC. ***Photo credits:*** p. 141: Bettmann/Corbis; pp. 143, 145: Koen Wessing, Photo Agency Hollandse Hoogte; p. 149:© William Klein, Courtesy Howard Greenberg Gallery, NYC; p. 152: © 1963 Richard Avedon; p. 153: Photograph by August Sander; p. 155: HRHRC, The University of Texas at Austin; p. 158: *Family Portrait, 1926* from the collection of Donna Mussenden VanDerZee; p. 159: © William Klein, Courtesy Howard Greenberg Gallery, NYC; p. 161: Estate of Andre Kertész; p. 162: Courtesy George Eastman House; p. 164: Centre des monuments nationaux de France; p. 165: *Wilson and Glass,* 1976 © Copyright The Estate of Robert Mapplethorpe. Used with permission; p. 168: *Self Portrait, 1975* © Copyright The Estate of Robert Mapplethorpe. Used with permission.

John Berger, "Appearances" from John Berger and Jean Mohr, *Another Way of Telling.* Copyright © 1982 by John Berger. Reprinted with the permission of Pantheon Books, a division of Random House, Inc. ***Photo credits:*** p. 178: Photograph by Jean Mohr, Geneva; p. 179: Imperial War Museum, NYP68567; p. 182: John Berger; p. 187: Estate of Andre Kertész; p. 194: Saul Landau; pp. 201, 202, 204: Estate of Andre Kertész.

Robert Coles, "The Tradition: Fact and Fiction" from *Doing Documentary Work.* Copyright © 1997 by Robert Coles. Reprinted with the permission of Oxford University Press, Inc. ***Photo credits:*** All photographs Library of Congress.

Marianne Hirsch, "Projected Memory: Holocaust Photographs in Personal and Public Fantasy" from *Acts of Memory,* edited by Mieke Bal, Jonathan Crewe, and Leo Spitzer. Copyright © 1998 by the Trustees of Darmouth College. Reprinted with the permission of the University Press of New England. ***Photo credits:*** p. 262: *From the Stroop Report on the Destruction of the Warsaw ghetto,* Liaison Agency/Getty Images; p. 264: *Past Lives (for the Children of Izieu),* copyright Lorie Novak, 1987, color photograph.

Dorothea Lange and Paul S. Taylor, "Foreword," "Old South," and "Plantation Under the Machine" from *An American Exodus: A Record of Human Erosion.* Copyright © 1939 by Dorothea Lange and Paul Schuster Taylor. Reprinted with the permission of Yale University Press. ***Photo credits:*** pp. 291, 294, 302, 303, 305, 306, 307, 309, 313, 314, 315, 317: Copyright the Dorothea Lange Collection, Oakland Museum of California, City of Oakland. Gift of Paul S. Taylor; pp. 292, 293, 295, 299, 308 (top), 308 (bottom), 312, 318: Courtesy the Dorothea Lange Collection, Oakland Museum of California, City of Oakland; pp. 296, 297, 298, 301, 304, 310, 316: Library of Congress.

W. J. T. Mitchell, "The Photographic Essay: Four Case Studies" from *Picture Theory.* Copyright © 1994 by W. J. T. Mitchell. Reprinted with the permission of The University of Chicago Press. This essay contains excerpts from Malek Alloula, *The Colonial Harem,* translated by Myrna and Wlad Godzich. Copyright © 1986 by Myrna and Wlad Godzich. Reprinted with the permission of University of Minnesota Press. ***Photo credits:*** p. 336: Jacob Riis, "Lodgers in Bayard St. Tenement," from *How the Other Half Lives* (1890); p. 340: Photo reproduced courtesy of the Museum of the City of New York. "Parade—Hoboken, New Jersey," copyright *The Americans,* Robert Frank, courtesy PaceWildenstein-MacGill Gallery, New York; pp. 341, 342, 344, 345, 346, 347, 348: Walker Evans, photographs from *Let Us Now Praise Famous Men* (1939) by James Agee and Walker Evans. Photographs courtesy of the Library of Congress; p. 343: Walker Evans, "Annie Mae Gudger." HRHRC, The University of Texas at Austin; p. 349: Margaret Bourke-White, HAMILTON, ALABAMA. Courtesy of Jonathan Toby White, PLC; p. 351: Daniel Boudinet, "Polaroid, 1979," from Roland Barthes, *Camera Lucida* (1981). Patrimoine Photographique, Paris; p. 353: Nadar, "The Artist's Mother (Or Wife)," in Roland Barthes, *Camera Lucida* (1981). Cliché Paul Nadar/Arch.Phot. © Centre des monuments nationaux, Paris. Courtesy of the University of Minnesota Press; p. 358: "Scenes and Types: Arabian Women with the Yachmak" from *The Colonial Harem* by Malek Alloula; p. 360: Jean Mohr, "Mayor of Jerusalem"; pp. 364 and 365: "Amman, 1984. Mrs. Farraj" and "Elderly Palestinian Villager, Ramallah, 1984" from *After the Last Sky,* by Edward Said. Photographs by Jean Mohr, Geneva.

Edward Said, "States" from Edward W. Said, *After the Last Sky: Palestinian Lives.* Copyright © 1986 by Edward W. Said. Reprinted with the permission of The Wylie Agency, Inc. ***Photo credits:*** All photographs by Jean Mohr, Geneva.